# ENGLISH FOOTBALL
## IN THE MODERN ERA

First published in 2015 by New Holland Publishers Pty Ltd
London • Sydney • Auckland

The Chandlery, Unit 9, 50 Westminster Bridge Road, London SE1 7QY, UK
1/66 Gibbes Street, Chatswood, NSW 2067, Australia
5/39 Woodside Avenue, Northcote, Auckland 0627, New Zealand

www.newhollandpublishers.com

A record of this book is held at the British Library and the National Library of Australia.

ISBN 978 1 74257 809 5

Managing Director: Fiona Schultz
Publisher: Alan Whiticker
Project Editor: Bill Twyman
Designer: Thomas Casey
Production Director: Olga Dementiev
Printer: Toppan Leefung Printing Ltd

1 3 5 7 9 10 8 6 4 2

Keep up with New Holland Publishers on Facebook
www.facebook.com/NewHollandPublishers

# ENGLISH FOOTBALL
## IN THE MODERN ERA

ALL THE ACTION
SEASON BY SEASON

## JON REEVES

IN ASSOCIATION WITH

SHOOT®
The voice of football

NH
NEW
HOLLAND

## DEDICATION

For my beloved wife Katie, my precious son George and 'baby' Reeves.

## ACKNOWLEDGEMENTS

I would like to thank Alan Whiticker and everybody at *New Holland* who helped with the publishing and design of this book. I would also like to thank Bill Twyman for his proofreading expertise and Dan Tyler and **Shoot** for their assistance with sourcing the fantastic images that adorn the covers and each of the chapters, and for aiding my trip down football memory lane with the inclusion of classic *Shoot* magazine covers from the last 23 years. I would also like to thank Colin Mitchell for his advice and assistance throughout the years.

Without the patience and understanding of my wife, Katie, it simply would not have been possible to complete this project. The support of other family members has also been greatly appreciated and I would like to thank them all again for their help and support.

As a football fan growing up in the 1990s witnessing the inception of the Premier League, working on this book made me realise even more clearly just how seismic the transformation of the English game has been in the last two decades.

Reliving the classic games, memorable goals and heart-wrenching drama that the highest level of English football provides has been a hugely enjoyable experience.

From stoppage-time title deciders to relegation devastation, FA Cup giant killing feats to Champions League glory – each of the last 24 seasons has its own story to tell. I hope that I've done each campaign justice and that the next 24 chapters will evoke as much nostalgia and enjoyment for the reader as they have done for the author.

# CONTENTS

# INTRODUCTION

English football has been transformed almost unrecognisably in the last quarter of a century. The Premier League brand is now eagerly devoured in over 50 countries and 212 different territories across the world, reaching a global television audience of 4.7 billion.

The irresistible progression of the game that England gave to the world first started to flourish after the Premier League was created in 1992. Decisions taken in the corridors of power of English football to revamp the organisation of the national sport proved to be both inspired and irreversible. Almost overnight the identity and profile of the beautiful game exploded onto the world stage.

A 24-team top flight, previously known as the First Division, was replaced by a 22-team Premier League, with the next three tiers rebranded as Division One, Division Two and Division Three respectively. A year later, the Premier League was cut down to 20 teams, ensuring fewer games but double the excitement, as English football's makeover continued apace.

The dawning of the Premier League era coincided with the emergence of BSkyB as the primary broadcaster of live top-flight action. The additional money pumped into the game, alongside countless new sponsors, funded a revolution in thinking, spending and the cultural makeup of the English game.

From a top division that struggled for quality and was out of contention when it came to enticing the world's best players – its clubs out of European competition for over five years – the EPL erupted in the late 1990s and charged into the new millennium, becoming one of the world's best leagues and arguably the most entertaining and captivating competition in global sport.

Alongside the ever-developing Premier League, the rest of English football has experienced exponential growth in the last 20 years. Logistical league changes, classic cup moments, a period of dominance at European football's top table, entertainment, energy and sheer drama have been the buzz words as the standard and profile of every level of the game has increased significantly.

From Manchester United's lifting of the inaugural trophy to Chelsea's latest Premier League title victory, this book charts the changing waters of the English game, highlighting the heroes, celebrating the glory and recapturing the drama of the last 23 seasons in 23 chapters of facts, stats and memorable images.

# ENGLISH FOOTBALL'S BIG BANG

**N**ow headlined by a league frequently feted as the most entertaining in the world, it's easy to forget that English football spent much of the last century lagging behind its European competitors in terms of quality, stature and reputation.

The inception of the Premier League in 1992 provided the launch pad for English football to reposition itself once again at the forefront of the global game's progression. In May 1992, the breakaway league signed a broadcasting rights contract with British Sky Broadcasting and the BBC valued at £304 million. The commercial exposure provided by satellite television, in addition to increased sponsorship, was key to the game's progression, even though the EPL's debut season began without an official sponsor.

OPPOSITE PAGE:
*Manchester United club captain Bryan Robson lifts the inaugural Premier League title at Old Trafford following the Red Devils' 3–1 victory over Blackburn.*

LEFT: *Nottingham Forest's classy striker Teddy Sheringham (pictured right, alongside Liverpool's Mark Wright) scored the first Premier League goal captured by the BSkyB cameras as Forest secured a 1-0 opening weekend victory over the Reds. Sheringham went on to sign for Tottenham Hostpur later in the season.*

# TRANSFER TALES

The figures invested by even the biggest clubs remained relatively modest and in-line with those spent in previous seasons ahead of the 1992–93 campaign. Newly promoted Blackburn Rovers signalled their intention by breaking the British transfer record to sign England striker Alan Shearer, while his international partner, Teddy Sheringham, was also the subject of a big money move, departing Nottingham Forest for Tottenham Hotspur.

The most significant deals continued to take place between top-flight clubs, including Manchester United's headline capture of Eric Cantona from rivals Leeds United. The French striker remained in the minority when it came to players from outside of the United Kingdom plying their trade in England's top flight. The impact of additional revenue would change this but in the early 1990s English clubs still struggled to compete with teams from Italy, Spain, Germany and even France when it came to the wages they could afford or were willing to pay. Indeed, many of England's best players were still departing for foreign shores, as Des Walker joined Paul Gascoigne and David Platt in Italy, following a move to Sampdoria in August.

Among the exceptions to the scarcity of foreign imports during the 1992–93 season were Denmark's European Championship winner John Jensen, who joined Arsenal from Brondby, Norwegian left-back Stig Inge Bjornebye, who signed for Liverpool and Russian goalkeeper Dmitri Kharine who arrived at Chelsea.

## BIGGEST TRANSFERS

**ALAN SHEARER** – from Southampton to Blackburn Rovers – £3.3m

**DEAN SAUNDERS** – from Liverpool to Aston Villa – £2.5m

**TERRY PHELAN** – from Wimbledon to Manchester City – £2.5m

**KEVIN GALLAGHER** – from Coventry City to Blackburn Rovers – £2.5m

**TEDDY SHERINGHAM** – from Nottingham Forest to Tottenham Hotspur – £2.1m

**ROBERT FLECK** – from Norwich City to Chelsea – £2.1m

**DAVID ROCASTLE** – from Arsenal to Manchester City – £2m

**MARTIN KEOWN** – from Everton to Arsenal – £2m

**EARL BARRETT** – from Oldham Athletic to Everton – £1.7m

**STUART RIPLEY** – from Middlesbrough to Blackburn Rovers – £1.3m

LEFT: *Alan Shearer, who became Britain's most expensive player ahead of the season, developed into the Premier League's most lethal marksman at Blackburn Rovers.*

The 1992–93 campaign saw the return of the iconic BBC highlights show, *Match of the Day*, to a regular Saturday night slot on British terrestrial television, ensuring that the national game was again more accessible to a mainstream audience.

The vast majority of top-flight stadiums required major surgery, with many still featuring standing areas despite the haunting memories of the Hillsborough tragedy that had occurred three years earlier. The Premier League's debut season saw immediate development at some of the country's most celebrated stadiums as standing areas were demolished at Manchester United's Old Trafford, Manchester City's Maine Road and Arsenal's Highbury.

At the end of 1991–92 season, the Football League's final campaign in its previous guise, Leeds United sealed a famous championship, pipping Manchester United to the First Division crown following a thrilling finale. Managed by Howard Wilkinson, who remains the last English manager to win the title, Leeds played a direct but effective style of football that maximised the talents of target man Lee Chapman and the sprightly Rod Wallace, whilst also showcasing the silky skills of Eric Cantona, Gary McAllister and Gary Speed.

Three teams that had dominated for much of the 1980s, Arsenal, Liverpool and Everton, were in decline in terms of league consistency and all three clubs continued that form in the Premier League. Two of London's most famed teams, Tottenham Hotspur and Chelsea, tasted occasional success in the cup competitions and Manchester City were still very much in the shadow of Manchester United.

Promoted Blackburn Rovers, Middlesbrough and Ipswich Town were the fortunate latecomers to the Premier League party, as the likes of Notts County, Luton Town and West Ham United missed out after relegation to the second tier.

The first ever Premier League comprised 22 clubs: Arsenal, Aston Villa, Blackburn Rovers, Chelsea, Coventry City, Crystal Palace, Everton, Ipswich Town, Leeds United, Liverpool, Manchester City, Manchester United, Middlesbrough, Norwich City, Nottingham Forest, Oldham Athletic, Queens Park Rangers, Sheffield Wednesday, Sheffield United, Southampton, Tottenham Hotspur, Wimbledon.

The dawning of a new division also coincided with the introduction of a new rule, which meant that goalkeepers could no longer pick up the ball if it had been intentionally passed back to them by a team-mate. Instead, the men between the posts had to use their feet to clear or pass the ball, which led to increased pressure from opposing forwards and some interesting miss-kicks and slices out of play in the opening weeks of the season.

## TALES OF THE TURF

Tipped as favourites for the title, Manchester United showed relegation form at the beginning of the season, losing away to Sheffield United in a game where Blades striker Brian Deane grabbed the first ever goal of the Premier League with a close-range header. A 3–0 loss at home to Everton and a home draw with Ipswich Town followed before United finally got their season started with a late 1–0 victory over Southampton, courtesy of Dion Dublin.

The Premier League's first live televised game on BSkyB came on the opening weekend of the season, when Nottingham Forest hosted Liverpool in an inaugural 'Super Sunday' clash. The game was settled by a fine Teddy Sheringham finish, as the home side defeated Liverpool 1–0. The next day saw the English top flight's first ever Monday night fixture, as Manchester City played Queens Park Rangers in a game that ended in a 1–1 draw.

Reigning champions Leeds United began the season in promising fashion, beating Wimbledon 2–1 at Elland Road but it soon became clear that their title defence would be unsuccessful as the Yorkshire club struggled for form, suffering a 4–1 thumping to newly promoted Middlesbrough in the third game of the season. The first clash of the campaign between two of the division's big guns, came when Arsenal beat Liverpool 2–0 at Anfield thanks to goals from Anders Limpar and Ian Wright.

The new division's early pace setters were Norwich City who beat Arsenal at Highbury on the opening day before a 2–1 victory over Chelsea at Carrow Road sent them to the top of the table. Managed by Mike Walker and featuring a nice blend of experience, with the likes of Mark Bowen, Bryan Gunn and Jeremy Goss, and youth, through Chris Sutton and Ruel Fox, as well as the predatory instincts of Mark Robins up front, the Canaries claimed top spot at the end of the first month of the season and became one of the surprise packages of the season.

Inspired by the goals of Alan Shearer, the managerial nous of Kenny Dalglish and millions of pounds worth of investment from owner Jack Walker, Blackburn Rovers also impressed during what was their first season back in the top flight for nearly 30 years. However, Blackburn's title challenge floundered in the second half of the season after the prolific Shearer was sidelined with a serious knee injury.

ABOVE: *The goals of former Manchester United striker Mark Robins helped Norwich City put up an unexpected title challenge.*

OPPOSITE PAGE: *The energetic Dean Saunders developed an impressive partnership with powerful striker Dalian Atkinson that saw Aston Villa enjoy a goal-filled first season in the Premier League.*

## INTERESTING INFO

Reigning champions Leeds United failed to win a single away game throughout the 1992–93 season.

LEFT: *Manchester United captain Steve Bruce popped up with two crucial goals during a last-gasp win over Sheffield Wednesday. The victory, combined with the positive influence of new signing, Eric Cantona, propelled the Red Devils to their first league title in 26 years.*

Manchester United soon found their feet, emphasised by a 2–0 home victory over Leeds United at the beginning of September. Aston Villa, who went on to lead the division for much of the season, showed their title credentials with a 4–2 win against Liverpool that featured two goals from Dean Saunders against his old club and a memorable miss from Reds striker Ronnie Rosenthal, who dribbled past Villa keeper Nigel Spink but crashed his shot against the crossbar with an open goal at his mercy.

Towards the end of November, Manchester United made a significant move in the transfer market, parting with what proved to be a bargain £1.2m to capture French forward Eric Cantona from rivals Leeds United. Hugely skilled and with the personality and confidence to flourish on the stage of the 'Theatre of Dreams', Cantona took the Red Devils' performances to another level, creating chances for his team-mates and scoring spectacular and crucial goals as the season progressed.

United took a giant leap towards winning the inaugural Premier League title during a dramatic home clash with Sheffield Wednesday in April 1993 when Ferguson's men trailed the Owls 1–0, following a John Sheridan penalty, with less than five minutes to play. The Red Devils' inspirational captain, Steve Bruce popped up with two headed goals, the first in the 86th minute and the second after an amazing six minutes of injury time, to turn the tide and give United's title run in the lift off it needed. The club's first championship for 26 years was sealed with two games remaining and without United kicking a ball, as Aston Villa lost 1–0 at home to Oldham Athletic in a game they needed to win to maintain their title challenge.

United's fierce local rivals Liverpool finished sixth in the table for the second season running, after a strong last two months of the season. Defending champions Leeds United fared even worse and came close to becoming embroiled in a relegation scrap before eventually finishing 17th.

*Wimbledon striker Dean Holdsworth fired 19 goals to help Joe Kinnear's side to a respectable mid-table placing.*

## ⚽ INTERESTING INFO

The only manager to lose his job during the 1992–93 season was Chelsea boss Ian Porterfield who was sacked in February and replaced by Dave Webb.

Two of the division's surprise packages were Queens Park Rangers and Wimbledon. Both London clubs exceeded expectations with QPR, inspired by the pace and power of Les Ferdinand in attack, finishing as high as fifth. The Dons, helped by the goal-scoring prowess of Dean Holdsworth, ended 12th.

Brian Clough's Nottingham Forest struggled for the majority of the campaign, occupying the foot of the table on a regular basis and failed to fill the void left by departing stars like Des Walker and Teddy Sheringham. Forest dropped out of the top flight for the first time in 26 years at the end of the season, their fate sealed after a home loss to Sheffield United.

Having led Forest to the summit of English and European football, relegation was a sad end to Clough's 18-year tenure as manager. Middlesbrough, managed by Lennie Lawrence, soon followed them into the second tier with Crystal Palace suffering demotion on the final day of the season, only finishing below Oldham Athletic on goal difference and a point further back from Southampton.

# HONOURS LIST

## FA Premier League

**CHAMPIONS:** Manchester United
Alex Ferguson's Red Devils became English champions for the first time in 26 years, finishing the season with a total of 84 points, clocking up 24 victories and finishing 10 clear of their nearest challengers.
**RUNNERS-UP:** Aston Villa
**RELEGATED:** Crystal Palace, Middlesbrough, Nottingham Forest
**TOP GOAL SCORER:** Teddy Sheringham (22 goals for Nottingham Forest and Tottenham Hotspur)

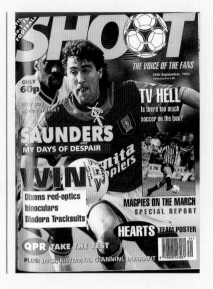

SHOOT MAGAZINE
1992–93

*The cover star was Aston Villa striker Dean Saunders who spoke candidly about his frustrating spell with former club Liverpool. Other features included a focus on promotion chasing Newcastle United and an article questioning whether there was too much football on television!*

# 1992–93 SEASON TABLE

| | | M | W | D | L | GF | GA | GD | PTS |
|---|---|---|---|---|---|---|---|---|---|
| 1 | Manchester United | 42 | 24 | 12 | 6 | 67 | 31 | +36 | 84 |
| 2 | Aston Villa | 42 | 21 | 11 | 10 | 57 | 40 | +17 | 74 |
| 3 | Norwich City | 42 | 21 | 9 | 12 | 61 | 65 | -4 | 72 |
| 4 | Blackburn Rovers | 42 | 20 | 11 | 11 | 68 | 46 | +22 | 71 |
| 5 | Queens Park Rangers | 42 | 17 | 12 | 13 | 63 | 55 | +8 | 63 |
| 6 | Liverpool | 42 | 16 | 11 | 15 | 62 | 55 | +7 | 59 |
| 7 | Sheffield Wednesday | 42 | 15 | 14 | 13 | 55 | 51 | +4 | 59 |
| 8 | Tottenham Hotspur | 42 | 16 | 11 | 15 | 60 | 66 | -6 | 59 |
| 9 | Manchester City | 42 | 15 | 12 | 15 | 56 | 51 | +5 | 57 |
| 10 | Arsenal | 42 | 15 | 11 | 16 | 40 | 38 | +2 | 56 |
| 11 | Chelsea | 42 | 14 | 14 | 14 | 51 | 54 | -3 | 56 |
| 12 | Wimbledon | 42 | 14 | 12 | 16 | 56 | 55 | +1 | 54 |
| 13 | Everton | 42 | 15 | 8 | 19 | 53 | 55 | -2 | 53 |
| 14 | Sheffield United | 42 | 14 | 10 | 18 | 54 | 53 | +1 | 52 |
| 15 | Coventry City | 42 | 13 | 13 | 16 | 52 | 57 | -5 | 52 |
| 16 | Ipswich Town | 42 | 12 | 16 | 14 | 50 | 55 | -5 | 52 |
| 17 | Leeds United | 42 | 12 | 15 | 15 | 57 | 62 | -5 | 51 |
| 18 | Southampton | 42 | 13 | 11 | 18 | 54 | 61 | -7 | 50 |
| 19 | Oldham Athletic | 42 | 13 | 10 | 19 | 63 | 74 | -11 | 49 |
| 20 | Crystal Palace | 42 | 11 | 16 | 15 | 48 | 61 | -13 | 49 |
| 21 | Middlesbrough | 42 | 11 | 11 | 20 | 54 | 75 | -21 | 44 |
| 22 | Nottingham Forest | 42 | 10 | 10 | 22 | 41 | 62 | -21 | 40 |

# PLAYERS OF THE SEASON

**PROFESSIONAL FOOTBALLERS' ASSOCIATION (PFA) PLAYER OF THE YEAR:** Paul McGrath, Aston Villa
**PFA YOUNG PLAYER OF THE YEAR:** Ryan Giggs, Manchester United
**FOOTBALL WRITERS' PLAYER OF THE YEAR:** Chris Waddle, Sheffield Wednesday

*Swindon Town, led by player-manager Glenn Hoddle (pictured centre right) celebrating their dramatic play-off final victory over Leicester City.*

**FOOTBALL LEAGUE DIVISION ONE CHAMPIONS:**
Newcastle United
**PROMOTED:** West Ham United
**DIVISION ONE PLAY-OFF WINNERS:** Swindon Town
**RELEGATED:** Brentford, Cambridge United, Bristol Rovers
**TOP GOAL SCORER:** Guy Whittingham (42 goals for Portsmouth)

Having returned to the club in February 1992, Kevin Keegan saved Newcastle United from relegation to the third tier at the end of 1991–92 campaign before implementing an attacking brand of football that saw the Magpies storm to the Division One title the following season. Healthily backed by owner Sir John Hall, Keegan invested significantly and successfully in the transfer market, signing the likes of goal-scoring midfielder Rob Lee from Charlton Athletic and prolific poacher Andy Cole from Bristol City, as the North East giants gained promotion and a return to the top flight for the first time in four seasons.

West Ham United, led by Billy Bonds, spent just a single season in Division One after sealing runners-up spot in 1993. Managed by Jim Smith, Portsmouth were unlucky to miss out on promotion, finishing level on 88 points with West Ham but with an inferior goal difference. Pompey also suffered play-off disappointment, losing in the semi-finals to sixth placed Leicester City. The Foxes faced fifth-placed Swindon Town in the final and lost a dramatic game 4–3 thanks to a winning penalty kick from Swindon's Paul Bodin.

**DIVISION TWO CHAMPIONS:** Stoke City
**PROMOTED:** Bolton Wanderers
**DIVISION TWO PLAY-OFF WINNERS:** West Bromwich Albion
**RELEGATED:** Preston North End, Mansfield Town, Wigan Athletic, Chester City
**TOP GOAL SCORER:** Bob Taylor (30 goals for West Bromwich Albion)

Maintaining the momentum of an impressive 1991–92 campaign, Lou Macari's Stoke City claimed the Division Two title in record breaking style by going 25 league matches without defeat and gaining a goal difference of plus 39, largely thanks to the goal-scoring exploits of Mark Stein who netted 33 in all competitions.

After five successive seasons in the third tier, Bolton Wanderers, managed by Bruch Rioch, gained automatic promotion. West Bromwich Albion, buoyed by the goal-scoring exploits of Bob Taylor, defeated Port Vale in the Play-off final at Wembley.

**DIVISION THREE CHAMPIONS:** Cardiff City
**PROMOTED:** Wrexham, Barnet
**DIVISION THREE PLAY-OFF WINNERS:** York City
**RELEGATED:** Halifax Town
**TOP GOAL SCORER:** Darren Foreman (Scarborough) and Carl Griffiths (Shrewsbury Town) – both 27 goals.

Two teams from Wales fought for the title in Division Three as Cardiff City and Wrexham both secured automatic promotion, with the former

ABOVE TOP: *Manager Lou Macari (holding the champagne) celebrates with his title-winning Stoke City players.*

ABOVE BOTTOM: *Wycombe Wanderers manager Martin O'Neill, who led the club into the Football League for the first time in their history, plots tactics from the dugout.*

as champions. Despite the late season departure of charismatic manager Barry Fry, Barnet claimed third and the final automatic promotion place while York City defeated Crewe Alexandra on penalties to win the play-offs. After 72 seasons in the Football League, Halifax Town were relegated after Gillingham's fine end of season run.

**FOOTBALL CONFERENCE CHAMPIONS:** Wycombe Wanderers

Guided by the enigmatic Martin O'Neill, Wycombe reached the Football League for the first time in their history and also won the FA Trophy.

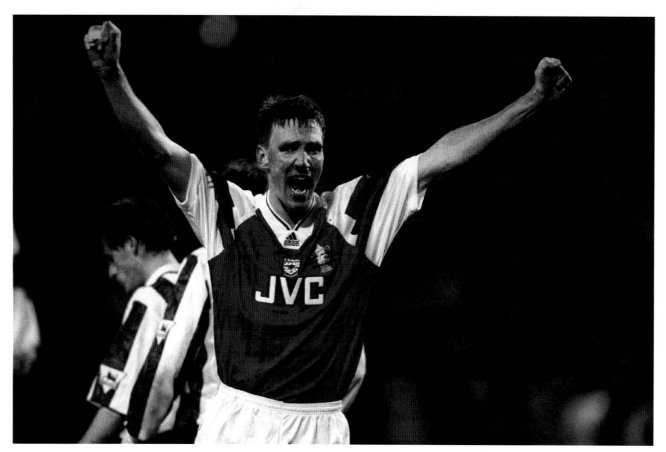

*Arsenal defender Andy Linighan celebrates his FA Cup final winning header against Sheffield Wednesday.*

# UP FOR THE CUP

**FA CUP WINNERS:** Arsenal

After the traditional Saturday afternoon final ended in a 1–1 draw, Arsenal and Sheffield Wednesday replayed the contest five days later. The replay at Wembley stadium saw the scores level again at 1–1 after 90 minutes, thanks to goals from Ian Wright and Chris Waddle. With 119 minutes on the clock Arsenal defender Andy Linighan powered a header past Chris Woods to seal the sixth FA Cup in the club's history.

Arsenal had defeated their North London rivals Tottenham Hotspur 1–0 in the semi-finals, thanks to Tony Adams' goal, whilst Wednesday overcame their city rivals Sheffield United after goals from Chris Waddle and Mark Bright.

Other notable results in the competition came when Sheffield United shocked Manchester United in the fifth round thanks to a Glyn Hodges winner and Liverpool were knocked out by Division Two Bolton Wanderers.

**LEAGUE (COCA COLA) CUP WINNERS:** Arsenal

The Gunners claimed the first domestic silverware of the season following a gritty 2–1 victory over Sheffield Wednesday. John Harkes had given the Owls an early lead before Paul Merson equalised for Arsenal. Unlikely hero, Steve Morrow, scored the winner in the second half with his first goal for the club before being notoriously dropped by Tony Adams during the post-match celebrations and suffering a broken arm. En route to the final, Arsenal defeated Crystal Palace over a two-legged semi-final, whilst Sheffield Wednesday overcame Blackburn at the same stage.

Shock results earlier in the competition included Crystal Palace knocking out Liverpool, Watford defeating Leeds and Scarborough overcoming Coventry City.

**CHARITY SHIELD WINNERS:** Leeds United
The reigning champions defeated FA Cup holders Liverpool 4–3 in an entertaining encounter that featured an Eric Cantona hat-trick and a comical own goal from Gordon Strachan.

**THE FOOTBALL LEAGUE (AUTOGLASS) TROPHY:** Port Vale
John Rudge's men gained some consolation for missing out on promotion by defeating Stockport County at Wembley, with Bernie Slaven grabbing the winning goal.

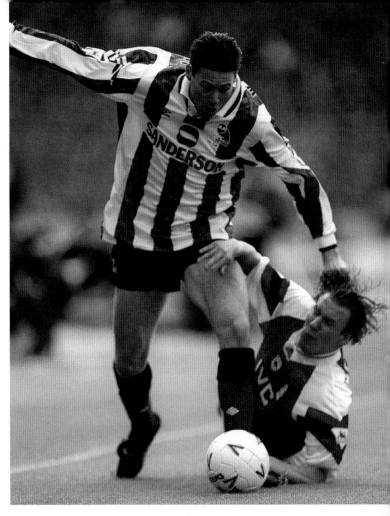

RIGHT: *Sheffield Wednesday's mesmerising winger Chris Waddle glides past Arsenal's Paul Merson in the FA Cup final. Waddle scored a spectacular free kick against Wednesday's city rivals Sheffield United in the semi-final.*

BELOW: *Arsenal utility man Steve Morrow drills the ball home to settle the League Cup in the Gunners favour. The Northern Irishman was later injured following some over exuberant post-match celebrations.*

LEFT: *Leeds United captain Gordon Strachan battles against Scottish champions Rangers during the Yorkshire club's failed Champions League campaign.*

OPPOSITE PAGE: *Even the individual brilliance of Paul 'Gazza' Gascoigne (pictured here during a 2–0 loss to Norway) failed to inspire England as Graham Taylor's side struggled to qualify for the 1994 World Cup.*

# INTO EUROPE

## European Champions League

Leeds United were England's sole entrants in a season when the European Cup was rebranded as the Champions League. The tournament was transformed from a succession of two-legged knockout ties as two mini leagues were added in the latter stages of the competition. Leeds were drawn against German champions Stuttgart in the first round, and the first leg ended in a 3–0 away defeat. Howard Wilkinson's men turned things round in the home tie, winning 4–1 with goals from Eric Cantona, Lee Chapman and Gary Speed. The 4–4 aggregate scoreline should've sent Stuttgart through on away goals, but it was later discovered that the Germans had fielded an illegible player, causing the game to be replayed. Leeds won the extra game 2–1 with Carl Shutt scoring the winning goal to set up a second round tie against Scottish giants Glasgow Rangers that was dubbed by the press as the 'Battle of Britain'. Another entertaining two-legged affair saw Leeds crash out of the tournament 4–2 on aggregate, with Rangers strikers Mark Hately and Ally McCoist in fine form. It meant the English side missed out on competing in the league stages of the competition.

## European Cup Winners' Cup

Liverpool began their Cup Winners' Cup campaign with a bang, thumping Cypriot side Apollon Limassol 8–2 on aggregate in a tie that featured five goals from Ian Rush. However, the Reds' progress stalled in the next round following a 6–2 loss to Russia's Spartak Moscow over two legs.

## UEFA Cup

Both English representatives made heavy work of the UEFA Cup with Manchester United crashing out on penalties to Torpedo Moscow in the first round and Sheffield Wednesday losing to German side Kaiserslautern in the second stage.

## The International Scene

The English national team continued to struggle under the guidance of Graham Taylor and began their qualification campaign for the 1994 World Cup in stuttering fashion, as home draws against Holland and Norway and a shock 2–0 away defeat to the Scandinavians left their progress in serious doubt.

# CHAPTER 2 // 1993-94
# A DOMINANT FORCE EMERGES

The second ever Premier League, which was now sponsored by Carling and labelled as the FA Carling Premiership, was eagerly anticipated. More money was invested in the game and the increased television exposure helped develop interest in English football both at home and abroad. The Football League was also attracting increased sponsorship interest, emphasised by the announcement of the Endsleigh insurance company as the primary sponsor of tiers two to four.

Champions Manchester United were widely tipped to retain their trophy with improved campaigns expected from Arsenal and Liverpool, as well as the emerging Blackburn Rovers. There were a number of new managerial appointments ahead of the season, as a couple of celebrated Tottenham midfielders began their first Premiership jobs. Argentine World Cup winner Ossie Ardiles took charge at White Hart Lane while Glenn Hoddle departed newly-promoted Swindon Town for Chelsea. One of the earliest casualties of the season was Manchester City manager Peter Reid who was replaced by Brian Horton.

Of the promoted teams, Newcastle United looked the most likely to succeed. Managed by the charismatic Kevin Keegan, the Magpies possessed a potent attacking threat through prolific young striker Andy Cole and his veteran partner Peter Beardsley.

OPPOSITE PAGE: *The precociously talented Ryan Giggs was a key element in Manchester United's title winning side of 1993–94. Creating countless chances for team-mates and scoring plenty of top drawer goals of his own, the dynamic winger regularly gave opposing defenders nightmares.*

BELOW: *Coventry City's Mick Quinn (centre) celebrates an opening day hat-trick against Arsenal with his team-mates.*

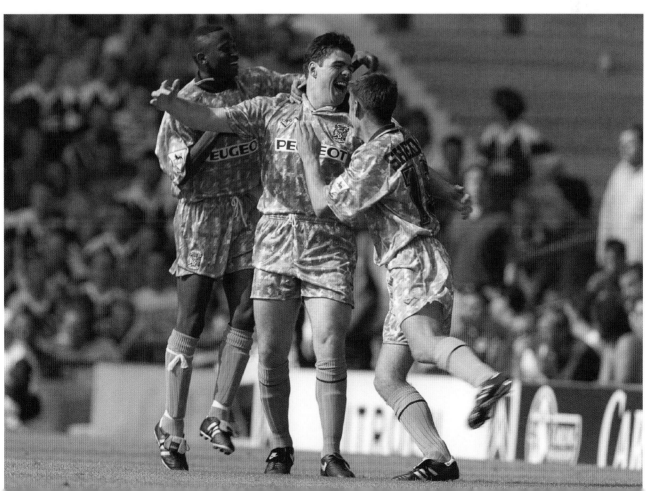

# TRANSFER TALES

Manchester United strengthened by breaking the British transfer record to sign Nottingham Forest midfielder Roy Keane. With the legendary Bryan Robson approaching the end of his playing days, the energetic and domineering Keane was a canny addition by Alex Ferguson. United's main rivals from the previous season, Aston Villa and Norwich City, didn't invest significantly, but Kenny Dalglish's Blackburn continued to splash the cash, securing the multi-million pound signings of David Batty, Paul Warhurst and Tim Flowers, the latter breaking the British record fee for a goalkeeper.

The dominant market was again the domestic one, with the biggest transfers taking place between English clubs. The foreign market was still relatively untapped and just a sprinkling of continental footballers arrived, such as Cypriot midfielder Nikki Papavasiliou who joined Newcastle, Norwegian striker Jan Age Fjortoft, who scored 13 goals in the last 17 games of the season for Swindon, his countryman Jostein Flo who provided a physical attacking presence for Sheffield United and Danish defender Jakob Kjeldbjerg, who signed for Chelsea. In fact, the majority of continental arrivals in the early years of the division continued to be from Scandinavian countries.

Transfer fees in the Football League were slowly beginning to creep up, emphasised by the £2m Nottingham Forest paid Southend United for the services of young striker, Stan Collymore.

## BIGGEST TRANSFERS

**ROY KEANE** – from Nottingham Forest to Manchester United – £3.75m

**BRIAN DEANE** – from Sheffield United to Leeds United £2.9m

**DAVID BATTY** – from Leeds United to Blackburn Rovers – £2.75m

**PAUL WARHURST** – from Sheffield Wednesday to Blackburn Rovers – £2.75m

**ANDY SINTON** – from Queens Park Rangers to Sheffield Wednesday £2.7m

**RUEL FOX** – from Norwich City to Newcastle United – £2.5m

**TIM FLOWERS** – from Southampton to Blackburn Rovers – £2.5m

**NEIL RUDDOCK** – from Tottenham Hotspur to Liverpool – £2.5m

**NIGEL CLOUGH** – from Nottingham Forest to Liverpool – £2.28m

**ANDY TOWNSEND** – from Chelsea to Aston Villa – £2.1m

LEFT: *The long-term replacement for Bryan Robson, young midfielder Roy Keane headlined the summer transfer activity after joining Manchester United from Nottingham Forest.*

# TALES OF THE TURF

Manchester United began their defence with a straightforward away victory over Norwich City that featured goals from heroes old and new in Bryan Robson and Ryan Giggs, before defeating Sheffield United at Old Trafford in a game that saw Roy Keane grab his first goals for the club. One of the opening weekend's surprise results took place at Highbury where Coventry City shocked Arsenal 3–0 with striker Mick Quinn scoring all three goals. New Liverpool signing Nigel Clough began the season well, notching twice against Sheffield Wednesday on his debut. The Reds' impressive start to the season continued with a crushing 5–0 victory over Swindon Town.

Everton were the division's early pacesetters and hit top spot towards the end of August, largely thanks to the goals of Tony Cottee. Manchester United and Aston Villa took part in an enthralling end-to-end encounter at Villa Park in the opening weeks, which United eventually won 2–1 following a clinical double from Lee Sharpe.

As the season progressed, Arsenal and Blackburn, boosted by the return to fitness of Alan Shearer, both showed good form as they tried to keep pace with Manchester United. An eventful Merseyside derby in September saw Liverpool goalkeeper Bruce Grobelaar square up to team-mate Steve McManaman after the Reds conceded the first goal during a 2–0 loss.

Newcastle striker Andy Cole had no problem stepping up to Premiership level and soon hit the goal trail, firing against Manchester United at Old Trafford, a brace against Sheffield Wednesday and a home hat-trick against Liverpool. Another young English striker making a mark was Liverpool's talented teenager, Robbie Fowler, who helped himself to a hat-trick against Southampton.

October saw Alan Shearer return to his best with a hat-trick against Leeds United in a 3–3 draw and Coventry City manager Bobby Gould resign from his job following a 5–1 defeat at QPR. Significant change in the boardroom at Manchester City led to the resignation of chairman Peter Swales who was replaced by former star player Francis Lee. The first Manchester derby of the season proved to be a memorable encounter as City stormed to a 2–0 lead before Manchester United produced the sort of dramatic comeback they were becoming famed for, winning the game 3–2 thanks to a late winner from Roy Keane.

Howard Kendall departed the Everton hot seat in December with the Toffees languishing in the bottom half of the table. Norwich grabbed a deserved 2–2 draw against Manchester United at Old Trafford while struggling Swindon were minutes away from a famous victory over Liverpool at Anfield, only for Reds defender Mark Wright to head home a late equaliser. Tottenham, playing an increasingly attacking style under Ossie Ardiles, shared six goals with Liverpool as both clubs struggled for defensive stability. Meanwhile, a 3–1 victory over Aston Villa and a heavy win against Oldham Athletic gave Manchester United 14 point's worth of breathing space at the top of the table as 1993 drew to a close.

January witnessed United and Liverpool share one of the more memorable games of the season as Liverpool fought back from three goals down to secure a dramatic 3–3 draw at Anfield. United's first-half performance had been phenomenal as a close range Steve Bruce header and spectacular goals from Ryan Giggs and Denis Irwin gave them the advantage before Nigel Clough bagged a brace and Neil Ruddock headed home in response for Liverpool.

Merseyside hogged the headlines in the opening months of 1994 as Graeme Souness resigned as Liverpool boss and was replaced by Roy Evans, before Mike Walker, who had worked miracles with Norwich City, was appointed the new Everton manager.

As the month drew to a close, Alan Ball replaced Ian Branfoot as Southampton boss and began his reign with a 2–1 win at Newcastle that featured a beautifully struck free-kick from Matt Le Tissier, while ever improving Blackburn Rovers defeated Leeds United by the same scoreline thanks to two typical poacher's goals from Alan Shearer. With games in hand, the Lancashire club appeared to be the only side capable of challenging Manchester United for the title. United, however, maintained their form with an away victory at QPR, which featured a memorable individual goal from Ryan Giggs.

Legendary Liverpool striker Ian Rush scored his 200th league goal for Liverpool in 2–0 victory over Leeds United at Anfield in April.

Relegation threatened Southampton and Swindon started to pick up form, as the Saints beat Liverpool and the Robins overcame Norwich. The goals of Mark Stein and John Spencer helped Chelsea beat Tottenham and ease clear of relegation worries, but Spurs remained embroiled in a fight to maintain their Premiership status, as did Everton under new boss Mike Walker who went on to lose 3–0 to his former club Norwich.

Champions Manchester United suffered a rare defeat and their only home loss of the season when Chelsea's Gavin Peacock grabbed the winning goal in a 1–0 victory that narrowed the lead at the top of the table to four points. Newcastle and Andy Cole continued their impressive run with a 7–1 victory over Swindon, as they and Blackburn put pressure on United.

United dropped a further two points against bottom placed Swindon in a game marred by a sending off for Eric Cantona following a nasty stamp on John Moncur. A few days later, Cantona again made the headlines for the wrong reasons as he was given another relatively harsh red card following an awkward clash with Arsenal's Tony Adams. The Gunners started to move up the table and close in on United, as Ian Wright's goals, including two hat-tricks in two games, and the dependable defensive unit that had served the Londoners so well for years, helped them pick up a succession of victories.

Goals from Robbie Earle and Dean Holdsworth helped Wimbledon complete a shock 4–1 victory over Blackburn at Selhurst Park, but Rovers kept up the pressure on Manchester United with a 2–0 victory over the Red Devils at the beginning of April. Wimbledon again had their say in the title race, beating United 1–0, while Blackburn defeated Aston Villa by the same margin.

RIGHT: *A frequent scorer of spectacular goals, Southampton's Matt Le Tissier was crucial to the Saints maintaining their Premiership status during the 1990s.*

A season already blessed with high-scoring games continued in that fashion in April as Southampton defeated Norwich 5–4 at Carrow Road. Boosted by Cantona's return to the side, Manchester United took a big step towards retaining the title with a derby day victory over Manchester City that featured a brace from the Frenchman.

With four games to play, Wimbledon sealed Swindon's fate with a 4–2 victory that included a long-range lob from Jon Fashanu, as the Wiltshire club dropped out of the top flight after a single season. Managing on a shoestring budget with unfashionable Wimbledon, Joe Kinnear guided the south London club to an impressive sixth place finish.

*ABOVE: The prolific Ian Wright, pictured here celebrating a goal against Swindon Town, was Arsenal's talismanic attacking presence during the early Premier League years.*

Blackburn crucially dropped two points at home to QPR, leaving Manchester United to increase their advantage at the top of the table with a hard-fought victory at Ipswich Town which featured a well-taken goal by Ryan Giggs. Rovers then went in to an away clash with Coventry City knowing they had to win to prevent United lifting the title, but the Sky Blues denied them thanks to two goals from Julian Darby in a 2–1 victory, helping to ensure that Manchester United achieved back to back titles.

At the other end of the table and with a single game remaining, two relegation places were still to be confirmed. One of the most dramatic and heart-wrenching final days in Premier League history followed with five clubs in contention for demotion, including Everton who had not been relegated since the Football League was founded in 1888. The Toffees completed the great escape, coming back from two goals down to defeat Wimbledon 3–2. The game was lit up by a splendid strike from Barry Horne and featured two goals from Graham Stuart, including a nerveless pressure cooker penalty. Southampton also stayed up by the skin of their teeth thanks to a 3–3 draw with West Ham. A 2–0 defeat to Spurs sent Oldham, who had avoided relegation on goal difference the previous season, down, before Sheffield United took the dreaded final spot, following a 3–2 defeat at Chelsea.

## ⚽ INTERESTING INFO

Since their relegation in 1994 only one of the three clubs that dropped out of the division that term have returned to the Premier League; Sheffield United, who spent a single season in the top flight in 2006–07.

'Goal king' Andy Cole took to the Premiership like a duck to water, helping newly-promoted Newcastle United storm up the table.

# HONOURS LIST

## FA Carling Premiership

**CHAMPIONS:** Manchester United
United sealed back to back titles thanks to a return of 92 points and scored 80 goals. They lost just four out of their 42 games and finished eight points clear of their rivals.
**RUNNERS-UP:** Blackburn Rovers
**RELEGATED:** Sheffield United, Oldham Athletic, Swindon Town
**TOP GOAL SCORER:** Andy Cole (34 goals for Newcastle United)

SHOOT MAGAZINE
1993–94

*Sheffield Wednesday winger Chris Waddle adorned the front cover while former England captain Gary Lineker gave a critical interview about under-pressure Three Lions manager Graham Taylor. Two of the stars of the day, Eric Cantona and Andy Cole, were celebrated in a pair of bumper posters.*

# 1993–94 SEASON TABLE

|   |   | M | W | D | L | GF | GA | GD | PTS |
|---|---|---|---|---|---|----|----|----|-----|
| 1 | Manchester United | 42 | 27 | 11 | 4 | 80 | 38 | +42 | 92 |
| 2 | Blackburn Rovers | 42 | 25 | 9 | 8 | 63 | 36 | +27 | 84 |
| 3 | Newcastle United | 42 | 23 | 8 | 11 | 82 | 41 | +41 | 77 |
| 4 | Arsenal | 42 | 18 | 17 | 7 | 53 | 28 | +25 | 71 |
| 5 | Leeds United | 42 | 18 | 16 | 8 | 65 | 39 | +26 | 70 |
| 6 | Wimbledon | 42 | 18 | 11 | 13 | 56 | 53 | +3 | 65 |
| 7 | Sheffield Wednesday | 42 | 16 | 16 | 10 | 76 | 54 | +22 | 64 |
| 8 | Liverpool | 42 | 17 | 9 | 16 | 59 | 55 | +4 | 60 |
| 9 | Queens Park Rangers | 42 | 16 | 12 | 14 | 62 | 61 | +1 | 60 |
| 10 | Aston Villa | 42 | 15 | 12 | 15 | 46 | 50 | -4 | 57 |
| 11 | Coventry City | 42 | 14 | 14 | 14 | 43 | 45 | -2 | 56 |
| 12 | Norwich City | 42 | 12 | 17 | 13 | 65 | 61 | +4 | 53 |
| 13 | West Ham United | 42 | 13 | 13 | 16 | 47 | 58 | -11 | 52 |
| 14 | Chelsea | 42 | 13 | 12 | 17 | 49 | 53 | -4 | 51 |
| 15 | Tottenham Hotspur | 42 | 11 | 12 | 19 | 54 | 59 | -5 | 45 |
| 16 | Manchester City | 42 | 9 | 18 | 15 | 38 | 49 | -11 | 45 |
| 17 | Everton | 42 | 12 | 8 | 22 | 42 | 63 | -21 | 44 |
| 18 | Southampton | 42 | 12 | 7 | 23 | 49 | 66 | -17 | 43 |
| 19 | Ipswich Town | 42 | 9 | 16 | 17 | 35 | 58 | -23 | 43 |
| 20 | Sheffield United | 42 | 8 | 18 | 16 | 42 | 60 | -18 | 42 |
| 21 | Oldham Athletic | 42 | 9 | 13 | 20 | 42 | 68 | -26 | 40 |
| 22 | Swindon Town | 42 | 5 | 15 | 22 | 47 | 100 | -53 | 30 |

# PLAYERS OF THE SEASON

**PFA PLAYER OF THE YEAR:** Eric Cantona, Manchester United
**PFA YOUNG PLAYER OF THE YEAR:** Andy Cole, Newcastle United
**FOOTBALL WRITERS PLAYER OF THE YEAR:** Alan Shearer, Blackburn Rovers

**FOOTBALL LEAGUE DIVISION ONE CHAMPIONS:**
Crystal Palace
**PROMOTED:** Nottingham Forest
**DIVISION ONE PLAY-OFF WINNERS:** Leicester City
**RELEGATED:** Birmingham City, Oxford United,
Peterborough United
**TOP GOAL SCORER:** John McGinlay (25 goals for
Bolton Wanderers)

In his first managerial assignment, Crystal Palace boss Alan Smith took the Eagles back into the top flight as Division One champions. Inspired by the goals of Chris Armstrong and a reliable defence, featuring the likes of Gareth Southgate, Richard Shaw and Dean Gordon, Crystal Palace topped Division One with 90 points, finishing seven clear of runners-up Nottingham Forest. Like Palace, the Nottingham club ensured their stay in the second tier was restricted to a single season, as Frank Clark erased memories of relegation under his predecessor Brian Clough. The third club to reach the Premiership was Leicester City who finally gained promotion via the play-offs having suffered two final defeats in the previous two seasons. The Foxes defeated their East Midlands rivals Derby Country 2–1 in the final thanks to two goals from their inspirational captain Steve Walsh.

**DIVISION TWO CHAMPIONS:** Reading
**PROMOTED:** Port Vale
**DIVISION TWO PLAY-OFF WINNERS:** Burnley
**RELEGATED:** Fulham, Exeter City, Hartlepool United,
Barnet
**TOP GOAL SCORER:** Jimmy Quinn (35 goals for
Reading)

Mark McGhee guided his emerging Reading team to the Division Two championship and promotion, as the goals of experienced striker Jimmy Quinn helped them finish a point ahead of second placed Port Vale. Managed by John Rudge, Vale made up for play-off final defeat the previous season by gaining automatic promotion. Burnley completed the trio of promoted teams, defeating Stockport County 2–1 in the play-off final.

ABOVE TOP LEFT: *Leicester City captain Steve Walsh celebrates his play-off final winning goal against Derby County at Wembley.*

ABOVE TOP RIGHT: *Veteran front man Jimmy Quinn was influential in Reading's Division Two title-winning campaign.*

**DIVISION THREE CHAMPIONS**: Shrewsbury Town
**PROMOTED**: Chester City, Crewe Alexandra
**DIVISION THREE PLAY-OFF WINNERS**: Wycombe Wanderers
**RELEGATED**: None
**TOP GOAL SCORER**: Tony Ellis (27 goals for Preston North End).
Shrewsbury Town, managed by Fred Davies, were promoted as champions. Chester City, led by Graham Barrow, were second and Crewe Alexandra continued their progression under the guidance of long-serving coach Dario Gradi to finish third. Martin O'Neill's Wycombe Wanderers defeated Preston North End 4–2 in the play-off final to seal back-to-back promotions.

**FOOTBALL CONFERENCE CHAMPIONS**: Kidderminster Harriers.
Managed by Graham Allner, the Midlands club finished clear at the top of the table but missed out on promotion after their Aggborough stadium failed to meet safety requirements.

BELOW: *Long-serving Crewe Alexandra boss Dario Gradi, famed for his ability to bring through talented young players, guided the Railwaymen to automatic promotion into Division Two.*

## UP FOR THE CUP

**FA CUP WINNERS:** Manchester United

The Red Devils completed the first league and cup double in their history with a routine 4–0 victory over Chelsea at Wembley. The Blues shaded a tight first half but United showed their class after the interval with Eric Cantona calmly dispatching two penalties and Mark Hughes and Brian McClair adding gloss to the scoreline.

United had beaten Oldham Athletic in a semi-final replay held at Maine Road. The first game at Wembley ended 1–1 after extra time with Mark Hughes scoring a dramatic late volley to level Neil Pointon's opener for Oldham. The replay was one-way traffic and resulted in a 4–1 victory for the Manchester club. Chelsea's passage to the final was more straightforward as they defeated Division Two side Luton Town 2–0 thanks to a Gavin Peacock double.

Luton had previously knocked out Premiership opposition in Newcastle United and West Ham United, with youngsters Scott Oakes, John Hartson and Paul Telfer the star men. Second tier Bolton Wanderers also enjoyed a spirited cup run, clocking up famous victories against Everton, Aston Villa and Arsenal. Other shock results included Bristol City's 1–0 win against Liverpool, Oxford United's replay victory over Leeds United and Manchester City's loss to Cardiff City.

ABOVE: *Manchester United's man for the big occasion, Mark Hughes, celebrates his FA Cup final goal against Chelsea. Bullish yet immensely skilled, the Welsh striker also scored a crucial match-saving volley against Oldham Athletic in the tournament's semi-final.*

## LEAGUE (COCA COLA) CUP WINNERS: Aston Villa

Ron Atkinson's Villa tasted revenge over their 1992–93 title rivals Manchester United with a dominant 3–1 victory at Wembley to deny the Red Devils a treble of domestic trophies. The goals came from Dalian Atkinson, Dean Saunders and Andy Townsend. Mark Hughes grabbed a consolation goal for the Reds to maintain his impressive goal-scoring record in major finals. To reach the final, United thumped Sheffield Wednesday 5–1 over a two–legged semi-final while Villa dispatched second tier Tranmere Rovers on penalties.

## CHARITY SHIELD WINNERS: Manchester United

The league champions defeated FA Cup winners Arsenal on penalties following a 1–1 draw at Wembley that featured spectacular goals from Ian Wright and Mark Hughes. Gunners stopper David Seaman had his penalty saved by his United counterpart Peter Schmeichel in the shootout to confirm United's victory.

## THE FOOTBALL LEAGUE (AUTOGLASS) TROPHY: Swansea City

The Welsh club tasted glory at Wembley thanks to a penalty shootout victory over Huddersfield Town.

OPPOSITE PAGE: *Young Luton Town forward Scott Oakes played a starring role as David Pleat's Hatters progressed to the FA Cup semi-final.*

ABOVE: *Aston Villa's Atkinson's, manager Ron (pictured left) and striker Dalian, cradle the League Cup trophy after defeating Manchester United 3–1 at Wembley.*

## INTO EUROPE

### European Champions League

Manchester United began their first campaign in European football's premier competition for 27 years with a 5–3 aggregate victory over Hungarian champions Kispest Honved that featured two-goals from skipper Steve Bruce. However, the Red Devils' run was ended in the second round after an away goal defeat to Turkish side Galatasaray following a 3–3 draw.

### European Cup Winners' Cup

ABOVE: *Arsenal striker Alan Smith guides home the strike that sealed European Cup Winners' glory for the Gunners.*

Arsenal enjoyed a memorable run in the competition, winning the first European trophy in their history following a 1–0 victory over Italian side Parma in the Copenhagen final. The winning goal was scored by Alan Smith who slammed a low long-rage effort into the net after 22 minutes. En route to the final George Graham's men defeated a number of impressive sides, including Paris Saint-Germain, Torino and Standard Liege.

## UEFA Cup

Of the two teams representing England, Aston Villa and Norwich City, it was the Canaries who grabbed the headlines following a shock victory over German giants Bayern Munich. Both clubs successfully negotiated their first round ties as Norwich overcame Vitesse 3–0 on aggregate and Villa defeated Slovan Bratislava 2–1. Norwich were paired with Bayern in the next stage, travelling to Munich's Olympic Stadium as clear underdogs for the first leg. However, inspired by a spectacular long-range volley from Jeremy Goss and a further goal from Mark Bowen, the English club claimed a famous 2–1 victory. In the home leg, Norwich secured a 1–1 draw at Carrow Road, which featured another goal from Goss and a top-drawer goalkeeping performance from Bryan Gunn, to reach the next round. Mike Walker's men were then knocked out by eventual winners Inter Milan following two narrow 1–0 defeats. Aston Villa lost 2–1 on aggregate to Spanish side Deportivo La Coruna in the second round.

### INTERESTING INFO

Norwich's 2–1 victory over Bayern Munich was the only time the European giants ever lost a home tie in the Olympic Stadium.

ABOVE TOP: *Norwich City's Jeremy Goss celebrates the memorable long-range volley that inspired the Canaries to a shock 2–1 UEFA Cup victory over Bayern Munich on their own patch.*

ABOVE BOTTOM: *An enraged Graham Taylor watches on helplessly as England slump to defeat against the Netherlands.*

## THE INTERNATIONAL SCENE

The final nails in the coffin of England's World Cup qualifying campaign were hammered home by Holland, who defeated the Three Lions 2–0 largely thanks to the efforts of defender Ronald Koeman. A 7–1 victory over San Marino in the final group game was too little too late and manager Graham Taylor was replaced by Terry Venables.

# WALKER'S MILLIONS FIRE ROVERS TO GLORY

**T**he Premiership was preparing to streamline from 22 to 20 teams for the 1995–96 season, meaning that four teams would drop through the relegation trapdoor at the end of the campaign. This also had a direct impact on Division One, as only two teams rather than the usual three would be in contention for promotion to the top flight.

Having claimed back to back Premiership titles, Manchester United were again expected to challenge at the top of the table, with Blackburn Rovers, who had broken the British transfer record with the £5m capture of Chris Sutton, looking like their most likely rivals.

In many ways the 1994–95 campaign represented a watershed for the English top flight, as clubs began to spend significantly in the transfer market. Fees and wages rose significantly, emphasised by the significant financial clout of Blackburn Rovers and Manchester United, and the foreign market became more popular than the domestic one, particularly in the aftermath of the 1994 World Cup in America.

Before the season started, Billy Bonds stepped down as West Ham manager following a dispute with the club's owners and was replaced by his assistant, Harry Redknapp.

Away from the increasingly captivating action on the pitch, the 1994–95 campaign was one filled with off-field controversy and speculation. Arsenal hit the headlines on more than one occasion – firstly when Paul Merson publically announced his battles with gambling, alcohol and drug addictions and secondly when manager George Graham was embroiled in a scandal involving the alleged acceptance of illegal payments from agents, which eventually led to his departure from the club.

Later on the season, Manchester United's Eric Cantona caused a nationwide stir for an on-field misdemeanour. His kung-fu kick aimed at a Crystal Palace supporter saw him sentenced to community service and banned from the game for nine months.

OPPOSITE PAGE: *One part of the much feted 'SAS' strike partnership, alongside Alan Shearer, Chris Sutton added even more firepower to Blackburn Rovers' dangerous frontline.*

LEFT: *Seconds before a moment of madness ended his season, Eric Cantona fixes his gaze on the Crystal Palace supporter he was about to attack, Matthew Simmonds (pictured gesticulating at the Frenchman).*

# TRANSFER TALES

Tottenham, with Ossie Ardiles still at the helm, spent heavily in the transfer market, bringing in a number of high-profile foreign players, including the German striker Jurgen Klinsmann, who became one of the first globally renowned players to play in the fledgling division. Spurs spent £2m to entice Klinsmann from AS Monaco and also captured the Romanian World Cup pair of Ilie Dumitrescu and Gheorghe Popescu.

Newcastle also added foreign class to their squad, capturing Swiss right-back Mark Hottiger and Belgian central defender Philippe Albert. Everton spent heavily on Nigerian striker Daniel Amokachi and Arsenal dipped their toes further into the continental market with the addition of Swedish midfielder Stefan Schwarz, who joined from Benfica.

The Scandinavian invasion into English football gathered pace as Klass Ingesson joined Sheffield Wednesday, who also added Romanian right-back Dan Petrescu, while the Danish trio of striker Ronnie Ekelund, who was loaned to Southampton from Barcelona, defender Marc Rieper, who joined West Ham and defender Claus Thomsen, who was signed by Ipswich Town, all arrived during the summer.

The domestic market remained strong, with the British transfer record breached twice during the season, first with Blackburn's capture of Chris Sutton and later on in the campaign when Manchester United spent £6m on Newcastle's Andy Cole. Newcastle added Derby County striker Paul Kitson while Liverpool invested a record figure for a defender, signing Coventry City centre back Phil Babb for £3.6m.

Manchester United brought in Blackburn defender David May but allowed powerful striker Dion Dublin to depart for Coventry City for £2m. A similarly styled English centre forward, Paul Furlong, joined Chelsea from second tier Watford for £2.3m while another promising front man, John Hartson, swapped the Football League for the top flight, when Arsenal paid Luton Town £2.3m to make the Welshman Britain's most expensive teenager.

*Germany striker Jurgen Klinsmann represented a real coup for the Premiership when Tottenham secured his services. The dead-eye finisher developed a superb partnership with Teddy Sheringham and became one of the most dangerous all-round front men in the division.*

## BIGGEST TRANSFERS

**ANDY COLE** – from Newcastle United to Manchester United – £6m (plus Keith Gillespie)

**CHRIS SUTTON** – from Norwich City to Blackburn Rovers – £5m

**DUNCAN FERGUSON** – from Glasgow Rangers to Everton – £4.2m

**PHIL BABB** – from Coventry City to Liverpool – £3.6m

**JOHN SCALES** – from Wimbledon to Liverpool £3.5m

**TONY YEBOAH** – from Eintracht Frankfurt to Leeds United – £3.4m

**DANIEL AMOKACHI** – from Club Brugge to Everton – £3m

**JOHN SCALES** – from Wimbledon to Liverpool – £3m

**BRYAN ROY** – from Foggia to Nottingham Forest – £2.9m

**GHEORGHE POPESCU** – from PSV Eindhoven to Tottenham Hotspur – £2.9m

OPPOSITE PAGE: *Razor-sharp Ukrainian winger Andrei Kanchelskis added consistent end product to his game during the 1994–95 campaign and regularly hit the target for Manchester United.*

## TALES OF THE TURF

The season started with Tottenham's high-profile summer signing Jurgen Klinsmann hogging the headlines thanks to a debut goal against Sheffield Wednesday that he and his team-mates marked with a dive-themed celebration that cheekily nodded towards the German's reputation for simulation. Spurs lost a thrilling match 4–3 that saw Wednesday begin the season positively. Liverpool hammered newly promoted Crystal Palace 6–1 at Selhurst Park and Newcastle United began with a 3–1 win at Leicester City.

Nottingham Forest's only major signing, Bryan Roy, scored a cracking goal on his debut as the East Midlands club defeated Ipswich 1–0, before following that up with a hard fought 1–1 draw with Manchester United that featured a great finish from Stan Collymore. Another highly-rated young English striker, Chris Sutton, adapted to life at Blackburn Rovers quickly, getting off the mark with goals against Leicester and Coventry, including a hat-trick against the Sky Blues.

Tottenham were famed for their attacking formation and entertaining football at the start of the campaign as Ossie Ardiles fielded his 'famous five' of forward thinking players, which featured Jurgen Klinsmann, Teddy Sheringham, Nicky Barmby, Darren Anderton and Ilie Dumitrescu. But, with a relatively inexperienced defence often left exposed, Spurs often struggled for consistency.

Another team expressing themselves through free-flowing attacking football were Roy Evans' Liverpool, who were inspired by the youthful exuberance of hometown pair Steve McManaman and Robbie Fowler. Fowler announced himself on the Premiership scene with a record-breaking hat-trick in a 3–0 win against Arsenal.

ABOVE TOP: *In a season filled with lethal strike pairings, classy Dutch forward Bryan Roy was the perfect foil for the prolific Stan Collymore, as Nottingham Forest challenged for a European qualifying place.*

ABOVE BOTTOM: *Teenage striker Robbie Fowler, pictured celebrating his record-breaking hat-trick against Arsenal alongside club legend Ian Rush, firmly announced himself on the Premiership stage during the 1994–95 season.*

### ⊕ INTERESTING INFO

Robbie Fowler's first-half hat-trick against Arsenal, which he completed in four minutes twenty three seconds, remains the fastest ever scored in the Premier League.

*Pace, power and great close-control, Stan Collymore emerged as one of the division's most dangerous attacking talents as Nottingham Forest adapted seamlessly to life back in the Premiership.*

Newcastle United were the early season pace-setters and won each of their first six games thanks to the goals of Andy Cole and the increasingly impressive Rob Lee. Blackburn Rovers remained unbeaten into the second month of the campaign, but Manchester United suffered consecutive early season reversals against Leeds United at Elland Road and away to Ipswich Town, which left them trailing in fourth place.

United then lost to Sheffield Wednesday before defeating Blackburn Rovers 4–2 at Ewood Park in a thrilling encounter that featured great goals from Mark Hughes and Paul Warhurst, as well as a decisive double from Andrei Kanchelskis. United then inflicted Newcastle's first defeat of the campaign, while Blackburn ended Nottingham Forest's unbeaten start.

Off-field matters at Queens Park Rangers led to the departure of manager Gerry Francis, following ongoing disagreements with the board and the appointment of former Rangers player Rodney Marsh as Director of Football without Francis' consent. Ray Wilkins left his playing contract with Crystal Palace to take up the reins at Loftus Road while Francis succeeded the sacked Ossie Ardiles at Spurs.

As the managerial merry-go-round continued, Ron Atkinson was fired by struggling Aston Villa and Everton, who were rooted to the bottom of the table and had made their worst ever start to a season, dispensed with the services of Mike Walker. Former Oldham Athletic boss Joe Royle was next in the Goodison Park hot seat. Brian Little tendered his resignation at Leicester City to take the vacant Aston Villa job with former Reading boss Mark McGhee replacing him at Filbert Street.

Manchester United returned to form in the first Manchester derby of the season, recording their biggest win in a derby for over 100 years – a 5–0 win that featured an Andrei Kanchelskis hat-trick. Everton began life under Joe Royle with a 2–0 win over Liverpool and Wimbledon defeated Newcastle 3–2 and knocked Kevin Keegan's men off the top of the table.

December brought another managerial change, as John Lyall stepped down as Ipswich boss and was replaced by George Burley. Nottingham Forest continued their impressive campaign with a surprise 2–1 victory against Manchester United, achieved by a smartly taken goal from Stan Collymore. Blackburn capitalised on that slip-up with a convincing 3–1 Boxing Day victory over Manchester City to leave themselves three points clear at the top come the turn of the year.

A total of four players have scored five goals in a single Premier League match. In addition to Andy Cole, they are Alan Shearer, Jermain Defoe and Dimitar Berbatov.

United spent heavily in the transfer market in a bid to remedy that situation, enticing free-scoring Andy Cole from Newcastle in a deal that delighted Old Trafford but left thousands of Geordies apoplectic with Kevin Keegan for allowing their star player to leave. As Cole slowly settled into the team, United's season was under a dark cloud during January when Eric Cantona was given a lengthy ban by the FA after he attacked Crystal Palace fan Matthew Simmonds following his sending off in a league contest at Selhurst Park. The Frenchman did not play again that season.

A rejuvenated Paul Merson returned to the Arsenal team in February but the Gunners still struggled for consistency and George Graham paid the price, being replaced by his assistant Stewart Houston. Tottenham recorded an impressive 3–1 victory over Blackburn Rovers as Kenny Dalglish's men suffered their first dip in form of the season.

The relegation battle involved half of the teams in the division, including the likes of Arsenal, Aston Villa, Chelsea, West Ham, Everton, Crystal Palace and Coventry City, with the latter club soon in the market for a new manager following Phil Neal's resignation. Coventry opted for Ron Atkinson as his replacement.

Duncan Ferguson scored the winning goal as Manchester United went down 1–0 to Everton at Goodison, handing the title initiative back to Blackburn before the Red Devils returned to something approaching their best from with a Premier League record 9–0 victory over Ipswich Town at Old Trafford that featured a five goal salvo from Andy Cole.

In March, Liverpool recorded a 2–0 victory over Manchester United thanks to goals from Steve McManaman and Jamie Redknapp. Blackburn enjoyed better fortunes on Merseyside, defeating relegation threatened Everton 2–1 at Goodison Park. A win against QPR gave Rovers an eight point advantage with six games left to play.

In April, Leicester became the first club to be relegated following West Ham's victory over Wimbledon. They were followed through the trapdoor by Ipswich Town as a result of Everton's 2–0 victory over Newcastle. Gordon Strachan returned to playing action at Coventry City, also taking the assistant manager's job, after being persuaded out of retirement by Ron Atkinson. The Scotsman's experience and guile had a major bearing on the Sky Blues' survival hopes. Norwich manager John Deehan resigned with just five matches to go and Gary Megson stepped in as his replacement, but it proved too little too late and the Canaries became the third club to be relegated having gained just 10 points from their last 20 games.

Aston Villa continued to struggle, despite an initial upturn in form following Brian Little's appointment and the team went eight league games without a goal in the closing weeks of the season before confirming their safety with a home win over Liverpool. Coventry ensured their top-flight status with a Dion Dublin-inspired victory over Spurs. The fourth and final relegation place was filled by Crystal Palace, whose manager Alan Smith stepped down from his role. Further managerial casualties, in a season filled with changes in the dugout, came at Manchester City when Brian Horton was shown the door, and at Sheffield Wednesday, where Trevor Francis resigned.

ABOVE TOP LEFT: *George Graham (pictured right) finally lost his job following a season filled with speculation about off-field matters and was replaced by his assistant, Stewart Houston (pictured left).*

OPPOSITE PAGE: *The goals of towering Coventry City striker Dion Dublin were key to keeping the Sky Blues in the Premiership.*

Blackburn endured a late season stutter, dropping points at Leeds before suffering an unlikely 3–2 home loss to Manchester City and going down 2–0 against West Ham. Manchester United gained maximum points from their two games in hand against Coventry and Sheffield Wednesday to cut Blackburn's lead to two points. That advantage was retained going into the final day, following a tense 1–0 win against Newcastle and United's 2–1 win over Southampton, in a game the Old Trafford giants needed to win to take the title race to the most dramatic of final day deciders.

On that momentous final day of the season, both teams were playing away. Blackburn travelled to Anfield to face Liverpool and Manchester United were pitched against West Ham at Upton Park. Blackburn needed to avoid defeat to become champions with United knowing that only victory would do for them in London.

Rovers took an early lead through Alan Shearer while United went behind following a Michael Hughes goal. In the second half United levelled matters through Brian McClair and Liverpool squared the scores at Anfield courtesy of John Barnes, leaving nerves frayed in both title-chasing camps.

ABOVE: *The goals and the money. Alan Shearer (left) celebrates with club owner Jack Walker after Blackburn Rovers were crowned Premiership champions.*

United laid siege to the West Ham goal but a combination of superb last-ditch defending, great goalkeeping from Ludek Miklosko and profligate finishing, left Ferguson's men frustrated. Their disappointment was compounded when Jamie Redknapp fired home a late free-kick to win the game for Liverpool, meaning United ultimately missed out on the title by a single point.

# HONOURS LIST

## FA Carling Premiership

**CHAMPIONS:** Blackburn Rovers
Blackburn won their first top-flight title for 81 years, with strikers Alan Shearer and Chris Sutton in fine form, helping them clock up 80 goals and 89 points.
**RUNNERS-UP:** Manchester United
**RELEGATED:** Crystal Palace, Norwich City, Leicester City, Ipswich Town
**TOP GOAL SCORER:** Alan Shearer (34 goals for Blackburn Rovers)

SHOOT MAGAZINE
1994–95

*Ahead of his confirmed move to Newcastle United, the potential destination of much sought-after Queens Park Rangers striker Les Ferdinand took prominence. Speculation about the future of Manchester United's under-fire forward, Eric Cantona, also featured while the abilities of Leeds striker Tony Yeboah were showcased. England international David Platt provided an exclusive diary of his time in Italy with Sampdoria.*

## 1994–95 SEASON TABLE

|  |  | M | W | D | L | GF | GA | GD | PTS |
|---|---|---|---|---|---|---|---|---|---|
| 1 | Blackburn Rovers | 42 | 27 | 8 | 7 | 80 | 39 | +41 | 89 |
| 2 | Manchester United | 42 | 26 | 10 | 6 | 77 | 28 | +49 | 88 |
| 3 | Nottingham Forest | 42 | 22 | 11 | 9 | 72 | 43 | +29 | 77 |
| 4 | Liverpool | 42 | 21 | 11 | 10 | 65 | 37 | +28 | 74 |
| 5 | Leeds United | 42 | 20 | 13 | 9 | 59 | 38 | +21 | 73 |
| 6 | Newcastle United | 42 | 20 | 12 | 10 | 67 | 47 | +20 | 72 |
| 7 | Tottenham Hotspur | 42 | 16 | 14 | 12 | 66 | 58 | +8 | 62 |
| 8 | Queens Park Rangers | 42 | 17 | 9 | 16 | 61 | 59 | +2 | 60 |
| 9 | Wimbledon | 42 | 15 | 11 | 16 | 48 | 65 | -17 | 56 |
| 10 | Southampton | 42 | 12 | 18 | 12 | 61 | 63 | -2 | 54 |
| 11 | Chelsea | 42 | 13 | 15 | 14 | 50 | 55 | -5 | 54 |
| 12 | Arsenal | 42 | 13 | 12 | 17 | 52 | 49 | +3 | 51 |
| 13 | Sheffield Wednesday | 42 | 13 | 12 | 17 | 49 | 57 | -8 | 51 |
| 14 | West Ham United | 42 | 13 | 11 | 18 | 44 | 48 | -4 | 50 |
| 15 | Everton | 42 | 11 | 17 | 14 | 44 | 51 | -7 | 50 |
| 16 | Coventry City | 42 | 12 | 14 | 16 | 44 | 62 | -18 | 50 |
| 17 | Manchester City | 42 | 12 | 13 | 17 | 53 | 64 | -11 | 49 |
| 18 | Aston Villa | 42 | 11 | 15 | 16 | 51 | 56 | -5 | 48 |
| 19 | Crystal Palace | 42 | 11 | 12 | 19 | 34 | 49 | -15 | 45 |
| 20 | Norwich City | 42 | 10 | 13 | 19 | 37 | 54 | -17 | 43 |
| 21 | Leicester City | 42 | 6 | 11 | 25 | 45 | 80 | -35 | 29 |
| 22 | Ipswich Town | 42 | 7 | 6 | 29 | 36 | 93 | -57 | 27 |

## PLAYERS OF THE SEASON

**PFA PLAYER OF THE YEAR:** Alan Shearer, Blackburn Rovers
**PFA YOUNG PLAYER OF THE YEAR:** Robbie Fowler, Liverpool
**FOOTBALL WRITERS' PLAYER OF THE YEAR:** Jurgen Klinsmann, Tottenham Hotspur

**FOOTBALL LEAGUE DIVISION ONE CHAMPIONS:**
Middlesbrough
**DIVISION ONE PLAY-OFF WINNERS:** Bolton Wanderers
**RELEGATED:** Swindon Town, Burnley, Bristol City,
Norwich City
**TOP GOAL SCORER:** John Aldridge (27 goals for
Tranmere Rovers)

Bryan Robson won the Division One title with Middlesbrough and achieved promotion to the Premiership at the end of his debut campaign as a manager. Supported by the significant funds of chairman Steve Gibson, Robson added plenty of quality, including Norwegian striker, Jan Age Fjortoft who had been captured from Swindon.

With just one more promotion place available, the other top five teams, which included second placed Reading, went straight into a play-off competition that saw the Royals and Bolton Wanderers face-off in a memorable final. Tied at 2–2 after 90 minutes the contest went in to extra time and was eventually won 4–3 by Bolton, with powerful striker Fabien de Freitas grabbing a crucial brace.

**DIVISION TWO CHAMPIONS:** Birmingham City
**DIVISION TWO PLAY-OFF WINNERS:** Huddersfield Town
**RELEGATED:** Cambridge United, Plymouth Argyle,
Cardiff City, Chester City, Leyton Orient
**TOP GOAL SCORER:** Gary Bennett (29 goals for
Wrexham)

Under Barry Fry Birmingham sealed an immediate return to Division One by lifting the Division Two championship trophy. Fielding a number of experienced pros and plenty of attacking talent, including Steve Claridge, Kevin Francis and Jose Dominguez, the Blues clocked up 89 points and scored 84 goals. As with Division One, the third tier was limited to just two promotion places, with the final spot taken by Huddersfield Town, who defeated Bristol Rovers 2–1 in the play-off final.

**DIVISION THREE CHAMPIONS:** Carlisle United
**PROMOTED:** Walsall
**DIVISION THREE PLAY-OFF WINNERS:** Chesterfield
**RELEGATED:** None
**TOP GOAL SCORER:** Dougie Freedman (24 goals for
Barnet)

Backed by the finances of Michael Knighton and managed by Melvin Day, Carlisle United stormed to the title, gaining 91 points and finished eight clear of second placed Walsall. The Cumbrians also made their first appearance at Wembley during the season, suffering a narrow loss to Birmingham City in the Auto Windscreens Shield final. The second automatic promotion place was taken by Chris Nicholl's Walsall, with John Duncan's Chesterfield victorious in the play-offs.

**FOOTBALL CONFERENCE CHAMPIONS:** Macclesfield Town, like Kidderminster Harriers the season before, were denied promotion to the Football League after their Moss Rose stadium was deemed insufficient to host league football.

OPPOSITE PAGE: *Dependable defender Neil Cox was a key man as Middlesbrough returned to the Premiership under the guidance of Bryan Robson.*

RIGHT: *Charismatic manager Barry Fry celebrates another goal as Birmingham City head for promotion.*

# UP FOR THE CUP

**FA CUP WINNERS:** Everton

Just days after the crushing blow of losing the league title to Blackburn Rovers, Manchester United again suffered disappointment as Everton defeated them 1–0 at Wembley in a closely fought contest. The game's only goal came from experienced striker Paul Rideout who headed home from close-range after Graham Stuart's powerful effort came crashing back off the cross-bar following a swift counter-attack led by Anders Limpar. The Toffees' experienced skipper Dave Watson lifted the club's first major trophy for eight years.

To reach the final, Everton thrashed Spurs 4–1 at Elland Road in a game featuring two goals from Daniel Amokachi while Manchester United overcame Crystal Palace following a replay comprising two feisty encounters. Shock results earlier in the season came when non-league Marlow beat Oxford United, Wrexham overcame Ipswich, Wolverhampton Wanderers knocked out Sheffield Wednesday on penalties and Millwall shocked Arsenal with a 2–0 win at Highbury before defeating Chelsea in the next round.

BELOW: *Experienced striker Paul Rideout celebrates his winning header against Manchester United in the FA Cup final.*

**LEAGUE (COCA COLA) CUP WINNERS:** Liverpool

Roy Evans lifted his first trophy as Liverpool boss and secured the Reds' first honour of the Premier League era with a 2–1 victory over Bolton Wanderers. Liverpool sailed into a two-goal lead thanks to two superb individual goals from winger Steve McManaman, who finished neatly following a mazy run on both occasions. Bolton responded through Alan Thompson but the Merseyside club held them off to capture the cup. The beaten semi-final finalists were Crystal Palace, who lost 2–0 on aggregate to Liverpool and Swindon Town who went down 4–3 to Bolton. Earlier in the tournament, shock results included Mansfield Town defeating Leeds United over two legs, Portsmouth's victory over Everton and Notts County's win over Spurs.

**CHARITY SHIELD WINNERS:** Manchester United

As double winners, Manchester United were paired with league runners-up Blackburn Rovers in the Wembley showpiece and went on to defeat their rivals 2–0 thanks to an Eric Cantona penalty and an overhead kick from Paul Ince.

**THE FOOTBALL LEAGUE (AUTO WINDSCREENS) SHIELD:** Birmingham City

Led by the charismatic Barry Fry, Birmingham defeated Carlisle United 1–0 at Wembley thanks to an extra-time winner from Paul Tait.

### ⚽ INTERESTING INFO

Paul Tait's football League Trophy winner for Birmingham was the first sudden death 'golden goal' ever scored in British football.

*Man of the match Steve McManaman poses with the League Cup after his two goals for Liverpool defeated Bolton Wanderers.*

## INTO EUROPE

### European Champions League

Manchester United's second season in the Champions League saw them drawn in a group featuring Spanish giants Barcelona, Swedish champions IFK Gothenburg and Turkey's Galatasaray. Despite an impressive home record that saw them defeat Gothenburg 4–2 and Galatasaray 4–0, and grab an entertaining 2–2 draw with Barcelona that featured memorable goals from Mark Hughes and Lee Sharpe, the Red Devils struggled on their travels, losing 3–1 in Sweden and suffering a humbling 4–0 defeat to Barcelona. Alex Ferguson's men failed to progress and their struggles in Europe's premier club competition continued.

## European Cup Winners' Cup

As holders of the trophy, Arsenal gained automatic entry into the competition and enjoyed another memorable campaign, once again reaching the final. Along the way the Gunners completed impressive victories over Brondby, Auxerre and Sampdoria, and Ian Wright was in fine goal-scoring form. Summer signing Stefan Schwarz was another key man, grabbing a crucial late goal in the semi-final with Sampdoria to take the tie to penalties. During the shootout, England goalkeeper David Seaman saved three of the Italians' five kicks. However, the final against Real Zaragoza proved to be a disappointing one for the Arsenal stopper, as he was beaten by a long-range lob from former Tottenham midfielder, Nayim, whose extra-time strike sealed the trophy for the Spanish club.

The eventual winners also put paid to the hopes of another English club, Chelsea, who qualified as FA Cup runners-up and went on their own impressive run. The Blues reached the semi-finals but missed out 4–3 on aggregate to Zaragoza, having earlier tasted victory over the likes of Club Brugge and Austria Vienna.

## UEFA Cup

The trio of English entrants experienced mixed fortunes, as Blackburn Rovers crashed out in the first round to Swedish side Trelleborg. Aston Villa, who recorded an impressive penalty shootout victory over an all-star Inter Milan side, were knocked out by Turkey's Trabzonspor and Newcastle United, who thumped Royal Antwerp 10–2 over two legs, suffered a second round defeat to Athletic Bilbao.

## THE INTERNATIONAL SCENE

Terry Venables presided over a number of friendlies as the Three Lions prepared to host the 1996 European Championships. Positive results included home victories over the USA and Nigeria with the only major disappointment coming off the pitch when England's friendly contest with the Republic of Ireland had to be abandoned due to disturbances involving English fans.

BELOW: *Arsenal goalkeeper David Seaman's desperate attempt to back pedal for the ball is to no avail, as Nayim's speculative long-range effort wins the European Cup Winners' Cup for Real Zaragoza.*

# WINNING EVERYTHING WITH KIDS AS THE FOREIGN INVASION TAKES GRIP

Cut from 22 to 20 teams ahead of the 1995–96 campaign, the Premiership lost none of its intensity. Before the season even began, controversy lingering from the previous campaign continued to mar the division's reputation. In July, former Arsenal boss George Graham was given a year-long ban from football as punishment for accepting illegal payments, while Bruce Grobbelaar, Hans Segers and John Fashanu were formally charged with being involved in match-fixing and bribery.

Manchester City appointed Southampton's Alan Ball as manager, as the Saints promoted long-serving coach, Dave Merrington to the hot seat. There was also significant change at Ewood Park as Kenny Dalglish swapped the manager's job at Blackburn for a Director of Football role, leaving first team coach Ray Harford to fill the void. There was another new appointment at Arsenal where Bruce Rioch took up the managerial reins, succeeding caretaker boss Stewart Houston, and Sheffield Wednesday replaced Trevor Francis with former Luton Town manager David Pleat.

OPPOSITE PAGE:
*Manchester United's Eric Cantona celebrates his successfully converted penalty against Liverpool in the Frenchman's first game back after being sidelined for nine months.*

LEFT: *Leeds United's Ghanaian striker Tony Yeboah celebrates a second goal of the season contender in a matter of weeks after he slammed home an unstoppable left-footed half-volley against Wimbledon.*

# TRANSFER TALES

The trend of more transfers and increased fees continued into the 1995–96 campaign, as did the propensity for a higher proportion of foreign-based players to enter the division. While the Premiership had attracted highly-regarded continental players in the past, including the likes of Eric Cantona and Jurgen Klinsmann, it remained rare for an English team to entice the world's best during their peak years.

However, this pattern was broken in the summer of 1995 when Arsenal completed the £7.5m signing of Dutch international striker Dennis Bergkamp from Inter Milan. Italy's top division, Serie A, had been Europe's highest profile league throughout the 1980s and into the 90s, but the capture of Bergkamp, as well as the ability of English clubs to hold onto their star players, emphasised by the likes of Eric Cantona and Ryan Giggs remaining at Manchester United, pointed towards a progressive change in power across the continent.

Other big name arrivals during the campaign added to the increasingly cosmopolitan feel of the Premiership as several South American stars were tempted to ply their trade in England, including Brazilian wonder kid Juninho, who shocked the world of football when he joined Middlesbrough, and Colombian forward, Faustino Asprilla, who joined Newcastle from Parma. Another big name from European football was Dutch forward Ruud Gullit, who was snapped up on a free transfer by Chelsea.

*Dutch forward Ruud Gullit joined Chelsea on a free transfer and was originally played as a sweeper by Glenn Hoddle.*

## BIGGEST TRANSFERS

**STAN COLLYMORE** – from Nottingham Forest to Liverpool – £8.4m

**DENNIS BERGKAMP** – from Inter Milan to Arsenal – £7.5m

**FAUSTINO ASPRILLA** – from AS Parma to Newcastle United – £6.7m

**LES FERDINAND** – from Queens Park Rangers to Newcastle United – £6m

**NICKY BARMBY** – from Tottenham Hotspur to Middlesbrough – £5.25m

**ANDREI KANCHELSKIS** – from Manchester United to Everton – £5m

**JUNINHO** – from Sao Paulo to Middlesbrough – £4.75m

**DAVID PLATT** – from Juventus to Arsenal – £4.75m

**CHRIS ARMSTRONG** – from Crystal Palace to Tottenham Hotspur – £4.5m

**TOMAS BROLIN** – from AS Parma to Leeds United – £4.5m

LEFT: *Brazilian playmaker Juninho caused a stir when he signed for Middlesbrough signifying the turning tide of the world's most sought after talents opting to move to England.*

## INTERESTING INFO

The 1995–96 season brought the introduction of the 'Bosman' ruling, after a successful legal challenge in the European Court of Human Rights by Belgian midfielder Jean-Marc Bosman gave out-of-contract players aged 23 or above the right to become free agents and move to other clubs for no transfer fee.

Further foreign captures during the 1995–96 season included Newcastle's addition of French winger David Ginola for £2.5m from Paris Saint-Germain, Leeds United's signing of Swedish international striker Tomas Brolin and Sheffield Wednesday's move for Anderlecht's Marc Degryse. Andrea Silenzi became the first Italian to play in the Premier League when he swapped Torino for Nottingham Forest and Manchester City brought in the magically gifted Georgian playmaker Georgi Kinkladze.

Big money domestic deals remained prominent, none more so than the one which saw Liverpool part with £8.4million to bring in Nottingham Forest striker Stan Collymore in a deal that broke the English transfer record for the third time in 12 months. Newcastle completed the £6m capture of QPR's talismanic striker Les Ferdinand, the £4m signing of Warren Barton and the £3.75m addition of David Batty.

Using the money generated from the Collymore deal, Nottingham Forest twice broke their transfer record to bring in Sheffield Wednesday's Chris Bart-Williams and Arsenal's Kevin Campbell. Middlesbrough invested a club record £5.25m fee to secure the services of Tottenham's Nicky Barmby, while Spurs broke their transfer record to bring in Chris Armstrong from Crystal Palace.

*The flair of French winger David Ginola added to Newcastle's irresistible pool of attacking talent.*

# TALES OF THE TURF

Some of the biggest transfer headlines ahead of the season came from Old Trafford, but for the departure of high-profile players rather than new arrivals. Alex Ferguson took the controversial decision to allow fans' favourites and established performers Paul Ince, Mark Hughes and Andrei Kanchelskis to depart the club. Causing even more of a stir, the Manchester United boss decided against bringing in big-money replacements, preferring to place his trust in an emerging group of young English players that included David Beckham, Paul Scholes and Gary Neville. The talented crop of youngsters went on to form the basis of the Manchester United team for the next decade.

Ferguson's bold move received widespread criticism and was put under further scrutiny when United were beaten convincingly by Aston Villa on the opening day of the season. With Eric Cantona still banned and other more experienced players out injured, an extremely young side went down 3–1 at Villa Park, prompting *Match of the Day* pundit Alan Hansen to famously assert 'You can't win anything with kids,' a view that was shared by many of the tabloid press but was later dispelled by the Red Devils.

While it was a slow start for Ferguson's men, Newcastle United flew out of the blocks, defeating Coventry City 3–0 in a game that featured Les Ferdinand's first goal for the club. Reigning champions Blackburn began their campaign with a 1–0 victory over QPR. Elsewhere a Matt Le Tissier hat-trick wasn't enough to prevent Southampton losing 4–3 to Nottingham Forest, while Bolton's first top-flight encounter for 15 years ended in a 3–2 defeat to Wimbledon.

The opening month was lit up by a memorable long-range volley by Tony Yeboah for Leeds United in their 1–0 win over Liverpool and also featured a debut goal for Middlesbrough's Nicky Barmby as the Teesiders grabbed a 1–1 draw against Arsenal. Boro's purpose-built Riverside Stadium held its first competitive contest as the home side defeated Chelsea 2–0 with Craig Hignett scoring the ground's first Premiership goal.

The month ended with a fiery contest between Manchester United and Blackburn Rovers that saw the Red Devils win 2–1 and Roy Keane sent off for two bookable offences. However, Newcastle topped the table having returned maximum points from their first three games.

In September Robbie Fowler scored four goals for Liverpool in their 5–0 league win over Bolton Wanderers, while Newcastle remained at the summit following a 2–0 win over Chelsea. Alan Shearer scored his 100th competitive goal for Blackburn, as his hat-trick lit up a 5–1 victory over Coventry while Tony Yeboah scored another spectacular goal, this time during a 4–2 win over Wimbledon at Selhurst Park.

October saw the highly-anticipated return to action of Eric Cantona who completed his nine month ban in a Premiership grudge match against Liverpool at Old Trafford. Cantona had an instant impact setting up Nicky Butt for the opening goal inside the first minute but was then overshadowed by a top class double from Liverpool striker Robbie Fowler. However, the Frenchman had the last laugh, calmly slotting home a pressure cooker penalty to ensure a share of the spoils for United.

Newcastle, playing some of the most free-flowing football the Premiership had witnessed, continued to impress as their attacking prowess garnered a 6–1 victory over Wimbledon which featured a hat-trick from the on-form Les Ferdinand. Manchester United maintained the title pace with 4–1 victory at Chelsea that showcased the goal-scoring ability of 20-year-old Paul Scholes. Liverpool also enjoyed a thumping victory, beating struggling Manchester City 6–0 at Anfield. The month ended with Bolton's surprise 1–0 victory over

*A summer signing from QPR, Les Ferdinand soon hit the goal trail for Newcastle United and spearheaded the Magpies Premiership title challenge.*

*Manchester United goalkeeper Peter Schmeichel was at the peak of his powers throughout the season and just as instrumental in the Red Devils' title success as the talismanic Eric Cantona. Schmeichel put in a match-saving master class in United's crucial 1–0 victory at Newcastle.*

Arsenal thanks to a solitary John McGinlay goal.

Blackburn's title defence stuttered as they found themselves marooned in mid-table and significantly off the pace. Manchester City remained in the relegation zone as another of the division's traditionally bigger clubs, Everton, sat at the wrong end of the table once again. During November Newcastle extended their lead at the top of the table following a 2–1 victory over Liverpool, while Manchester United slipped up at Arsenal.

Blackburn showed signs of improvement with a comprehensive 7–0 win over lowly Nottingham Forest at Ewood Park. A 2–0 defeat against a Robbie Fowler-inspired Liverpool and a loss at Leeds saw Manchester United trailing Newcastle by 10 points as Kevin Keegan's men remained in irresistible form. Ahead of the turn of the year, United did cut Newcastle's advantage to four points following a crucial 2–0 victory over the Magpies at Old Trafford and a 2–1 win at QPR.

The New Year brought a new low for Manchester United as they suffered their heaviest Premier League defeat – a 4–1 loss to Spurs. Newcastle re-established a seven-point lead over the Red Devils with a 2–0 victory over Arsenal while, at the other end of the table, struggling Bolton parted company with manager Roy McFarland.

In January, Liverpool stormed to a 5–0 victory over Leeds and Newcastle extended their lead at the top of the division to nine points. Manchester City, Bolton and QPR continued to struggle and Bryan Robson's Middlesbrough experienced an alarming drop down the table, going on to lose 5–0 Chelsea in February.

Newcastle slumped to a 3–3 draw with Manchester City as Manchester United's 6–0 humbling of Bolton narrowed the gap at the top to four points. March brought a clash between Newcastle and Manchester United at St James' Park dubbed as the title decider. Newcastle dominated the first half but the game ended in a 1–0 victory for the visitors, which was achieved through a precise Eric Cantona volley and a heroic goalkeeping performance from Peter Schmeichel.

The goals of Andrei Kanchelskis helped Everton climb the table as QPR defeated Southampton in a relegation six-pointer. Manchester United ended March three points clear of Newcastle but the Magpies had two games in hand.

April brought one of the most entertaining games of the season and arguably the most memorable clash of the Premier League era as title contenders Newcastle and Liverpool played out a thrilling encounter at Anfield. Les Ferdinand equalised Robbie Fowler's opener for the Reds, before David Ginola put Newcastle in front, only for Fowler to level matters at 2–2. Faustino Asprilla put Newcastle back ahead with a nicely placed lob before a late double from Stan Collymore, which featured a dramatic stoppage time strike sealed a 4–3 win for Liverpool and dealt a hefty psychological blow to Kevin Keegan's men. Manchester United capitalised with a 3–2 victory over Manchester City at Maine Road before completing a narrow 1–0 win against Coventry.

Newcastle's hopes took another big blow when two late goals from Graham Fenton saw them beaten 2–1 by Blackburn. QPR kept their survival bid alive by beating Everton 3–1, a result which damaged the visiting side's hopes of European qualification. Manchester United suffered a shock 3–1 defeat to Southampton before Newcastle completed a 1–0 win over Aston Villa to cut the gap at the top of the table to three points.

Bolton's relegation was confirmed after a home loss to Southampton. They were soon followed through the exit door by QPR, whose run of 13 years in the top flight came to an end despite a 3–0 win over West Ham.

Manchester United edged closer to their third league title in four seasons with a thumping 5–0 win over Nottingham Forest while Newcastle remained on their coat-tails with a 1–0 win at Leeds, which prompted an aggressive post-match reaction from Kevin Keegan. Infuriated by comments made by Alex Ferguson in the build up to the fixture, which inferred that Leeds wouldn't put in the same effort against the Magpies as they had against his side, and under severe pressure to claim the club's first league title since 1927, Keegan let rip live on Sky Sports.

The Englishman's impassioned tirade culminated in the memorable quote, 'You can tell him (Ferguson)… he'll be watching this now… we're still fighting for this title and he's got to go to Middlesbrough and get something… and I'll tell you, honestly… I would love it if we beat them… love it!'

Keegan's mention of United having to go to Middlesbrough and get something referred to the final day of the season, when Ferguson's men travelled to the Riverside Stadium knowing that avoiding defeat would see them crowned champions. Following a disappointing 1–1 draw at Nottingham Forest, Newcastle needed to beat Tottenham at home to keep their hopes alive.

In reality, the final day lacked any real drama as the Manchester club raced into a 3–0 lead over Middlesbrough thanks to goals from David May, Andy Cole and Ryan Giggs, while Newcastle were held by Spurs, meaning the Red Devils' eventual winning margin was four points. Newcastle were joined in the UEFA Cup by third place Liverpool and fourth place Arsenal.

United's local rivals, Manchester City were experiencing a much more intense and significantly less enjoyable final fixture. Relegation looked on the cards as they faced in-form Liverpool at Maine Road with City knowing they needed to better the results of Southampton and Coventry to survive. The Blues were holding Liverpool 2–2 when word came through that Coventry were behind.

City kept possession and attempted to run the clock down to preserve a point before striker Niall Quinn, who had been substituted, discovered that Coventry were in fact drawing and bolted down the touchline to pass on the news to his team-mates. City tried to attack and grab a vital winner, but the momentum was lost and their relegation confirmed.

## ⚽ INTERESTING INFO

Liverpool's Steve McManaman racked up a Premier League record 25 assists during the season.

OPPOSITE PAGE: *Stan Collymore, who joined Liverpool during the summer, hit the winning goal in the season's most enthralling clash, which saw the Reds defeat Newcastle 4–3 at Anfield.*

# HONOURS LIST

## FA Carling Premiership
**CHAMPIONS:** Manchester United
United claimed the Premiership crown for the third time in four seasons, following a monumental battle with Newcastle United. The Red Devils garnered 82 points from 38 games.
**RUNNERS-UP:** Newcastle United
**RELEGATED:** Manchester City, Queens Park Rangers, Bolton Wanderers
**TOP GOAL SCORER:** Alan Shearer (31 goals for Blackburn Rovers)

SHOOT MAGAZINE
1995–96

*Front cover star Juninho was the subject of an in-depth interview following his impressive start to life in England with Middlesbrough, as Shoot gave away three magazines for the price of one. Also pictured on the cover were Tottenham winger Andy Sinton, Everton's Duncan Ferguson and Manchester United's Eric Cantona.*

## 1995–96 SEASON TABLE

| | | M | W | D | L | GF | GA | GD | PTS |
|---|---|---|---|---|---|---|---|---|---|
| 1 | Manchester United | 38 | 25 | 7 | 6 | 73 | 35 | +38 | 82 |
| 2 | Newcastle United | 38 | 24 | 6 | 8 | 66 | 37 | +29 | 78 |
| 3 | Liverpool | 38 | 20 | 11 | 7 | 70 | 34 | +36 | 71 |
| 4 | Aston Villa | 38 | 18 | 9 | 11 | 52 | 35 | +17 | 63 |
| 5 | Arsenal | 38 | 17 | 12 | 9 | 49 | 32 | +17 | 63 |
| 6 | Everton | 38 | 17 | 10 | 11 | 64 | 44 | +20 | 61 |
| 7 | Blackburn Rovers | 38 | 18 | 7 | 13 | 61 | 47 | +14 | 61 |
| 8 | Tottenham Hotspur | 38 | 16 | 13 | 9 | 50 | 38 | +12 | 61 |
| 9 | Nottingham Forest | 38 | 15 | 13 | 10 | 50 | 54 | -4 | 58 |
| 10 | West Ham United | 38 | 14 | 9 | 15 | 43 | 52 | -9 | 51 |
| 11 | Chelsea | 38 | 12 | 14 | 12 | 46 | 44 | +2 | 50 |
| 12 | Middlesbrough | 38 | 11 | 10 | 17 | 35 | 50 | -15 | 43 |
| 13 | Leeds United | 38 | 12 | 7 | 19 | 40 | 57 | -17 | 43 |
| 14 | Wimbledon | 38 | 10 | 11 | 17 | 55 | 70 | -15 | 41 |
| 15 | Sheffield Wednesday | 38 | 10 | 10 | 18 | 48 | 61 | -13 | 40 |
| 16 | Coventry City | 38 | 8 | 14 | 16 | 42 | 60 | -18 | 38 |
| 17 | Southampton | 38 | 9 | 11 | 18 | 34 | 52 | -18 | 38 |
| 18 | Manchester City | 38 | 9 | 11 | 18 | 33 | 58 | -25 | 38 |
| 19 | Queens Park Rangers | 38 | 9 | 6 | 23 | 38 | 57 | -19 | 33 |
| 20 | Bolton Wanderers | 38 | 8 | 5 | 25 | 39 | 71 | -32 | 29 |

## PLAYERS OF THE SEASON

**PFA PLAYER OF THE YEAR:** Les Ferdinand, Newcastle United
**PFA YOUNG PLAYER OF THE YEAR:** Robbie Fowler, Liverpool
**FOOTBALL WRITERS' PLAYER OF THE YEAR:** Eric Cantona, Manchester United

*Sunderland boss Peter Reid celebrating his team's promotion on the Roker Park pitch.*

*Swindon boss Steve McMahon, who guided the Robins to promotion, takes a training session in wintery conditions.*

**FOOTBALL LEAGUE DIVISION ONE CHAMPIONS:**
Sunderland
**PROMOTED:** Derby County
**DIVISION ONE PLAY-OFF WINNERS:** Leicester City
**RELEGATED:** Millwall, Watford, Luton Town
**TOP GOAL SCORER:** John Aldridge (27 goals for Tranmere Rovers)

With Peter Reid in the dugout, Sunderland enjoyed one of their most successful campaigns to confirm their first appearance in the Premier League. The North East club amassed 83 points and finished four clear of second placed Derby. The Rams, under the charge of veteran boss Jim Smith, finally reached the top flight after years of significant investment in the transfer market. Leicester, managed by Martin O'Neill, sealed their return to the top flight following a last-gasp play-off final victory over Crystal Palace achieved thanks to a long-range strike from Steve Claridge.

**DIVISION TWO CHAMPIONS:** Swindon Town
**PROMOTED:** Oxford United
**DIVISION TWO PLAY-OFF WINNERS:** Bradford City
**RELEGATED:** Carlisle United, Swansea City, Brighton & Hove Albion, Hull City
**TOP GOAL SCORER:** Marcus Stewart (21 goals for Bristol Rovers)

Swindon, who had been in the Premier League just two seasons previously, completed an immediate return to Division One after a dominating display in Division Two that saw Steve McMahon's men clock up 92 points. Denis Smith inspired Oxford to automatic promotion while Chris Kamara's debut season in management ended in play-off final glory for Bradford City thanks to a 2–0 victory over Notts County, achieved through goals from Des Hamilton and Mark Stallard.

**DIVISION THREE CHAMPIONS:** Preston North End
**PROMOTED:** Gillingham, Bury
**DIVISION THREE PLAY-OFF WINNERS:** Plymouth Argyle
**RELEGATED:** None
**TOP GOAL SCORER:** Steve White (21 goals for Hereford United)

Managed by Garry Peters, Preston began their resurgence through the divisions by claiming the Division Three title with a total of 86 points, beating Gillingham, bossed by Tony Pulis, and Stan Ternent's Bury into second and third place respectively. Neil Warnock's Plymouth Argyle enjoyed play-off final success, defeating Darlington 1–0 thanks to a goal from Ronnie Mauge.

**FOOTBALL CONFERENCE CHAMPIONS:** Stevenage Borough. For the third consecutive season the Conference champions were denied entry to the Football League due to the quality of their stadium.

# UP FOR THE CUP

**FA CUP WINNERS:** Manchester United

Manchester United were pitted against their great rivals Liverpool in the Wembley final. In truth, a pretty turgid affair followed in a game that was lit up by one piece of genuine class from Eric Cantona. After David James failed to deal with an out-swinging David Beckham corner, the Frenchman – positioned just outside the area – nimbly adjusted his feet before aiming a volley through an almost impenetrable gaggle of bodies and into the vacant net. United became the first English club to have won the league and cup double on two occasions.

The Red Devils reached the final following a 2–1 win over Chelsea that featured a winning goal from David Beckham, while Liverpool overcame Aston Villa 3–0 thanks to a Robbie Fowler brace in the other semi-final.

Earlier in the competition, Hitchin Town pulled off an upset by defeating Bristol Rovers 2–1 while other shocks included Sheffield United's 1–0 replay win over Arsenal, West Ham's loss to Grimsby Town and Everton's defeat to Port Vale.

BELOW: *Eric Cantona, who scored the only goal of the game, lifts the FA Cup after Manchester United's 1–0 triumph over Liverpool at Wembley.*

## LEAGUE (COCA COLA) CUP WINNERS: Aston Villa

Aston Villa convincingly defeated Leeds United 3–0 at Wembley thanks to goals from Savo Milosevic, Ian Taylor and Dwight Yorke. The victory saw Villa equal Liverpool's record of five League Cups. Brian Little's men advanced to the final following an away goal victory over Arsenal, while runners-up Leeds overcame Birmingham City 5–1 on aggregate.

The biggest shock of the tournament came in the early rounds when third tier York City achieved a 3–0 away win over Manchester United, eventually knocking out the Premier League side 4–3 on aggregate. Other surprises came when Bradford City defeated Nottingham Forest and Millwall ousted Everton.

## CHARITY SHIELD WINNERS: Everton

Everton completed a 1–0 victory over Blackburn thanks to a goal from midfielder Vinny Samways.

## THE FOOTBALL LEAGUE (AUTO WINDSCREENS) SHIELD: Rotherham United.

The Millers enjoyed a 2–1 success over Shrewsbury Town with both goals coming from Nigel Jemson.

ABOVE: *Aston Villa striker Savo Milosevic slams home the opening goal as the Villains comprehensively defeat Leeds United in the Coca Cola Cup final.*

# INTO EUROPE

## European Champions League

Drawn in a group with Spartak Moscow, Legia Warsaw and Rosenburg, English champions Blackburn were expected to qualify for the knockout stages but after a series of disappointing results they ended up bottom of the table with a return of just four points. The low point came in a 3–0 away defeat to Spartak Moscow that saw Rovers' Graeme Le Saux and David Batty come to blows.

## European Cup Winners' Cup

Everton overcame Icelandic side KR Reykjavik 6–3 over two legs before being knocked out by Dutch club Feyenoord 1–0 over two legs in the second round.

## UEFA Cup

The English representatives were Manchester United, Liverpool, Nottingham Forest and Leeds. The biggest disappointment came at Old Trafford when Manchester United slumped to an away goal defeat to Russian side Rotor Volgograd, despite a goal from goalkeeper Peter Schmeichel.

Leeds enjoyed a 3–1 win over AS Monaco largely achieved thanks to the free-scoring Tony Yeboah before crashing out 8–3 over two legs to PSV Eindhoven in the second round. Liverpool progressed to the same stage, defeating Spartak Vladikavkaz before being knocked out by Brondby. Nottingham Forest were the most successful English side, advancing to the quarter-finals thanks to victories over Malmo, Auxerre and Lyon before eventual winners Bayern Munich defeated them 7–2 on aggregate.

*Blackburn striker Mike Newell completes a nine-minute hat-trick against Rosenburg in a rare high-point of Rovers' disastrous Champions League campaign.*

## THE INTERNATIONAL SCENE

The summer of 1996 saw football come home as England hosted the European Championships and came within a whisker of reaching the final of a major international tournament for the first time in 30 years. Benefiting from the tactical nous of coach Terry Venables and given licence to express themselves, the Three Lions completed famous victories over Scotland and Holland, with the Dutch stunned 4–1, thanks to doubles from Teddy Sheringham and Alan Shearer. Both strikers were in excellent form and Shearer ended as the tournament's top scorer with a final tally of five goals. Following a quarter-final victory over Spain, England were knocked out in the semi-finals by Germany following a penalty shootout.

ABOVE: *Alan Shearer adds gloss to the scoreline with one of the most flowing passing moves completed by an England team in living memory. Shearer arrowed home from Teddy Sheringham's clever assist to extend the Three Lions' lead against the Netherlands.*

# CUP COMPETITIONS CAPTURE THE IMAGINATION

The euphoria of Euro '96, labelled as the summer when English football came home, brought even more optimism about the country's most popular game ahead of the 1996–97 season. Entertaining football played in front of sold out stadiums gave the outside world an even more emphatic glimpse of the appeal of the English game and many of the globe's best players continued to make a beeline for the Premiership.

New rules brought in by the Premier League meant that teams could name five substitutes on the bench during matches, with three permitted to enter the pitch during the 90 minutes.

Of the promoted sides, Derby County looked most likely to survive after adding continental class to their side during the summer. Leicester City and Sunderland were expected by most observers to struggle.

The first managerial departure took place before a ball was kicked when Bruce Rioch left Arsenal following a dispute with the board. Stewart Houston was again appointed as caretaker boss.

OPPOSITE PAGE: *The very picture of focus and technique, young Manchester United midfielder David Beckham lets fly with a drive from his own half that beats Wimbledon goalkeeper Neil Sullivan and transports the England international's career and profile to a stratospheric level.*

LEFT: *Just moments before he famously covered his face with his shirt, Middlesbrough's Italian striker Fabrizio Ravenelli celebrates scoring a hat-trick against Liverpool on his Premiership debut.*

# TRANSFER TALES

The foreign invasion of the Premiership continued apace during the season, beginning in May with an addition to Middlesbrough's list of cosmopolitan names following the £4m signing of Brazilian midfielder Emerson. Headline arrivals included many of Italy's finest, such as Fabrizio Ravenelli who joined Middlesbrough, Benito Carbone, who signed for Sheffield Wednesday, as well as classy midfielder Roberto Di Matteo and the mercurial Gianfranco Zola, both of whom joined Chelsea.

Chelsea continued their cosmopolitan recruitment drive with the signing of French defender Frank Leboeuf, Spurs added Norwegian striker Steffen Iversen and Aston Villa brought in Portuguese full-back Fernando Nelson. Manchester United also invested heavily in the European market, bringing in Norwegian pair Ronnie Johnsen and Ole Gunnar Solskjaer, two Dutchmen in Raimond van der Gouw and Jordi Cruyff and the Czech Republic star Karel Poborsky. Derby brought in Croatian class, signing attacking midfielder Aljosa Asanovic from Hajduk Split.

The domestic transfer market remained strong, emphasised by the world record £15m capture of Alan Shearer, who signed for his hometown club Newcastle from Blackburn. The Magpies allowed young English striker Darren Huckerby to join Coventry, who also brought in Gary McAllister from Leeds. The Elland Road club invested heavily in Manchester United winger Lee Sharpe and Crystal Palace goalkeeper Nigel Martyn. Aston Villa splashed out £7m on Liverpool striker Stan Collymore, who joined the club he supported as a boy.

## BIGGEST TRANSFERS

**ALAN SHEARER** – from Blackburn Rovers to Newcastle United – £15m

**FABRIZIO RAVANELLI** – from Juventus to Middlesbrough – £7m

**STAN COLLYMORE** – from Liverpool to Aston Villa – £7m

**NICKY BARMBY** – from Middlesbrough to Everton – £5.75m

**ROBERTO DI MATTEO** – from Lazio to Chelsea – £4.9m

**SLAVEN BILIC** – from Karlsruher to West Ham United – £4.5m

**PIERRE VAN HOOIJDONK** – from Celtic to Nottingham Forest – £4.5m

**GIANFRANCO ZOLA** – from AS Parma to Chelsea – £4.5m

**KAREL POBORSKY** – from Slavia Prague to Manchester United – £3.5m

**PATRICK VIEIRA** – from AC Milan to Arsenal – £3.5m

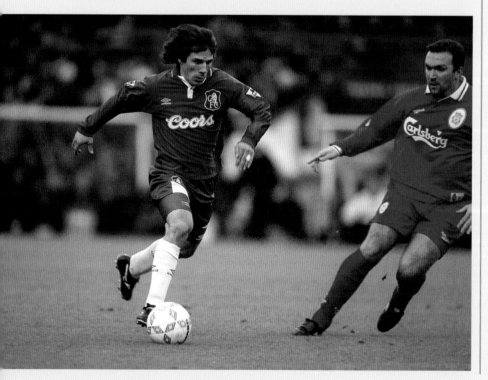

LEFT: *One of the first World stars to arrive in the Premiership during the peak years of his career, Italian forward Gianfranco Zola added even more star quality to Chelsea's richly skilled squad.*

# TALES OF THE TURF

The opening weekend of the season was crowned with a memorable goal from David Beckham who scored from the halfway line in Manchester United's 3–0 victory over Wimbledon. Fabrizio Ravenelli made an immediate impact at Middlesbrough scoring a debut hat-trick during a 3–3 draw with Liverpool. Alan Shearer's highly anticipated debut for Newcastle saw the Magpies go down 2–0 at Everton. The England man didn't have to wait long for his first Newcastle goals, slamming home a powerful free-kick against Wimbledon during a 2–0 victory in his next match. David Pleat's Sheffield Wednesday were the surprise leaders at the end of the month after winning their first three games, including an impressive victory at Newcastle.

Middlesbrough enhanced their reputation as one of the Premiership's most entertaining teams, defeating Coventry 4–0 thanks to braces from Ravenelli and Juninho. Another 4–0 defeat, this time for Leeds against Manchester United, signalled the end of Howard Wilkinson's eight year reign as manager. Stewart Houston stepped down as Arsenal's caretaker boss to take charge at QPR before Frenchman Arsene Wenger was appointed Gunners manager.

Liverpool's summer signing Patrik Berger announced his arrival in the Premiership with two goals against Leicester and a hat-trick against Chelsea, in a game that saw the Reds emerge as 5–1 winners. Two goals from Matt Le Tissier slowed Middlesbrough's early season progress as Southampton beat the Teesiders 4–0 at the Dell. Liverpool ended September as league leaders, closely followed by Arsenal, Manchester United and surprise package, Wimbledon in fourth.

A David Beckham goal enabled Manchester United to defeat Liverpool 1–0 at Old Trafford, but the Red Devils soon suffered their heaviest defeat in the Premiership to date, as they were crushed 5–0 by Newcastle at St James' Park. Goals from Darren Peacock, David Ginola, Les Ferdinand and Alan Shearer put the hosts 4–0 up before Belgian defender Philippe Albert beautifully placed a long-range lob over Peter Schmeichel.

United followed that loss with another heavy away defeat, this time a 6–3 thrashing at the hands

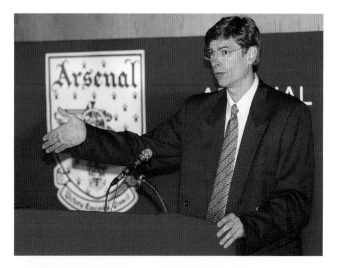

ABOVE TOP: *Unknown to the majority of English supporters, Frenchman Arsene Wenger speaks at the press conference unveiling him as the new manager of Arsenal.*

ABOVE BOTTOM: *After an incredible Euro '96 for England, Alan Shearer returned 'home' to Newcastle United for £15m and, alongside Les Ferdinand, terrorised the Manchester United defence during a 5–0 home victory for the Magpies.*

*After struggling to cope with the pressure he placed on himself, as well as with the increasing expectations associated with the Newcastle job, fans' favourite Kevin Keegan stepped down as manager midway through the season.*

*A mid-season signing from Arsenal, John Hartson and his striker partner Paul Kitson, scored the goals that fired West Ham United to survival.*

of Southampton. The Saints stormed all over the reigning champions and Norwegian striker Egil Ostenstadt grabbed a hat-trick. As well as the result the game was noteworthy for United's decision to change their grey away kit at half-time, as the players claimed they were struggling to see each other.

New Arsenal boss Arsene Wenger enjoyed a great start to his Gunners career, finishing October at the top of the table on goal difference from Newcastle. Manchester United sat fifth, a position behind Liverpool who had two games in hand. Blackburn remained rock bottom having failed to record a single victory in the first 11 games.

Manchester United's struggles continued into November as their two-year unbeaten home run was ended by Chelsea. A resurgent Chris Sutton inspired Blackburn to their first victory of the season during a 3–0 win over Liverpool as Newcastle beat local rivals Middlesbrough 3–1. Boro then suffered another heavy defeat, losing 5–1 to Liverpool at Anfield.

Leicester City continued to surprise many observers, stabilising their top half standing with a 3–1 win at Aston Villa. Everton reignited their season with a 7–1 crushing of Southampton, which featured a Gary Speed hat-trick and goals from record signing Nicky Barmby and Andrei Kanchelskis. Manchester United ended their three-match losing run with a scrappy 1–0 victory over Arsenal, achieved thanks to an own goal from Nigel Winterburn.

Arsenal ended a second consecutive month on top of the Premiership, closely followed by a batch of clubs. Nottingham Forest found themselves adrift at the foot of the division having recorded just one win in 15 games. Manager Frank Clark soon left his role to be replaced by club legend Stuart Pearce as player-manager until the end of the season.

Middlesbrough's woes continued during December as they were beaten by Leicester and Liverpool, before making headlines by opting to cancel a fixture against Blackburn amidst claims from Bryan Robson that they were unable to field a team due to 23 of his players suffering with illness. It proved to be a costly mistake, as the three points docked from 'Boro as a punishment by the FA after they are charged with bringing the game into disrepute turned out to be crucial in sealing their eventual relegation fate.

Boxing Day saw Manchester United strengthen their title credentials with a 4–0 win over Nottingham Forest. Wimbledon and Newcastle maintained their good form, with the Dons overcoming Everton 3–1 and the Magpies firing seven against Spurs, but Liverpool ended the year at the top of the division following a 1–0 win at Southampton.

The city of Newcastle was rocked to its foundations during the first week of 1997 when Magpies manager Kevin Keegan made the surprise decision to walk away from the club, stating 'I feel I have taken this club as far as I can.' With Newcastle still within touching distance of the title, the board moved quickly and appointed former Blackburn boss Kenny Dalglish as Keegan's successor.

The end of January saw Manchester United reach the summit of the table following a 2–1 win against Wimbledon. Newcastle remained close to United with an entertaining 4–3 victory over Leicester, inspired by an Alan Shearer hat-trick. Another Magpies striker, Paul Kitson, departed the club to aid West Ham's survival battle as the Hammers paid a club record £2.3m for his services before also investing significantly to secure Arsenal striker John Hartson.

Leicester enjoyed a satisfying 4–2 win over East Midlands rivals Derby County thanks to a hat-trick from Ian Marshall before a rare Vinnie Jones goal ensured all three points for Wimbledon against Arsenal. As the month drew to a close, experienced manager Dave Bassett took over at struggling Nottingham Forest.

ABOVE: *The gangly but ultra-skilled Costa Rican Paulo Wanchope starts on a speculative yet searing individual run that saw him take on the entire Manchester United defence before scoring a remarkable goal during Derby County's 3–2 victory over the Red Devils at Old Trafford.*

*One of the most dependable defenders England has produced for decades, Manchester United right-back Gary Neville drove home a rare but vital goal against Middlesbrough at Old Trafford.*

In March Newcastle suffered home defeats to Southampton while Spurs, inspired by three Steffen Iversen goals, beat lowly Sunderland at Roker Park. Peter Reid's men went on to record a surprise 2–1 win over Manchester United, which ended the Red Devil's four-month unbeaten run. Sunderland's fellow North East strugglers, Middlesbrough, enjoyed a 6–1 win over Derby.

Liverpool and Newcastle again illuminated the season with a thrilling encounter at Anfield. The game – remarkable because it ended 4–3 to the home side once again, saw Liverpool race into a 3–0 lead through goals from Steve McManaman, Patrik Berger and Robbie Fowler. Newcastle clawed back the deficit thanks to Keith Gillespie, Faustino Asprilla and Warren Barton before a late strike from Fowler settled the game in favour of the home side.

The goals of Paul Kitson and John Hartson dramatically helped Harry Redknapp's West Ham improve their survival hopes while back-to-back wins helped Middlesbrough climb the table despite a failed appeal to restore the three points they had been docked earlier in the season. Manchester United ended a third month in a row at the top of the table as Liverpool provided their most consistent challenge. With Everton struggling for form, manager Joe Royle tendered his resignation and was replaced by club captain Dave Watson on a temporary basis.

At the beginning of April, Derby County, inspired by a piece of individual brilliance from Costa Rican striker Paulo Wanchope, achieved a shock 3–2 win at Manchester United but Liverpool failed to capitalise on that slip, losing 2–1 against Coventry at Anfield.

Manchester United took a big step towards reclaiming the title following a 3–1 win against Liverpool in a game that featured two rare goals from defender Gary Pallister. The reigning champions were firmly in the box seat after ending the penultimate month of the campaign five points clear.

Manchester United and Middlesbrough shared six goals in a thrilling 3–3 draw at Old Trafford, in a game that featured a rare goal from defender Gary Neville. Despite the dropped points United soon became champions after Newcastle drew with West Ham and Liverpool lost 2–1 to Wimbledon, in a game that featured a first senior goal from teenage striker Michael Owen.

With Nottingham Forest already demoted, the final day of the season was filled with drama over the remaining two relegation places. Coventry City achieved unlikely survival following a 2–1 win against Tottenham at White Hart Lane but the Sky Blues' ecstasy was matched by the agony of Middlesbrough, who were relegated following a 0–0 draw at Leeds. Meanwhile Sunderland's loss to Wimbledon ensured their immediate return to the second tier.

## INTERESTING INFO

Michael Owen's debut goal for Liverpool made him the club's youngest ever league goal scorer at the age of 17 years and 144 days.

# HONOURS LIST

## FA Carling Premiership

**CHAMPIONS:** Manchester United
United completed back to back Premiership titles for the second time, clocking up 82 points and finishing four clear of second placed Newcastle.
**RUNNERS-UP:** Newcastle United
**RELEGATED:** Sunderland, Middlesbrough, Nottingham Forest
**TOP GOAL SCORER:** Alan Shearer (25 goals for Newcastle United)

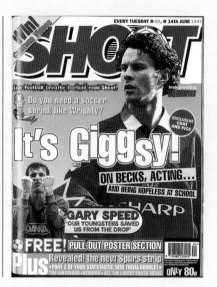

**SHOOT MAGAZINE**
**1996–97**

*The increasingly marketable Ryan Giggs was emblazoned on the cover after the Manchester United winger spoke exclusively about his team-mate David Beckham, going into acting and his experiences at school. Everton's Gary Speed was also interviewed about the Toffees narrowly avoiding relegation while the new Tottenham kit was revealed inside the magazine.*

## 1996–97 SEASON TABLE

|   |   | M | W | D | L | GF | GA | GD | PTS |
|---|---|---|---|---|---|----|----|----|-----|
| 1 | Manchester United | 38 | 21 | 12 | 5 | 76 | 44 | +32 | 75 |
| 2 | Newcastle United | 38 | 19 | 11 | 8 | 73 | 40 | +33 | 68 |
| 3 | Arsenal | 38 | 19 | 11 | 8 | 62 | 32 | +30 | 68 |
| 4 | Liverpool | 38 | 19 | 11 | 8 | 62 | 37 | +25 | 68 |
| 5 | Aston Villa | 38 | 17 | 10 | 11 | 47 | 34 | +13 | 61 |
| 6 | Chelsea | 38 | 16 | 11 | 11 | 58 | 55 | +3 | 59 |
| 7 | Sheffield Wednesday | 38 | 14 | 15 | 9 | 50 | 51 | -1 | 57 |
| 8 | Wimbledon | 38 | 15 | 11 | 12 | 49 | 46 | +3 | 56 |
| 9 | Leicester City | 38 | 12 | 11 | 15 | 46 | 54 | -8 | 47 |
| 10 | Tottenham Hotspur | 38 | 13 | 7 | 18 | 44 | 51 | -7 | 46 |
| 11 | Leeds United | 38 | 11 | 13 | 14 | 28 | 38 | -10 | 46 |
| 12 | Derby County | 38 | 11 | 13 | 14 | 45 | 58 | -13 | 46 |
| 13 | Blackburn Rovers | 38 | 9 | 15 | 14 | 42 | 43 | -1 | 42 |
| 14 | West Ham United | 38 | 10 | 12 | 16 | 39 | 48 | -9 | 42 |
| 15 | Everton | 38 | 10 | 12 | 16 | 44 | 57 | -13 | 42 |
| 16 | Southampton | 38 | 10 | 11 | 17 | 50 | 56 | -6 | 41 |
| 17 | Coventry City | 38 | 9 | 14 | 15 | 38 | 54 | -16 | 41 |
| 18 | Sunderland | 38 | 10 | 10 | 18 | 35 | 53 | -18 | 40 |
| 19 | Middlesbrough | 38 | 10 | 12 | 16 | 51 | 60 | -9 | 39 |
| 20 | Nottingham Forest | 38 | 6 | 16 | 16 | 31 | 59 | -28 | 34 |

## PLAYERS OF THE SEASON

**PFA PLAYER OF THE YEAR:** Gianfranco Zola, Chelsea
**PFA YOUNG PLAYER OF THE YEAR:** David Beckham, Manchester United
**FOOTBALL WRITERS' PLAYER OF THE YEAR:** Gianfranco Zola, Chelsea

*Scottish striker John McGinlay top scored for Bolton Wanderers as they lifted the Division One title.*

**FOOTBALL LEAGUE DIVISION ONE CHAMPIONS:** Bolton Wanderers
**PROMOTED:** Barnsley
**DIVISION ONE PLAY-OFF WINNERS:** Crystal Palace
**RELEGATED:** Grimsby Town, Oldham Athletic, Southend United
**TOP GOAL SCORER:** John McGinlay (24 goals for Bolton Wanderers)

Bolton Wanderers returned to the Premiership in convincing fashion with a dominant title win that saw them score a century of goals and amass 98 points. Achieved under the guidance of Colin Todd, it was the first time that Wanderers had ever finished top of a division. A total of 18 points further back were runners-up Barnsley, managed by Danny Wilson, who reached the top flight for the first time in their history. The third promotion place was taken by Steve Coppell's Crystal Palace, who defeated Sheffield United 1–0 at Wembley thanks to a goal from captain David Hopkin.

**DIVISION TWO CHAMPIONS:** Bury
**PROMOTED:** Stockport County
**DIVISION TWO PLAY-OFF WINNERS:** Crewe Alexandra
**RELEGATED:** Peterborough United, Shrewsbury Town, Rotherham United, Notts County
**TOP GOAL SCORER:** Tony Thorpe (28 goals for Luton Town)

Bury won their second successive promotion under Stan Ternent, returning to the second tier for the first time in 30 years. Dave Jones' Stockport capped a fantastic season that also saw them reach the League Cup semi-finals by taking the second automatic promotion berth. After defeating Brentford 1–0 in the Play-off final, Crewe Alexandra reached the second tier for the first time since 1896.

**DIVISION THREE CHAMPIONS:** Wigan Athletic
**PROMOTED:** Fulham, Carlisle United
**DIVISION THREE PLAY-OFF WINNERS:** Northampton Town
**RELEGATED:** Hereford United
**TOP GOAL SCORER:** Graeme Jones (31 goals for Wigan Athletic)

With the investment of owner Dave Whelan starting to bear fruit Wigan Athletic won the title and gained promotion to Division Two after four years in the basement tier. Former Norwich City boss John Deehan was the man in the dugout as Graeme Jones' finishing proved crucial for the Latics who claimed the title by virtue of their impressive goal-scoring return. Fulham, managed by Micky Adams, gained promotion from second place as they began their journey back up the divisions. Carlisle claimed third and the final automatic promotion spot while Northampton Town were triumphant in the play-offs, defeating Swansea City 1–0 through John Frain's last minute winner. A dramatic last day of the season saw Brighton & Hove Albion avoid relegation at the expense of Hereford United who dropped into the Conference.

**FOOTBALL CONFERENCE CHAMPIONS:** Macclesfield Town.

Managed by former Manchester United player Sammy McIlroy, Macclesfield Town claimed the Conference title for the second time in three years, this time earning promotion thanks to upgrades that had been made to their Moss Rose ground.

# UP FOR THE CUP

**FA CUP WINNERS:** Chelsea

The Blues claimed their first major trophy since 1971 thanks to a comfortable 2–0 victory over relegated Middlesbrough. Chelsea enjoyed the perfect start after Roberto Di Matteo slammed home a powerful strike after just 42 seconds. The Londoners extended their lead in the second half through Eddie Newton to condemn 'Boro to their second major final defeat of the season.

## ⚽ INTERESTING INFO

Chelsea's FA Cup win saw Ruud Gullit become the first non British or Irish manager to lift a major English trophy.

Chelsea reached the final after overcoming Wimbledon 3–0 at Highbury thanks to goals from Mark Hughes and Gianfranco Zola. It was less straightforward for Middlesbrough who needed a replay to defeat Second Division Chesterfield. The first encounter at Old Trafford ended 3–3 in a game that Chesterfield led twice before 'Boro took went ahead in extra time only to be denied a minute from the end by a dramatic late header from Chesterfield-born, Jamie Hewitt. In the replay at Hillsborough, Bryan Robson's men made light work of their opponents, winning 3–0.

Chesterfield provided one of the stories of that season's competition having defeated the likes of Bolton and Nottingham Forest to advance to the quarter-finals where they overcame another Division Two side, Wrexham. The Welsh club enjoyed shock victories over West Ham and Birmingham City. Several non-league clubs ousted league opposition, including Woking who disposed of Millwall and Cambridge United; Sudbury Town who saw off Brighton and Hednesford Town who beat York City. Other headline makers were Bradford City who shocked Everton with a 3–2 win at Goodison Park, Wimbledon who put paid to Manchester United's hopes following a replay victory at Selhurst Park and Portsmouth who knocked out Leeds.

*Chelsea midfielder Roberto Di Matteo celebrates scoring a spectacular strike inside the first minute of the FA Cup final. The Blues went on to defeat Middlesbrough 2–0 at Wembley.*

## LEAGUE (COCA COLA) CUP WINNERS: Leicester City

Capping an impressive first season back in the Premiership that saw Martin O'Neill's men finish in the top ten, the Foxes defeated Middlesbrough following a replay to lift their first major honour since 1964. After the first game ended 1–1 Wembley and featured extra-time goals from Leicester's Emile Heskey and 'Boro's Fabrizio Ravanelli, both teams replayed at Hillsborough 10 days later. Another tight encounter went into extra time before Steve Claridge's smart strike settled matters.

Leicester overcame Wimbledon in the semi-finals thanks to an away goal from Simon Grayson after the aggregate score ended 1–1, while Middlesbrough defeated Third Division Stockport County 3–0 across the two games. Stockport had been the competition's surprise package, clocking up victories over Premiership Blackburn, West Ham and Southampton. Other shock results came when Division Three Lincoln City defeated second tier Manchester City 5–1 on aggregate and Oxford United dumped Sheffield Wednesday out of the competition, while York City followed up their victory over Manchester United the previous season with a 4–3 aggregate win against Everton.

## CHARITY SHIELD WINNERS: Manchester United

The champions defeated the previous season's runners-up Newcastle 4–0 thanks to goals from Eric Cantona, Nicky Butt, David Beckham and Roy Keane.

## THE FOOTBALL LEAGUE (AUTO WINDSCREENS) SHIELD: Carlisle United.

Following a 0–0 draw after extra time, the Cumbrians defeated Colchester United 4–3 on penalties.

LEFT TOP AND BOTTOM: *Chesterfield's famous FA Cup run captured the imagination of the town, as well as the wider British public. One of the Spireites' heroes, Kevin Davies, is pictured in action (top); fans (bottom) enjoy their team's remarkable 3–3 FA Cup semi-final draw against Premiership Middlesbrough.*

## INTO EUROPE

### European Champions League

Manchester United showed a marked improvement on their recent attempts in Europe, qualifying through a group that featured Juventus, Fenerbache and Rapid Vienna. The Red Devils then enjoyed a memorable 4–0 home victory over FC Porto in the quarter-finals to set up a semi-final tie with German champions Borussia Dortmund. Following two keenly contested encounters, Dortmund came out on top 2–0 on aggregate, eventually going on to win the trophy.

### European Cup Winners' Cup

Liverpool reached the semi-finals, having defeated FC Sion, Brann and Finish side MYPA, before losing out 3–2 on aggregate to Paris Saint-German despite a 2–0 home win that featured goals from Robbie Fowler and Mark Wright.

ABOVE: *Leicester City striker Steve Claridge riffles home to settle the League Cup final in the Foxes' favour. The contest went to a replay after the East Midlands side had drawn 1–1 with Middlesbrough at Wembley.*

# UEFA Cup

The Premiership's representatives were Aston Villa, who were eliminated by Sweden's Helsingborg on away goals in the first round; Arsenal, who crashed out to Borussia Monchengladbach of Germany at the same stage and Newcastle, who progressed to the quarter-finals before being soundly beaten 4–0 on aggregate by AS Monaco.

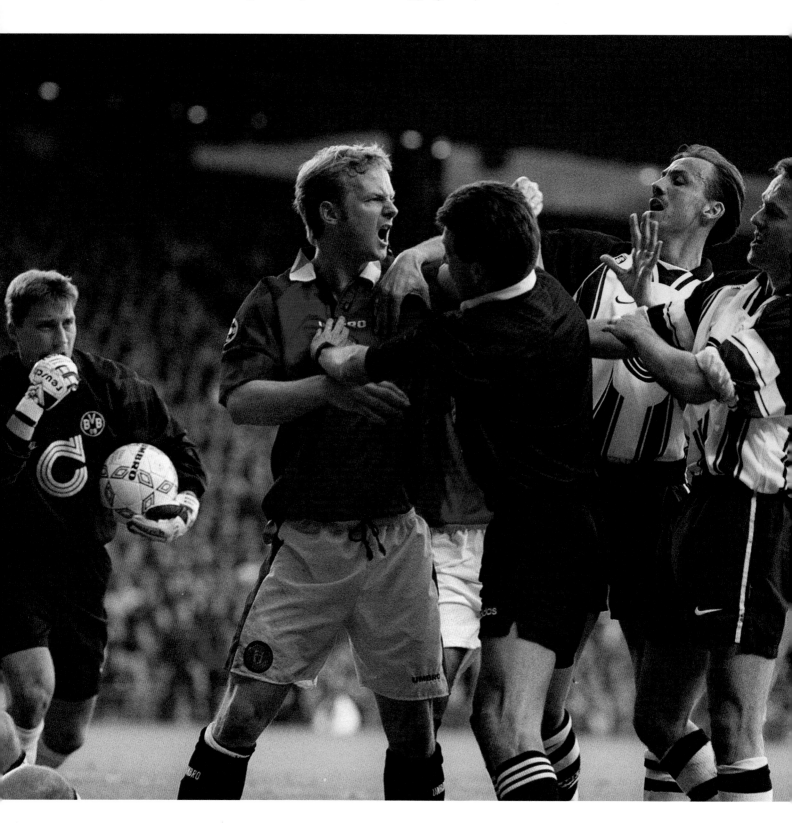

# THE INTERNATIONAL SCENE

Following the post Euro 96 euphoria, new England manager Glenn Hoddle gave debuts to a number of players, including Manchester United youngsters David Beckham and Paul Scholes. The Three Lions' World Cup qualifying campaign began well with three consecutive victories before they suffered a home loss to Italy. England remained nicely placed in their group and went on to impress in the 1997 Le Tournoi tournament held in France. Hoddle's men enjoyed victories over both Italy and France before narrowly losing to Brazil, but still topped the four team group to lift the trophy.

ABOVE: *England's Ian Wright celebrates a typically clinical finish that helped the Three Lions to an impressive 2–0 victory over Italy in 'Le Tournoi'.*

OPPOSITE: *Manchester United defender David May pictured during the heat of the battle against Borussia Dortmund in the Champions League semi-final. The Red Devils eventually exited to the German side as their struggles in Europe continued.*

# FRENCH REVOLUTION FIRES GUNNERS

**W**ith Manchester United chasing a record third championship in a row, their main challengers looked to be two of London's biggest clubs, as the continental influences at Arsenal and Chelsea left both sides looking well equipped. Stamford Bridge exuded glamour, hosting some of the biggest names in the division, while Arsene Wenger's Arsenal combined English grit through the immovable defensive unit instilled by George Graham with the irresistible pace and skill of forward-thinking players from across Europe.

New managerial appointments ahead of the campaign included Howard Kendall who departed Sheffield United to take charge of Everton for the third time and Roy Hodgson, who had previously coached Inter Milan, took up the reins at Blackburn Rovers. Before the campaign commenced, Bruce Grobbelaar, Hans Segers and John Fashanu, along with a Thai businessman, were cleared of any involvement with match-fixing following a legal trial.

OPPOSITE PAGE: *The ice man of Arsenal's superb double-winning side, PFA and Football Writers' Player of the Year Dennis Bergkamp oozed class and composure and his goals and vision provided the Gunners' creative spark.*

LEFT: *Joining Spurs for a second spell, German striker Jurgen Klinsmann may have been in the autumn years of his career, but his goals were vital to preserving the London club's Premiership status.*

# TRANSFER TALES

Arsenal strengthened their squad significantly with the addition of Dutch winger Marc Overmars and scheming French midfielder Emmanuel Petit. Arsene Wenger allowed Paul Merson to leave the club, as the England international signed for Middlesbrough in a £4.5m deal that represented a record fee paid by an English club outside of the top flight.

Further evidence of the increased financial power of clubs outside of the Premiership was provided by Fulham who spent £1.1m on striker Paul Peschisolido to make him the first player to join a third-tier club for a seven-figure sum. The Cottagers later broke the Division Two record for a second time after shelling out £2m on Blackburn defender Chris Coleman. Rovers also sold another defender, allowing Ian Pearce to join West Ham. Harry Redknapp's Hammers were typically active in the market, and also brought in Israeli international Eyal Berkovic and French World Cup winning goalkeeper, Bernard Lama.

The foreign market remained popular, as Blackburn snapped up Swiss defender Stephane Henchoz and Swedish striker Martin Dahlin, Crystal Palace added Italian stars Attilio Lombardo and Michele Padovano from Juventus and Derby also raided Serie A to capture Francesco Baiano and Stefan Eranio.

Returning to the Premiership from Italy, following a two-year spell with Inter Milan, was England midfielder Paul Ince. The former Manchester United favourite controversially chose to move to Liverpool in a £4.2m deal. The Anfield club also boosted their midfield ranks with the signings of Oyvind Leonhardsen and Danny Murphy, as well as strengthening their attack with the capture of Karl-Heinz Riedle.

Other players swapping clubs domestically included Graeme Le Saux who rejoined Chelsea in a record £5m deal for a defender, Les Ferdinand and David Ginola who both joined Spurs from Newcastle and David Hirst who signed for Southampton from Sheffield Wednesday.

Leeds United made what proved to be a significant addition, with the £2m capture of Netherlands striker Jimmy Floyd Hasselbaink from Boavista, while another Dutchman, George Boateng, joined Coventry City, alongside Romanian striker Viorel Moldovan.

Newcastle were the busiest club of the summer and throughout the campaign, bringing in experienced heads Stuart Pearce, John Barnes and Ian Rush on a free transfer, as well as investing £5.5m in Everton's Gary Speed and signing several players from the European market, including Greek defender Nikos Dabizas, Swedish striker Andreas Andersson, Italy defender Alessandro Pistone and Danish front man John Dahl Tomasson.

Sheffield Wednesday swelled their ranks with the £4.2m signing of Paolo Di Canio and the £3m addition of Everton's Andy Hinchcliffe. Manchester United spent relatively modestly, parting with £5m for Blackburn's Norwegian defender Henning Berg and snapping up Spurs and England forward Teddy Sheringham to fill the boots of the recently retired Eric Cantona.

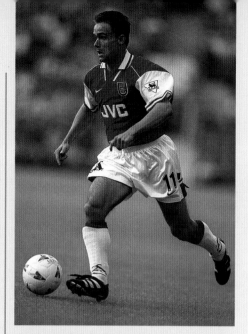

*Lightning-quick Dutch winger Marc Overmars brought another dimension to Arsenal's attack as his goals and craft were crucial to the Gunners' success.*

## BIGGEST TRANSFERS

**MARC OVERMARS** – from Ajax to Arsenal – £7m

**LES FERDINAND** – from Newcastle United to Tottenham Hotspur – £6m

**GARY SPEED** – from Everton to Newcastle United – £5.5m

**HENNING BERG** – from Blackburn Rovers to Manchester United – £5m

**GRAEME LE SAUX** – from Blackburn Rovers to Chelsea – £5m

**PAUL MERSON** – from Arsenal to Middlesbrough – £4.5m

**ALESSANDRO PISTONE** – from Inter Milan to Newcastle United – £4.5m

**PAOLO DI CANIO** – from Celtic to Sheffield Wednesday – £4.2m

**PAUL INCE** – from Inter Milan to Liverpool – £4.2m

**DEAN HOLDSWORTH** – from Wimbledon to Bolton Wanderers – £3.5m

**OYVIND LEONHARDSEN** – from Wimbledon to Liverpool – £3.5m

**EMMANUEL PETIT** – from AS Monaco to Arsenal – £3.5m

**TEDDY SHERINGHAM** – from Tottenham Hotspur to Manchester United – £3.5m

# TALES OF THE TURF

Barnsley, playing top-flight football for the first time, suffered a 2–1 defeat to West Ham while Coventry gained another first day shock victory, beating Chelsea 2–1. Another early season surprise came when Leicester defeated Liverpool 2–1 at Anfield, while Manchester United and Newcastle enjoyed positive starts to the campaign.

Chelsea got their campaign up and running with a 6–0 victory over Barnsley at Oakwell and Blackburn went one better, hitting seven past Sheffield Wednesday at Ewood Park to end August top of the table on goal difference from Manchester United.

September saw newly promoted Bolton play their first fixture at their purpose built 27,500-seat Reebok Stadium. Their first home fixture away from Burnden Park for 102 years ended in a 0–0 draw with Everton. Wimbledon enjoyed a 3–1 win against Newcastle at St. James' Park as Kenny Dalglish's team, missing the injured Alan Shearer, struggled for form. Meanwhile, former Magpies boss Kevin Keegan announced his return to football, taking up a role as Second Division Fulham's Chief Operating Officer.

Leeds and Blackburn shared seven goals in a game where the visitor's triumphed by a 4–3 scoreline but the Elland Road supporters were soon buzzing again when the Whites defeated Manchester 1–0 in a game that saw Roy Keane tangle with Alf-Inge Haaland and suffer a cruciate ligament injury that ruled him out for the rest of the season.

Arsenal took top spot at the end of the month, a place ahead of Manchester United in second and a point above third place Leicester City. The Gunners continued their great form into October, slamming five past Barnsley at Highbury in the same month that the Yorkshire club were hammered 7–0 by Manchester United. The Red Devils finished the month top of the pile with Arsenal in second and Blackburn third. Chelsea and Liverpool, who benefitted from the goal-scoring prowess of Michael Owen, were close behind, with the unfashionable trio of Leicester, Wimbledon and Derby County also making their mark in the top half of the table. In the bottom half, Sheffield Wednesday appointed former boss Ron Atkinson as manager after sacking David Pleat.

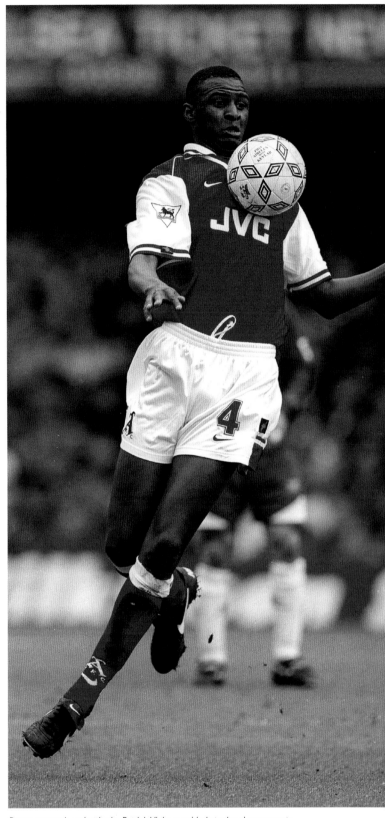

*Power, strength and attitude, Patrick Vieira provided steel and presence to Arsenal's double-winning side, forming an awesome midfield partnership with his countryman, Emmanuel Petit.*

*Italian striker Gianluca Vialli was the shock appointment as Chelsea manager following the mid-season sacking of Ruud Gullit.*

*Arsene Wenger and his players celebrate on the Highbury turf after Arsenal lifted the Premiership trophy for the first time.*

Manchester United began November with a crushing 6–1 win over Sheffield Wednesday but their lead at the top of the table was cut when Arsenal defeated them 3–2 at Highbury. The Gunners grabbed a late winner through David Platt after two goals from Teddy Sheringham pegged back Arsenal's two goal lead, which had been achieved through Nicolas Anelka and Patrick Vieira. United got back on track with a 5–2 win at Wimbledon while Arsenal suffered a shock loss to Sheffield Wednesday, meaning United ended the month on top of the table. At the foot of the division, Everton occupied 20th place, putting at risk their record of 44 successive seasons in the English top flight.

Spurs changed managers during November after Gerry Francis resigned and was replaced by Christian Gross from Switzerland, who famously claimed to have taken the London Underground to the press conference that unveiled him as boss.

Tottenham suffered a 6-1 home loss to Chelsea at the beginning of December but went on to make the headline signing of Jurgen Klinsmann from Sampdoria, and his goals proved key to their eventual survival. Spurs went on to make the headline signing of Jurgen Klinsmann from Sampdoria, and his goals goals proved key to their eventual survival. Manchester United enjoyed a 3–1 win at rivals Liverpool and the reigning champions

ended 1997 top by five points, with Arsenal lagging behind in sixth place.

Arsenal got back on track in the New Year with victories over Leeds and Southampton while Manchester United remained top of the table despite a 1–0 home loss to Leicester City, whose winning goal was scored by Tony Cottee.

February brought the shock dismissal of Chelsea boss Ruud Gullit, who departed the club after a disagreement with owner Ken Bates. One of Gullit's signings, Italian striker Gianluca Vialli, was installed as player-manager. Another managerial change came at Aston Villa, where Brian Little stepped down and was replaced by John Gregory. Manchester ended the month at the top thanks to a hard fought 1–0 win at Chelsea achieved through a rare Phil Neville goal that left them 11 points clear of second placed Blackburn. Arsenal lay a single point further back in third, but crucially had three games in hand on the leaders.

March brought one of the biggest league matches of the season, as Arsenal beat Manchester United 1–0 on their own turf through a well-taken goal from Marc Overmars. The Gunners continued to cut United's gap, clocking up successive 1–0 wins against Sheffield Wednesday and Bolton and completing an eighth successive clean sheet to set a new Premiership record. Crystal Palace manager Steve Coppell became director of football with players Attilio Lombardo and Tomas Brolin taking over first team affairs.

Manchester United remained in the title hunt until draws in April, against Liverpool and Newcastle, handed Arsenal the advantage. Controversy hit England captain Alan Shearer, who was investigated by the FA for aiming what appeared to be a deliberate kick to the face of Leicester's Neil Lennon. The Newcastle striker eventually escaped without charge.

Victories against Wimbledon, Derby and Barnsley meant that Arsenal needed to win just one of their final three fixtures to lift the title. Manchester United did all they could to maintain their challenge with a scrappy 3–0 win at Crystal Palace, a result that saw the Eagles become the first club to be relegated. However, the title was decided in emphatic fashion on May 3 when Arsenal thumped Everton 4–0 in a game made famous by defender and club captain Tony Adams' beautifully taken left-footed half-volley. The Gunners had stormed to the championship thanks to a Premiership record ten successive victories.

### ⊚ INTERESTING INFO

Arsenal's 1997–98 Premiership victory saw Arsene Wenger become the first non-British manager to win the division.

The trio of clubs that had gained promotion to the Premiership the previous summer, Crystal Palace, Bolton and Barnsley, all went on to drop out of the division. Everton again escaped relegation with a spot of last-day drama following a 1–1 draw against Coventry, which featured a long-range half-volley from Toffees midfielder Gareth Farrelly and edged them to safety following Bolton's defeat to Chelsea. Manager Howard Kendall resigned his post at the end of the campaign. The UEFA Cup places were filled by Liverpool, Chelsea, Leeds United, Blackburn Rovers and Aston Villa.

*Everton's inspiration, Duncan Ferguson caused defenders nightmares with his aerial prowess and tough man persona. The physically imposing striker was instrumental in keeping the Toffees in the top flight.*

# HONOURS LIST

## FA Carling Premiership
**CHAMPIONS:** Arsenal – At the end of his first full season in English football, Arsene Wenger guided the Gunners to the second league and cup double in their history.
**RUNNERS-UP:** Manchester United
**RELEGATED:** Bolton Wanderers, Barnsley, Crystal Palace
**TOP GOAL SCORERS:** Dion Dublin (Coventry City), Michael Owen (Liverpool) and Chris Sutton (Blackburn Rovers) – all 18 goals.

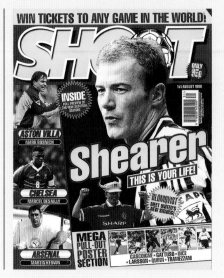

SHOOT MAGAZINE
1997–98

*Newcastle's Alan Shearer took centre stage while focus was also given to Manchester United's latest summer signing, Swedish winger Jesper Blomqvist. Other Premiership players featured in the publication included Aston Villa goalkeeper Mark Bosnich, Chelsea's Marcel Desailly and Arsenal defender Martin Keown.*

# 1997–98 SEASON TABLE

|  |  | M | W | D | L | GF | GA | GD | PTS |
|---|---|---|---|---|---|---|---|---|---|
| 1 | Arsenal | 38 | 23 | 9 | 6 | 68 | 33 | +35 | 78 |
| 2 | Manchester United | 38 | 23 | 8 | 7 | 73 | 26 | +47 | 77 |
| 3 | Liverpool | 38 | 18 | 11 | 9 | 68 | 42 | +26 | 65 |
| 4 | Chelsea | 38 | 20 | 3 | 15 | 71 | 43 | +28 | 63 |
| 5 | Leeds United | 38 | 17 | 8 | 13 | 57 | 46 | +11 | 59 |
| 6 | Blackburn Rovers | 38 | 16 | 10 | 12 | 57 | 52 | +5 | 58 |
| 7 | Aston Villa | 38 | 17 | 6 | 15 | 49 | 48 | +1 | 57 |
| 8 | West Ham United | 38 | 16 | 8 | 14 | 56 | 57 | -1 | 56 |
| 9 | Derby County | 38 | 16 | 7 | 15 | 52 | 49 | +3 | 55 |
| 10 | Leicester City | 38 | 13 | 14 | 11 | 51 | 41 | +10 | 53 |
| 11 | Coventry City | 38 | 12 | 16 | 10 | 46 | 44 | +2 | 52 |
| 12 | Southampton | 38 | 14 | 6 | 18 | 50 | 55 | -5 | 48 |
| 13 | Newcastle United | 38 | 11 | 11 | 16 | 35 | 44 | -9 | 44 |
| 14 | Tottenham Hotspur | 38 | 11 | 11 | 16 | 44 | 56 | -12 | 44 |
| 15 | Wimbledon | 38 | 10 | 14 | 14 | 34 | 46 | -12 | 44 |
| 16 | Sheffield Wednesday | 38 | 12 | 8 | 18 | 52 | 67 | -15 | 44 |
| 17 | Everton | 38 | 9 | 13 | 16 | 41 | 56 | -15 | 40 |
| 18 | Bolton Wanderers | 38 | 9 | 13 | 16 | 41 | 61 | -20 | 40 |
| 19 | Barnsley | 38 | 10 | 5 | 23 | 37 | 82 | -45 | 35 |
| 20 | Crystal Palace | 38 | 8 | 9 | 21 | 37 | 71 | -34 | 33 |

# PLAYERS OF THE SEASON

**PFA PLAYER OF THE YEAR:** Dennis Bergkamp, Arsenal
**PFA YOUNG PLAYER OF THE YEAR:** Michael Owen, Liverpool
**FOOTBALL WRITERS' PLAYER OF THE YEAR:** Dennis Bergkamp, Arsenal

**FOOTBALL LEAGUE DIVISION ONE CHAMPIONS:**
Nottingham Forest
**PROMOTED:** Middlesbrough
**DIVISION ONE PLAY-OFF WINNERS:** Charlton Athletic
**RELEGATED:** Manchester City, Stoke City, Reading
**TOP GOAL SCORER:** Kevin Phillips (Sunderland) and
Pierre van Hooijdonk (Nottingham Forest) – both
29 goals.

With the experienced Dave Bassett at the helm,
Nottingham Forest steamrollered the majority of their
league opposition, largely thanks to the impressive
goal-scoring exploits of powerful strike pairing Pierre
van Hooijdonk and Kevin Campbell. Forest clocked
up a total of 94 points, winning 28 of their 46 games
and scoring 84 goals. Second place went to Bryan
Robson's Middlesbrough, which ensured they spent
just a single season outside the top flight.

The last promotion place went to Alan Curbishley's
Charlton Athletic who ensured their first Premiership
participation after arguably the most entertaining
play-off finals of all-time. Facing Peter Reid's
Sunderland, the Addicks took an early lead through
Clive Mendonca before goals from Niall Quinn
and Kevin Phillips put the Black Cats 2–1 ahead.
Mendonca then levelled matters before Quinn
scored again to edge Sunderland back in front. A
late Richard Rufus goal sent the contest into extra
time, where Nicky Summerbee put Sunderland back
on the front foot before Mendonca completed his
hat-trick to send the match to penalties. Following
a marathon shootout, Michael Gray's spot kick was
comfortably saved by Charlton's Sasa Ilic to send
the London club into the top flight.

*ABOVE TOP LEFT: After moving south of the border from Celtic, Dutch striker Pierre van Hooijdonk formed an imposing striker partnership with Kevin Campbell that fired Nottingham Forest back into the big time.*

*ABOVE TOP RIGHT: Former England boss Graham Taylor returned to the Vicarage Road dugout for a second spell as Watford manager and again enjoyed great success while working on a limited budget.*

**DIVISION TWO CHAMPIONS:** Watford
**PROMOTED:** Bristol City
**DIVISION TWO PLAY-OFF WINNERS:** Grimsby Town
**RELEGATED:** Brentford, Plymouth Argyle, Carlisle
United, Southend United
**TOP GOAL SCORER:** Barry Hayles (23 goals for Bristol
Rovers)

Back in his second spell as Watford boss, former
England manager Graham Taylor guided the Hornets
to the title, returning 88 points and finishing three
clear of second place Bristol City, who gained
automatic promotion under the guidance of John
Ward. Grimsby completed the promotion picture
after defeating Northampton 1–0 in the play-off final.

**DIVISION THREE CHAMPIONS:** Notts County
**PROMOTED:** Macclesfield Town, Lincoln City
**DIVISION THREE PLAY-OFF WINNERS:** Colchester United
**RELEGATED:** Doncaster Rovers
**TOP GOAL SCORER:** Gary Jones (28 goals for Notts
County)

With Sam Allardyce at the helm, Notts County
enjoyed an unprecedented campaign, achieving a
record breaking early promotion in March, as well
as achieving an all-time high 17-point margin at the
top of the table. Sammy McIlroy's Macclesfield
Town maintained the momentum of their previous
season's success to seal back to back promotions
as runners-up. Lincoln City took the third automatic
promotion spot while Colchester moved up a level
following a 1–0 play-off final win over Torquay United.

**FOOTBALL CONFERENCE CHAMPIONS:** Halifax Town.
Under manager George Mulhall, the Shaymen
sealed a return to the Football League largely thanks
to the free-scoring form of striker Geoff Horsfield.

# UP FOR THE CUP

**FA CUP WINNERS:** Arsenal

Claiming the second double in their history, Arsene Wenger's men completed a comfortable 2–0 victory over Newcastle United thanks to goals from Marc Overmars and Nicolas Anelka. As they had done all season, the Gunners dominated possession and showed great pace and precision in attack.

Arsenal reached the Wembley showpiece following a tight 1–0 win over second tier Wolverhampton Wanderers at Villa Park, which was achieved thanks to an early finish from Christopher Wreh. Newcastle also won their semi-final by the same scoreline, beating Sheffield United at Old Trafford thanks to Alan Shearer's goal.

Headline results during the competition included Coventry overcoming Liverpool in the third round following a 3–1 win at Anfield; Manchester United's 5–3 mauling of Chelsea at Stamford Bridge, before the Red Devils later went out of the competition to Barnsley; non-league Stevenage Borough holding Newcastle to a 1–1 draw, before narrowly being defeated in the replay and Wolves knocking out both Wimbledon and Leeds United.

**LEAGUE (COCA COLA) CUP WINNERS:** Chelsea

The Blues lifted the League Cup following a 2–0 victory that featured extra-time goals from Frank Sinclair and Roberto Di Matteo. Under the guidance of newly-appointed Gianluca Vialli, Chelsea defeated Arsenal 5–3 on aggregate in a semi-final tie that saw Mark Hughes score twice and end the Gunners' hopes of a domestic treble. In the other semi-final Middlesbrough overcame Liverpool 3–2 on aggregate with Paul Merson bagging a brace across the tie.

Earlier in the competition, shock results included victories for Grimsby over Sheffield Wednesday and Leicester City, Hull's defeat of Crystal Palace, Ipswich's win against Manchester United and Reading's triumph over Leeds

ABOVE: *French youngster Nicolas Anelka belied his tender years with some measured and elegant finishing during Arsenal's successful season. Here he celebrates scoring the Gunners' second goal against Newcastle in the FA Cup final.*

OPPOSITE PAGE TOP: *Chelsea defender Frank Sinclair heads home against Middlesbrough during the Blues' 2–0 League Cup final victory.*

OPPOSITE PAGE BOTTOM: *Striker Giuliano Grazioli draws non-league Stevenage Borough level against Newcastle to take the Premiership side to a third round replay.*

**CHARITY SHIELD WINNERS:** Manchester United
United overcame Chelsea 4–2 on penalties after the game ended 1–1 following 90 minutes and extra time. The Blues had taken the lead through former Red Devils favourite Mark Hughes before Ronnie Johnsen levelled matters.

**THE FOOTBALL LEAGUE (AUTO WINDSCREENS) SHIELD:**
Grimsby Town defeated Bournemouth 2–1 at Wembley after extra time thanks to Wayne Burnett's winning goal.

# INTO EUROPE

## European Champions League

1997–98 was the first season to feature runners-up from some of Europe's highest profile leagues as the competition grew to feature six groups rather than four. As Premiership champions, Manchester United once again gained entry but were also joined by second placed Newcastle United, who progressed through the qualifying round 4–3 on aggregate against Croatia Zagreb before being drawn in a tricky group alongside Barcelona, PSV Eindhoven and Dynamo Kiev. The Magpies gave a reasonable account of themselves, achieving notable home victories over Barcelona and Kiev, but only picked up a single point away from home and finished third in the group. Manchester United fared better in the group stages, finishing top of the pile over Juventus, Feyenoord and MFK Kosice, and achieving a memorable 3–2 victory over the Italian champions at Old Trafford. However, Alex Ferguson's men flattered to deceive in the knockout rounds, losing 1–0 to AS Monaco to depart at the quarter-final stage.

## European Cup Winners' Cup

Chelsea, who began the tournament under the stewardship of Ruud Gullit, went on to lift the trophy to seal the second European honour in the club's history. The Blues enjoyed a steady progression through the competition, defeating Slovan Bratislava and FC Tromso in the early rounds before being paired with Spain's Real Betis in the quarter-finals. A brace from Tore Andre Flo set them up for a 2–1 away win before a 3–1 home victory featuring goals from Trevor Sinclair, Roberto Di Matteo and Gianfranco Zola ensured their progress to the semi-finals. Up against Vicenza of Italy, the Blues came back from a 1–0 first leg deficit to win the tie 4–2 on aggregate thanks to goals from Mark Hughes, Gus Poyet and another from Zola. The diminutive Italian was once again the hero in the final storming onto a Dennis Wise through ball before dispatching a right-footed half-volley into the roof of the net. It proved to be the only goal as the English club defeated Germany's VfB Stuttgart in Stockholm.

## UEFA Cup

Representing England were Arsenal, who fell at the first round to PAOK of Greece; Leicester City who were also knocked out at the same stage to highly-rated Atletico Madrid and Aston Villa and Liverpool, who both fared slightly better. Liverpool reached the second round but were defeated by Strasbourg after overcoming Celtic 2–2 on away goals in a first round tie that featured a memorable solo finish from Steve McManaman. League Cup winners Villa were England's most impressive performers and enjoyed victories over Bordeaux, Athletic Bilbao and Steaua Bucharest before suffering quarter-final defeat on away goals to Atletico Madrid.

*Match-winner Gianfranco Zola holds onto the European Cup Winners' Cup after his strike helped Chelsea to a 1–0 win over VfB Stuttgart.*

# THE INTERNATIONAL SCENE

Having sealed qualification for the 1998 World Cup as group winners after a hard-fought 0–0 draw against Italy in Rome, Glenn Hoddle's England went into the tournament itself in good shape. After defeating Tunisia 2–0 in their opening game, thanks to goals from Alan Shearer and Paul Scholes, the Three Lions lost 2–1 to Romania in a game that saw teenage Michael Owen come off the bench and grab a goal. England then overcame Colombia 2–0 thanks to powerful Darren Anderton strike and a swerving David Beckham free-kick.

ABOVEE: *Bloodied and bruised, Paul Ince was one of England's warriors during a spirited 0–0 with Italy in Rome that confirmed the Three Lions' qualification for the 1998 World Cup.*

*Micheal Owen, who went on to score one of the finest goals in World Cup history, celebrates his first goal of the tournament for England against Romania. David Beckham (pictured with his arm around Owen) went on to score a classy free-kick against Colombia before being sent off against Argentina as the Three Lions crashed out of the tournament.*

Pitted against great rivals Argentina in the second round, Hoddle's side gave a spirited performance to draw the game 2–2 after being reduced to 10 men following David Beckham's red card. The Three Lions eventually exited on penalties after David Batty missed the crucial kick. The game had featured one of the great England goals when Michael Owen picked up the ball on the halfway line, slalomed in and out of challenges and slammed the ball into the net.

# RECORD BREAKING TREBLE FOR UNITED

**A**head of the new season Liverpool appointed former French national coach Gerard Houllier as joint manager alongside Roy Evans. It was all change on the other side of Stanley Park as Everton replaced Howard Kendall with Scottish manager Walter Smith. Reigning champions Arsenal again looked likely to challenge for major honours, as did Manchester United who were boosted by the return of long-term injury absentee Roy Keane.

As a club, Manchester United rallied around David Beckham after the talented midfielder was on the receiving end of a torrent of abuse from the national press and supporters of other teams following his dismissal whilst playing for England in the World Cup. In contrast, another of the Three Lions' World Cup contingent, Michael Owen, was billed as the new golden boy of English football after making a goal-scoring impact at the tournament.

The pre-season preparations of promoted Nottingham Forest were thrown into disarray when Dutch striker, Pierre van Hooijdonk, their top scorer during the previous campaign went on strike and refused to play following a dispute with the club. Middlesbrough and Charlton Athletic, who gained promotion alongside Forest, began the season on a much more stable footing.

OPPOSITE PAGE: *A picture of concentration, Manchester United striker Andy Cole lobs the ball over advancing Tottenham goalkeeper Ian Walker to score United's winning goal in the game the clinched the Premiership title.*

BELOW: *The prodigiously talented Michael Owen has the entire Newcastle United defence under his spell on the way to completing a devastatingly clinical hat-trick during Liverpool's 4–1 victory over the Magpies.*

# TRANSFER TALES

Stinging from their first season without a trophy since 1994–95, Manchester United spent heavily in the transfer market, bringing in Dwight Yorke for a club record £12.6m, Jaap Stam for £10.75m and Jesper Blomqvist for £4.4m. United allowed long-serving defender Gary Pallister to rejoin his hometown club Middlesbrough for £3m. Boro also brought in Colin Cooper, Brian Deane from Benfica and Dean Gordon.

Aston Villa reinvested the funds they received for Dwight Yorke, adding the likes of Paul Merson, Dion Dublin, Steve Watson, Alan Thompson and Steve Stone. Coventry City made several significant signings, including John Aloisi and Paul Hall from Portsmouth, as well as Morocco midfielder Youssef Chippo and Bosnian defender Mo Konjic.

Newcastle invested heavily with the captures of Everton striker Duncan Ferguson for £8m, Peruvian winger Nolberto Solano for £2.48m and German international midfielder Dietmar Hamann from Bayern Munich for £5.25m. The Magpies also swelled their ranks with the likes of Stephane Guivarch and Didier Domi.

Southampton made over 10 new signings, including Mark Hughes from Chelsea, Stuart Ripley from Blackburn, Morrocan international Hassan Kachloul and Latvian striker Marian Pahars. Blackburn were also a busy club in the transfer market and added 11 new players, including Matt Jansen from Crystal Palace, Keith Gillespie from Newcastle, Jason McAteer from Liverpool and Barnsley striker Ashley Ward.

Everton signed Ivorian striker Ibrahima Bakayoko from Montpellier for £4.5million as well as French midfielder Olivier Dacourt from Strasbourg for £3.8m and young Italian defender Marco Materazzi from Perugia.

# BIGGEST TRANSFERS

**DWIGHT YORKE** – from Aston Villa to Manchester United – £12.6m

**JAAP STAM** – from PSV Eindhoven to Manchester United – £10.75m

**DUNCAN FERGUSON** – from Everton to Newcastle United – £8m

**KEVIN DAVIES** – from Southampton to Blackburn Rovers – £7.5m

**JOHN HARTSON** – from West Ham United to Wimbledon – £7.5m

**PAUL MERSON** – from Middlesbrough to Aston Villa – £6.75m

**DION DUBLIN** – from Coventry City to Aston Villa – £5.75m

**STEVE STONE** – from Nottingham Forest to Aston Villa – £5.5m

**CHRISTIAN DAILY** – from Derby County to Blackburn Rovers – £5.4m

**PIERLUIGI CASIRAGHI** – from Lazio to Chelsea – £5.4m

LEFT: *One of Manchester United's key summer additions and a man mountain of a defender, Dutch international Jaap Stam formed a rock solid partnership with Ronnie Johnsen that provided the foundations for a season of unprecedented success for the Red Devils.*

Arsenal were less extravagant than closest rivals Manchester United, investing just £3m in Swedish midfielder Freddie Ljungberg. The Gunners' record scorer Ian Wright joined West Ham in a cut price deal, while Marc-Vivien Foe, Neil Ruddock, Javier Margas, Scott Minto and Paolo Di Canio also joined the Hammers.

Andy Impey departed West Ham for Leicester, who also brought in Frank Sinclair from Chelsea and Icelandic midfielder Arnar Gunnlaugsson. Tottenham's most significant piece of business came in the form of the £4m signing of Blackburn midfielder Tim Sherwood. Dutch World Cup midfielder Wim Jonk arrived at Sheffield Wednesday from PSV Eindhoven in a £2.5m deal while Wimbledon broke their transfer record to entice Welsh striker John Hartson from West Ham for £7.5m.

Chelsea signed French World Cup winner Marcel Desailly for £4.6m from AC Milan, Pierluigi Casiraghi from Lazio for £5.4m, Albert Ferrer from Barcelona, Bjarne Goldbaek from FC Copenhagen and Brian Laudrup on a free transfer from Rangers. Liverpool added Rigobert Song in a £2.7m deal, Veggard Heggem from Rosenborg and South African-born striker, Sean Dundee for £2m.

ABOVE: *French World Cup winning defender Marcel Desailly represented a real coup for Chelsea when they brought him from AC Milan. An athlete, expert man-marker and all-round talented footballer, the powerful defender instantly strengthened the Blues' back four.*

# TALES OF THE TURF

Reigning champions Arsenal began the campaign strongly with a 2–1 victory over Nottingham Forest, while Manchester United were held at home by Leicester City. Chelsea suffered a surprise opening day loss to Coventry for the second successive season. Newly promoted Charlton achieved an impressive 5–0 win over Southampton at the Valley while Tottenham endured a disappointing first month to the campaign that included a 3–1 defeat to Spurs and a 3–0 home loss to Sheffield Wednesday.

Liverpool's Michael Owen further enhanced his reputation with a clinical hat-trick against Newcastle during a 4–1 victory for the Reds. Magpies boss Kenny Dalglish was sacked in the build-up to the game and replaced by former Chelsea manager Ruud Gullit.

Manchester United's slow start continued with a 0–0 draw at West Ham as Charlton Athletic were the surprise early season leaders, ending August at the top of the table after winning one and drawing two of their opening games.

September brought the sacking of Spurs manager Christian Gross after just nine months in charge. New Manchester United signing Dwight Yorke grabbed two goals against Charlton on his debut as United won 4–1. The Red Devils remained in the headlines throughout the month as the club accepted a takeover bid from BSkyB. However, the takeover was eventually thrown out by the Monopolies and Mergers Commission, who deemed BSkyB's ownership would represent a conflict of interest.

Ruud Gullit inspired a resurgence of form at Newcastle who defeated Coventry 5–1 while Charlton picked up another impressive result, drawing 3–3 with Liverpool at Anfield. Arsenal followed up their Charity Shield victory over Manchester United with a league win by the same 3–0 margin, which was achieved through goals from Tony Adams, Nicolas Anelka and Freddie Ljungberg.

One of the season's most bizarre incidents took place during a fixture between Sheffield Wednesday and Arsenal in September. Wednesday's enigmatic forward Paolo Di Canio, disgruntled at a series of refereeing decisions, lost his cool after receiving a red card and pushed official Paul Alcock in the chest. The referee was off-balance anyway and stumbled to the ground in a comical fashion but the ramifications for the Italian playmaker were serious. Di Canio was given an 11 game ban by the FA and fined £10,000.

John Gregory's Aston Villa ended September on top of the table, with new signings Dion Dublin and Paul Merson in particularly impressive form. Derby County found themselves in second place with Manchester United third and Liverpool fourth.

October saw another managerial departure as George Graham quit his role at Leeds to take charge of Tottenham. Bryan Robson's Middlesbrough continued to adapt well to life back in the top flight, recording a 4–0 win over Sheffield Wednesday while Leicester City, who continued to defy the odds with some impressive results under Martin O'Neill, were delighted to announce that their much sought-after manager would not be taking over at Leeds, following impassioned pleas from Foxes fans. Leeds opted to give temporary boss David O'Leary the job on a full-time basis. The month ended with Aston Villa top of table but Manchester United and Arsenal were hot on their heels.

At the beginning of November Manchester United goalkeeper Peter Schmeichel announced his intention to depart the club at the end of the season while Liverpool joint manager Roy Evans resigned to leave Gerard Houllier in sole charge. Roy Hodgson stepped down as Blackburn boss a few weeks later after a 2–0 home loss to Southampton saw Rovers sink to the bottom of the table. Manchester United suffered a surprise 3–1 defeat at Sheffield Wednesday as they ended the month a point behind Aston Villa.

OPPOSITE PAGE: *A consistent scorer for Leeds United throughout the campaign, Dutch centre forward Jimmy Floyd Hasselbaink headed home a crucial goal that significantly impacted upon the title race when he found the net in a 1–0 win against Arsenal.*

At the beginning of December, United lost assistant manager Brian Kidd who succeeded Roy Hodgson at Blackburn. Alex Ferguson later brought in Derby coach Steve McClaren as his number two but not before the Red Devils suffered a home loss to Middlesbrough, in what proved to be United's final defeat of the campaign. Aston Villa ended 1998 as league leaders but Manchester United, Arsenal, Chelsea, Leeds and West Ham were close behind.

A few days into the New Year, struggling Nottingham Forest sacked manager Dave Bassett. His temporary replacement was Micky Adams before Ron Atkinson took permanent charge. Manchester United hammered Leicester 6–2 at Filbert Street on the same weekend as Liverpool thrashed Southampton 7–1 at Anfield. Liverpool midfielder Steve McManaman announced his intention to depart the club on a free transfer, much to the frustration of Reds fans.

At the bottom of the table Ron Atkinson inspired Nottingham Forest to their first win in 19 matches, with a 1–0 victory at Everton but the East Midlanders remained stranded in 20th position. At the top of the division, Manchester United ended the month in pole position, with Arsenal just two points adrift in fourth. In February United recorded the Premier League's highest ever away win with a thumping 8–1 victory against Nottingham Forest at the City Ground. The game featured four goals from second-half substitute Ole Gunnar Solskjaer and helped the Red Devils end the month four points clear. However, second place Chelsea had a game in hand.

In March Nottingham Forest recorded their third victory of the season, winning 3–1 at Wimbledon. Arsenal secured three consecutive victories, defeating Sheffield Wednesday, Everton and Coventry to ramp up the pressure on Manchester United, who won all four of their fixtures.

As the month drew to a close, Nottingham Forest became the first team to be relegated following a 2–0 loss to Aston Villa. In the title race, Arsenal led the way, a point ahead of Manchester United who had a game in hand. Joe Kinnear left his role as Wimbledon boss due to ill health and was replaced by Terry Burton and Mick Harford until the end of the season.

Manchester United again took the title initiative in May when Arsenal lost their penultimate game of the season by a single Jimmy Floyd Hasselbaink goal against Leeds. United's game in hand against Blackburn ended in a draw as Rovers became the second team to drop into Division One, just four years after being English champions. The result left United needing to win their last game of the season, at home to Tottenham, to claim the league.

On the final day, United clinched their fifth Premier League title in seven seasons after beating Tottenham 2–1 thanks to a swerving David Beckham drive and a precisely placed Andy Cole lob. Arsenal's 1–0 win over Aston Villa wasn't enough as Alex Ferguson's men picked up the first of three trophies in a week. Chelsea ended in third with Leeds fourth. West Ham secured their highest finish for 13 years, after cementing fifth place and European qualification for this first time in 19 years. Final day heartbreak was suffered by Charlton, who lost 1–0 at home to Sheffield Wednesday and dropped out of the division as Southampton claimed survival with victory over Everton.

## ⚽ INTERESTING INFO

During his 27 games for Everton, Marco Materazzi was sent off an incredible four times.

# HONOURS LIST

## FA Carling Premiership

**CHAMPIONS:** Manchester United – Alex Ferguson's men returned to the summit of English football winning the championship by a single point.
**RUNNERS-UP:** Arsenal
**RELEGATED:** Charlton Athletic, Blackburn Rovers, Nottingham Forest
**TOP GOAL SCORERS:** Jimmy Floyd Hasselbaink (Leeds United), Michael Owen (Liverpool), Dwight Yorke (Manchester United) – all 18 goals.

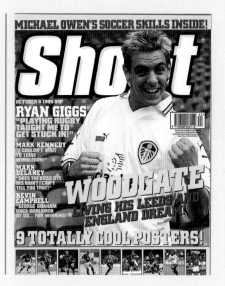

SHOOT MAGAZINE
1998–99

*Cover star Jonathan Woodgate talked about his fantasy Leeds United and England teams while the magazine again contained a whole host of features and a plethora of action-filled posters. Also previewed on the front cover were interviews with Manchester United's Ryan Giggs, Manchester City winger Mark Kennedy, Mark Delaney of Aston Villa and Everton's Kevin Campbell.*

# 1998–99 SEASON TABLE

| | | M | W | D | L | GF | GA | GD | PTS |
|---|---|---|---|---|---|---|---|---|---|
| 1 | Manchester United | 38 | 22 | 13 | 3 | 80 | 37 | +43 | 79 |
| 2 | Arsenal | 38 | 22 | 12 | 4 | 59 | 17 | +42 | 78 |
| 3 | Chelsea | 38 | 20 | 15 | 3 | 57 | 30 | +27 | 75 |
| 4 | Leeds United | 38 | 18 | 13 | 7 | 62 | 34 | +28 | 67 |
| 5 | West Ham United | 38 | 16 | 9 | 13 | 46 | 53 | -7 | 57 |
| 6 | Aston Villa | 38 | 15 | 10 | 13 | 51 | 46 | +5 | 55 |
| 7 | Liverpool | 38 | 15 | 9 | 14 | 68 | 49 | +19 | 54 |
| 8 | Derby County | 38 | 13 | 13 | 12 | 40 | 45 | -5 | 52 |
| 9 | Middlesbrough | 38 | 12 | 15 | 11 | 48 | 54 | -6 | 51 |
| 10 | Leicester City | 38 | 12 | 13 | 13 | 40 | 46 | -6 | 49 |
| 11 | Tottenham Hotspur | 38 | 11 | 14 | 13 | 47 | 50 | -3 | 47 |
| 12 | Sheffield Wednesday | 38 | 13 | 7 | 18 | 41 | 42 | -1 | 46 |
| 13 | Newcastle United | 38 | 11 | 13 | 14 | 48 | 54 | -6 | 46 |
| 14 | Everton | 38 | 11 | 10 | 17 | 42 | 47 | -5 | 43 |
| 15 | Coventry City | 38 | 11 | 9 | 18 | 39 | 51 | -12 | 42 |
| 16 | Wimbledon | 38 | 10 | 12 | 16 | 40 | 63 | -23 | 42 |
| 17 | Southampton | 38 | 11 | 8 | 19 | 37 | 64 | -27 | 41 |
| 18 | Charlton Athletic | 38 | 8 | 12 | 18 | 41 | 56 | -15 | 36 |
| 19 | Blackburn Rovers | 38 | 7 | 14 | 17 | 38 | 52 | -14 | 35 |
| 20 | Nottingham Forest | 38 | 7 | 9 | 22 | 35 | 69 | -34 | 30 |

# PLAYERS OF THE SEASON

**PFA PLAYER OF THE YEAR:** David Ginola, Tottenham Hotspur
**PFA YOUNG PLAYER OF THE YEAR:** Nicolas Anelka, Arsenal
**FOOTBALL WRITERS' PLAYER OF THE YEAR:** David Ginola, Tottenham Hotspur

FOOTBALL LEAGUE DIVISION ONE CHAMPIONS: Sunderland
PROMOTED: Bradford City
DIVISION ONE PLAY-OFF WINNERS: Watford
RELEGATED: Bury, Oxford United, Bristol City
TOP GOAL SCORER: Lee Hughes (31 goals for West Bromwich Albion)

Peter Reid's Sunderland put the disappointment of play-off final defeat from the previous season behind them in devastating fashion, storming to the Division One title with a record breaking points tally of 105. Inspired by the strike partnership of Niall Quinn and Kevin Phillips the Black Cats scored an impressive 91 goals in 46 games and conceded just 28.

Bradford City boss Paul Jewell worked wonders to achieve automatic promotion with the unfancied Bantams, returning the Yorkshire club to English football's highest level for the first time in 80 years. Another surprise came in the play-off final when Graham Taylor's Watford defeated Bolton Wanderers 2–0 thanks to goals from Nick Wright and Allan Smart.

OPPOSITE PAGE: *Despite Manchester United's domestic dominance, it was the individual Gallic flair of David Ginola that attracted the plaudits, as the Tottenham winger secured both the PFA and Football Writers' accolades.*

ABOVE: *As part of a classic little and large strike partnership with Niall Quinn, young English centre forward Kevin Phillips fired Sunderland to the Division One title. The clinical Phillips went on star in the Premiership the following season*

Fulham captain Chris Coleman lifts the Division Two trophy after the Cottagers stormed to the title.

Brentford chairman and manager Ron Noades proudly hoists the Division Three 'champions' banner at Griffin Park.

**DIVISION TWO CHAMPIONS:** Fulham
**PROMOTED:** Walsall
**DIVISION TWO PLAY-OFF WINNERS:** Manchester City
**RELEGATED:** York City, Northampton Town, Lincoln City, Macclesfield Town
**TOP GOAL SCORER:** Jamie Cureton (25 goals for Bristol Rovers)

With Kevin Keegan at the helm, Fulham stormed to the title despite their charismatic boss combining his duties with the England manager's job during the second half of the season. The Cottagers achieved their second promotion in three seasons in impressive fashion. Joining the London club in Division One was surprise package Walsall, who gained promotion for just the second time in their history, under the stewardship of boss Colin Lee. Joe Royle ensured Manchester City spent just a single season in the third tier following a dramatic play-off final victory over Tony Pulis' Gillingham. A stoppage time equaliser from Paul Dickov levelled the scores at 2–2 before a goalless period of extra time was followed by a 3–1 penalty shootout victory for the Manchester club.

**DIVISION THREE CHAMPIONS:** Brentford
**PROMOTED:** Cambridge United, Cardiff City
**DIVISION THREE PLAY-OFF WINNERS:** Scunthorpe United
**RELEGATED:** Scarborough
**TOP GOAL SCORER:** Marco Gabbiadini (24 goals for Darlington)

Brentford, who were managed by club chairman Ron Noades, achieved promotion as champions. Star performers for the Bees included defender Hermann Hreidarsson and midfielder Paul Evans. Cambridge United, managed by Roy McFarland, finished second despite topping the table for much of the season while the third automatic promotion place went to Frank Burrows' Cardiff City. Scunthorpe United won the play-offs, earning their first promotion since 1983, thanks to a 1–0 win against Scunthorpe United in the final, achieved through Alex Calvo Garcia's goal.

Dropping out of the league in dramatic fashion were Scarborough, who fell into the Conference on the last day of the season after Carlisle United scored an injury-time winner through goalkeeper Jimmy Glass. The on loan custodian ran up the pitch for a last gasp corner and slammed home a close range volley to complete a 2–1 victory over Plymouth Argyle that saved the Cumbrian club but sealed Scarborough's fate.

**FOOTBALL CONFERENCE CHAMPIONS:** Cheltenham Town

Led by boss Steve Cotterill, Cheltenham reached the Football League for the first time in their history after finishing top of the pile with 80 points and 71 goals.

# UP FOR THE CUP

**FA CUP WINNERS:** Manchester United

The champions completed their third league and cup double under Alex Ferguson with a 2–0 victory over Newcastle at Wembley. A first-half injury to captain Roy Keane saw him replaced by Teddy Sheringham who went on to open the scoring with a typically classy finish. The Red Devils extended their lead in the second period when Paul Scholes drilled one home from the edge of the box.

One of the games of the season came in the semi-finals when Manchester United were paired with Arsenal. After a first 90 minutes at Villa Park ended goalless the subsequent replay provided one of the classic FA Cup ties. An early goal from David Beckham gave United the lead before Dennis Bergkamp levelled matters for the Gunners. Roy Keane was sent off for a second bookable offence and Arsenal were awarded a last minute penalty when Phil Neville felled Ray Parlour in the area.

With the chance to settle the tie, Bergkamp saw his shot saved by Peter Schmeichel and the game went into extra time. As the game ebbed and flowed the ten men of United took an unlikely lead when substitute Ryan Giggs capitalised on a weary, misguided pass from Patrick Vieira. The Welshman waltzed in and out of several challenges as he stormed from the half-way line to inside the Arsenal box before slamming home a left-footed shot high into the net past David Seaman to send United to the final. Newcastle's semi-final clash saw them defeat Tottenham 2–0 at Old Trafford with both goals coming in extra time from Alan Shearer.

Other standout results during the competition included Bedlington Terriers' shock 4–1 win over Colchester United, Swansea City overcoming West Ham, Fulham's 1–0 win against Southampton and 2–0 victory at Aston Villa, Rushden & Diamonds taking Leeds to a replay and Portsmouth's 1–0 win at Nottingham Forest.

ABOVE: *Manchester United's FA Cup final goal scorers, Teddy Sheringham and Paul Scholes, lift the trophy following the Red Devils' 2–0 victory against Newcastle. It was Scholes last game of the season as he, like United skipper Roy Keane missed the Champions League final through suspension.*

## LEAGUE (WORTHINGTON) CUP WINNERS:
Tottenham Hotspur

George Graham guided Spurs to their first major trophy in eight years following a bad tempered final against Leicester City. Tottenham's Justin Edinburgh became the last man to be sent off at the old Wembley stadium when he threw a punch at Leicester's Robbie Savage after 63 minutes. Ten man Spurs went on to grab a last minute winner when Danish midfielder Allan Nielsen powered home a diving header from close-range.

Tottenham reached the final thanks to a 1–0 two-legged semi-final victory over Wimbledon achieved thanks to Steffen Iversen's goal. Leicester overcame Sunderland 3–2 on aggregate with Tony Cottee scoring all of their goals.

Earlier in the competition the headline grabbers included Cambridge United who ousted Sheffield Wednesday, Fulham who saw off Southampton, Northampton Town who knocked out West Ham, Luton Town who accounted for Coventry and Barnsley, and Wimbledon who edged Chelsea out at the quarter-final stage.

## CHARITY SHIELD WINNERS: Arsenal
The Gunners tore into a Manchester United side bedding in several new signings with a devastating display of attacking football. Arsene Wenger's side enjoyed a 3–0 victory thanks to goals from Marc Overmars, Christopher Wreh and Nicolas Anelka.

## THE FOOTBALL LEAGUE (AUTO WINDSCREENS) SHIELD:
Wigan Athletic

The Latics, managed by Ray Mathias, defeated Millwall 1–0 at Wembley thanks to a stoppage time winner from Paul Rogers.

ABOVE TOP: *Shirt in his hand and surrounded by joyous team-mates and fans, Manchester United winger Ryan Giggs celebrate his miraculous winning goal that sent United into the FA Cup final at the expense of great rivals Arsenal.*

ABOVE BOTTOM: *Tottenham skipper Sol Campbell hoists the League Cup after the North London club defeated Leicester City in the final.*

# INTO EUROPE

## European Champions League

Manchester United and Arsenal were England's two representatives in the competition. The Gunners, competing in the tournament for the first time since it had changed format and playing their home matches at Wembley stadium, struggled and finished third in a group that also included Dynamo Kiev, Racing Club Lens and Panathinaikos.

Manchester United fared much better, going on to reach the final before lifting the trophy in memorable circumstances. Having progressed through a tough group that also featured Barcelona and Bayern Munich, United negotiated tricky knockout clashes against Inter Milan and Juventus to reach the final. Standout moments along the way, included Dwight Yorke and Andy Cole tearing Barcelona's defence to shreds at the Nou Camp, Paul Scholes' crucial away goal against Inter at the San Siro and an inspirational captain's performance by Roy Keane away at Juventus in a match United won 3–2 despite going two goals down early in the game.

ABOVE: *Manchester United captain Roy Keane heads home the goal that turned the tide during the Champions League semi-final clash with Juventus. The Irishman had received a booking that ruled him out of the final should the Red Devils get there, but went on to put in one of his most commanding and inspiring displays in a red shirt.*

The final itself saw Alex Ferguson's men paired with Bayern Munich and proved to be an edgy affair. The German side took an early lead through Mario Basler and looked likely to extend that advantage on the counter-attack after the half-time interval as United surged forward in search of an equaliser. As the clock ticked down, two second-half substitutes did the damage as first Teddy Sheringham and then Ole Solskjaer scored late goals from corners to seal United's second European Cup crown and complete an unprecedented treble of Premiership title, FA Cup victory and Champions League success.

## European Cup Winners' Cup

Representing England in the competition, in the last year before it was scrapped and incorporated into an increased UEFA Cup, were holders of the trophy Chelsea and the previous season's FA Cup runners-up, Newcastle.

The Magpies' involvement proved short-lived as they exited in the first round following an away goals defeat to FK Partizan. Chelsea faired significantly better, defeating the Scandanavian trio of Helsingborg, Copenhagen and Valeranga to reach the semi-finals, where they were eventually eliminated 2–1 on aggregate by Real Mallorca.

## UEFA Cup

Blackburn Rovers departed after a single round following a two-legged defeat to Lyon and Leeds exited in the second round after a 1–0 loss to Roma, Aston Villa were knocked out at the same stage against Celta Vigo while Liverpool enjoyed the most success. The Reds advanced to the third round, having beaten MFK Kosice and Valencia, before Celta Vigo halted their progress.

# THE INTERNATIONAL SCENE

Glenn Hoddle saw his team lose at Sweden and draw at home to Bulgaria but off-field matters led to him losing his job after an article appeared in the Times attributing quotes to him that suggested disabled people were being punished for sins in previous lives. The story sparked national outrage and the FA cancelled Hoddle's contract. After Howard Wilkinson stepped in on a caretaker basis, Fulham boss Kevin Keegan was appointed Hoddle's successor.

OPPOSITE PAGE TOP:
*Supersub Ole Gunnar Solskjaer turns away in joyous disbelief after his close-range finish hit the roof of the net to complete a remarkable stoppage time turn around that saw Manchester United defeat Bayern Munich 2–1 in the Champions League final.*

OPPOSITE PAGE BOTTOM:
*Manchester United's treble winning players celebrate on the Nou Camp pitch with the Champions League trophy.*

# ADVANCING INTO THE 21ST CENTURY

Still known as the FA Carling Premiership, the division's eighth year was once again met with eager anticipation right across the world. It was a season of relatively few managerial changes, with just two new bosses, Egil Olsen, who replaced Joe Kinnear at Wimbledon and Danny Wilson, who came in at Sheffield Wednesday, taking charge of a new team ahead of the campaign.

Still basking in the glory of their treble triumph, Manchester United were the team on everyone's lips ahead of the new season as many observers tipped them to dominate both at home and abroad for many years to come.

European success for a Premiership side raised the profile of the game even further and players from across the continent continued to flock to England to ply their trade.

LEFT: *A goal-scoring success at Blackburn Rovers, English striker Chris Sutton found the going harder at Chelsea after joining the Blues for a £10m fee.*

OPPOSITE PAGE: *Ryan Giggs remained one of Manchester United's key performers during the campaign as he and David Beckham continued to supply a glut of chances for their team-mates.*

# TRANSFER TALES

Spending remained at a high level but didn't increase dramatically ahead of the new season, with the majority of deals being conducted under the £5m mark. Chelsea continued to show their financial strength by breaking their transfer record to sign Blackburn's Chris Sutton for £10m. The Blues also brought in France's World Cup winning captain Didier Deschamps, Emerson Thome from Sheffield Wednesday, Mario Melchiot from Ajax and Danish defender Jes Hogh.

Liverpool acquired Finnish defender Sami Hyppia, as well as Vladimir Smicer, Sander Westerveld, Titi Camara and Stephane Henchoz; allowing the likes of David James, Paul Ince, Rob Jones and Karl-Heinz Riedle to depart. As the campaign progressed, Liverpool also parted with £11m to sign young Leicester striker Emile Heskey. That fee that was equalled by Arsenal when they captured French forward Thierry Henry from Juventus. The Gunners also swelled their continental ranks with the signings of Silvinho, Davor Suker and Oleg Luzhny. Manchester United also spent in the European market, adding Quinton Fortune, Mikael Silvestre and Massimo Taibi.

Leeds United continued to spend big, investing £5m in Sunderland's Michael Bridges as well as bringing in Danny Mills from Charlton Athletic, Jason Wilcox from Blackburn and Michael Dueberry from Chelsea. Newcastle showed their intent by splashing £6.5m on Ipswich youngster Kieron Dyer while their North East rivals Middlesbrough added German international Christian Ziege.

Some of the biggest headlines were made by outgoing deals, as two of the division's most talented strikers moved to Spain when Arsenal sold Nicolas Anelka to Real Madrid for £23 million and Jimmy Floyd Hasselbaink also headed to the Spanish capital, departing Leeds for Atletico Madrid in a £12 million deal.

West Ham signed the Derby duo of Igor Stimac and Paulo Wanchope while across London, Spurs brought in Chris Perry from Wimbledon for £4m and Oyvind Leonhardsen from Liverpool. Everton completed the permanent signing of Kevin Campbell following his successful loan spell at the tail end of the previous campaign.

Coventry City experienced one of their busiest summers, sealing several high-profile signings, including Moroccan international midfielder Mustapha Hadji from Deportivo La Coruna and young Irish striker Robbie Keane from Wolves for £6m.

The free transfer addition of Dean Richards added steel to Southampton's defence, while the Saints also re-signed Kevin Davies from Blackburn with Egil Ostenstad moving in the opposite direction. Wimbledon boss Egil Olsen added five Norwegian's to his squad, including Trond Andersen and Andreas Lund.

*Pictured playing for Leicester City, talented young English striker Emile Heskey was snapped up by Liverpool during the season.*

## BIGGEST TRANSFERS

**THIERRY HENRY** – from Juventus to Arsenal – £11m

**EMILE HESKEY** – from Leicester City to Liverpool – £11m

**CHRIS SUTTON** – from Blackburn Rovers to Chelsea – £10m

**DEITMAR HAMMAN** – from Newcastle United to Liverpool – £8m

**KIERON DYER** – from Ipswich Town to Newcastle United – £6.5m

**ROBBIE KEANE** – from Wolverhampton Wanderers to Coventry City – £6m

**MICHAEL BRIDGES** – from Sunderland to Leeds United – £5m

**GEORGE BOATENG** – from Coventry City to Aston Villa – £4.5m

**DARREN HUCKERBY** – from Coventry City to Leeds United – £4.4m

**CHRISTIAN ZIEGE** – from AC Milan to Middlesbrough – £4m

**CHRIS PERRY** – from Wimbledon to Tottenham Hotspur – £4m

# TALES OF THE TURF

Big spending Chelsea began the season with a bang, defeating newly promoted Sunderland 4–0 at Stamford Bridge, while Bradford engineered a surprise 1–0 win at Middlesbrough. The third promoted side, Watford, lost their first two games against Wimbledon and then Sunderland. The Black Cats' first win came courtesy of two goals from prolific striker Kevin Phillips. Watford went on to record a shock 1–0 win against Liverpool at Anfield thanks to a Tommy Mooney goal.

Manchester United began strongly, recording a 4–0 win over Sheffield Wednesday and defeating Arsenal 2–1 at Highbury thanks to two goals from Roy Keane. New Leeds signing Michael Bridges began his career with a bang, notching a hat-trick in the club's 3–0 win at Southampton.

Bridges' former club Sunderland enjoyed a 2–1 win against local rivals Newcastle at St James' Park in a game that featured goals from Kevin Phillips and Niall Quinn, and became notorious for Magpies boss Ruud Gullit's decision to drop club captain Alan Shearer and his strike partner Duncan Ferguson ahead of the game. Gullit left the club just three days later before the Magpies were crushed 5–1 by Manchester United at Old Trafford, with former Newcastle striker Andy Cole grabbing four goals.

September brought the appointment of former England manager Bobby Robson as Newcastle United boss. At 66 years old Robson was the oldest manager in all four divisions of the English game. He went on to make an instant impact as the Magpies thumped Sheffield Wednesday 8–0 – the second highest victory in Premier League history – in his first game in charge. Restored to the team, Alan Shearer scored five of the eight goals. Sunderland's Kevin Phillips maintained his hot streak in front of goal with a hat-trick in a 5–0 win over Derby.

Manchester United claimed a 3–2 win over Liverpool at Anfield that featured two own goals by Jamie Carragher. In the same game, new United goalkeeper Massimo Taibi was handed his debut and won the man of the match award. However, Taibi's first game at Old Trafford the following week ended in disaster as he allowed a tame long-range effort from Southampton's Matt Le Tissier to squirm through his legs in a 3–3 draw. The Italian was then culpable for a couple of goals in United's subsequent 5–0 hammering at Chelsea. The loss at Stamford Bridge was the Red Devils' first domestic defeat for almost nine months.

ABOVE: *The unfortunate Liverpool Jamie Carragher stoops, but not to conquer, as he inadvertently heads the ball into his own net for his second own goal during the Reds' 3–2 loss to Manchester United.*

*Italian goalkeeper Massimo Taibi looks crestfallen as he concedes another goal during Chelsea's 5–0 thumping of Manchester United at Stamford Bridge.*

## INTERESTING INFO

The 1999–00 campaign was one filled with entertainment and saw a new season high for goals scored, with the ball hitting the back of the net on 1,060 occasions in the Premiership.

Despite their poor form United began October at the top of the table as Leeds, who had won their previous six games, played out a thrilling 4–4 draw with Everton at Goodison Park. Leeds ended the month top of the pile, with Manchester United two points off the pace in second. Arsenal sat third with the impressive Sunderland and Leicester City completing the top five.

Arsenal and Manchester United started to show their class during November as the Gunners, inspired by a Marc Overmars hat-trick, hammered Middlesbrough 5–1 at Highbury. United completed a run of three wins on the bounce with a 2–1 triumph at Derby that saw them end the month at the top of the division. Liverpool also found some form during the month and broke into the top five at the expense of Leicester.

Bill Kenwright completed his takeover of Everton at the beginning of December but the Toffees' fortunes on the pitch didn't change as they went down 5–1 at Manchester United. Leeds United enjoyed an impressive December, winning six of their seven league games to usurp the Red Devils at the top of the table at the beginning of the new Millennium.

In January Chelsea brought in Liberian striker George Weah on loan from AC Milan to add another world renowned name to the Premiership. Sheffield Wednesday enjoyed a change in fortunes, drawing with Arsenal and defeating Bradford and Spurs to ease their relegation concerns. Southampton manager Dave Jones departed the club and was replaced by former England manager Glenn Hoddle.

February brought Manchester United's first defeat in four months as they went down 3–0 at Newcastle, but the Red Devils completed a vital 1–0 win at Leeds a few weeks later. The Yorkshire club, who also suffered defeat against Liverpool and dropped points at Middlesbrough, started to drop off the pace, leaving Manchester United with a six-point lead at the end of the month.

OPPOSITE PAGE: *Manchester United's captain Roy Keane scored two crucial goals against Arsenal during the Red Devils' 2–1 victory. The clash at Highbury was a typically heated contest that saw Keane and his midfield adversary Patrick Vieira competing right on the edge.*

*One of Bradford City's heroes as the Bantams completed an unlikely bid for Premiership survival, hardworking forward Dean Windass became a firm fans' favourite at Valley Parade.*

Leicester City's new addition, Stan Collymore marked his debut with a memorable hat-trick against Sunderland at the beginning of March as the Foxes once again looked on course for a top ten finish. Spurs recorded a thumping 7–2 win over Southampton, which featured a Steffen Iversen hat-trick as Manchester United ended the month seven points clear at the top of the table. Sheffield Wednesday ended Danny Wilson's time in charge, replacing him with Peter Shreeves until the end of the season.

April brought a touching tribute to the Hillsborough tragedy when on April 15, all Premiership and Football League matches kicked off at 3.06 pm, to commemorate the 96 Liverpool supporters who lost their lives in the 1989 disaster. A 4–3 win at Middlesbrough and 4–2 victory at Southampton sealed Manchester United's sixth Premier League title in eight seasons, with four games left to play.

Leeds overcame an end-of-season slump to claim third place and join Manchester United and Arsenal in the Champions League while Liverpool and Chelsea, who occupied fourth and fifth respectively, qualified alongside League Cup winners Leicester for the UEFA Cup. Sunderland recorded an impressive seventh place standing in their first season back in the top flight.

At the bottom of the table Watford, who were the first team to be relegated, finished bottom of the pile, recording a record low of 24 points. In their penultimate game of the campaign, Sheffield Wednesday slipped to relegation after a 3–3 draw with Arsenal. The final day brought delight for Bradford, who recorded a 1–0 home win over Liverpool thanks to David Wetherall's goal, and despair for Wimbledon, who were being managed by caretaker boss Terry Burton following the sacking of Egil Olsen. The Dons lost 3–0 at Southampton and dropped into Division One for the first time in 14 years.

## INTERESTING INFO

Coventry City completed the whole 1999–00 season without recording a single away win, but still finished 14th thanks to an impressive home record that saw them win 12 of their 19 matches.

# HONOURS LIST

## FA Carling Premiership

**CHAMPIONS:** Manchester United – United completed back to back titles for the third time, achieving a points total of 91 that left them 18 clear of second place Arsenal. The Red Devils lost just three league games all season for the second successive campaign.
**RUNNERS-UP:** Arsenal
**RELEGATED:** Wimbledon, Sheffield Wednesday, Watford
**TOP GOAL SCORERS:** Kevin Phillips (30 goals for Sunderland)

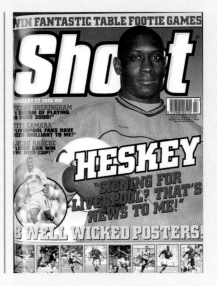

SHOOT MAGAZINE
1999–00

*Leicester City striker Emile Heskey (pictured) played down speculation about him leaving the club to sign for Liverpool – a move that came to fruition later in the season. The magazine also caught up with England striker Teddy Sheringham, Liverpool forward Titi Camara and Leeds United captain Lucas Radebe.*

# 1999–00 SEASON TABLE

|   |   | M | W | D | L | GF | GA | GD | PTS |
|---|---|---|---|---|---|---|---|---|---|
| 1 | Manchester United | 38 | 28 | 7 | 3 | 97 | 45 | +52 | 91 |
| 2 | Arsenal | 38 | 22 | 7 | 9 | 73 | 43 | +30 | 73 |
| 3 | Leeds United | 38 | 21 | 6 | 11 | 58 | 43 | +15 | 69 |
| 4 | Liverpool | 38 | 19 | 10 | 9 | 51 | 30 | +21 | 67 |
| 5 | Chelsea | 38 | 18 | 11 | 9 | 53 | 34 | +19 | 65 |
| 6 | Aston Villa | 38 | 15 | 13 | 10 | 46 | 35 | +11 | 58 |
| 7 | Sunderland | 38 | 16 | 10 | 12 | 57 | 56 | +1 | 58 |
| 8 | Leicester City | 38 | 16 | 7 | 15 | 55 | 55 | 0 | 55 |
| 9 | West Ham United | 38 | 15 | 10 | 13 | 52 | 53 | -1 | 55 |
| 10 | Tottenham Hotspur | 38 | 15 | 8 | 15 | 57 | 49 | +8 | 53 |
| 11 | Newcastle United | 38 | 14 | 10 | 14 | 63 | 54 | +9 | 52 |
| 12 | Middlesbrough | 38 | 14 | 10 | 14 | 46 | 52 | -6 | 52 |
| 13 | Everton | 38 | 12 | 14 | 12 | 59 | 49 | +10 | 50 |
| 14 | Coventry City | 38 | 12 | 8 | 18 | 47 | 54 | -7 | 44 |
| 15 | Southampton | 38 | 12 | 8 | 18 | 45 | 62 | -17 | 44 |
| 16 | Derby County | 38 | 9 | 11 | 18 | 44 | 57 | -13 | 38 |
| 17 | Bradford City | 38 | 9 | 9 | 20 | 38 | 68 | -30 | 36 |
| 18 | Wimbledon | 38 | 7 | 12 | 19 | 46 | 74 | -28 | 33 |
| 19 | Sheffield Wednesday | 38 | 8 | 7 | 23 | 38 | 70 | -32 | 31 |
| 20 | Watford | 38 | 6 | 6 | 26 | 35 | 77 | -42 | 24 |

# PLAYERS OF THE SEASON

**PFA PLAYER OF THE YEAR:** Roy Keane, Manchester United
**PFA YOUNG PLAYER OF THE YEAR:** Harry Kewell, Leeds United
**FOOTBALL WRITERS' PLAYER OF THE YEAR:** Roy Keane, Manchester United

ABOVE LEFT: *As well as finishing the Premiership's top marksmen, Sunderland striker Kevin Phillips was awarded the European Golden Boot after scoring the highest number of goals in all of the continent's top-flight divisions.*

ABOVE RIGHT: *Just one of Leeds United's crop of exciting youngsters, skilful winger Harry Kewell was named PFA Young Player of the Year.*

**FOOTBALL LEAGUE DIVISION ONE CHAMPIONS:** Charlton Athletic
**PROMOTED:** Manchester City
**DIVISION ONE PLAY-OFF WINNERS:** Ipswich Town
**RELEGATED:** Walsall, Port Vale, Swindon Town
**TOP GOAL SCORER:** Andy Hunt (21 goals for Charlton Athletic)

Alan Curbishley's Charlton ensured their top-flight exile was a brief one as they sealed the title to claim automatic promotion just a year after suffering relegation. The Addicks accumulated 91 points, losing just nine of their 46 league games. The goals of Andy Hunt and Clive Mendonca were key as promotion was achieved with weeks of the campaign to spare.

Guided again by Joe Royle, Manchester City finished second to complete successive promotions and a return to the Premier League for the first time in five years. George Burley's Ipswich reached the play-offs for the fourth successive campaign and triumphed 4–2 over Barnsley in a thrilling final at Wembley. The Suffolk club sealed the win with goals from Tony Mowbray, Richard Naylor, Marcus Stewart and Martin Reuser.

**DIVISION TWO CHAMPIONS:** Preston North End
**PROMOTED:** Burnley
**DIVISION TWO PLAY-OFF WINNERS:** Gillingham
**RELEGATED:** Cardiff City, Blackpool, Scunthorpe United, Chesterfield
**TOP GOAL SCORER:** Andy Payton (27 goals for Burnley)

David Moyes continued his transformation of Preston North End as he guided the Lancashire club back into English football's top two divisions for the first time in 19 years. The surprise package of the season was Stan Ternent's Burnley who, tipped by many for relegation at the start of the campaign, went on to finish second and achieve automatic promotion. With Peter Taylor at the helm, Gillingham extinguished some of the previous campaign's play-off misery with a 3–2 extra-time play-off final victory over Wigan Athletic, with the winning goal provided by Andy Thomson.

**DIVISION THREE CHAMPIONS:** Swansea City
**PROMOTED:** Rotherham United, Northampton Town
**DIVISION THREE PLAY-OFF WINNERS:** Peterborough United
**RELEGATED:** Chester City
**TOP GOAL SCORER:** Marco Gabbiadini (25 goals for Darlington)

Swansea, managed by John Hollins, and Rotherham, led by Ronnie Moore, faced off in a dramatic title battle that went down to the final day of the season. The Division was eventually won by the Swans who achieved the point they needed following a last day clash against the Millers. Kevin Wilson guided Northampton to third place and automatic promotion while Peterborough overcame Darlington 1–0 in the play-off final thanks to Andy Clarke's goal. At the wrong end of the table Chester lost their 69-year long Football League status having occupied bottom place for the majority of the season.

**FOOTBALL CONFERENCE CHAMPIONS:** Kidderminster Harriers

Managed by former Liverpool midfielder Jan Molby, Kidderminster claimed the title with a nine point advantage from second placed Rushden & Diamonds.

ABOVE TOP: *A predator in the six yard box, Charlton striker Clive Mendonca formed a threatening partnership with Andy Hunt that fired the Addicks back into the Premiership.*

ABOVE BOTTOM: *Swansea City's title winning manager John Hollins is mobbed by ecstatic supporters.*

# UP FOR THE CUP

**FA CUP WINNERS:** Chelsea

With Manchester United famously not taking part in the tournament, as they focused on playing in the inaugural World Club Championship in Brazil, the 1999–00 competition was one of the most open for years. To keep the correct numbers of teams involved at the right stage, the FA allowed one of the lower-division sides that had already been knocked out to be reinterred into the competition. Following a draw of lots, Darlington were afforded progress into the third round as 'lucky losers'.

The final, which was last to be held at the old Wembley Stadium, was contested between Chelsea and Aston Villa, and was eventually won 1–0 by the London club, who once again owed a debt of gratitude to the big game goal-scoring exploits of Roberto Di Matteo.

The Blues reached the final following a 2–1 win over Newcastle that featured a brace from Gus Poyet, while Aston Villa overcame Bolton Wanderers 4–1 on penalties following a 0–0 draw in their semi-final tie.

Tranmere, under the guidance of John Aldridge, enjoyed another impressive cup run, beating both West Ham and Sunderland to reach the quarter-finals. Gillingham also reached the last eight of the competition, recording victories against Bradford and Sheffield Wednesday. Other shock results included Cambridge United's victory over Crystal Palace, Burnley's win over Derby, Newcastle's 6–1 demolition of Spurs and Wrexham's 2–1 success against Middlesbrough.

## INTERESTING INFO

Manchester United became the first FA Cup holders not to defend their trophy when they withdrew from the 1999–00 competition.

**LEAGUE (WORTHINGTON) CUP WINNERS:** Leicester City

Martin O'Neill's Leicester City won their second League Cup in four seasons after defeating Tranmere 2–1 at Wembley thanks to two headed goals from captain Matt Elliott. Division One Tranmere replied through David Kelly but couldn't level matters.

Managed by John Aldridge, Tranmere overcame Bolton 4–0 over two legs in their semi-final having already disposed of Premiership Middlesbrough in the quarter-finals, while Leicester defeated Aston Villa 1–0 on aggregate, with the only goal of the tie coming from Matt Elliott.

Standout results in that season's tournament included Oxford's victory over Everton, Aston Villa's 3–0 win against Manchester United and Birmingham's 2–0 success against Newcastle.

**CHARITY SHIELD WINNERS:** Arsenal

The Gunners defeated Manchester United 2–1 at Wembley thanks to goals from Nwankwo Kanu and Ray Parlour, after Dwight Yorke had given United a first-half lead.

**THE FOOTBALL LEAGUE (AUTO WINDSCREEN) SHIELD:** Stoke City

Managed by Gudjon Thordarson, Stoke City defeated Bristol City 2–1 at Wembley through goals from Graham Kavanagh and Peter Thorne.

OPPOSITE PAGE TOP: *Leicester City captain heads home the second of his two League Cup final goals as the Foxes defeat Tranmere Rovers 2–1 at Wembley.*

OPPOSITE PAGE BOTTOM: *Leicester City supporters enjoy another trip to Wembley during the Martin O'Neill era, this time for their victorious 2000 League Cup final victory over Tranmere Rovers.*

# INTO EUROPE

### European Champions League

A new format during 1999–00 saw the Champions League become even harder to win than ever before following the introduction of a second group stage, meaning teams would have to play 12 group games before even reaching the knockout stages. Reigning champions Manchester United negotiated both their groups as the first placed team, defeating the likes of Marseille, Fiorentina and Valencia. A tough quarter-final draw saw United paired with Real Madrid, who went on to defeat them 3–2 on aggregate thanks to two goals from Raul.

Chelsea, participating in the Champions League for the first time, progressed to the same stage, topping their first group, which featured AC Milan, Galatasaray and Hertha Berlin, and finishing runners-up to Lazio in the second. The Blues eventually exited after being eliminated 6–4 on aggregate by Barcelona. Arsenal continued to struggle in the Champions League and departed the competition at the end of the first group stage. The Gunners missed out at the expense of Barcelona and Fiorentina and dropped into the UEFA Cup as a result.

### UEFA Cup

England's representatives in the extended competition included West Ham, who progressed to the second round where they were knocked out by Steaua Bucharest; Spurs, who exited at the same stage to Kaiserslautern and Newcastle, who went one step further before losing out to Roma.

David O'Leary's young Leeds side gained many new admirers, defeating the likes of Spartak Moscow, Roma and Slavia Prague. They eventually exited the competition amidst tragic circumstances against Galatasaray. The tie, which was lost 4–2 on aggregate, was overshadowed by the death of two Leeds fans at the hands of Galatasaray supporters.

Arsenal entered the competition at the fourth round stage after being knocked out of the Champions League, and went on to defeat Deportivo La Coruna, Werder Bremen and Lens to reach the final. Following a disappointing contest that ended 0–0 after extra-time, the Gunners lost 4–1 on penalties after both Davor Suker and Patrick Vieira failed to convert their spot kicks.

ABOVE: *Roy Keane slides the ball into his own net to put Manchester United on the back foot during their home loss to Real Madrid in the Champions League.*

OPPOSITE PAGE TOP: *A typically dramatic European night under the lights at Old Trafford ultimately ended in disappointment for Manchester United as they were upstaged by an impressive Real Madrid and exited the Champions League.*

OPPOSITE PAGE BOTTOM: *An anguished Patrick Vieira hits the deck during Arsenal's UEFA Cup final loss to Galatasaray.*

# THE INTERNATIONAL SCENE

Having qualified for Euro 2000 via a 2–1 two-legged play-off victory over Scotland, achieved through two Paul Scholes goals at Hampden Park, Kevin Keegan's England endured a dismal showing at the competition itself. England flattered to deceive in their first group stage game, storming into a 2–0 goal lead through Scholes and Steve McManaman, before eventually losing 3–2. A hard fought 1–0 over Germany, thanks to an Alan Shearer header followed, before the Three Lions suffered a 3–2 loss to Romania and exited the competition.

**A**head of the campaign, ITV announced a new multi million pound deal to televise Premier League highlights for the 2001–02 season. The new agreement meant that the BBC *Match of the Day* programme would once again disappear from the small screen at the end of the current campaign.

Following several seasons of more consistent performances in European competition, English teams were awarded an extra qualifying place in the Champions League, which meant clubs finishing in the Premiership top four would have the opportunity to participate in the ever-growing tournament.

Leicester City manager Martin O'Neill departed the club to take over as Celtic manager. The successful Northern Irishman was replaced by former England Under 21 boss, Peter Taylor. Paul Jewell stepped down as Bradford boss with his assistant Chris Hutchings taking over.

LEFT: *Leeds shocked English football when they broke the British transfer record to sign young West Ham defender Rio Ferdinand for £18m. After a shaky start to life at Elland Road, Ferdinand soon became a key element in the Whites' impressive displays in both the Premiership and the Champions League.*

OPPOSITE PAGE: *Arguably the most intense competitor the Premier League has ever seen, Manchester United captain Roy Keane drove the Red Devils on to further heights through a mixture of incredible talent and an unrivalled will to win.*

# TRANSFER TALES

Before the season started, the British record transfer fee was broken when Chelsea parted with £15m to bring in Jimmy Floyd Hasselbaink from Atletico Madrid. During an active summer for the Blues, further additions included Mario Stanic, Eidur Gudjohnsen, Winston Bogarde, Carlo Cudicini and Mark Bosnich.

Arsenal spent significantly, breaking their transfer record to sign French striker Sylvain Wiltord for £13m and investing heavily in the likes of Cameroon right-back Lauren and another Frenchman, Robert Pires. The Gunners did, however, lose Emmanuel Petit and Marc Overmars to Barcelona.

Manchester United looked to France's successful national squad to fill their problem goalkeeper position, splashing an English record £7.8m for a stopper on Monaco's Fabien Barthez.

Leeds United were again amongst the biggest spenders, emphasised by their mid-season British record addition of Rio Ferdinand from West Ham for £18m. The fee broke the world record for a defender. Leeds also spent heavily on the likes of Mark Viduka and Olivier Dacourt.

Liverpool and Gerard Houllier were also active in the market, bringing in the likes of Nicky Barmby, Igor Biscan and Christian Zeige for significant fees and Jari Litmanen, Gary McAllister and Marcus Babbel on free transfers. The Anfield club allowed Rigobert Song and Titi Camara to join West Ham, who also brought in Nigel Winterburn and Davor Suker on free transfers from Arsenal.

Tottenham and Aston Villa broke their transfer records to bring in strikers, as Sergei Rebrov arrived at White Hart Lane for £11m and Juan Pablo Angel made the move to Villa Park for £9.5m. Villa also added Alpay Ozalan, David Ginola and Luc Nilis.

Everton re-signed Duncan Ferguson from Newcastle and added the likes of Alex Nyarko, Niclas Alexandersson, Thomas Gravesen and Alessandro Pistone. The Toffees also added former England international midfielder Paul Gascoigne on a free transfer from Middlesbrough.

Middlesbrough showed glimpses of their glamorous spending of previous seasons with the additions of Croatian international striker Alen Boksic from Lazio and France international midfielder Christian Karembeu from Real Madrid. Newcastle spent £7m on Wimbledon's Carl Cort while Coventry added young Welsh forward Craig Bellamy for £6.25m from Norwich.

New Leicester manager Peter Taylor broke the club's transfer record to sign Ade Akinbiyi for £5.5m from Wolverhampton Wanderers and also brought in the likes of Gary Rowett, Matt Jones, Callum Davidson and Junior Lewis. Bradford City took a big gamble with their finances, capturing players like Stan Collymore, Dan Petrescu and Benito Carbone on high salaries.

*The less celebrated half of a devastating Dynamo Kiev strike pairing – that also featured Andrei Shevchenko – Ukrainian forward Sergei Rebrov caused a stir when he joined Tottenham in a big money deal.*

## BIGGEST TRANSFERS

**RIO FERDINAND** – from West Ham United to Leeds United – £18m

**JIMMY FLOYD HASSELBAINK** – from Atletico Madrid to Chelsea – £15m

**SYLVAIN WILTORD** – from Lyon to Arsenal – £13m

**SERGEI REBROV** – from Dynamo Kiev to Tottenham Hotspur – £11m

**JUAN PABLO ANGEL** – from River Plate to Aston Villa – £9.5m

**UGO EHIOGU** – from Aston Villa to Middlesbrough – £8m

**FABIEN BARTHEZ** – from AS Monaco to Manchester United – £7.8m

**JESPER GRONKJAER** – from Ajax to Chelsea – £7.8m

**OLIVIER DACOURT** – from Lens to Leeds United – £7.2m

**LAUREN** – from Real Mallorca to Arsenal – £7.2m

# TALES OF THE TURF

The season began with a meeting between two newly promoted teams, as Charlton hosted Manchester City at the Valley in a game that ended in a 4–0 win for the Addicks. Jimmy Floyd Hasselbaink scored a debut goal as Chelsea started with a 4–2 home win against West Ham.

Manchester City got their campaign up and running with a 4–2 home win against Sunderland that featured a hat-trick from Paulo Wanchope. Despite an opening day loss to Sunderland, Arsenal finished August top of the pile following victories against Liverpool and Charlton. A win and two draws for Manchester United left them just a point behind the Gunners.

September saw United hit form for the first time with a thumping 6–0 victory over Bradford at Old Trafford. After a slow start to the campaign, Chelsea sacked manager Gianluca Vialli and replaced him with fellow Italian Claudio Ranieri. Manchester United ended the month top the pile, followed by surprise early season title challengers, Leicester and Charlton, as well as the usual suspects of Arsenal and Liverpool.

Leicester hit top spot at the beginning of October. It was the first time the Foxes had been at the summit of English football since the 1963–64 season. However, it proved short-lived as Manchester United steamrollered past them 3–0 at Filbert Street to reclaim first place.

ABOVE TOP LEFT: *With Manchester United still struggling to find an adequate successor for Peter Schmeichel between the posts, Sir Alex Ferguson moved for French stopper Fabien Barthez during the summer.*

ABOVE TOP RIGHT: *A significant addition by Chelsea ahead of the season, Jimmy Floyd Hasselbaink brought presence and pace to the Blues' attack.*

*Having played a bit part role in Manchester United's successes of seasons gone by, England striker Teddy Sheringham performed a starring role during the 1999–00 season. The experienced forward expertly linked up play and showed ice cool composure in front of goal.*

## 🌐 INTERESTING INFO

Ledley King scored the fastest goal in Premier League history when he netted after just 10 seconds in a league fixture against Bradford in December.

Chelsea adapted well to life under Claudio Ranieri, sealing a 6–1 win over Coventry at Stamford Bridge. Arsenal hit five against Manchester City, as did Manchester United against Southampton, thanks to a hat-trick from the in-form Teddy Sheringham that helped the champions retain top spot.

Liverpool's new signings blended well to provide arguably the Reds most promising title challenge for over a decade, while surprise package Ipswich Town were in touching distance of a Champions League qualifying place. Without a win in their first 11 games, Derby County propped up the table and were joined in the bottom three by Bradford City and Southampton.

November brought a thrilling encounter between Leeds and Liverpool at Elland Road, as Mark Viduka scored all four of the home side's goals in a 4–3 win. David Beckham settled the first Manchester derby in five seasons with a typically majestic free-kick before Les Ferdinand rolled back the years with a smartly taken hat-trick in Spurs' 3–0 win over Leicester. Struggling Bradford sacked manager Chris Hutchings and replaced him with Jim Jefferies.

Manchester United remained at the top of the division in December, closely followed by Arsenal, Liverpool and Ipswich. With the team struggling for consistency, Middlesbrough chairman Steve Gibson brought in former England coach Terry Venables to work alongside Bryan Robson. The loss of inspirational midfielder Neil Lennon to Celtic coincided with a drop in form for Leicester, who dropped down the table despite their promising start.

A rare Ray Parlour hat-trick inspired Arsenal to a 5–0 home win over Newcastle while Manchester United were held to a 3–3 draw by Charlton. A first home league defeat for two years followed for United when Danny Murphy scored Liverpool's only goal in a 1–0 victory. However, the Red Devils ended 2000 eight points clear at the top of the table. Sunderland edged themselves into European contention but big-spending Leeds were stagnating in 14th place. Bradford ended the year at the foot of the table, having returned just 12 points from their opening 20 games.

While their rivals faltered, Manchester United showed dominant form during January, winning all four of their league games to increase the gap at the top to 15 points. Chelsea moved up the table and edged closer to a top four placing while Middlesbrough moved out of the bottom three as Alen Boksic found his form in front of goal.

February effectively brought the end of the title race as nearest challengers Arsenal were hammered 6–1 by Manchester United at Old Trafford in a game that featured a quick-fire hat-trick from Dwight Yorke. The win left United 16 points clear of the Gunners and odds on for their third Premiership title in a row.

Despite dropping points at both Leeds and Liverpool during March, Manchester United remained on course for the title. As the month drew to a close, Glenn Hoddle resigned as Southampton manager to replace the sacked George Graham at Tottenham. Hoddle's vacancy at Southampton was filled by Stuart Gray. The month was a lit up by a remarkable goal from West Ham's Paolo Di Canio who met a deep Trevor Sinclair cross with a technically brilliant scissor volley that flew into the net as the Hammers defeated Wimbledon 2–1 at Upton Park.

ABOVE: *A sound passer, who possessed great work ethic, Ray Parlour wasn't renowned for his goal-scoring exploits but the box to box midfielder is pictured here heading home one of the three goals he scored for Arsenal against Newcastle*

Manchester United began April with a 13 point advantage at the top and went on to seal their seventh title in nine seasons following wins against Charlton and Coventry. Bradford City's relegation was confirmed at the end of the month while Manchester City, who later sacked boss Joe Royle, and Coventry City soon followed them through the trapdoor after failing to win their final two fixtures.

The end of the season brought two further managerial changes as Harry Redknapp surprisingly left West Ham and Bryan Robson resigned from Middlesbrough.

The Champions League places went to Arsenal and Liverpool, while Leeds, Ipswich and Chelsea qualified for the UEFA Cup. The final day of the season saw Southampton play their final game at the Dell, their home of 103 years. The Saints signed-off in style with a 3–2 win over Arsenal crowned with a winning goal from Matt Le Tissier.

ABOVE TOP LEFT: *Spending an increasing amount of time outside of the Manchester United first team, Dwight Yorke reminded supporters of his qualities with a quick fire hat-trick against Arsenal at Old Trafford. United thumped the Gunners 6–1 to emphasise a growing gap between the fierce rivals.*

ABOVE BOTTOM LEFT: *The often controversial forward, Paolo Di Canio, fired home one of the most talked about goals in Premiership history when his powerfully placed scissor kick inspired West Ham to a home victory against Wimbledon.*

ABOVE RIGHT: *Part of the surprise package of the season, young defender Titus Bramble helped Ipswich Town achieve a UEFA Cup place in their first campaign back in the Premiership since 1995.*

OPPOSITE PAGE: *Set-piece specialist Danny Murphy curled home a free-kick to inspire Liverpool to a 1–0 victory against Manchester United at Old Trafford. The ballplaying midfielder developed a happy habit of scoring crucial goals against the Reds' fierce rivals.*

# HONOURS LIST

## FA Carling Premiership

**CHAMPIONS:** Manchester United – Sir Alex Ferguson finally realised the feat of winning three consecutive Premier League titles in what was arguably their easiest championship victory to date.

**RUNNERS-UP:** Arsenal

**RELEGATED:** Manchester City, Coventry City, Bradford City

**TOP GOAL SCORER:** Jimmy Floyd Hasselbaink (23 goals for Chelsea)

SHOOT MAGAZINE
2000–01

*Despite a lack of consistency and playing time, Paul 'Gazza' Gascogne remained one of the stars of English football and adorned this front cover in the blue of Everton. The former England man spoke about his injury woes and helping the Toffees to achieve Premiership survival. Arsenal's Latvian defender Igors Stepanovs gave his first English interview while Sunderland goalkeeper Thomas Sorensen and Leeds United boss David O'Leary were also featured.*

# 2000–01 SEASON TABLE

|    |                     | M  | W  | D  | L  | GF | GA | GD  | PTS |
|----|---------------------|----|----|----|----|----|----|-----|-----|
| 1  | Manchester United   | 38 | 24 | 8  | 6  | 79 | 31 | +48 | 80  |
| 2  | Arsenal             | 38 | 20 | 10 | 8  | 63 | 38 | +25 | 70  |
| 3  | Liverpool           | 38 | 20 | 9  | 9  | 71 | 39 | +32 | 69  |
| 4  | Leeds United        | 38 | 20 | 8  | 10 | 64 | 43 | +21 | 68  |
| 5  | Ipswich Town        | 38 | 20 | 6  | 12 | 57 | 42 | +15 | 66  |
| 6  | Chelsea             | 38 | 17 | 10 | 11 | 68 | 45 | +23 | 61  |
| 7  | Sunderland          | 38 | 15 | 12 | 11 | 46 | 41 | +5  | 57  |
| 8  | Aston Villa         | 38 | 13 | 15 | 10 | 46 | 43 | +3  | 54  |
| 9  | Charlton Athletic   | 38 | 14 | 10 | 14 | 50 | 57 | -7  | 52  |
| 10 | Southampton         | 38 | 14 | 10 | 14 | 40 | 48 | -8  | 52  |
| 11 | Newcastle United    | 38 | 14 | 9  | 15 | 44 | 50 | -6  | 51  |
| 12 | Tottenham Hotspur   | 38 | 13 | 10 | 15 | 47 | 54 | -7  | 49  |
| 13 | Leicester City      | 38 | 14 | 6  | 18 | 39 | 51 | -12 | 48  |
| 14 | Middlesbrough       | 38 | 9  | 15 | 14 | 44 | 44 | 0   | 42  |
| 15 | West Ham United     | 38 | 10 | 12 | 16 | 45 | 50 | -5  | 42  |
| 16 | Everton             | 38 | 11 | 9  | 18 | 45 | 59 | -14 | 42  |
| 17 | Derby County        | 38 | 10 | 12 | 16 | 37 | 59 | -22 | 42  |
| 18 | Manchester City     | 38 | 8  | 10 | 20 | 41 | 65 | -24 | 34  |
| 19 | Coventry City       | 38 | 8  | 10 | 20 | 36 | 63 | -27 | 34  |
| 20 | Bradford City       | 38 | 5  | 11 | 22 | 30 | 70 | -40 | 26  |

# PLAYERS OF THE SEASON

**PFA PLAYER OF THE YEAR:** Teddy Sheringham, Manchester United

**PFA YOUNG PLAYER OF THE YEAR:** Steven Gerrard, Liverpool

**FOOTBALL WRITERS' PLAYER OF THE YEAR:** Teddy Sheringham, Manchester United

*A real athlete of a striker, Fulham's Louis Saha took Division One by storm to fire Jean Tigana's Fulham into the Premiership for the first time.*

*Millwall striker Neil Harris was Division Two's joint top goal scorer and played an influential role in the Lions' championship success.*

**FOOTBALL LEAGUE DIVISION ONE CHAMPIONS:** Fulham
**PROMOTED:** Blackburn Rovers
**DIVISION ONE PLAY-OFF WINNERS:** Bolton Wanderers
**RELEGATED:** Huddersfield Town, Queens Park Rangers, Tranmere Rovers
**TOP GOAL SCORER:** Louis Saha (27 goals for Fulham)
Under high-profile boss Jean Tigana, Fulham's continued investment in the transfer market was rewarded with the Division One title. The Cottagers claimed top spot at a canter, clocking up an impressive 101 points. Second place went to Blackburn Rovers, managed by Graeme Souness, who pipped Sam Allardyce's Bolton Wanderers to automatic promotion. Wanderers later reached the top flight following a comprehensive 3–0 victory over David Moyes' Preston in the play-off final.

**DIVISION TWO CHAMPIONS:** Millwall
**PROMOTED:** Rotherham United
**DIVISION TWO PLAY-OFF WINNERS:** Walsall
**RELEGATED:** Bristol Rovers, Luton Town, Swansea City, Oxford United
**TOP GOAL SCORERS:** Jamie Cureton (Reading) and Neil Harris (Millwall) – both 27 goals
Managed by Mark McGhee, Millwall topped Division Two to return to the second tier for the first time since 1996. Tipped by many to struggle, Ronnie Moore's Rotherham United enjoyed a remarkable season that saw them push Millwall all the way before finishing second and claiming automatic promotion. The third promotion place went to Ray Graydon's Walsall who defeated Reading 3–2 after extra time in the play-off final.

**DIVISION THREE CHAMPIONS:** Brighton & Hove Albion
**PROMOTED:** Cardiff City, Chesterfield
**DIVISION THREE PLAY-OFF WINNERS:** Blackpool
**RELEGATED:** Barnet
**TOP GOAL SCORER:** Bobby Zamora (28 goals for Brighton & Hove Albion)
Brighton, who had been struggling both financially and on the pitch for a number of years, experienced an upturn in fortunes as the managerial nous of Micky Adams and the goals of Bobby Zamora took them to the title. Joining them via the automatic promotion places were Alan Cork's Cardiff City and Nicky Law's Chesterfield. Blackpool, managed by Steve McMahon, defeated Leyton Orient 4–2 in the play-off final. Barnet, under the guidance of Tony Cottee, finished bottom of the pile and dropped out of the division after losing a final day relegation decider against Torquay United.

**FOOTBALL CONFERENCE CHAMPIONS:** Rushden & Diamonds
The strongly backed Northamptonshire club reached the Football League for the first time in their history under the guidance of manager Brian Talbot.

## INTERESTING INFO

Despite Alex Ferguson winning a third straight title with Manchester United and Gerard Houllier lifting three trophies for Liverpool, Ipswich Town boss George Burley was named Manager of the Year after leading the Suffolk club to a surprise fifth place finish.

# UP FOR THE CUP

**FA CUP WINNERS:** Liverpool

In the first FA Cup final to be played at the Millennium Stadium in Wales, Liverpool clinched the Cup after beating Arsenal 2–1. The Gunners took the lead after 72 minutes through Freddie Ljungberg before two late goals from Michael Owen enabled Liverpool to lift their sixth FA Cup.

The Reds reached the final following a 2–1 victory over Second Division Wycombe Wanderers while Arsenal progressed to the showpiece with a 2–1 win against North London rivals Tottenham.

Two of the most impressive performers in the competition were lower league Wycombe Wanderers and Tranmere. Managed by Lawrie Sanchez, Wycombe advanced to the semi-finals after defeating the likes of Wolves, Wimbledon and most famously, Leicester City in the quarter-final. Wanderers' winning goal was scored by Roy Essandoh, whose agent had responded to an advert placed on Ceefax, appealing for a fit, non-cup-tied striker to sign for the club ahead of the clash with Leicester. Tranmere reached the quarter-finals and enjoyed victories over Everton and Southampton. Other shock results during the tournament included West Ham's 1–0 win against Manchester United at Old Trafford when Paolo Di Canio scored a memorable goal; non-league Kingstonian's win against Southend and Nuneaton's victory over Stoke City.

BELOW: *Liverpool's Michael Owen wheels away in delight, followed by his joyous team mates, after completing a dramatic late brace against Arsenal to win the FA Cup.*

**LEAGUE (WORTHINGTON) CUP WINNERS:** Liverpool

Liverpool became the first English team to win a major domestic trophy on penalties after they defeated First Division Birmingham City 5–4 on spot kicks. The game ended 1–1 after extra time with Liverpool opening the scoring through Robbie Fowler before the Blues grabbed a last minute equaliser through Darren Purse. The lottery from 12 yards ended in Liverpool's favour after Sander Westerveld saved penalties from Martin Grainger and Andy Johnson.

Liverpool reached the final following a 7–1 aggregate victory over Crystal Palace, while Birmingham overcame Ipswich Town 4–1 after extra time in their semi-final clash. Standout results earlier in the tournament included Sunderland knocking out Manchester United, Liverpool scoring eight against Stoke and Birmingham beating Newcastle.

**CHARITY SHIELD WINNERS:** Chelsea

FA Cup winners Chelsea defeated champions Manchester United in a bad tempered contest that saw United captain Roy Keane sent off after an hour. In the last ever Charity Shield played at the old Wembley, The Blues won 2–0 thanks to goals from Jimmy Floyd Hasselbaink and Mario Melchiot.

**THE FOOTBALL LEAGUE (LDV VANS) TROPHY:** Port Vale

Guided by former Manchester City manager, Brian Horton, Port Vale lifted the trophy following a 2–1 victory over Ray Lewington's Brentford thanks to goals from Marc Bridge-Wilkinson and Steve Brooker.

*Liverpool goalkeeper Sander Westerveld was the Reds' hero in the League Cup final as his penalty saves delivered the club's first trophy of the season.*

## INTO EUROPE

### European Champions League

Manchester United again progressed to the latter stages of the tournament, qualifying through two group stages that featured the likes of PSV Eindhoven, Anderlecht and Valencia. The Red Devils were eliminated in the quarter-finals to eventual winners Bayern Munich. Arsenal also progressed to the same stage, having topped their first group, finishing above Lazio and runners-up to Bayern Munich in their second. The Gunners lost out on away goals to Valencia in the quarter-finals.

Going one step better and providing the Premier League's best showing in the competition were David O'Leary's Leeds United who played some superb football to overcome the likes of AC Milan, Lazio and Barcelona in the group stages before recording an impressive 3–2 aggregate victory over Spain's Deportivo La Coruna in the quarter-final. The Whites' dreams of European glory were ended by Valencia in the semi-finals following a 3–0 aggregate loss.

### UEFA Cup

ABOVE: *Leeds midfielder David Batty battles for possession during the Whites' semi-final clash with Valencia.*

Gerard Houlier's Liverpool won their third cup competition of the season following a 5–4 extra-time victory over Spanish side Alaves in the final. The end to end encounter featured goals from Markus Babbel, Steven Gerrard, Gary McAllister and Robbie Fowler before a late own goal from Alaves' Delfi Geli settled the contest in Liverpool's favour.

The Reds showed impressive form throughout the competition, defeating the likes of Roma, Porto and Barcelona en route to the final. Star players during the continental campaign included the evergreen Gary McAllister who grabbed a memorable winning goal against Barcelona at Anfield and Robbie Fowler who showed good goal-scoring form throughout the campaign.

England's other representatives in the tournament were Leicester, who were eliminated in the first round by Red Star Belgrade, and Chelsea, who surprisingly crashed out at the same stage at the hands of Swiss side St. Gallen.

*BELOW: Liverpool players celebrate their UEFA Cup success, the third trophy they had lifted during the season.*

# THE INTERNATIONAL SCENE

Kevin Keegan's reign as England manager came to an end in ignominious fashion after the Three Lions were defeated 1–0 by Germany in the last ever international played at the old Wembley Stadium. After Howard Wilkinson and then Peter Taylor stepped in as caretaker managers, Swedish coach Sven-Goran Eriksson was announced as Keegan's successor. The Swede's first match in charge ended in a 3–0 friendly win over Spain before England got their World Cup qualifying campaign back on track with a series of victories.

# CHAPTER 10 // 2001–02
# ANOTHER DOUBLE FOR ARSENAL

**S**ir Alex Ferguson announced his intention to retire from football at the end of the 2001–02 campaign. The effect of this news seemed devastating for the team as United struggled alarmingly during the opening months of the campaign before Ferguson made a public u-turn and confirmed he would remain at Old Trafford for many more years.

Former England boss Kevin Keegan returned to football ahead of the campaign, succeeding Joe Royle as manager of recently relegated Manchester City. Another managerial change came at Middlesbrough, where Bryan Robson and Terry Venables were replaced by Manchester United assistant manager Steve McClaren. Following the departure of Harry Redknapp, West Ham promoted youth team coach Glenn Roeder to the position of manager.

OPPOSITE PAGE: *French forward Thierry Henry matured during the season. Combining a blend of pure speed and expert technique, Henry finished the campaign as the Premiership's most prolific marksmen.*

BELOW: *After injury delayed his dream transfer for a year, Dutch goal machine Ruud van Nistelrooy finally joined Manchester United ahead of the new season and soon made up for lost time, scoring twice on his debut.*

# TRANSFER TALES

The biggest spenders were Manchester United who finally completed the £19m signing of Dutch striker Ruud van Nistlerooy, a year after a deal had been agreed but he subsequently failed a medical and suffered a serious knee injury. Van Nistlelrooy was joined at Old Trafford by Argentina international midfielder Juan Sebastien Veron as United broke the British transfer record to secure his services from Lazio in a £28.1m deal. To balance the books, Sir Alex Ferguson surprisingly allowed commanding central defender Jaap Stam to leave the club and brought in French defender Laurent Blanc as his replacement. Later on in the season, Andy Cole departed United for Blackburn and the Red Devils brought in Uruguayan striker Diego Forlan.

Liverpool continued to add to their squad in an attempt to build upon their treble trophy success of the previous campaign. The Reds brought in the likes of Norway defender John Arne Riise, Polish stopper Jerzy Dudek, Czech Republic striker Milan Baros and young English goalkeeper Chris Kirkland.

Arsenal experienced a relatively quiet summer in terms of expenditure but did make the key defensive addition of England international central defender Sol Campbell. The move made headlines as Campbell had allowed his contract with the Gunners' North London rivals Tottenham to run down before joining the club on a free transfer. Arsene Wenger also invested £6m in young Ipswich goalkeeper Richard Wright.

Tottenham splashed out a club record £8.1m on Campbell's replacement, bringing in Dean Richards from Southampton and also swelled their ranks with the signings of Gus Poyet from Chelsea and Christian Ziege from Liverpool.

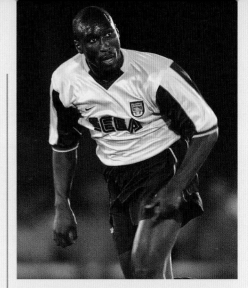

*England defender Sol Campbell made the bold but controversial move of singing for Arsenal on a free transfer after letting his contract with their North London rivals, Tottenham, run down.*

## BIGGEST TRANSFERS

**JUAN SEBASTIEN VERON** – from Lazio to Manchester United – £28.1m

**RUUD VAN NISTELROOY** – from PSV Eindhoven to Manchester United – £19m

**ROBBIE KEANE** – from Inter Milan to Leeds United – £12m

**STEVE MARLET** – from Lyon to Fulham – £11.5m

**ROBBIE FOWLER** – from Liverpool to Leeds United – £11m

**FRANK LAMPARD** – from West Ham United to Chelsea – £11m

**LAURENT ROBERT** – from Paris Saint Germain – £9.5m

**DEAN RICHARDS** – from Southampton to Tottenham Hotspur – £8.1m

**ANDY COLE** – from Manchester United to Blackburn Rovers – £8m

**DIEGO FORLAN** – from Independiente to Manchester United £7.5m

**EMMANUEL PETIT** – from Barcelona to Chelsea – £7.5m

**BOUDEWIJN ZENDEN** – from Barcelona to Chelsea – £7.5m

LEFT: *Manchester United continued their spending spree with the big name signing Sir Alex Ferguson had craved for years, as Argentinean playmaker Juan Sebastien Veron arrived at Old Trafford from Lazio.*

Buoyed by their Champions League qualification, Leeds continued to write exorbitant cheques, shelling out £11m for both Robbie Fowler from Liverpool and Robbie Keane from Inter Milan, as well as £7m on young Derby County midfielder Seth Johnson. Chelsea also splashed the cash, investing £11m in West Ham midfielder Frank Lampard, £6.2m in French defender William Gallas and a total of £15m in the services of Barcelona pair Emmanuel Petit and Boudewijn Zenden.

Promoted Fulham showed their intent with the club record £11m capture of French striker Steve Marlet and the £7m signing of Dutch international goalkeeper Edwin van Der Sar from Juventus. The Cottagers also brought in Steed Malbranque and Sylvain Legwinski. Elsewhere, Newcastle signed Craig Bellamy from Coventry and Jermaine Jenas from Nottingham Forest, while Middlesbrough reunited Gareth Southgate with Ugo Ehiogu at the heart of their defence, spending £6.5m on the England international.

West Ham brought in England goalkeeper David James from Aston Villa, Czech Republic defender Tomas Repka and re-signed Don Hutchinson from Sunderland in a £5m deal. Several high profile players joined clubs on free transfers, including Peter Schmeichel who returned to the Premier League with Aston Villa, Fabrizio Ravanelli who joined Derby and Youri Djorkaeff who arrived at Bolton.

Clubs in Division One continued to splash the cash, with the transfer record for the second tier first broken by Coventry when they parted with £5m for West Brom's Lee Hughes and then equalled by Manchester City who added Preston's Jon Macken for the same fee. Division Two side Cardiff City also got in on the big-spending action, parting with £1.7m for Stoke striker Peter Thorne, as the Premier League's mega money slowly started to trickle down the league pyramid.

*Kevin Nolan (left) celebrates with Michael Ricketts as Bolton shock Leicester City with a 5–0 victory on the opening day of the season.*

## TALES OF THE TURF

Newly promoted Bolton announced their arrival back in the top flight with a thumping 5–0 win against Leicester at Filbert Street on the opening day of the season. Another recently promoted side, Fulham, gave a good account of themselves a day later, pushing Manchester United close at Old Trafford in a game that the champions eventually won 3–2, thanks to two debut goals from Ruud van Nistelrooy.

Bolton won their third consecutive game thanks to a 2–1 home victory over Liverpool and ended the opening month of the season top of the table. Everton and Leeds also enjoyed good starts, with Arsenal and Manchester United in close attendance.

Liverpool, struggling to recapture their impressive form from the previous season, lost further ground in September following a shock 3–1 home defeat to Aston Villa. The month's standout contest came at White Hart Lane, where Tottenham cruised into a three goal half-time lead against Manchester United, before eventually losing 5–3. With Leicester struggling at the foot of the table, the club's board opted to sack Peter Taylor.

### INTERESTING INFO

Manchester United's third place standing in 2001–02 was their first finish outside of the top two in the Premier League era.

October brought another managerial change as Jim Smith stepped down after six years at Derby to be replaced by his assistant Colin Todd, while Leicester appointed the managerial team of Dave Bassett and Micky Adams to succeed Peter Taylor, and Southampton replaced Stuart Gray with Gordon Strachan.

Liverpool's season was thrown into disarray when manager Gerard Houllier had to undergo emergency heart surgery after complaining of chest pains during a home draw with Leeds United. Assistant boss Phil Thompson took charge on a caretaker basis while the Frenchman recuperated.

West Ham's slow start under Glenn Roeder continued when the Hammers were hammered 7–1 by Blackburn at Ewood Park. Another team playing in claret and blue, Aston Villa, fared much better as a 3–2 win over Bolton sent them top of the table for the first time in nearly three years.

*ABOVE: Liverpool's Norwegian left-back John Arne Riise, pictured competing with Manchester United's Gary Neville, scored a stunning long-range strike as the Reds defeated their rivals 3–1 at Anfield.*

November began with a shock home defeat for Arsenal, who went down 4–2 to Charlton. However, the Gunners soon turned things round with a 3–1 victory over Manchester United. The Red Devils continued to struggle for form, and also lost 3–1 to Liverpool at Anfield in a game that featured a long-range bullet from left-back John Arne Riise. The Merseyside club moved top of the table despite allowing fans' favourite Robbie Fowler to depart for Leeds. George Burley's Ipswich – so impressive the previous season – found themselves routed to the bottom of the table with just a single victory.

December failed to bring a change in fortunes for Manchester United who were stunned by consecutive home defeats to Chelsea and West Ham that completed a run of six losses from seven league fixtures. The Red Devils sat ninth in the league and 11 points behind leaders Liverpool, prompting Sir Alex Ferguson to write off the team's chances of retaining the title.

United showed signs of recovery, winning five games in a row, including a 5–0 home win over Derby, a 6–1 defeat of Southampton and 2–0 victory at Everton, but 2001 drew to a close with Arsenal top of the table on goal difference from Bobby Robson's on-song Newcastle and a point clear of Leeds in third place.

Manchester United's resurgence continued into January with a 3–1 win against Newcastle before a 3–1 victory over Southampton sent them top on goal difference. The Red Devils remained top at the end of the month, having created a four-point lead over Arsenal in second.

Struggling Derby parted company with manager Colin Todd after just three months in charge and Aston Villa boss John Gregory resigned from his post, eventually succeeding Todd at Derby. Former Villa boss Graham Taylor was given a second chance to manage the club. A poor run of form saw Leicester cemented in bottom place and eight points from safety. The Foxes were joined in the bottom three by Derby and Ipswich.

Manchester United extended their winning run to nine games at the beginning of February, the same month that Sir Alex Ferguson announced his decision to continue as manager beyond the end of the season. Arsenal, who claimed back to back wins against Everton and Fulham, remained firmly in contention for the title.

BELOW: *Not quite Fergie's time to wave goodbye. Half way through the season Manchester United manager Sir Alex Ferguson made a remarkable u-turn on his decision to retire from football.*

RIGHT: *Arsenal striker Sylvain Wiltord celebrates scoring the goal that secured the Premiership title for the Gunners. The Frenchman prodded home a close-range rebound to secure a 1–0 victory over nearest rivals Manchester United at Old Trafford.*

Derby County enjoyed better form under new boss John Gregory and held Manchester United to a 2–2 draw at the beginning of March, thanks to a double from Malcolm Christie. Everton parted company with boss Walter Smith, appointing the highly rated David Moyes as his successor.

Liverpool, boosted by the return to the dugout of Gerard Houllier, remained close to the leaders with a late victory over Chelsea, but Manchester United's chances were damaged by a 1–0 home loss to Middlesbrough. United recorded a thrilling 4–3 victory over Leeds at Elland Road but the Arsenal juggernaut continued to destroy everything in front of it, with the Gunners picking up crucial wins at Newcastle and Aston Villa. Liverpool ended the month top of the table, with Manchester United in second and Arsenal third.

The opening day of April saw the Gunners top the table with a 3–0 win at Charlton and 1–0 victory over Spurs, while Leicester's decision to move Dave Bassett into a director of football role and name Micky Adams as manager was too late to save them relegation, which was confirmed following a 1–0 home loss to Manchester United.

Germany striker Fredi Bobic proved a crucial late season loan addition for Bolton, as he grabbed a hat-trick in a crunch 4–1 victory over relegation rivals Ipswich. Derby County were the next team to have their relegation confirmed after losing seven of their last eight games.

May brought a title decider at Old Trafford, when favourites Arsenal visited Manchester United knowing a win would confirm the championship.

In a tense encounter, Sylvain Wiltord grabbed the only goal from close range to silence the home support and confirm the Gunners' second Premier League crown. United went on to suffer further disappointment on the final day of the season, drawing 0–0 at home to Charlton while Liverpool triumphed 5–0 over Ipswich to claim second place and force United into the third.

That Anfield defeat sent Ipswich down and ensured the safety of Sunderland and Bolton. Bottom place Leicester signed off the season with a 2–1 victory over Tottenham in the last game to played in the 111 year history of their Filbert Street home. The stadium's final goal was fittingly scored by local youngster Matt Piper.

May brought serious financial concerns for a whole host of Football League clubs after the debt-ridden ITV Digital channel, which intended to televise a number of matches and pay handsomely to do so, collapsed. A number of clubs, including former Premier League sides Bradford City, Nottingham Forest and Watford, who had set their budgets based on the forecasted extra revenue, filed for administration in a bid to avoid going out of business following such a significant loss of finance.

## ⚽ INTERESTING INFO //

Bucking the trend of recent campaigns, the 2001–02 season saw all three of the promoted teams; Bolton, Blackburn and Fulham, retain their Premiership status at the end of the term.

# HONOURS LIST

## FA Barclaycard Premiership

**CHAMPIONS:** Arsenal – A remarkable late season surge saw the Gunners claim their second Premiership title under Arsene Wenger. The lethal attacking pairing of Thierry Henry and Dennis Bergkamp helped the North London club win 26 of their 38 games.
**RUNNERS-UP:** Liverpool
**RELEGATED:** Ipswich Town, Derby County, Leicester City
**TOP GOAL SCORER:** Thierry Henry (24 goals for Arsenal)

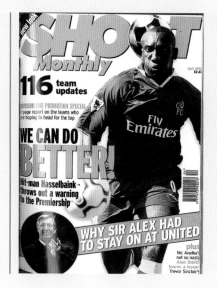

SHOOT MAGAZINE 2001–02

*Front page billing was given to new Chelsea signing Jimmy Floyd Hasselbaink who also outlined his ambitions to win the Premiership with the Blues. The magazine also examined the reasons why Sir Alex Ferguson performed a dramatic u-turn to snub retirement and remain as Manchester United manager and focused on the teams competing for promotion from the second tier.*

## 2001–02 SEASON TABLE

|    |                      | M  | W  | D  | L  | GF | GA | GD  | PTS |
|----|----------------------|----|----|----|----|----|----|-----|-----|
| 1  | Arsenal              | 38 | 26 | 9  | 3  | 79 | 36 | +43 | 87  |
| 2  | Liverpool            | 38 | 24 | 8  | 6  | 67 | 30 | +37 | 80  |
| 3  | Manchester United    | 38 | 24 | 5  | 9  | 87 | 45 | +42 | 77  |
| 4  | Newcastle United     | 38 | 21 | 8  | 9  | 74 | 52 | +22 | 71  |
| 5  | Leeds United         | 38 | 18 | 12 | 8  | 53 | 37 | +16 | 66  |
| 6  | Chelsea              | 38 | 17 | 13 | 8  | 66 | 38 | +28 | 64  |
| 7  | West Ham United      | 38 | 15 | 8  | 15 | 48 | 57 | -9  | 53  |
| 8  | Aston Villa          | 38 | 12 | 14 | 12 | 46 | 47 | -1  | 50  |
| 9  | Tottenham Hotspur    | 38 | 14 | 8  | 16 | 49 | 53 | -4  | 50  |
| 10 | Blackburn Rovers     | 38 | 12 | 10 | 16 | 55 | 51 | +4  | 46  |
| 11 | Southampton          | 38 | 12 | 9  | 17 | 46 | 54 | -8  | 45  |
| 12 | Middlesbrough        | 38 | 12 | 9  | 17 | 35 | 47 | -12 | 45  |
| 13 | Fulham               | 38 | 10 | 14 | 14 | 36 | 44 | -8  | 44  |
| 14 | Charlton Athletic    | 38 | 10 | 14 | 14 | 38 | 49 | -11 | 44  |
| 15 | Everton              | 38 | 11 | 10 | 17 | 45 | 57 | -12 | 43  |
| 16 | Bolton Wanderers     | 38 | 9  | 13 | 16 | 44 | 62 | -18 | 40  |
| 17 | Sunderland           | 38 | 10 | 10 | 18 | 29 | 51 | -22 | 40  |
| 18 | Ipswich Town         | 38 | 9  | 9  | 20 | 41 | 64 | -23 | 36  |
| 19 | Derby County         | 38 | 8  | 6  | 24 | 33 | 63 | -30 | 30  |
| 20 | Leicester City       | 38 | 5  | 13 | 20 | 30 | 64 | -34 | 28  |

# PLAYERS OF THE SEASON

**PFA PLAYER OF THE YEAR:** Ruud van Nistelrooy, Manchester United
**PFA YOUNG PLAYER OF THE YEAR:** Craig Bellamy, Newcastle United
**FOOTBALL WRITERS' PLAYER OF THE YEAR:** Robert Pires, Arsenal

**FOOTBALL LEAGUE DIVISION ONE CHAMPIONS:** Manchester City
**PROMOTED:** West Bromwich Albion
**DIVISION ONE PLAY-OFF WINNERS:** Birmingham City
**RELEGATED:** Crewe Alexandra, Barnsley, Stockport County
**TOP GOAL SCORER:** Shaun Goater (28 goals for Manchester City)

Playing an attacking brand of football in line with his philosophy at Newcastle United, Kevin Keegan guided Manchester City to the title and back into the Premier League at the first time of asking. The Blues, fielding the attacking talents of Ali Benarbia, Eyal Berkovic and Shaun Goater, won 31 games, scored 108 goals and claimed 99 points. Second place went to Gary Megson's West Brom who achieved promotion to the Premier League for the first time. The Baggies returned to the top flight after a 16-year exile and finished just above local rivals Wolves. The third promotion place went to Birmingham City, who defeated Norwich City on penalties in the play-off final after the scores finished 1–1 after extra time. The crucial spot kick was converted by Birmingham's Darren Carter and returned the Blues to the top flight for the first time since 1986.

OPPOSITE PAGE: *After topping the Premier League's goalscoring charts and impressing with his all-round play, Dutch striker Ruud van Nistelrooy was named PFA Player of the Year.*

ABOVE: *Linking up brilliantly with the equally skilled and diminutive Eyal Berkovic, Algerian midfielder Ali Bernarbia was crucial to Manchester City's Division One success.*

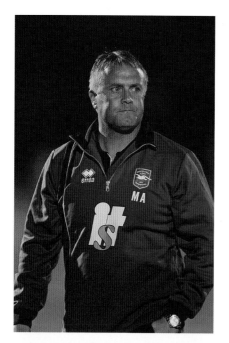

**DIVISION TWO CHAMPIONS:** Brighton & Hove Albion
**PROMOTED:** Reading
**DIVISION TWO PLAY-OFF WINNERS:** Stoke City
**RELEGATED:** Bournemouth, Bury, Wrexham, Cambridge United
**TOP GOAL SCORER:** Bobby Zamora (28 goals for Brighton & Hove Albion)

Brighton sealed the title despite losing manager Micky Adams to Leicester City during the campaign. His replacement, former Foxes boss Peter Taylor, maintained the momentum built up by Adams as Bobby Zamora again showed red-hot form in front of goal. Reading ended four successive seasons in Division Two, gaining promotion in second place under Alan Pardew while Stoke City, bossed by Gudjon Thordarson, triumphed over Brentford in the play-off final.

**DIVISION THREE CHAMPIONS:** Plymouth Argyle
**PROMOTED:** Luton Town, Mansfield Town
**DIVISION THREE PLAY-OFF WINNERS:** Cheltenham Town
**RELEGATED:** Halifax Town
**TOP GOAL SCORER:** Steve Howard (24 goals for Luton Town)

A two-way battle for the title between Plymouth and Luton ended with the Devon club as champions. Managed by Paul Sturrock, Argyle amassed 102 points, losing just six of their 46 games. Five points behind in second were Joe Kinnear's Luton with Mansfield Town claiming third. The play-off final was won by Cheltenham Town who defeated Rushden & Diamonds 3–1. Halifax Town dropped out of the league after spending the majority of the campaign rooted to the foot of the table.

**FOOTBALL CONFERENCE CHAMPIONS:** Boston United

Managed by Steve Evans, Boston won the title on goal difference after finishing level on points with Dagenham & Redbridge. However, the Lincolnshire club were later found guilty of breaking the Football Association's rules over the registration of players. The Pilgrims were fined and docked four points ahead of their first ever season in the Football League.

RIGHT TOP: *Seasoned lower league boss Micky Adams worked miracles to guide Brighton into Division One as champions.*

RIGHT MIDDLE: *Plymouth Argyle manager Paul Sturrock patrols his dugout during the Pilgrims' Division Three title-winning campaign.*

RIGHT BOTTOM: *Outspoken Boston United manager Steve Evans guided the controversy shrouded Lincolnshire club into the Football League for the first time in their history.*

# UP FOR THE CUP

### FA CUP WINNERS: Arsenal

With the Cup final taking place ahead of the final game of the season, Arsenal actually lifted the first part of the double before winning the Premier League. The Gunners enjoyed a convincing 2–0 victory over Chelsea at the Millennium Stadium thanks to impressive finishes from Freddie Ljungberg and Ray Parlour.

Arsenal reached the final following a narrow 1–0 win over Middlesbrough while Chelsea were also victorious by the same scoreline, knocking West London rivals Fulham out of the competition.

Earlier in tournament, a number of lower league sides made the headlines for ousting higher ranked sides, including Bristol Rovers who defeated Derby and Cardiff City who disposed of Leeds.

### LEAGUE (WORTHINGTON) CUP WINNERS: Blackburn Rovers

Graeme Souness' Blackburn Rovers won the League Cup for the first time in their history after overcoming Spurs 2–1 at the Millennium Stadium. Rovers' goals came from Matt Jansen and Andy Cole, with Christian Zeige on the scoresheet for Tottenham.

Blackburn progressed to the final with a 6–3 aggregate victory over Sheffield Wednesday that featured two goals apiece for Andy Cole and Craig Hignett, while Spurs overcame Chelsea by the same two-legged scoreline.

Shock results earlier in the competition included holders Liverpool crashing out to fourth tier Grimsby Town thanks to an extra-time winner from former Everton striker Phil Jevons; Sheffield Wednesday's victory over Aston Villa: Reading overcoming West Ham and Blackburn's 4–0 home thumping of Arsenal in the quarter-finals.

*Blackburn Rovers striker Andy Cole celebrates with the only domestic trophy he hadn't won with Manchester United, the League Cup. Cole was on target as Graeme Souness' battling side defeated Tottenham 2–1 in Cardiff.*

ABOVE: *Arsenal's Ray Parlour looks on as his curling effort arrows into the top corner past stranded Chelsea goalkeeper Carlo Cuidicini. The Gunners defeated the Blues 2–0 in the FA Cup final.*

**CHARITY SHIELD WINNERS:** Liverpool

Liverpool beat fierce rivals Manchester United 2–1 thanks to goals from Gary McAllister and Michael Owen. United's consolation came from Ruud van Nistelrooy.

**THE FOOTBALL LEAGUE (LDV VANS) TROPHY:** Blackpool

Steve McMahon's Blackpool defeated Cambridge United by a convincing 4–1 scoreline that featured goals from John Murphy, Chris Clarke, John Hills and Scott Taylor.

# INTO EUROPE

### European Champions League
With the final to be played in his home city of Glasgow in what could've been his last game in charge of Manchester United, Sir Alex Ferguson was fully focussed on lifting his second Champions League crown for the club. And, United came close, advancing as far as the semi-finals where they were knocked out over two legs by Germany's Bayer Leverkusen. During the competition, the goals of Ruud van Nistelrooy inspired the Red Devils through the group stages and to an impressive quarter-final victory over Deportivo La Coruna.

Of England's other representatives, Arsenal failed to make it past the second group stage and Liverpool, participating in their first campaign in the competition since its change of format, enjoyed a more successful campaign. The Reds recorded victories against the likes of Borussia Dortmund and Roma and progressed to the quarter-final where they were defeated by Bayer Leverkusen.

### UEFA Cup
Aston Villa again struggled to make an impression in the competition, crashing out on away goals to Croatia's NK Varteks in the first round. Chelsea were ousted at the same stage, suffering a shock 3–1 aggregate loss to Israel's Hapoel Tel Aviv. Faring better were Ipswich Town, who progressed to the third round before suffering a brave defeat to Inter Milan and Leeds, who reached the fourth round before losing to PSV Eindhoven.

ABOVE: *Their faces drenched in anguish, Laurent Blanc and Ruud van Nistelrooy curse another missed opportunity as Manchester United crash out of Europe against Bayer Leverkusen.*

RIGHT: *With disbelief and delight etched on his face, Michael Owen celebrates his hat-trick sealing goal during England's famous 5–1 victory over Germany in Munich.*

OPPOSITE PAGE: *Time seemed to stand still at Old Trafford as David Beckham prepared to strike a crucial free-kick. Exerting expert technique, Beckham's curling effort flew into the net to salvage a 2–2 draw with Greece and secure England's qualification for the World Cup.*

BELOW: *David Beckham celebrates England's 1–0 victory over Argentina at the World Cup. The Three Lions captain calmly converted a pressure cooker penalty to win the game.*

# THE INTERNATIONAL SCENE

England stormed to a memorable 5–1 win over Germany in Munich. A smartly taken hat-trick by Michael Owen, added to goals from Steven Gerrard and Emile Heskey as the Three Lions put in one of their most complete performances for decades. Despite that victory, England still needed a dramatic late free-kick from David Beckham in their final qualification clash against Greece, to grab a draw and send the Three Lions to the 2002 World Cup.

Affected by a number of injuries, England failed to progress to the later stages of the tournament proper in Japan and South Korea. A famous 1–0 victory over Argentina, achieved through a David Beckham penalty against the nation he saw red against four years earlier, helped Sven-Goran Eriksson's men progress through the group stages. However, eventual winners Brazil put paid to England's hopes following a 2–1 victory in the quarter-final.

# A FAREWELL TITLE FOR DAVID BECKHAM

Following a dominant campaign from Arsenal, Manchester United announced their intentions with the record addition of England international defender Rio Ferdinand from Leeds. The Elland Road club's bubble had burst following three seasons of progression that had ultimately been achieved through playing roulette with the club's finances. After Leeds failed to reach the 2002–03 Champions League, the huge investment in transfer fees and wages, coupled with outstanding loan debts, provided a perfect financial storm and meant their best players would have to be sold to ensure the very future of the club.

The summer of 2002 saw manager David O'Leary pay for that Champions League qualification failure with his job. The Irishman had invested over £100m in new players and despite crafting a team filled with exciting young footballers, the club's future looked bleak. His replacement was former England boss Terry Venables who inherited the daunting task of rebuilding a club with scarce resource and shorn of its most talented players.

The 2002–03 campaign also saw the introduction of compulsory transfer windows to ensure English football met FIFA regulations. The new rules meant that players could only be transferred between clubs during dedicated transfer windows, one during the summer close season and another in January.

OPPOSITE PAGE: *In what proved to be his last appearance at Old Trafford as a Manchester United player David Beckham celebrates scoring a crucial goal during the Red Devils' end of season victory over Charlton Athletic.*

BELOW: *Bermudan striker Shaun Goater capitalises on an uncharacteristic error from Gary Neville to give Manchester City the advantage against Manchester United at Maine Road.*

# TRANSFER TALES

In addition to the headline signing of Rio Ferdinand, Manchester United brought in Spanish goalkeeper Ricardo. The second highest transfer fee was spent by United's local rivals, Manchester City, who splashed £13m on former Arsenal striker Nicolas Anelka.

The Gunners, meanwhile, strengthened their squad with the signings of French defender Pascal Cygan and World Cup winning Brazil midfielder Gilberto Silva. Liverpool continued to spend big, obtaining Senegal striker El-Hadji Diouf for £10m and his international team-mate, Salif Diao, for £5m. Also arriving at Anfield was French midfielder Bruno Cheyrou. The Reds allowed Jamie Redknapp to join Tottenham on a free transfer and Nicky Barmby to sign for Leeds.

Newcastle again invested heavily before and during the campaign, adding Jonathan Woodgate from Leeds, Portuguese youngster Hugo Viana and Ipswich defender Titus Bramble for significant fees. Their North East rivals Sunderland spent £6.75m on Norway striker Tore Andre Flo and also added Marcus Stewart, Matt Piper, Mart Poom and Stephen Wright, while Middlesbrough where again amongst the division's highest spenders, breaking their transfer record to add Italian striker Massimo Maccarone for £8.15m and re-signing fans' favourite Juninho for £6m. Franck Queudrue and George Boateng also joined during the summer and Boro boosted their bid for a UEFA Cup place during the season by bringing in Chris Riggott, Malcolm Christie and Michael Ricketts.

West Ham acquired the likes of Lee Bowyer, Raimond van der Gouw and Les Ferdinand while Aton Villa added Ronnie Johnsen, Ulises de la Cruz and Marcus Allback. Bolton made two headline additions, obtaining Jay Jay Okocha on a free transfer and Ivan Campo on loan from Real Madrid.

## BIGGEST TRANSFERS

**RIO FERDINAND** – from Leeds United to Manchester United – £30m

**NICOLAS ANELKA** – from Paris Saint Germain to Manchester City – £13m

**EL HADJI DIOUF** – from Lens to Liverpool – £10m

**JONATHAN WOODGATE** – from Leeds United to Newcastle United – £9m

**HUGO VIANA** – from Sporting Lisbon to Newcastle United – £8.5m

**MASSIMO MACCARONE** – from Empoli to Middlesbrough – £8.15m

**ROBBIE KEANE** – from Leeds United to Tottenham Hotspur – £7m

**TORE ANDRE FLO** – from Rangers to Sunderland – £6.75m

**JUNINHO** – from Atletico Madrid to Middlesbrough – £6m

**GEORGE BOATENG** – from Aston Villa to Middlesbrough – £5m

**TITUS BRAMBLE** – from Ipswich Town to Newcastle United – £5m

LEFT: *An impressive performer for England at the 2002 World Cup, Rio Ferdinand, pictured in action against his former employers Leeds United, joined Manchester United in the summer for £30m.*

# TALES OF THE TURF

The opening day of the season saw West Brom lose their first top-flight game in 17 years, 1–0 against Manchester United at Old Trafford. Glenn Hoddle's Tottenham began the campaign strongly, winning three of their opening four games and ended August as league leaders. Arsenal and Liverpool also started well, as did Leeds and Charlton.

Manchester United began their title challenge in stuttering form, losing 1–0 at home to Bolton, when Kevin Nolan scored the only goal, and going down away to Leeds by the same scoreline.

September brought the first second city derby in league competition for 15 years, when Birmingham defeated Aston Villa 3–0 at St Andrew's. Manchester United achieved a narrow victory at Spurs thanks to a penalty from Ruud van Nistelrooy while Arsenal sealed a fifth consecutive victory in the league with a 3–1 win over Sunderland at Highbury to end the month top of the table.

The first Premier League manager to lose his job that season was Sunderland's Peter Reid who was ousted at the beginning of October and replaced by the managerial duo of former Leeds boss Howard Wilkinson and Stoke's Steve Cotterill.

One of the most exiting young talents England had seen for years announced his arrival to the Premiership on October 19 when 16-year-old Everton striker, Wayne Rooney, scored a spectacular long-range winner against reigning champions Arsenal at Goodison Park. The powerful curling effort left England stopper David Seaman beaten all ends up and destroyed the Gunners' 30 match unbeaten run. Liverpool recorded a seven game winning streak that saw them top the table at the end of October and open up a four point gap over Arsenal.

Manchester United endured another poor result in November when Manchester City, inspired by the work rate and goals of Shaun Goater, recorded a 3–1 victory in the last ever Manchester derby held at Maine Road. The Red Devils showed some signs of recovery with a 5–3 home victory over Newcastle at Old Trafford in a fixture lit-up by a Ruud van Nistelrooy hat-trick.

Sunderland's first win under Howard Wilkinson came against Spurs, but league leaders Liverpool endured a wretched run of results that included defeats at Middlesbrough and Fulham, allowing Arsenal to reclaim top spot at the end of the month. David Moyes' Everton stormed up to third place while Chelsea and Manchester United remained in close attendance.

December was a good month for United, who recorded a 2–0 home win against Arsenal in a game that featured a rare goal for Juan Sebastien Veron and a 3–0 victory over West Ham. The Gunners got back on track with wins over Middlesbrough and West Brom to end the year as league leaders. In-form Southampton edged closer to a European place in seventh.

Leeds United's financial struggles were highlighted in January when the Whites sold Jonathan Woodgate to Newcastle and Robbie Fowler to Manchester City. Another former Leeds striker, Robbie Keane, continued to find his feet at Spurs, scoring a hat-trick in a 4–3 victory over Everton. Thierry Henry also bagged a treble in Arsenal's 3–1 win over West Ham in a month that saw the Gunners defeat Chelsea and Birmingham. Manchester United won all three of their league fixtures but ended the month two points behind the Gunners. Liverpool dropped down to eighth, while West Brom and West Ham looked certainties for relegation.

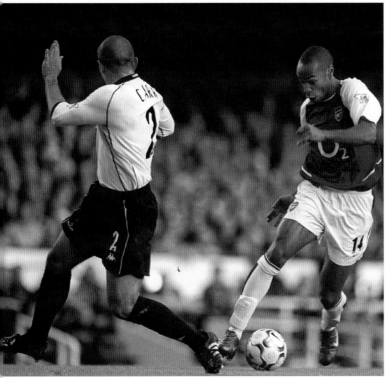

ABOVE TOP: *Manchester United hotshot Ruud van Nistelrooy celebrates his goal of the season contender against Fulham at Old Trafford.*

ABOVE BOTTOM: *Arsenal's main attacking threat once again, Thierry Henry scored twice during the top of the table clash with Manchester United at Highbury.*

February saw Manchester City frustrate Manchester United once more as they grabbed a 1–1 draw at Old Trafford, while the Red Devils also dropped points against Bolton in a 1–1 draw. Both results saw the title initiative handed to Arsenal who recorded wins against Fulham, Manchester City and Charlton, and engineered a five point advantage over United. Bobby Robson's Newcastle showed their top four credentials, moving up to third following positive results against Leeds and Spurs.

Arsenal extended their lead to eight points at the top of the table at the beginning of March. The gap decreased when United defeated Leeds and Aston Villa and Arsenal lost 2–0 at Blackburn. At the other end of the table, Sunderland sacked their second manager of the season when Howard Wilkinson departed the club after the Black Cats had recorded just two wins from his 20 games in charge. Two days later, former Republic of Ireland boss Mick McCarthy was appointed as manager and given the seemingly impossible task of keeping the club in the Premier League.

March brought another managerial casualty when Leeds disposed of Terry Venables. The team were placed 16th in the division as the club's debts of £120m provided an alarmingly bleak outlook for the future. Peter Reid was appointed as manager until the end of the season, as a team that had starred in Europe just a season earlier, looked in genuine danger of dropping into the second tier of English football.

Manchester United and Arsenal traded places at the top, as the Red Devils defeated Fulham 3–0 at Old Trafford in game that featured a superb individual goal from Ruud van Nistelrooy, who later completed a hat-trick. Arsenal defeated Everton 2–1 at Highbury and ended the month a point behind United with a game in hand.

A key moment in the race for the title came during the first weekend of April when Manchester United cruised to a 4–0 victory over Liverpool while Arsenal were held to a 1–1 draw by Aston Villa. United once again found their best run of form at the perfect time, and went on to hammer Newcastle 6–2 at St James Park when Paul Scholes hit a hat-trick. Meanwhile, after a run of poor results, Fulham sacked manager Jean Tigana and appointed Chris Coleman.

Peter Reid began to make an impact with Leeds, inspiring the Whites to a 6–1 victory at Charlton. On April 12, Reid's former club Sunderland became the first team to suffer relegation following a 2–0 defeat at Birmingham. A few days later Arsenal and Manchester United met at Highbury in a game billed as a title decider. A ferocious encounter ensued and saw United take an early lead from the prolific Ruud van Nistelrooy, only for Arsenal to claw level and go in front through two Thierry Henry goals before a late Ryan Giggs header meant the game ended 2–2. That result suited the visitors better than the hosts and left United three points clear, while the Gunners had a game in hand.

The following weekend, Paul Scholes was coolness personified when he grabbed a brace in United's tense 3–1 home victory over Blackburn as Arsenal claimed a crucial 2–0 win at Middlesbrough. The next team to drop out of the division was West Brom, who suffered relegation despite a 2–1 win at Sunderland.

Struggling West Ham were thrown into turmoil when manager Glenn Roeder was hospitalised with a brain tumour. Director of Football Trevor Brooking stepped into the breach while Roeder recuperated.

The vital turning point in a continually twisting title saga took place with just three games left to play when Arsenal surrendered a two goal lead against Bolton to draw 2–2. On the same weekend Manchester United recorded a 2–0 victory over Spurs, achieved through goals from the in-form Scholes and van Nistelrooy.

ABOVE LEFT: *Manchester United's Ryan Giggs celebrates a vital headed equaliser against Arsenal at Highbury during the season-defining 2–2 draw between the two clubs.*

ABOVE RIGHT: *A teenage force of nature, Everton striker Wayne Rooney announced himself to the rest of English football with a spectacular long-range effort that curled into David Seaman's net to defeat reigning champions Arsenal.*

At the beginning of May another hat-trick from Ruud van Nistelrooy put Manchester United on the verge of title glory, as the Red Devils beat Charlton 4–1 at Old Trafford. The following day, the Premiership crown was theirs as Arsenal suffered a shock 3–2 home defeat to lowly Leeds in a result that ensured the Yorkshire club's safety. Sir Alex Ferguson's men lifted the Premiership trophy for the eighth time in 11 seasons. The Red Devils' final game of the season was a 2–1 victory over Everton that featured a typically clinical free-kick from David Beckham.

The final day of the season brought heartbreak for West Ham who were relegated for the first time in 10 years despite a 2–2 draw at Birmingham City and clocking up 42 points; a total that in most seasons would have comfortably seen them stay up.

BELOW: *Mark Viduka wheels away in delight after scoring the goal that edged Leeds United to safety and ended Arsenal's title challenge.*

Bolton secured their Premiership status thanks to 2–1 win over Middlesbrough while bottom placed Sunderland finished the season with record lows of four wins, 19 points and 21 goals. Their North East rivals, Newcastle, enjoyed their best season for years, as Bobby Robson led the Magpies to a third place finish and into the Champions League. Chelsea also qualified for Europe's premier competition after finishing fourth.

# HONOURS LIST

## FA Barclaycard Premiership
**CHAMPIONS:** Manchester United
The Red Devils claimed back the trophy they had become so accustomed to winning with a superb late season surge, to finish five points clear of second placed Arsenal.
**RUNNERS-UP:** Arsenal
**RELEGATED:** West Ham United, West Bromwich Albion, Sunderland
**TOP GOAL SCORER:** Ruud van Nistelrooy (25 goals for Manchester United)

SHOOT MAGAZINE
2002–03

*Southampton's in-form striker James Beattie was pictured celebrating another goal as Shoot speculated whether the young forward deserved a chance in the England team. Tottenham's Darren Anderton pledged his loyalty to the club and explained why he turned down the chance to join Manchester United. The prospects of England's Champions League hopefuls were also assessed.*

## 2002–03 SEASON TABLE

| | | M | W | D | L | GF | GA | GD | PTS |
|---|---|---|---|---|---|---|---|---|---|
| 1 | Manchester United | 38 | 25 | 8 | 5 | 74 | 34 | +40 | 83 |
| 2 | Arsenal | 38 | 23 | 9 | 6 | 85 | 42 | +43 | 78 |
| 3 | Newcastle United | 38 | 21 | 6 | 11 | 63 | 48 | +15 | 69 |
| 4 | Chelsea | 38 | 19 | 10 | 9 | 68 | 38 | +30 | 67 |
| 5 | Liverpool | 38 | 18 | 10 | 10 | 61 | 41 | +20 | 64 |
| 6 | Blackburn Rovers | 38 | 16 | 12 | 10 | 52 | 43 | +9 | 60 |
| 7 | Everton | 38 | 17 | 8 | 13 | 48 | 49 | -1 | 59 |
| 8 | Southampton | 38 | 13 | 13 | 12 | 43 | 46 | -3 | 52 |
| 9 | Manchester City | 38 | 15 | 6 | 17 | 47 | 54 | -7 | 51 |
| 10 | Tottenham Hotspur | 38 | 14 | 8 | 16 | 51 | 62 | -11 | 50 |
| 11 | Middlesbrough | 38 | 13 | 10 | 15 | 48 | 44 | +4 | 49 |
| 12 | Charlton Athletic | 38 | 14 | 7 | 17 | 45 | 56 | -11 | 49 |
| 13 | Birmingham City | 38 | 13 | 9 | 16 | 41 | 49 | -8 | 48 |
| 14 | Fulham | 38 | 13 | 9 | 16 | 41 | 50 | -9 | 48 |
| 15 | Leeds United | 38 | 14 | 5 | 19 | 58 | 57 | +1 | 47 |
| 16 | Aston Villa | 38 | 12 | 9 | 17 | 42 | 47 | -5 | 45 |
| 17 | Bolton Wanderers | 38 | 10 | 14 | 14 | 41 | 51 | -10 | 44 |
| 18 | West Ham United | 38 | 10 | 12 | 16 | 42 | 59 | -17 | 42 |
| 19 | West Bromwich Albion | 38 | 6 | 8 | 24 | 29 | 65 | -36 | 26 |
| 20 | Sunderland | 38 | 4 | 7 | 27 | 21 | 65 | -44 | 19 |

# PLAYERS OF THE SEASON

**PFA PLAYER OF THE YEAR:** Thierry Henry, Arsenal
**PFA YOUNG PLAYER OF THE YEAR:** Jermaine Jenas, Newcastle United
**FOOTBALL WRITERS' PLAYER OF THE YEAR:** Thierry Henry, Arsenal

ABOVE TOP: *Box to box midfielder Jermaine Jenas showed great promise under Sir Bobby Robson at Newcastle and was awarded with the PFA Young Player of the Year accolade.*

ABOVE BOTTOM: *Portsmouth manager Harry Redknapp deep in discussion with owner Milan Mandaric during Pompey's title-winning campaign.*

## ⚽ INTERESTING INFO

Sheffield Wednesday were relegated to Division Two, just 10 years after reaching the FA Cup final and 11 years after finishing third in the Premier League.

**FOOTBALL LEAGUE DIVISION ONE CHAMPIONS:**
Portsmouth
**PROMOTED:** Leicester City
**DIVISION ONE PLAY-OFF WINNERS:** Wolverhampton Wanderers
**RELEGATED:** Sheffield Wednesday, Brighton & Hove Albion, Grimsby Town
**TOP GOAL SCORER:** Svetoslav Todorov (26 goals for Portsmouth)

With Harry Redknapp in charge and a team featuring the experience and creativity of players like Paul Merson, Steve Stone and Tim Sherwood. Portsmouth stormed to the League One title with a total of 98 points and 97 goals. Leicester's City absence from the top flight proved a brief one as Micky Adams guided the Foxes to second place and automatic promotion. The third promotion place was taken by Wolves who defeated Sheffield United 3–0 in the play-off final to return to the top flight for the first time in 19 years. The goals were scored by Mark Kennedy, Nathan Blake and Kevin Miller.

**DIVISION TWO CHAMPIONS:** Wigan Athletic
**PROMOTED:** Crewe Alexandra
**DIVISION TWO PLAY-OFF WINNERS:** Cardiff City
**RELEGATED:** Cheltenham Town, Huddersfield Town, Mansfield Town, Northampton Town
**TOP GOAL SCORER:** Robert Earnshaw (31 goals for Cardiff City)

Wigan Athletic confirmed progression beyond the third tier for the first time in their history after clocking up 100 points to win the League Two title at a canter. Managed by Paul Jewell, the Latics were defeated just four times in the league. Veteran boss Dario Gradi inspired Crewe to automatic promotion in second place while Cardiff City, another club managed by an experienced manager – in the form of Lennie Lawrance – also progressed, following a play-off final victory over Queens Park Rangers.

**DIVISION THREE CHAMPIONS:** Rushden & Diamonds
**PROMOTED:** Hartlepool United, Wrexham
**DIVISION THREE PLAY-OFF WINNERS:** Bournemouth
**RELEGATED:** Exeter City, Shrewsbury Town
**TOP GOAL SCORER:** Andy Morrell (44 goals for Wrexham)

Brian Talbot's Rushden & Diamonds continued their meteoric rise through the Football League after claiming the League Two title following an end of season collapse by Hartlepool who had led the division for much of the campaign but ultimately had to settle for second place. The third automatic place went to Wrexham while Sean O'Driscoll's Bournemouth defeated Lincoln City 5–2 in the play-off final. Dropping out of the Football league were Shrewsbury Town and Exeter City, as two clubs were relegated from the fourth tier for the first time.

**FOOTBALL CONFERENCE CHAMPIONS:** Yeovil Town
**PROMOTED:** Doncaster Rovers

Gary Johnson's Yeovil reached the league for the first time in their history after lifting the Conference title. Joining them in League Two via the play-offs were Dave Penney's Doncaster who defeated Dagenham & Redbridge 3–2 in the final.

RIGHT TOP: *Speedy striker Robert Earnshaw ended the season as Division Two's top goal scorer and helped the Bluebirds achieve promotion via the play-offs.*

RIGHT BOTTOM: *Bournemouth manager Sean O'Driscoll inspired the Cherries back into Division Two following a 5–2 play-off final victory over Lincoln City.*

# UP FOR THE CUP

**FA CUP WINNERS:** Arsenal

Arsenal retained the FA Cup, lifting the trophy for the ninth time in their history, following a 1–0 defeat of Southampton. The only goal of the game was a close range first-half finish from Robert Pires.

The Gunners arrived at the final following a 1–0 semi-final win over Sheffield United while Southampton overcame Watford with a 2–1 victory. Earlier in the competition Arsenal ended Manchester United's interest following a 2–0 win at Old Trafford that featured goals from Edu and Sylvain Wiltford.

Earlier headlines in the tournament were made by League Two Shrewsbury Town, who beat Everton 2–1 thanks to a brace from experienced striker Nigel Jemson; Burnley, who defeated Fulham; Crystal Palace, who overcame Liverpool at Anfield and Vauxhall Motors, who knocked out QPR in the third round.

**LEAGUE (COCA COLA) CUP WINNERS:** Liverpool

Liverpool claimed another trophy under Gerard Houllier and lifted the League Cup for the seventh time in their history following a 2–0 win over Manchester United. The Reds' goals came from England duo Steven Gerrard and Michael Owen.

Liverpool progressed to the final after defeating Sheffield United 3–2 on aggregate in the semi-final while United overcame Blackburn 4–2 in their two-legged contest. Earlier in the competition Sheffield United picked up impressive victories over Sunderland and Leeds, Wigan overcame Fulham and West Brom, and Burnley knocked out Spurs.

**COMMUNITY SHIELD WINNERS:** Liverpool

In the first year the pre-season showpiece was renamed as the Community Shield, Liverpool lost 1–0 to Arsenal at the Millennium Stadium. The only goal of the game came from Gunners midfielder Gilberto Silva.

**THE FOOTBALL LEAGUE (LDV VANS) TROPHY:**

Danny Wilson's Bristol City overcame Carlisle United 2–0 thanks to goals from Lee Peacock and Liam Rosenior.

ABOVE TOP: *Arsenal's French winger Robert Pires possesses the FA Cup trophy after scoring the solitary goal of the Gunners' 1–0 victory over Southampton.*

ABOVE BOTTOM: *Liverpool's League Final goal scorers, Michael Owen (left) and Steven Gerrard celebrate with the trophy after the Merseyside club defeated Manchester United 2–0 at the Millennium Stadium.*

# INTO EUROPE

## European Champions League

Liverpool crashed out in the group stage, finishing third behind Valencia and Basel but Newcastle gave a better account of themselves, finishing second in a group that contained Juventus and Dynamo Kiev before failing to advance from the second group stage. Arsenal suffered the same fate, exiting following a third place finish, behind Ajax and Valencia. Manchester United were again the best performing English team, reaching the quarter-finals, where they were paired against Real Madrid. The Spanish giants recorded a 6–5 aggregate victory that featured a memorable hat-trick from Brazilian striker Ronaldo. The result denied United the opportunity to play in that season's final, which was being hosted at their Old Trafford home ground.

## UEFA Cup

Chelsea again exited the competition at an early stage, losing 5–4 to Norwegian side Viking FK in the first round. Of England's other representatives, Ipswich crashed out to Slovan Liberec in the second round, Blackburn lost to Celtic at the same stage and Leeds advanced to the third round before losing to Malaga and Fulham exited to Hertha Berlin. Liverpool, playing in the competition after being eliminated from the Champions League, advanced to the quarter-finals where they were defeated 3–1 on aggregate by Celtic.

ABOVE: *Ronaldo celebrates scoring for Real Madrid against Manchester United in the Champions League at Old Trafford. The Brazilian forward went on to complete a hat-trick and receive a standing ovation from the home fans when he departed the action.*

# THE INTERNATIONAL SCENE

With Sven-Goran Eriksson still at the helm, England began their qualification campaign for Euro 2004 in positive fashion, recording victories against Slovakia, Liechtenstein and Turkey.

# ARSENAL'S IRRESISTIBLE 'INVINCIBLES' MAKE HISTORY

In the season when the Premiership was declared the richest division in the Europe, the takeover of Chelsea by a Russian named Roman Abramovich completely changed the landscape of the English game. The Blues spent huge amounts in the transfer market, hoovering up some of the best young British talent while also bringing in several big names from across the continent.

Arguably the division's most high-profile player and English football's most iconic personality, David Beckham, departed England to become Real Madrid's latest 'Galactico'.

Ahead of the new season, the only managerial change saw former Leeds boss David O'Leary appointed as Aston Villa manager.

OPPOSITE PAGE: *One of the most feared centre forwards in Premier League history, Arsenal's Thierry Henry once again topped the season's scoring charts.*

LEFT: *The raw young talent of Cristiano Ronaldo added flair to the Manchester United ranks ahead of the season. Far from the finished article, the long-term replacement for David Beckham displayed twinkle toed dribbling brilliance but often frustrated with an inconsistent end product.*

# TRANSFER TALES

Chelsea's new-found riches hogged the transfer headlines ahead of the new campaign as the Blues broke their transfer record to sign Damien Duff from Blackburn for £17m. Chelsea also splashed the cash on established performers such as Claude Makelele, Hernan Crespo, Adrian Mutu, Geremi, Juan Sebastian Veron and Alexei Smertin. The Stamford Bridge outfit also acquired a quartet of promising young English players in the form of Wayne Bridge, Joe Cole, Glen Johnson and Scott Parker.

Following the sale of David Beckham, Manchester United recruited his long-term replacement, purchasing the prodigiously talented Portuguese winger, Cristiano Ronaldo from Sporting Lisbon. The Red Devils also brought USA goalkeeper Tim Howard, Brazilian World Cup winner Kleberson and Fulham striker Louis Saha.

Liverpool invested in the domestic market, with the additions of Harry Kewell from Leeds and Steve Finnan from Fulham. Blackburn brought in Rangers midfielder Barry Ferguson as a replacement for David Dunn who was snapped up by Birmingham.

Other major signings included Arsenal's £10.5m capture of Jose Antonio Reyes, Tottenham's £7m acquisition of Jermain Defoe from West Ham and Manchester City's addition of England goalkeeper, David James, who also departed the Hammers.

## BIGGEST TRANSFERS

**DAMIEN DUFF** – from Blackburn Rovers to Chelsea – £17m

**CLAUDE MAKELELE** – from Real Madrid to Chelsea – £16.6m

**HERNAN CRESPO** – from Inter Milan to Chelsea – £15.8m

**ADRIAN MUTU** – from Parma to Chelsea – £15.8m

**JUAN SEBASTIAN VERON** – from Manchester United to Chelsea – £15m

**LOUIS SAHA** – from Fulham to Manchester United – £12.8m

**CRISTIANO RONALDO** – from Sporting Lisbon to Manchester United – £12.24m

**JOSE ANTONIO REYES** – from Sevilla to Arsenal – £10.5m

**SCOTT PARKER** – from Charlton Athletic to Chelsea – £10m

**BARRY FERGUSON** – from Rangers to Blackburn Rovers – £7.5m

LEFT: *So good he had a position named after him, Claude Makelele was an expert exponent of the defensive midfield position and provided the perfect shield for Chelsea's already solid backline. The French international, who signed from Real Madrid, also helped transform Frank Lampard's fortunes at Stamford Bridge.*

# TALES OF THE TURF

The opening day of the season was lit up by a captivating debut display by Manchester United's Cristiano Ronaldo. The twinkled toed winger came off the bench to transform the tempo of United's 4–0 victory over Bolton.

The first month of the season ended with Arsenal and Manchester United at the top of the table, with both teams winning each of their opening three fixtures. Newly promoted Portsmouth also started strongly, as did Manchester City and big spending Chelsea.

Following a slow start to the season, Tottenham sacked manager Glenn Hoddle in September and placed Director of Football David Pleat in temporary charge. Arsenal finished the month at the top of the table, a single point clear of both Chelsea and Manchester United. Birmingham and Southampton, who had made surprisingly strong starts, completed the top five. Wolves were bottom of the table and were still to register their first win of the season, while the other relegation spots were occupied by Newcastle and Spurs.

As their new signings continued to acclimatise, Chelsea enjoyed an impressive September, recording victories against Spurs, Wolves and Aston Villa to finish the month top of the pile. Arsenal and Manchester United remained in close contention. The clubs met in a tinderbox of a fixture at the end of the month. In a game that ultimately ended 0–0, Patrick Vieira was sent off for a petulant kick at Ruud van Nistelrooy. The United striker remained at the centre of controversy when his missed penalty in the last minute of the game prompted ugly scenes as several Arsenal players barged and pushed the Dutchman.

Steve Bruce's Birmingham continued to impress in fourth while Fulham, managed by Chris Coleman, moved up into fifth. Improved displays from Spurs and Wolves saw them replaced in the bottom three by Leicester and Middlesbrough, while financially crippled Leeds dropped into the relegation zone.

BELOW: *Arsenal's Martin Keown was the main perpetrator as several Gunners players bundled into Manchester United striker Ruud van Nistelrooy after he missed a penalty. The aggression of Keown and his colleagues caused confrontations from players from both teams.*

Peter Reid's tenure as Leeds manager came to an end in November with Whites' legend Eddie Gray replacing him on a temporary basis. Chelsea maintained a slender one point led over Arsenal at the top of the division with Manchester United a little further off the pace.

Judgement day for Manchester United's Rio Ferdinand came on 19 December when the FA handed him an eight-month ban for forgetting to take a drug test earlier in the season. The ban also ruled the England international out of participating in Euro 2004.

Whilst Ferdinand's ban had a negative impact on United's performances towards the end of the campaign, they ended the year as league leaders following a positive run of results. Chelsea and Arsenal remained unbeaten in the league and firmly in the title picture while two other London clubs, Charlton and Fulham, completed the top five.

The New Year brought an announcement from Southampton manager Gordon Strachan that he would depart his role at the end of the season. In fact, he actually left the club at the beginning of March to be replaced by Plymouth Argyle boss Paul Sturrock. Arsenal hit top form between January and early March, winning nine league matches on the bounce to open up a significant gap over Chelsea and Manchester United. The Gunners' impressive run featured victories at Aston Villa and Chelsea and a 4–1 thumping of Middlesbrough at Highbury.

OPPOSITE PAGE: *Brazilian defensive midfielder Gilberto Silva added guile and aggression to the Arsenal midfield and afforded Patrick Vieira with more of an attacking licence.*

ABOVE: *Despite his advancing years, Dennis Bergkamp remained Arsenal's key creative force. Combining superbly with Thierry Henry and Robert Pires, the Dutchman was the architect of some of the most aesthetically pleasing football the Premiership had witnessed.*

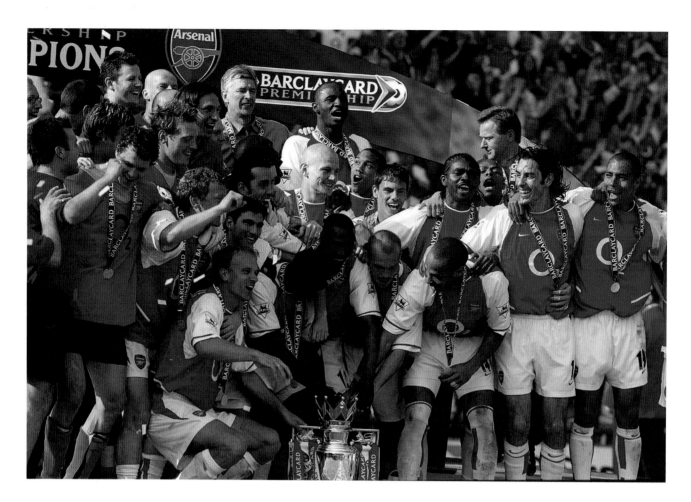

Arsenal's irresistible form continued throughout March as they became the first team in Premier League history to complete their first 30 matches without defeat. The Gunners weren't just unbeatable, they were playing breathtaking attacking football as the likes of Thierry Henry, Dennis Bergkamp and Robert Pires illuminated the English game. Arsenal's lead stretched to seven points over Chelsea by the end of the month, with reigning champions Manchester United a further seven points off the pace.

With their displays going from strength to strength and the players' confidence at an all-time high, Arsenal clinched the title on 25 April following a 2–2 draw against local rivals Tottenham at White Hart Lane. Arsene Wenger's side went on to complete the campaign undefeated, following a final-day victory over Leicester City at Highbury. It was only the third time since the formation of the Football League in 1888 that any club had achieved such a feat.

The Gunners ended the season with a total of 90 points, having won 26 and drawn 12 of their 38 games. Chelsea pipped Manchester United to second place, meaning Sir Alex Ferguson's team finished outside the division's top two for just the second time in 12 seasons. The final Champions League place was claimed by Liverpool.

ABOVE: *Arsenal's 'Invincibles' celebrate with the Premiership trophy after becoming the first team to remain unbeaten during a Premier League season.*

Leicester City's relegation from the top flight was confirmed at the beginning of May following a 2–2 draw at Charlton. They were joined a day later by Leeds who were hammered 4–1 by Bolton. That loss meant the Whites suffered relegation exactly three years after they had competed in a Champions League semi-final. Wolverhampton Wanderers, who had failed to win a single away game all season, had their fate confirmed a week later following a 1–1 draw at Newcastle, while David Moyes' Everton, who endured a frustrating campaign finished in 17th, just six points above the bottom three.

# HONOURS LIST

## FA Barclaycard Premiership

**CHAMPIONS:** Arsenal

The first team in the Premier League era to complete a league campaign without defeat, Arsenal's 'Invincibles' claimed their third league title under Arsene Wenger in emphatic fashion.

**RUNNERS-UP:** Chelsea

**RELEGATED:** Leicester City, Leeds United, Wolverhampton Wanderers

**TOP GOAL SCORER:** Thierry Henry (30 goals for Arsenal)

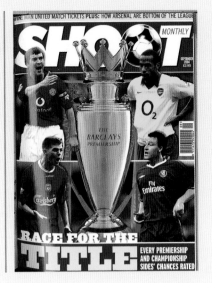

**SHOOT MAGAZINE 2003–04**

*A special pre-season preview edition concentrated on the clubs that were likely to challenge for the title. Key players from the main protagonists were featured as Manchester United captain Roy Keane was pictured alongside Arsenal striker Thierry Henry, Liverpool captain Steven Gerrard and Chelsea talisman John Terry.*

## 2003–04 SEASON TABLE

|  | | M | W | D | L | GF | GA | GD | PTS |
|---|---|---|---|---|---|---|---|---|---|
| 1 | Arsenal | 38 | 26 | 12 | 0 | 73 | 26 | +47 | 90 |
| 2 | Chelsea | 38 | 24 | 7 | 7 | 67 | 30 | +37 | 79 |
| 3 | Manchester United | 38 | 23 | 6 | 9 | 64 | 35 | +29 | 75 |
| 4 | Liverpool | 38 | 16 | 12 | 10 | 55 | 37 | +18 | 60 |
| 5 | Newcastle United | 38 | 13 | 17 | 8 | 52 | 40 | +12 | 56 |
| 6 | Aston Villa | 38 | 15 | 11 | 12 | 48 | 44 | +4 | 56 |
| 7 | Charlton Athletic | 38 | 14 | 11 | 13 | 51 | 51 | 0 | 53 |
| 8 | Bolton Wanderers | 38 | 14 | 11 | 13 | 48 | 56 | -8 | 53 |
| 9 | Fulham | 38 | 14 | 10 | 14 | 52 | 46 | +6 | 52 |
| 10 | Birmingham City | 38 | 12 | 14 | 12 | 43 | 48 | -5 | 50 |
| 11 | Middlesbrough | 38 | 13 | 9 | 16 | 44 | 52 | -8 | 48 |
| 12 | Southampton | 38 | 12 | 11 | 15 | 44 | 45 | -1 | 47 |
| 13 | Portsmouth | 38 | 12 | 9 | 17 | 47 | 54 | -7 | 45 |
| 14 | Tottenham Hotspur | 38 | 13 | 6 | 19 | 47 | 57 | -10 | 45 |
| 15 | Blackburn Rovers | 38 | 12 | 8 | 18 | 51 | 59 | -8 | 44 |
| 16 | Manchester City | 38 | 9 | 14 | 15 | 55 | 54 | +1 | 41 |
| 17 | Everton | 38 | 9 | 12 | 17 | 45 | 57 | -12 | 39 |
| 18 | Leicester City | 38 | 6 | 15 | 17 | 48 | 65 | -17 | 33 |
| 19 | Leeds United | 38 | 8 | 9 | 21 | 40 | 79 | -39 | 33 |
| 20 | Wolverhampton Wanderers | 38 | 7 | 12 | 19 | 38 | 77 | -39 | 33 |

## PLAYERS OF THE SEASON

**PFA PLAYER OF THE YEAR:** Thierry Henry, Arsenal

**PFA YOUNG PLAYER OF THE YEAR:** Scott Parker, Charlton Athletic and Chelsea

**FOOTBALL WRITERS PLAYER OF THE YEAR:** Thierry Henry, Arsenal

**FOOTBALL LEAGUE DIVISION ONE CHAMPIONS:**
Norwich City
**PROMOTED:** West Bromwich Albion
**DIVISION ONE PLAY-OFF WINNERS:** Crystal Palace
**RELEGATED:** Walsall, Bradford City, Wimbledon
**TOP GOAL SCORER:** Andy Johnson (27 goals for
Crystal Palace)

Norwich topped the table to ensure a Premier League return after almost a decade away. Managed by Nigel Worthington, the Canaries amassed 94 points, finishing eight clear of runners-up West Brom, who secured an immediate return to the Premier League under Gary Megson.

Iain Dowie masterminded a remarkable transformation of Crystal Palace. When the young manager took over just before Christmas the Eagles were 19th in the division. The team's turnaround under Dowie was completed when they qualified for the play-offs and defeated West Ham 1–0 in the final, with Neil Shipperley scoring the winning goal. Dropping out of the division were former Premier League side Wimbledon, who completed their last season before being renamed as MK Dons.

**DIVISION TWO CHAMPIONS:** Plymouth Argyle
**PROMOTED:** Queens Park Rangers
**DIVISION TWO PLAY-OFF WINNERS:** Brighton & Hove
Albion
**RELEGATED:** Grimsby Town, Rushden & Diamonds,
Notts County, Wycombe Wanderers
**TOP GOAL SCORER:** Leon Knight (Brighton & Hove
Albion) and Stephen McPhee (Port Vale) – both
25 goals

Plymouth Argyle finished top of the pile, winning 26 of their 46 matches and scoring 85 goals, despite losing manager Paul Sturrock to Southampton in March. His replacement, Bobby Williams, steadied the ship and ensured promotion for the Devon club. Second place went to Ian Holloway's QPR who finished a point ahead of Bristol City in the third. The Robins went on to suffer further disappointment in the play-off final, losing 1–0 to Mark McGhee's Brighton & Hove Albion.

**DIVISION THREE CHAMPIONS:** Doncaster Rovers
**PROMOTED:** Hull City, Torquay United
**DIVISION THREE PLAY-OFF WINNERS:** Huddersfield
Town
**RELEGATED:** Carlisle United, York City
**TOP GOAL SCORER:** Steve MacLean (23 goals for
Scunthorpe United)

Dave Penny led Doncaster Rovers to a second successive promotion by completing a dominant league title victory. Hull City, who had invested heavily in their playing staff under the guidance of Peter Taylor, took the second automatic place and were joined by third-placed Torquay United. Huddersfield beat Mansfield in the play-off final. At the other end of the table, the two clubs dropping out of the Football League were York City and Carlisle United.

## ⚽ INTERESTING INFO

Carlisle's relegation from League Two in 2004 saw them become England's first former top-flight club to drop into the Conference.

**FOOTBALL CONFERENCE CHAMPIONS:** Chester City
**PROMOTED:** Doncaster Rovers

Managed by former England defender Mark Wright, Chester City lifted the Conference title. Shrewsbury Town also gained promotion after defeating Aldershot Town 3–0 on penalties in the play-off final.

OPPOSITE PAGE TOP: *The embodiment of hard work and tenacity, Charlton midfielder Scott Parker was in superb form during the 2003–04 campaign, prompting a big money move to Chelsea at the end of the season.*

OPPOSITE PAGE BOTTOM: *Crystal Palace striker Neil Shipperley in action during the Division One play-off final victory over West Ham. The experienced forward scored the game's only goal to send the Eagles soaring back into the Premiership.*

LEFT: *Cameroon forward Joseph-Desire Job bagged one of Middlesbrough's goals as they defeated Bolton Wanderers 2–1 in the Carling Cup final.*

# UP FOR THE CUP

**FA CUP WINNERS:** Manchester United

Manchester United eased the disappointment of losing the league to Arsenal with a routine 3–0 victory over League One Millwall in the FA Cup final. The Red Devils' goals were shared between Cristiano Ronalo, who scored once and Ruud van Nistelrooy, who found the net twice. With Champions League football already assured, confirmation of the 11th FA Cup success in United's history meant that Millwall would participate in European competition, in the form of the UEFA Cup, for the first time.

United reached the final following a hard fought semi-final victory over Arsenal at Villa Park, achieved courtesy of a Paul Scholes thunderbolt while Millwall overcome Sunderland 1–0 thanks to Tim Cahill's goal.

In the earlier rounds of the competition Colchester defeated Coventry, Gillingham knocked out Charlton and Manchester City overcame a 3–0 half-time deficit and playing 45 minutes with 10 men to beat Spurs 4–3.

**LEAGUE (CARLING) CUP WINNERS:** Middlesbrough

Managed by Steve McClaren Middlesbrough lifted the first major honour in the history following a 2–1 victory over Sam Allardyce's Botlon in the final. Boro struck twice in the opening seven minutes of the game through Joseph-Desire Job and Boudewijn Zenden.

Middlesbrough reached the final following a 3–1 aggregate victory over Arsenal that featured goals from Zenden and Juninho while Bolton overcame Aston Villa 5–4 in their semi-final contest.

Earlier in the tournament West Brom halted both Newcastle and Manchester United's progress while Bolton accounted for Liverpool's involvement in the competition. Lower league sides making the headlines included Rotherham, who narrowly lost to Arsenal on penalties, Wigan, who knocked out Fulham and Blackpool, who defeated Birmingham.

**COMMUNITY SHIELD WINNERS:** Manchester United

In a bad tempered encounter that saw Arsenal's Francis Jeffers shown a red card, Manchester United triumphed on penalties after Thierry Henry equalised Mikael Silvestre's opening goal.

**THE FOOTBALL LEAGUE (LDV VANS) TROPHY:**

Steve McMahon enjoyed further success as Blackpool boss as his team defeated Southend United 2–0 in the final thanks to goals from John Murphy and Danny Coid.

## INTO EUROPE
### European Champions League

With the tournament returned to the more streamlined format of a single group stage, followed by an extra knockout round, English teams fared better during the 2003–04 campaign. The only team that struggled were Newcastle who crashed out in the third qualifying round following a penalty shootout defeat to Partizan Belgrade.

ABOVE: *Chelsea left-back Wayne Bridge sprints to celebrate with Blues fans after scoring the goal that knocked Arsenal out of the Champions League.*

The other three teams, Chelsea, Manchester United and Arsenal, each topped their groups but United exited at the first knockout stage following a shock defeat to Jose Mourinho's FC Porto. The charismatic coach introduced himself to the English game with an iconic sprint down the Old Trafford touchline to celebrate his side's winner before going on to lift an unlikely Champions League crown.

Chelsea defeated Stuttgart and Arsenal overcame Celta Vigo to set up an all English tie between the London clubs in the quarter-finals. Despite their peerless domestic form, Arsenal failed to get the better of the Blues, losing 3–2 on aggregate thanks to winning goal from Wayne Bridge. As the tournament appeared to open up for Chelsea they suffered a shock 5–3 aggregate semi-final defeat to Monaco.

## UEFA Cup

Blackburn and Southampton both experienced early disappointment, exiting in the first round. Manchester City lasted one round further before crashing out on away goals to Georgian side, Groclin, while Liverpool advanced to the fourth round, where they were defeated by eventual winners Marseille. The Premier League's standout performers were Newcastle United who overcame the likes of Real Mallorca and PSV Eindhoven to reach the semi-finals, where they were beaten by Marseille.

BELOW: *Newcastle captain Alan Shearer battles for possession against Inter Milan during the Magpies' impressive UEFA Cup run.*

## THE INTERNATIONAL SCENE

ABOVE: *England striker Wayne Rooney announced himself on The International Scene with four goals during Euro 2004. Here the Everton youngster is pictured scoring a header against Switzerland.*

Having secured a place at Euro 2004 with a combative 0–0 draw against Turkey in Istanbul, England put in some impressive performances at the tournament proper. Sven-Goran Eriksson's side got over the initial disappointment of an opening day defeat against France by defeating Switzerland 3–0 and Croatia 4–2. Both games featured two goals from Wayne Rooney who announced himself at the highest level in emphatic fashion.

The Three Lions reached the quarter-finals where they faced hosts Portugal in an epic encounter. Michael Owen's early goal was followed by an injury that forced Rooney off and a late equaliser from Helder Postiga. Rui Costa edged Portugal ahead in extra time but Frank Lampard levelled matters, before Sol Campbell harshly had a goal ruled out and the clash went to penalties. England once again put in a dire performance from 12 yards as both David Beckham and Darius Vassell failed to convert, allowing Portugal goalkeeper Ricardo to strike home the winning kick.

LEFT: *As usual England's supporters turned out in their numbers for a major tournament, this time Euro 2004 held in Portugal. However, they were once again left disappointed by their team's efforts on the pitch.*

BELOW: *England striker Darius Vassell sees his tame penalty saved by gloveless Portugal goalkeeper Ricardo as the Three Lions crash out of Euro 2004.*

# DRAMATIC EUROPEAN GLORY FOR LIVERPOOL AS THE 'SPECIAL ONE' ARRIVES

**T**he arrival of a new manager stole the headlines ahead of the 2004–05 season as Chelsea's appointment of Portuguese coach Jose Mourinho, coupled with continued investment from Roman Abramovich, saw many pundits tip the Blues for the title. In his first press conference, Mourinho, who had replaced the sacked Claudio Ranieri, famously labelled himself as the 'special one'; a moniker that followed him throughout his time in England.

It was all change at Anfield when Gerard Houllier was shown the door after six years in charge and replaced with former Valencia boss, Rafael Benitez. Tottenham appointed Frenchman Jacques Santini as their new manager to replace caretaker boss David Pleat.

In the Football League the second tier was re-branded as the Championship, with the third and fourth levels becoming League One and League Two respectively.

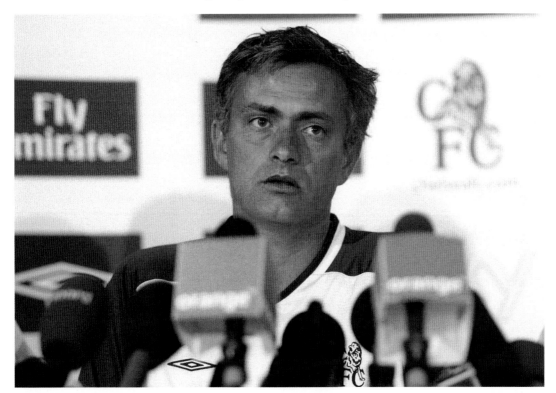

LEFT: *Facing the full glare of the English media, new Chelsea manager Jose Mourinho gave a typically polished performance, christening himself as the 'special one'.*

OPPOSITE PAGE: *Possessing strength, confidence and a dominant command of his area, Petr Cech developed into the Premiership's most consistent goalkeeper after joining Chelsea.*

# TRANSFER TALES

Following his heroics for England at Euro 2004, Wayne Rooney was snapped up by Manchester United and became the world's most expensive teenager following a £27m deal. United also added Argentine defender Gabriel Heinze and Leeds striker Alan Smith.

Liverpool, who sold England striker Michael Owen to Real Madrid, brought in the likes of Xabi Alonso, Luis Garcia and Djibril Cisse. Also leaving Anfield was England striker Emile Heskey, who joined Birmingham for £6.75m.

Jose Mourinho wasted little time putting his stamp on the Chelsea squad, spending heavily on Ivory Coast striker Didier Drogba, flying Dutch winger Arjen Robben, Serbian striker Mateja Kezman and the Portuguese trio of Ricardo Carvalho, Tiago and Paulo Ferreira. Czech Republic goalkeeper Petr Cech also arrived at Stamford Bridge.

A number of more experienced performers departed Stamford Bridge, including Jimmy Floyd Hasselbaink and Boudewijn Zenden, who both joined Middlesbrough. The Teesiders also added Barcelona's Michael Reiziger and Arsenal's Ray Parlour on free transfers and invested £4.5m in Leeds striker Mark Viduka.

The purge of talent departing Elland Road continued as James Milner left for Newcastle, Dominic Matteo signed for Blackburn and goalkeeper Paul Robinson joined Tottenham. Spurs also added Michael Carrick and Pedro Mendes, while across North London, Arsenal brought in Dutch forward Robin van Persie from Feyenoord.

Newcastle acquired French defender Jean-Alain Boumsong from Rangers for £8m, England midfielder Nicky Butt from Manchester United, Tottenham right-back Stephen Carr and Netherlands international striker Patrick Kluivert. Everton's most significant piece of pre-season business was the addition of Millwall's Tim Cahill, but the Toffees invested £6m in James Beattie during the season.

## BIGGEST TRANSFERS

**WAYNE ROONEY** – from Everton to Manchester United – £27m

**DIDIER DROGBA** – from Marseille to Chelsea – £24m

**RICARDO CARVALHO** – from FC Porto to Chelsea – £19.85m

**DJIBRIL CISSE** – from Auxerre to Liverpool – £14m

**PAULO FERREIRA** – from FC Porto to Chelsea – £13.2m

**ARJEN ROBBEN** – from PSV Eindhoven to Chelsea – £12m

**XABI ALONSO** – from Real Sociedad to Liverpool – £10.5m

**JEAN-ALAIN BOUMSONG** – from Rangers to Newcastle – £8m

**TIAGO** – from Benfica to Chelsea – £8m

**PETR CECH** – from Rennes to Chelsea – £7m

**ALAN SMITH** – from Leeds United to Manchester United – £7m

LEFT: *One of the hottest properties in English football, Wayne Rooney was snapped up by Manchester United during the summer. The England international departed Everton in a £27m deal.*

# TALES OF THE TURF

Just a week into the season, Southampton parted company with manager Paul Sturrock and replaced him with Steve Wigley. Chelsea won each of their opening four games, including a 1–0 victory over Manchester United while Arsenal set the all-time record for consecutive unbeaten matches in the top flight after a 3–0 win over Blackburn meant they had completed 43 league games without defeat.

Manchester United struggled to make an impact in the opening weeks, winning just one of their first four fixtures and ending the opening month in ninth place, way behind early pacesetters Chelsea and Arsenal who were level on points at the top of the league.

Despite transforming Newcastle's fortunes during his time in charge, taking the Magpies from relegation candidates to regular performers in European competition, Bobby Robson was surprisingly sacked by the club's board following a slow start to the league campaign. Graeme Souness was named as his replacement after he resigned his post at Blackburn Rovers. The Lancashire club named Wales boss Mark Hughes as their new manager.

Arsenal enjoyed a productive September, picking up maximum points against Fulham and Manchester City as Chelsea recorded consecutive 0–0 draws with Aston Villa and Spurs. The Gunners ended the month two points clear of the Blues with Everton, Bolton and Manchester United completing the top five. Liverpool, struggled to find their feet under Rafa Benitez and suffered early season defeats to Bolton, Manchester United and Chelsea.

October witnessed a highly-anticipated clash between Manchester United and Arsenal at Old Trafford. With the Gunners bidding to negotiate a 50th consecutive league match without defeat, United played with added intensity and desire and eventually won 2–0 thanks to goals from Wayne Rooney and Ruud van Nistelrooy.

The early season managerial changes continued when Gary Megson was dismissed by West Brom and replaced by former Baggies player, Bryan Robson, before Jacques Santini quit his role with Tottenham and was succeeded by Dutchman Martin Jol. Elsewhere, Chelsea striker Adrian Mutu tested positive for cocaine and had his contract cancelled by the club.

Arsenal and Chelsea continued to impress but the surprise package of the campaign was David Moyes' Everton, who occupied third place at the end of October. A 1–1 draw against Crystal Palace saw Arsenal drop down to second as Chelsea topped the table for the first time following a 1–0 victory over Everton.

November featured Sir Alex Ferguson's 1000th match in charge of Manchester United, as the Red Devils defeated Lyon 2–1 in the Champions League. Harry Redknapp walked away from Portsmouth following a disagreement with chairman Milan Mandaric over the appointment of new Director of Football Velimir Zajec. Zajec later succeeded Redknapp in the Pompey dugout.

Chelsea, with powerful striker Didier Drogba beginning to impress, retained top spot at the end of November, securing victories over Fulham and Charlton to open up a five point advantage over Arsenal. Tottenham, who had started well, dropped like a stone and stood just a point clear of the relegation zone.

Southampton sacked Steve Wigley in December after just 14 games at the helm and replaced him with Harry Redknapp, fresh from his departure as manager of Saints' bitter local rivals, Portsmouth. Chelsea's mean defence and ruthless attack returned a total of 13 of the 15 points available during the month to end 2004 eight points clear of

*A big money signing from Marseille, once Didier Drogba adapted to the ferocity of the Premiership he absolutely revelled in it.*

Arsenal. Resurgent Spurs rocketed into the top half of the table, where Charlton, Middlesbrough and Liverpool were all enjoying better fortunes. Bryan Robson's West Brom were bottom at Christmas having recorded just one win and 11 points.

Chelsea hit the headlines for the wrong reasons in February when they were investigated by the Premier League for an alleged illegal approach for Arsenal left-back Ashley Cole. Off the field matters also dominated the agenda at Manchester United, as the club confirmed that US businessman, Malcolm Glazer, had made an £800 million takeover bid.

In March, Kevin Keegan tendered his resignation at Manchester City and Stuart Pearce replaced him as caretaker boss. Chelsea's first league title since 1955 looked imminent as the Blues ended the month 11 points clear of Manchester United with just eight games left. Arsenal, Everton, Bolton and Liverpool were in competition for the Champions League places while Norwich, West Brom and Southampton made up the bottom three.

Newcastle caused a stir in April when teammates Lee Bowyer and Kieron Dyer were sent off for fighting each other during a Premier League contest with Aston Villa. Frenchman Alain Perrin was appointed Portsmouth manager, with Velimir Zajec reverting to his previous role as Director of Football, while Malcolm Glazer made a revised bid to takeover Manchester United based on saddling the club with a little less debt than he'd first outlined.

The final day of April saw Chelsea crowned champions after two Frank Lampard goals were enough to defeat Bolton at the Reebok Stadium. The Blues' inspirational captain John Terry went on to lift the club's first top-flight title for 50 years. A solid defence, protected by the consummate model of a defensive midfielder, Claude Makelele, provided the perfect foundations for the attacking instincts of Lampard, Arjen Robben, Damien Duff and Didier Drogba, as the Blues' combination of power, pace and ruthless determination, allowed them to dominate the division.

Stuart Pearce became Manchester City manager on a permanent basis in May while across Manchester, the Glazer family acquired enough shares to launch a successful takeover bid of United.

## INTERESTING INFO

April saw Everton striker James Vaughan become the youngest ever scorer in the Premier League when he netted against Crystal Palace at the tender age of 16 years and 271 days.

The relegation battle went down to the final day of the season and saw Crystal Palace, who were 10 minutes from safety before Charlton equalised against them, suffer the dreaded drop. Norwich, who were hammered 6–0 at Fulham, were also relegated alongside Southampton, as the Saints' 27-year stay in the top flight came to an end. Bryan Robson's West Brom completed a remarkable recovery after winning their final game against Portsmouth to become the first side in Premier League history to have been placed bottom at Christmas to avoid dropping out of the division.

Arsenal claimed runners-up spot and were joined in the Champions League places by Manchester United and Everton, who under David Moyes exceed all expectations to finish three points ahead of neighbours Liverpool. Bolton and Middlesbrough took the UEFA Cup qualifying spots while Boro sealed seventh place following a dramatic final day clash with Manchester City, which saw Mark Schwarzer save a stoppage time penalty from Robbie Fowler that, if converted, would've seen City take seventh instead.

ABOVE: *Chelsea midfielder Frank Lampard passionately celebrates scoring against Bolton in the game that confirmed the Blues' first Premiership title.*

RIGHT: *Chelsea skipper John Terry holds the Premiership trophy aloft as the Blues celebrate their dominant title success.*

# HONOURS LIST

## FA Barclays Premiership

**CHAMPIONS:** Chelsea

In his first season in English football, Jose Mourinho made quite an impact as his dominant Chelsea lost just one of their 38 games and conceded a Premier League record low of 15 goals.

**RUNNERS-UP:** Arsenal

**RELEGATED:** Crystal Palace, Norwich, Southampton

**TOP GOAL SCORER:** Thierry Henry (25 goals for Arsenal)

SHOOT MAGAZINE
2004–05

*In this season review edition, the successes of English teams was celebrated with a large image of Chelsea captain John Terry lifting the Premiership title emblazoned on the cover. Liverpool's dramatic Champions League glory was also covered as was Arsenal's FA Cup final victory over Manchester United.*

# 2004–05 SEASON TABLE

| | | M | W | D | L | GF | GA | GD | PTS |
|---|---|---|---|---|---|---|---|---|---|
| 1 | Chelsea | 38 | 29 | 8 | 1 | 72 | 15 | +57 | 95 |
| 2 | Arsenal | 38 | 25 | 8 | 5 | 87 | 36 | +51 | 83 |
| 3 | Manchester United | 38 | 22 | 11 | 5 | 58 | 26 | +32 | 77 |
| 4 | Everton | 38 | 18 | 7 | 13 | 45 | 46 | -1 | 61 |
| 5 | Liverpool | 38 | 17 | 7 | 14 | 52 | 41 | +11 | 58 |
| 6 | Bolton Wanderers | 38 | 16 | 10 | 12 | 49 | 44 | +5 | 58 |
| 7 | Middlesbrough | 38 | 14 | 13 | 11 | 53 | 46 | +7 | 55 |
| 8 | Manchester City | 38 | 13 | 13 | 12 | 47 | 39 | +8 | 52 |
| 9 | Tottenham Hotspur | 38 | 14 | 10 | 14 | 47 | 41 | +6 | 52 |
| 10 | Aston Villa | 38 | 12 | 11 | 15 | 45 | 52 | -7 | 47 |
| 11 | Charlton Athletic | 38 | 12 | 10 | 16 | 42 | 58 | -16 | 46 |
| 12 | Birmingham City | 38 | 11 | 12 | 15 | 40 | 46 | -6 | 45 |
| 13 | Fulham | 38 | 12 | 8 | 18 | 52 | 60 | -8 | 44 |
| 14 | Newcastle United | 38 | 10 | 14 | 14 | 47 | 57 | -10 | 44 |
| 15 | Blackburn Rovers | 38 | 9 | 15 | 14 | 32 | 43 | -11 | 42 |
| 16 | Portsmouth | 38 | 10 | 9 | 19 | 43 | 59 | -16 | 39 |
| 17 | West Bromwich Albion | 38 | 6 | 16 | 16 | 36 | 61 | -25 | 34 |
| 18 | Crystal Palace | 38 | 7 | 12 | 19 | 41 | 62 | -21 | 33 |
| 19 | Norwich City | 38 | 7 | 12 | 19 | 42 | 77 | -35 | 33 |
| 20 | Southampton | 38 | 6 | 14 | 18 | 45 | 66 | -21 | 32 |

# PLAYERS OF THE SEASON

**PFA PLAYER OF THE YEAR:** John Terry, Chelsea

**PFA YOUNG PLAYER OF THE YEAR:** Wayne Rooney, Manchester United

**FOOTBALL WRITERS' PLAYER OF THE YEAR:** Frank Lampard, Chelsea

ABOVE: *Young Luton defender Curtis Davies was one of the Hatters' star performers during their League One title winning campaign.*

OPPOSITE PAGE: *One part of a lethal Championship strike partnership, Jason Roberts, who linked up well with Jason Ellington, helped fire Wigan Athletic into the Premiership.*

**CHAMPIONSHIP CHAMPIONS:** Sunderland
**PROMOTED:** Wigan Athletic
**CHAMPIONSHIP PLAY-OFF WINNERS:** West Ham United
**RELEGATED:** Gillingham, Nottingham Forest, Rotherham United
**TOP GOAL SCORER:** Nathan Ellington (24 goals for Wigan Athletic)

Sunderland clinched a return to the top flight as emphatic champions. Mick McCarthy's side returned a total of 97 points to finish seven clear of second placed Wigan. Paul Jewell's Latics reached English football's top tier for the first time in their history to give the former Bradford boss his second promotion to the Premiership in six years. The third promotion place went to Alan Pardew's West Ham who defeated Preston North End in the play-off final courtesy of a single Bobby Zamora goal.

**LEAGUE ONE CHAMPIONS:** Luton Town
**PROMOTED:** Hull City
**LEAGUE ONE PLAY-OFF WINNERS:** Sheffield Wednesday
**RELEGATED:** Torquay United, Wrexham, Peterborough United, Stockport County
**TOP GOAL SCORER:** Stuart Elliot (Hull City) and Dean Windass (Bradford City) – both 27 goals.

Mike Newell led Luton Town to the title as the Hatters won 26 of their 46 games and accumulated 98 points. Peter Taylor secured back to back promotions for Hull City, who finished second, while Paul Sturrock, who arrived at Sheffield Wednesday during the campaign, guided the Owls to play-off final success following a 4–2 victory over Hartlepool after extra time.

*Yeovil Town celebrate another goal during their ultra-successful League Two campaign.*

**LEAGUE TWO CHAMPIONS:** Yeovil Town
**PROMOTED:** Scunthorpe United, Swansea City
**LEAGUE TWO PLAY-OFF WINNERS:** Southend United
**RELEGATED:** Kidderminster Harriers, Cambridge United
**TOP GOAL SCORER:** Phil Jevons (27 goals for Yeovil Town)

Just two years after gaining promotion to the Football League for the first time, Gary Johnson's Yeovil Town stormed to the League Two title thanks to an impressive goal scoring tally of 90. The Glovers finished three points clear of second place Scunthorpe and Swansea in third. Steve Tilson's Southend defeated Lincoln City 2–0 in the play-off final, through extra-time goals from Freddy Eastwood and Duncan Jupp. Cambridge United and Kidderminster Harriers dropped out of the division with the former also going into administration and being docked points.

**FOOTBALL CONFERENCE CHAMPIONS:** Barnet
**PROMOTED:** Carlisle United

Champions Barnet, managed by Paul Fairclough, and play-off winners Carlisle, who defeated Stevenage 1–0 in the final, both made returns to the Football League.

# UP FOR THE CUP

**FA CUP WINNERS:** Arsenal

In a game dominated by Manchester United's talented youngsters, Wayne Rooney and Cristiano Ronaldo, Arsenal came out on top following a penalty shootout. After the game ended 0–0 after extra time, Paul Scholes had his penalty saved by Jens Lehman and Patrick Vieira scored the decisive spot-kick and lifted the trophy in what proved to be his last appearance in an Arsenal shirt.

To reach the final, the Gunners overcame Blackburn 3–0 thanks to goals from Robin van Persie and Robert Pires. It was equally straightforward for Manchester United as they defeated Newcastle 4–0 in a game that featured goals from Ruud van Nistelrooy, Paul Scholes and Cristiano Ronaldo.

Teams making headlines earlier in the competition included Burnley, who knocked out Liverpool; Sheffield United, who defeated Aston Villa and Oldham, who overcame Manchester City.

## LEAGUE (CARLING) CUP WINNERS: Chelsea

Jose Mourinho's first trophy in English football was secured following a thrilling encounter against Liverpool at the Millennium Stadium. Rafa Benitez's Reds took a first minute lead through John Arne Riise before Steven Gerrard headed into his own net to level matters. Mourinho was sent to the stands for his questionable conduct on the touchline before Chelsea scored twice in extra time through Didier Drogba and Mateja Kezman. Antonio Nunez grabbed a late consolation for Liverpool to make the final score 3–2 to the Blues.

Chelsea reached the final following a 2–1 aggregate victory over Manchester United while Liverpool overcame Watford 2–0 thanks to two goals from Steven Gerrard. Earlier in the competition the main talking points were provided by Watford, who knocked out Southampton and Portsmouth; Burnley, who defeated Aston Villa and Crewe, who ended Sunderland's participation in the competition.

## COMMUNITY SHIELD WINNERS: Arsenal

Arsenal claimed the first silverware of the season after overcoming Manchester United 3–1. Adding to Mikael Silvestre's own goal, the Gunners' goal scorers were Gilberto Silva and Jose Antonio Reyes.

## THE FOOTBALL LEAGUE (LDV VANS) TROPHY: Wrexham

Vastly experienced manager Denis Smith led Wrexham to glory following a 2–0 victory over Southend that featured goals from Juan Ugarte and Darren Ferguson.

ABOVE: *Serbian striker Mateja Kezman prods home from close range during Chelsea's 3–2 Carling Cup final victory over Liverpool.*

OPPOSITE PAGE BOTTOM RIGHT: *With what proved to be his last kick in an Arsenal shirt, Gunners captain Patrick Vieira scored the penalty that delivered the FA Cup to the North London club's trophy cabinet.*

## INTO EUROPE

### European Champions League

The standout performers in 2004–05 were Liverpool, who shocked European football to the lift the Champions League trophy. Inspired by the tactical nous of Rafael Benitez, some fantastic team spirit and a little bit of luck along the way, the Reds completed the most unlikely of their five European crowns in the most dramatic of circumstances. It all began in the group stages when they were on the verge of going out of the competition in their final match against Greek side Olympiakos. Losing 1–0 at half-time, the Reds needed to score three goals without reply to go through. Florent Sinama Pongolle levelled, before Neil Mellor and then Steven Gerrard, both scored in the last ten minutes. Gerrard's thunderous long-range strike came with just four minutes remaining.

ABOVE: *Liverpool's Xabi Alonso forces the ball home after his penalty had been saved by AC Milan's Dida, to bring the Reds within one goal of the Italians.*

Liverpool defeated Bayer Leverkusen 6–2 on aggregate in the last 16 before grabbing a hard fought 2–1 quarter-final first leg win over Juventus through goals from Sami Hyypia and Luis Garcia. The Reds were paired with Chelsea in the semi-final in a tie settled by a single moment of controversy. With the first leg at Stamford Bridge drawn 0–0, the deadlock was broken inside the opening five minutes during the corresponding clash at Anfield when Luis Garcia prodded the ball towards the goal. As Chelsea defender William Gallas raced back towards his goal. It was unclear whether his attempted clearance was enough to stop the ball crossing the line, but the officials were certain and awarded what Jose Mourinho later described as a 'ghost goal' to the hosts, who progressed into the final.

BELOW: *Chelsea's William Gallas desperately tries to prevent Luis Garcia's effort from entering the Anfield net. However, the goal was awarded and helped Liverpool advance to the Champions League final at the expense of the Blues.*

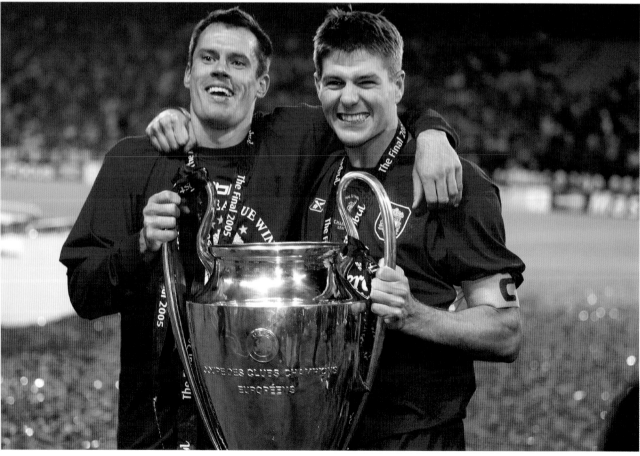

Playing in their first European Cup final since 1985, Liverpool were paired with the multi-talented AC Milan in Istanbul. The Italian side, filled with big name performers, stormed into a 3–0 lead before half-time. However, Liverpool were transformed after the interval and got back into the game when Steven Gerrard looped a header home in the 54th minute. The Reds scored again two minutes later through Vladimir Smicer before Xabi Alonso levelled the scores at 3–3 after an hour.

The game went into extra time with AC Milan and Andrei Shevchenko in particular coming close to regaining the lead but they found Liverpool defender Jamie Carragher and goalkeeper Jerzy Dudek in inspired form. The Polish stopper maintained those heroics in the penalty shootout when he saved from Serginho, Andrea Pirlo and the crucial kick from Shevchenko. Liverpool scored through Dietmar Hamann, Djibril Cisse and Vladimir Smicer to win the shootout 3–2 and lift the trophy.

Semi-finalists Chelsea overcame the likes of Barcelona and Bayern Munich before being knocked out by Liverpool, while Arsenal and Manchester United crashed out in the first knockout round.

## UEFA Cup

The tournament underwent a revamp with a group stage brought in after the first round of knockout ties. Championship Millwall crashed out before that stage, losing 4–2 on aggregate to Hungarian side Ferencvaros. The North East pair of Middlesbrough and Newcastle both stormed to the top of their groups, with the Magpies finishing above the likes of Sochaux and Sporting Lisbon, and Boro overcoming Lazio and Valencia.

In the next set of knockout games, Middlesbrough defeated Austria's Grazer AK 4–3 on aggregate while Newcastle beat Heerenveen by the same scoreline. Inspired by the goal-scoring exploits of Alan Shearer, who ended as the competition's top scorer with 11, the Magpies then hammered Olympiakos 7–1 in the last 16 but Boro faltered, losing 4–2 to Sporting Lisbon. The Portuguese side then accounted for Newcastle by the same scoreline in the quarter-finals.

# THE INTERNATIONAL SCENE

Given a favourable qualifying draw for the 2006 World Cup, England began their campaign with victories over Poland, Wales, Azerbaijan and Northern Ireland and also recorded friendly victories over the USA and Colombia.

OPPOSITE PAGE TOP:
*Liverpool goalkeeper Jerzy Dudek performed heroics during the penalty shootout to help the Reds lift their fifth European Cup.*

OPPOSITE PAGE BOTTOM:
*Local lads, Jamie Carragher (left) and Steven Gerrard, who both performed admirably during the final, celebrate Liverpool's Champions League success.*

# LONDON'S NOUVEAU RICHE CONTINUE TO DOMINATE

**C**helsea's purposeful title winning campaign highlighted the London club's statement of intent to be the next team to dominate English football, leaving the Premiership with four powerful clubs capable of challenging for major honours, both at home and abroad.

Before the season began, the Blues were charged with making an illegal approach for Arsenal's Ashley Cole. Chelsea, Cole and manager Jose Mourinho all received significant fines for their behaviour. However, the controversy didn't stop the London club's continued extravagance in the transfer market.

Relegated Southampton made the headlines when they brought in former England Rugby Union World Cup winning coach, Sir Clive Woodward, as the club's Director of Football. With the business aspect of the game becoming more and more crucial and ticket prices continuing to rise, the relationships between the biggest clubs and some of their most loyal supporters became strained. This was emphasised at Manchester United where a group of fans, disgusted and disillusioned by Malcolm Glazer's takeover, set up their own club called FC United of Manchester, which was entered into the second division of the North West Counties Football League.

OPPOSITE PAGE: *Ghanaian midfield maestro Michael Essien added even more strength and power to Chelsea's multi-talented squad. Captured from Lyon during the summer, Essien went on to form an impenetrable partnership with Claude Makelele.*

LEFT: *Pictured after slamming home one of the goals of the season, a blockbusting volley against Newcastle, Wayne Rooney continued to impress in the red of Manchester United and was voted the PFA Young Player of the Year.*

# TRANSFER TALES

Chelsea again broke their transfer record, with the capture of powerful Ghanaian midfielder Michael Essien from Lyon in a £24.4m deal. The Blues also invested heavily in Manchester City winger Shaun Wright-Phillips and Spanish left-back Asier Del Horno but allowed Finnish striker Mikael Forssell to join Birmingham City and Scott Parker to sign for Newcastle.

Graeme Souness' Newcastle also brought in Spanish forward Albert Luque for £9.5m and Turkish midfielder Emre. Meanwhile, Tottenham, who lost striker Freddie Kanoute to Sevilla, boosted their midfield with Newcastle's Jermaine Jenas and the free transfer signing of Edgar Davids.

Sir Alex Ferguson's transformation of Manchester United continued before and during the season as he brought in Dutch goalkeeper Edwin van Der Sar, French full-back Patrice Evra, Serbian centre back Nemanja Vidic and South Korean midfielder, Park Ji-Sung.

One major talent exiting the Premier League was Arsenal's talismanic midfielder Patrick Vieira who joined Juventus for £13.7m. The Gunners made a number of additions, including Belarus winger Alexander Hleb, 16-year-old Southampton forward Theo Walcott, Togolese striker Emmanuel Adebayor and French midfielder Abou Diaby.

The Spanish revolution continued apace at Liverpool with the arrival of goalkeeper Pepe Reina. The Reds also added Chilean winger Mark Gonzalez, Danish defender Daniel Agger and England striker Peter Crouch.

Blackburn brought in Craig Bellamy from Newcastle, while Everton splashed out £5m on Danish defender Per Kroldrup, £3.5m for Manchester United's Phil Neville and also enticed Dutch midfielder Andy van der Meyde.

Bolton continued to attract high-profile names from world football, signing Mexico striker Jared Borgetti and Japan midfielder Hidetoshi Nakata. Aston Villa added Wilfred Bouma and Milan Baros but allowed Darius Vassell to depart for Manchester City, who also paid Heerenveen £6m for Greek striker Georgios Samaras. West Ham acquired Israeli international Yossi Benayoun and Norwich striker Dean Ashton.

# BIGGEST TRANSFERS

**MICHAEL ESSIEN** – from Lyon to Chelsea – £24.4m

**SHAUN WRIGHT-PHILLIPS** – from Manchester City to Chelsea – £21m

**MICHAEL OWEN** – from Real Madrid to Newcastle United – £17m

**ALEXANDER HLEB** – from Stuttgart to Arsenal – £11.2m

**ALBERT LUQUE** – Deportivo La Coruna to Newcastle United – £9.5m

**ASIER DEL HORNO** – from Real Betis to Chelsea – £8m

**YAKUBU** – from Portsmouth to Middlesbrough – £7.5m

**DEAN ASHTON** – from Norwich City to West Ham United – £7.25m

**JERMAINE JENAS** – from Newcastle United to Tottenham Hotspur – £7m

**EMMANUEL ADEBAYOR** – from AS Monaco to Arsenal – £7m

# TALES OF THE TURF

Reigning champions Chelsea began the defence of their title in ominous fashion, winning each of their games in the opening month of the season without conceding a single goal. The Blues defeated Arsenal and Tottenham and once again looked in imperious form. Their surprise early challengers were Manchester City, who won three of their first four fixtures. Newly promoted Sunderland lost each of their first four games and sat bottom of the table. August saw Liverpool claim the UEFA Super Cup following a 3–1 extra-time victory over UEFA Cup winners CSKA Moscow, which was achieved through goals from Djibril Cisse and Luis Garcia.

Chelsea continued their impressive form throughout September, winning each of their three matches. Their closest challengers were surprisingly Bolton and Charlton who were followed by newly promoted West Ham in fourth and Manchester United in fifth.

United, who were still striving for consistency, became the first team to score 1,000 goals in the Premier League. However, the landmark, which was reached when Cristiano Ronaldo converted against Middlesbrough, came in a 4–1 defeat at the Riverside stadium. United and Arsenal found themselves down in sixth and seventh as Chelsea continued to impress and ended the month with 10 wins from their opening 11 games. The Blues' nearest challenge again came from an unexpected party, as Premier League debutants Wigan Athletic sat in second place.

November saw Manchester United end Chelsea's run of 41 Premier League games without defeat after Darren Fletcher's header secured a 1–0 victory at Old Trafford. The winner left the Red Devils as Chelsea's nearest challengers but they were still 10 points behind the Blues. A few weeks later, United club captain Roy Keane brought an end to 12 trophy-laden years at Old Trafford. The Irishman left the club by mutual consent after his relationship with manager Alex Ferguson became severely fractured.

Alain Perrin became the first managerial casualty of the season when he was sacked by Portsmouth after just eight months at the helm. Sunderland ended the month rooted to the bottom of the table having recorded just a single win and a paltry tally of five points.

The Premiership's dominant midfield force for over a decade and one of the most consistently excellent performers in Manchester United's history, Roy Keane departed the Red Devils in controversial circumstances during the opening months of the season.

## INTERESTING INFO

The 2005–06 campaign saw Thierry Henry collect the Football Writers' Player of the Year award for a record third time.

At the beginning of December the managerial vacancy at Portsmouth was filled by a familiar face as Harry Redknapp returned to the club after resigning his post with their Hampshire rivals Southampton. Chelsea ended 2005 top of the pile, boasting an 11-point lead over Manchester United. Liverpool sat in third, while Spurs and Wigan completed the top five.

It was a case of New Year, same old Chelsea, as Jose Mourinho's men increased their advantage at the top of the table to 14 points. The Blues recorded away victories at West Ham and Sunderland but were held at home by Charlton.

Graeme Souness was sacked by Newcastle in February with the caretaker managerial team of Glenn Roeder and Alan Shearer taking temporary charge. Shearer became the club's record goal scorer when he netted his 201st goal for the Magpies during a 2–0 victory over Portsmouth. The club captain beat a record held by Jackie Milburn that had stood for 49 years.

Chelsea showed they were fallible when they were defeated 3–0 by Middlesbrough. Boro's goals came from Fabio Rochemback, Stewart Downing and Yakubu. It was the first time the Blues had lost by more than a single goal under the guidance of Jose Mourinho.

Sunderland sacked manager Mick McCarthy in March after his side returned just 10 points from 28 matches. Kevin Ball was named caretaker boss until the end of the season. Five wins on the bounce allowed Manchester United to reduce Chelsea's lead at the top to nine points as Liverpool, Tottenham, Blackburn and Arsenal competed to finish in the top four.

Sunderland became the first team to be relegated on April 14th following a 0–0 draw against Manchester United at Old Trafford, which also dented the host's slim title hopes. The Black Cats then played host to Alan Shearer's last competitive fixture as a professional footballer, when he was injured in a Premier League clash at the Stadium of Light. Fittingly, the former England captain also marked the occasion with a goal.

RIGHT: *Converted from a creative free spirit into an effective, more disciplined wide midfielder by Jose Mourinho, Joe Cole enjoyed some of the best form of his career during the 2005–06 season and grabbed several crucial goals.*

Towards the end of the month, Chelsea hosted Manchester United knowing that victory would secure their second successive title. The Blues claimed maximum points in style, defeating Sir Alex Ferguson's side 3–0 thanks to goals from defenders William Gallas and Ricardo Carvalho and a beautiful piece of individual brilliance from Joe Cole.

On the same day, West Brom's relegation from the top flight was confirmed after Portsmouth grabbed a 2–1 win at Wigan. A 0–0 draw with Newcastle also sealed Birmingham's fate, as the Blues dropped into the second tier once more. Long-serving Charlton boss Alan Curbishley announced he would resign from the club at the end of the season, bringing to an end an extremely successful 15 years at The Valley.

The season ended with Manchester United as runners-up to Chelsea and Liverpool in third. The final Champions League place was decided on the last day of the season, with both Spurs and Arsenal in contention. Tottenham were in pole position going into their clash with West Ham, knowing all they needed was to better Arsenal's result.

BELOW: *England striker Jermain Defoe battles for possession as part of an under the weather Tottenham team that saw their Champions League qualification dreams shattered following a final day defeat to West Ham United.*

ABOVE: *Arsenal fans salute Thierry Henry during the Gunners' last ever game at Highbury. The Frenchman was again the difference as his goals inspired the North London club to a crucial 4–2 victory over Wigan which cemented a fourth place finish.*

In the build up to their contest at Upton Park, Tottenham's preparations were thrown into chaos when several players were hit by a stomach virus which was believed to have occurred through food poisoning. Manager Martin Jol struggled to field 11 players, with many of his side playing despite feeling unwell. A jaded Spurs went on to lose the game 2–1, as a Thierry Henry-inspired Arsenal defeated Wigan 4–2 to pip their rivals to fourth place and ensure the final game at Highbury, their home stadium since 1913, ended on a successful note.

# HONOURS LIST

## FA Barclays Premiership

**CHAMPIONS:** Chelsea

Jose Mourinho's men claimed back to back titles at a canter, accumulating 91 points and conceding just 22 goals.

**RUNNERS-UP:** Manchester United

**RELEGATED:** Birmingham City, West Bromwich Albion, Sunderland

**TOP GOAL SCORER:** Thierry Henry (27 goals for Arsenal)

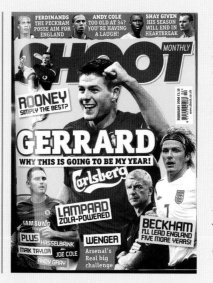

SHOOT MAGAZINE
2005–06

A revamped front cover previewed an interview with Liverpool star Steven Gerrard which forecasted a successful season for the Reds. With more than one image now featuring prominently, new Manchester United signing Wayne Rooney was also featured, as was Chelsea midfielder Frank Lampard, Arsenal manager Arsene Wenger and England captain David Beckham.

# 2005–06 SEASON TABLE

|  |  | M | W | D | L | GF | GA | GD | PTS |
|---|---|---|---|---|---|---|---|---|---|
| 1 | Chelsea | 38 | 29 | 4 | 5 | 72 | 22 | +50 | 91 |
| 2 | Manchester United | 38 | 25 | 8 | 5 | 72 | 34 | +38 | 83 |
| 3 | Liverpool | 38 | 25 | 7 | 6 | 57 | 25 | +32 | 82 |
| 4 | Arsenal | 38 | 20 | 7 | 11 | 68 | 31 | +37 | 67 |
| 5 | Tottenham Hotspur | 38 | 18 | 11 | 9 | 53 | 38 | +15 | 65 |
| 6 | Blackburn Rovers | 38 | 19 | 6 | 13 | 51 | 42 | +9 | 63 |
| 7 | Newcastle United | 38 | 17 | 7 | 14 | 47 | 42 | +5 | 58 |
| 8 | Bolton Wanderers | 38 | 15 | 11 | 12 | 49 | 41 | +8 | 56 |
| 9 | West Ham United | 38 | 16 | 7 | 15 | 52 | 55 | -3 | 55 |
| 10 | Wigan Athletic | 38 | 15 | 6 | 17 | 45 | 52 | -7 | 51 |
| 11 | Everton | 38 | 14 | 8 | 16 | 34 | 49 | -15 | 50 |
| 12 | Fulham | 38 | 14 | 6 | 18 | 48 | 58 | -10 | 48 |
| 13 | Charlton Athletic | 38 | 13 | 8 | 17 | 41 | 55 | -14 | 47 |
| 14 | Middlesbrough | 38 | 12 | 9 | 17 | 48 | 58 | -10 | 45 |
| 15 | Manchester City | 38 | 13 | 4 | 21 | 43 | 48 | -5 | 43 |
| 16 | Aston Villa | 38 | 10 | 12 | 16 | 42 | 55 | -13 | 42 |
| 17 | Portsmouth | 38 | 10 | 8 | 20 | 37 | 62 | -25 | 38 |
| 18 | Birmingham City | 38 | 8 | 10 | 20 | 28 | 50 | -22 | 34 |
| 19 | West Bromwich Albion | 38 | 7 | 9 | 22 | 31 | 58 | -27 | 30 |
| 20 | Sunderland | 38 | 3 | 6 | 29 | 26 | 69 | -43 | 15 |

# PLAYERS OF THE SEASON

**PFA PLAYER OF THE YEAR:** Steven Gerrard, Liverpool

**PFA YOUNG PLAYER OF THE YEAR:** Wayne Rooney, Manchester United

**FOOTBALL WRITERS' PLAYER OF THE YEAR:** Thierry Henry, Arsenal

**FOOTBALL LEAGUE CHAMPIONSHIP CHAMPIONS:**
Reading
**PROMOTED:** Sheffield United
**CHAMPIONSHIP PLAY-OFF WINNERS:** Watford
**RELEGATED:** Crewe Alexandra, Millwall, Brighton &
Hove Albion
**TOP GOAL SCORER:** Marlon King (21 goals for
Watford)

Steve Coppell's Reading reached the Premier
League in some style. The Royals topped the
table with a record 106 points and sealed the title
as early as April 1st. Second place and automatic
promotion went to Neil Warnock's Sheffield United.
Ady Boothroyd's unfancied Watford took the third
promotion place, defeating Leeds United 3–0 in the
play-off final.

**LEAGUE ONE CHAMPIONS:** Southend United
**PROMOTED:** Colchester United
**LEAGUE ONE PLAY-OFF WINNERS:** Barnsley
**RELEGATED:** Hartlepool United, MK Dons, Swindon
Town, Walsall
**TOP GOAL SCORER:** Billy Sharp (Scunthorpe United)
and Freddy Eastwood (Southend United) – both 23
goals

Andy Tilson's Southend United claimed the title and
a second successive promotion to ensure a return to
the second tier for the first time in nearly a decade.
In second place was another Essex-based club,
Colchester United, who reached the Championship
for the first time in their history, under the guidance
of Phil Parkinson. Andy Ritchie's Barnsley defeated
Swansea City 4–3 on penalties in the play-off final.

### ⚽ INTERESTING INFO

Swindon's 2006 relegation to League Two saw them
become the first club that had played in the Premier League
to have dropped down to English football's fourth tier.

ABOVE TOP: *Steve Coppell, backed by his Reading players, takes to the Walkers
Stadium pitch to accept the adulation of Royals supporters after the Berkshire
club lifted the Championship title to reach the Premiership for the first time.*

ABOVE BOTTOM: *Consistent striker Freddie Eastwood was League One's joint
leading marksman alongside Scunthorpe United's Billy Sharp.*

**LEAGUE TWO CHAMPIONS:** Carlisle United
**PROMOTED:** Northampton Town, Leyton Orient
**LEAGUE TWO PLAY-OFF WINNERS:** Cheltenham Town
**RELEGATED:** Oxford United, Rushden & Diamonds
**TOP GOAL SCORER:** Rickie Lambert (22 goals for Rochdale)

Carlisle United, managed by Paul Simpson, completed back-to-back promotions after lifting the League Two title just two years after their relegation from the Football League. Finishing three points off the pace in second were John Gorman's Northampton Town, who finished a couple of points clear of third placed Leyton Orient. Cheltenham Town defeated Grimsby Town 1–0 in the play-offs, thanks to a Steve Guinan goal. Oxford United dropped out of the Football League for the first time in 44 years and were joined in the Conference by Rushden & Diamonds.

LEFT: *Veteran Hereford United manager Graham Turner took the Bulls back into the Football League following Conference play-off success.*

## ⚽ INTERESTING INFO

By losing 3–1 to Grimsby in the play-off semi-finals, Lincoln City became the first club to have experienced disappointment in four consecutive play-off competitions.

**FOOTBALL CONFERENCE CHAMPIONS:** Accrington Stanley
**PROMOTED:** Hereford United

John Coleman's Accrington Stanley won the Conference title enabling the reincarnation of the club that previously competed in the Football League to rejoin the fourth tier for the first time in 44 years. Graham Turner's Hereford United defeated Halifax Town 3–2 after extra time in the play-off final.

# UP FOR THE CUP

### FA CUP WINNERS: Liverpool

The Reds defeated West Ham on penalties in the 125th FA Cup final following a topsy-turvy encounter. West Ham, managed by Alan Pardew, took an early lead after Jamie Carragher put through his own goal. The Hammers then doubled their advantage following a smart finish from Dean Ashton before Djibril Cisse and Steven Gerrard levelled matters for Liverpool. The balance tipped back in West Ham's favour when Paul Konchesky's cross looped over Pepe Reina and into the net. As the game ticked into stoppage time, the Merseysiders were rescued by the talismanic Gerrard once again as he let fly from 30 yards with a powerful half-volley that flew past Shaka Hislop. After 30 minutes of extra time ended goalless, Liverpool won 3–1 on penalties with Reina saving from Anton Ferdinand to settle the contest.

The Reds reached the final following a 2–1 victory over Chelsea that featured goals from John Arne Riise and Blues' nemesis Luis Garcia while West Ham overcame Middlesbrough 1–0 thanks to Marlon Harewood's second-half strike.

The headline makers in the early rounds of the tournament were Conference side Burton Albion, managed by Nigel Clough, who held Manchester United to 0–0 draw earned a lucrative replay at Old Trafford. Other shock results included Colchester United's victories over Sheffield United and Derby County; Brentford's win against Sunderland; Bolton's triumph over Arsenal and Leyton Orient knocking out Premiership Fulham.

### LEAGUE (CARLING) CUP WINNERS: Manchester United

Manchester United claimed their first major trophy for two years following a 4–0 victory over Paul Jewell's Wigan Athletic at the Millennium Stadium. United's emerging team provided a glimpse of future glories as two well taken goals from Wayne Rooney were accompanied by single strikes from Louis Saha and Cristiano Ronaldo.

United progressed to the final following a 3–1 aggregate victory over Blackburn, thanks to two goals from Saha and one from Ruud van Nistelrooy, while Wigan got the better of Arsenal after a Jason Roberts 'away' goal after the scores ended level at 2–2.

OPPOSITE PAGE BOTTOM: *Liverpool striker Djibril Cisse volleys home to claw the Reds back into contention during the 2006 FA Cup final.*

ABOVE TOP: *Steven Gerrard, who produced two moments of match-winning brilliance against West Ham in the final, lifts the FA Cup with Reds manager Rafael Benitez.*

ABOVE BOTTOM: *Louis Saha is mobbed by his Manchester United colleagues after finding the net against Wigan during the Red Devils' League Cup final victory.*

Noteworthy moments earlier in the tournament included Doncaster Rovers knocking out Manchester City and Aston Villa and taking Arsenal to penalties in the quarter-finals, before losing 3–1 on spot kicks, Crystal Palace defeating Liverpool, Charlton overcoming holders Chelsea on penalties at Stamford Bridge and Grimsby Town ending Tottenham's progress in the competition.

### COMMUNITY SHIELD WINNERS: Chelsea

The Blues beat Arsenal 2–1 in Cardiff after Didier Drogba scored both goals. Arsenal's response came from Cesc Fabregas.

### THE FOOTBALL LEAGUE (LDV VANS) TROPHY: Swansea City

The Welsh club, managed by Kenny Jackett, defeated Carlisle United 2–1 thanks to goals from Lee Trundle and Adebayo Akinfenwa.

# INTO EUROPE

## European Champions League

With five teams participating in the competition, including reigning champions Liverpool, the Premiership strength was evident to the whole of Europe. The standout performers were Arsenal who progressed to the final after achieving a host of memorable results.

On their way to the Paris showpiece, Arsenal recorded an impressive 1–0 aggregate victory over Real Madrid thanks to a typically clinical finish from Thierry Henry. The Gunners then ousted Juventus in the quarter-final thanks to goals from Henry and Cesc Fabregas, and overcame Villarreal in the semi-final following a solitary goal from Kolo Toure and a key penalty save from goalkeeper Jens Lehman.

The final was transformed in the 18th minute when Arsenal stopper Jens Lehman surged off his line to close down Samuel Eto'o but caused the Barcelona striker to topple to the ground. Despite Ludovic Giuly placing the ball into an empty net, a free-kick outside the area was awarded and Lehman was given his marching orders. The resulting free kick wasn't converted but Arsenal remained a goal behind, a man light and shorn of one of their most dangerous attacking talents – Robert Pires – who had been sacrificed to make way for substitute goalkeeper Manuel Almunia. The Gunners showed great character to take the lead before half-time when Sol Campbell leapt highest and headed home Henry's free-kick.

Arsenal continued to battle and despite Barcelona dominating possession, it took until the 76th minute for the Gunners defence to be breached when Samuel Eto'o scored from close range. The Catalan club continued to press and just five minutes later Brazilian right-back Juliano Belletti was the unlikely hero when he drove the ball home following Henrik Larsson's clever pass.

Of the other English teams, Liverpool and Chelsea exited in the last 16, with the Reds losing 3–0 to Benfica and the Blues suffering a 3–2 defeat to Barcelona. Manchester United suffered their worst Champions League campaign under Sir Alex Ferguson, finishing bottom of a group that also contained Benfica, Villarreal and Lille. Everton's progress in the competition was ended before the group stages even began, as David Moyes' men were beaten 4–2 on aggregate by Villarreal in the third qualifying round.

ABOVE TOP LEFT: *England defender Sol Campbell gives 10-man Arsenal a surprise 1–0 lead against Barcelona in the Gunners' first ever European Cup final appearance.*

ABOVE TOP RIGHT: *Arsenal keeper Jens Lehman cuts a forlorn figure following his early dismissal against Barcelona in the Champions League final.*

## UEFA Cup

Steve McClaren's Middlesbrough progressed all the way to the final of the UEFA Cup. Boro met a Sevilla side on top of their game in final, which was held in Eindhoven, and eventually lost 4–0 with the Spanish side's goals coming from Luis Fabiano, Maresca and former West Ham and Spurs striker Freddie Kanoute.

Middlesbrough's progress to the final had been memorable and included a couple of last gasp victories. The League Cup winners successfully negotiated a first round tie against Skoda Xanthi of Greece before finishing top of a group that contained AZ Alkmaar, Litex Lovech, Dnipro Dnipropetrovsk and Grasshopper Zurich. In the knockout stages Boro knocked out VfB Stuttgart and Roma on away goals.

In the quarter-final against FC Basel, McClaren's men left it late to seal their progress. Trailing 2–0 from the first leg, Boro went further behind when Eduardo scored what seemed to be a crucial away goal. However, a Mark Viduka brace put Boro back in contention before Jimmy Floyd Hasselbaink made it 3–3 on aggregate. The English club were still crashing out until Massimo Maccarone slid home the winning goal in the last minute to complete a remarkable comeback.

Buoyed by that performance, Middlesbrough weren't intimidated in the semi-final when they trailed Steaua Bucharest by a single goal following the first leg and went on to win the tie 4–2 thanks to two more goals from Maccarone and single strikes from Viduka and Chris Riggott. The final proved a step too far for Boro but Steve McClaren, who led the team for the last time during the showpiece before starting his new role as England manager, had helped place the club firmly on the European football map.

BELOW: *Middlesbrough boss Steve McClaren says goodbye to supporters following his team's UEFA Cup final loss to Sevilla. McClaren departed his role to succeed Sven-Goran Eriksson as England manager.*

OVERLEAF: *Middlesbrough striker Massimo Maccarone celebrates another crucial, last-gasp goal during the Teesside club's dramatic UEFA Cup campaign.*

# THE INTERNATIONAL SCENE

England once again achieved qualification for a major tournament under Sven-Goran Eriksson, reaching the 2006 World Cup. At the tournament England defeated Paraguay and Trinidad and Tobago, and drew with Sweden to ensure qualification into the knockout stages. A 1–0 victory over Ecuador, achieved through a long-range David Beckham free-kick, set up a quarter-final clash with Portugal. 120 minutes of goalless action followed, as England, hampered by Wayne Rooney's red card, battled bravely, with the ubiquitous Owen Hargreaves in particularly impressive form.

Following Rooney's dismissal, his club colleague and Portugal's star man, Cristiano Ronaldo, was seen to wink at the bench, signalling that his team's perceived attempts at winding Rooney up had proved successful. England took the game to penalties, but their deficiencies from 12 yards once again reared their ugly head, as Frank Lampard, Steven Gerrard and Jamie Carragher all missed their kicks, allowing Ronaldo to score the winner and send England home.

BELOW: *Wayne Rooney is incensed by the behaviour of Manchester United club-mate Cristiano Ronaldo in the build up to the England striker's red card against Portugal at the 2006 World Cup.*

# CHAPTER 15 // 2006–07

# R AND R
# REVITALISE UNITED

Ahead of the new season much of the paper talk was about Cristiano Ronaldo's return to Old Trafford following his highly publicised involvement with Wayne Rooney's sending off during the World Cup. Saddled with the pantomime villain label that always proved popular with the tabloid press following an England World Cup disaster, the Portuguese winger was prepared for a rocky ride from opposing fans throughout the campaign. Observers speculated about how his relationship with Rooney would be affected, but as the competitive action got under way it was abundantly clear that both men were on the same page and intent on taking their performances to another level.

New consortiums took over at both Southampton and Sunderland during the summer, with former Black Cats striker Niall Quinn leading the group that assumed full control at the Stadium of Light. It signified the growing trend of clubs at all levels attempting to get their finances in order to compete at the highest level and capitalise upon the growing riches the English game had to offer.

Before the season began, David O'Leary's tenure at Aston Villa came to an end when he was replaced by former Leicester City and Celtic manager Martin O'Neill. The man chosen to follow the long-serving Alan Curbishley at Charlton was former Crystal Palace boss Iain Dowie

OPPOSITE PAGE: *Wayne Rooney heads towards the Manchester United fans to celebrate after scoring a critical title-chasing goal against his former club Everton at Goodison Park.*

LEFT: *The hand of friendship. Wayne Rooney and Cristiano Ronaldo celebrate another goal as Manchester United tear into Fulham on the opening day of the season and dispel any myths of a rift between the hugely talented pair.*

# TRANSFER TALES

Chelsea again broke their transfer record to acquire AC Milan striker Andrei Shevchenko for £30m, but the biggest transfer story of the season emerged on the eve of the August transfer window when two high-profile Argentina internationals, Carlos Tevez and Javier Mascherano, were amazingly signed by West Ham United from Brazilian side Corinthians.

The deals represented somewhat of a coup for the Hammers. The transfer fees were undisclosed as was the controversial nature of the deals. During the season it became clear that third party ownership issues put the validity of both players' time at the club in doubt.

As well as bringing in Shevchenko, Chelsea also splashed the cash on Ivory Coast forward Salomon Kalou and Dutch defender Khalid Boulahrouz. The Blues also completed the protracted signing of Ashley Cole from Arsenal, but arguably Jose Mourinho's best addition came in the shape of German international midfielder Michael Ballack on a free transfer.

Manchester United invested heavily in the composure and vision of Spurs midfielder Michael Carrick but allowed striker Ruud van Nistelrooy to leave Old Trafford for Real Madrid. Halfway through the campaign, the Red Devils added to their attacking ranks with the short-term loan signing of veteran Swedish striker Henrik Larsson.

Arsenal brought in Czech midfielder Tomas Rosicky from Borussia Dortmund, Chelsea defender William Gallas and completed the season-long loan of Julio Baptista from Real Madrid; allowing Jose Antonio Reyes to move in the opposite direction.

Tottenham completed the £10.9m signing of classy Bulgarian forward Dimitar Berbatov and also brought in Ivorian midfielder Didier Zokora, Pascal Chimbonda from Wigan, Steed Malbranque from Fulham and Egyptian striker Mido.

Liverpool signed Dutch striker Dirk Kuyt for £9m and also spent heavily on Craig Bellamy and Jermaine Pennant. Across Merseyside, Everton signed Crystal Palace striker Andrew Johnson and Wolves defender Joleon Lescott, while Bolton broke their transfer record to bring in Nicolas Anelka.

Harry Redknapp's Portsmouth were very active in the market, adding quality and experience in the shape of Sol Campbell, Nwankwo Kanu, David James, David Thompson, Niko Kranjcar and Andy Cole.

*West Ham United caused a global sensation when they completed deals for the Argentine pair of Carlos Tevez and Javier Mascherano. Tevez went on to save the Hammers' season but the manner of both transfers would later see the club challenged in the courts.*

## BIGGEST TRANSFERS

**ANDREI SHEVCHENKO** – from AC Milan to Chelsea – £30m

**MICHAEL CARRICK** – from Tottenham Hotspur to Manchester United – £18.6m

**DIMITAR BERBATOV** – from Bayer Leverkusen to Tottenham Hotspur – £10.9m

**OBAFEMI MARTINS** – from Inter Milan to Newcastle United – £10.1m

**DIRK KUYT** – from Feyenoord to Liverpool – £10m

**ASHLEY YOUNG** – from Watford to Aston Villa – £9.65m

**ANDY JOHNSON** – from Crystal Palace to Everton – £8.6m

**DIDIER ZOKORA** – from Saint-Etienne to Tottenham Hotspur – £8.2m

**NICOLAS ANELKA** – from Fenerbahce to Bolton Wanders – £8m

**SALOMON KALOU** – from Feyenoord to Chelsea – £8m

## TALES OF THE TURF

Newly promoted Sheffield United achieved a credible opening day draw with Liverpool at Brammall Lane while Manchester United enjoyed an explosive start to the campaign, defeating Fulham 5–1 in a game that featured goals and superb performances from both Wayne Rooney and Cristiano Ronaldo.

Manchester United's impressive start continued with a 3–0 victory at Charlton which featured Ole Gunnar Solskjaer's first goal following three injury blighted years. The Red Devils ended August at the top of the table, after winning three of their opening four games.

Another high-profile takeover took place in the Premiership when Aston Villa were acquired by American businessman Randy Lerner, who succeeded the long-serving Doug Ellis as chairman.

A return to form for Chelsea featured wins against Liverpool and Fulham and saw them top the table at the end of September. Surprise package Bolton, inspired by the goals of Nicolas Anelka, were two points behind in second. A home defeat against Arsenal and 1–1 draw at a plucky Reading side, slowed Manchester United's progress.

Reading, who started the season in great form, hit the headlines in October following a bruising clash with Chelsea that saw two Blues goalkeepers, Petr Cech and Carlo Cuidicini, receive head injuries. Cech's, sustained during an awkward clash with Stephen Hunt's knee, was the most severe and saw him undergo surgery for a depressed skull fracture. The giant stopper was later ruled out for the rest of the season.

Aston Villa, the division's last unbeaten side, suffered defeat in October, losing 3–1 to Liverpool at Anfield. A resurgent Manchester United enjoyed a 2–0 victory over Liverpool and a 4–0 win against Bolton and returned to the top of the table, edging out Chelsea on goal difference.

ABOVE: *Chelsea again splashed the cash ahead of the new campaign, parting with £30m to sign AC Milan striker Andrei Shevchenko. However, the Ukrainian struggled to live up to the expectations placed on his shoulders.*

A Premier League all-time record attendance was set in March when Manchester United hosted Blackburn Rovers at Old Trafford in front of 76,098 supporters.

November brought another change of ownership when West Ham United were bought by Icelandic businessman Eggert Magnusson's for £85m. With the Hammers struggling at the wrong end of the table it wasn't long before the new regime lost patience with Alan Pardew, showing him the exit door and appointing former Charlton boss Alan Curbishley. Curbishley's former club brought an end to Iain Dowie's time at the Valley, replacing him with his assistant Les Reed.

The top two met in a tight encounter that ended in a 1–1 draw after Ricardo Carvalho equalised Louis Saha's opener. The results left United three points clear of Chelsea with Harry Redknapp's improving Portsmouth 11 off the pace in third.

The 15,000th goal in Premier League history was scored in December when Fulham's Moritz Volz netted against Chelsea in a game that ended 2–2 and saw the Blues lose further ground on Manchester United. The Red Devils enjoyed a productive festive period, defeating Aston Villa, Wigan and Reading, after suffering a shock 1–0 loss at West Ham while Chelsea stumbled to three successive draws. The year ended with Sir Alex Ferguson's team six points clear of their nearest challengers.

Watford remained firmly in the relegation picture as did West Ham, Charlton, Sheffield United, Wigan and Middlesbrough. After just a month in charge, Les Reed paid the price for the team's continued poor form and was replaced by former West Ham manager Alan Pardew.

LEFT TOP: *Following a magical and determined individual run, Cristiano Ronaldo powers home a later winner as Manchester United take a crucial step towards the title.*

LEFT MIDDLE: *Manchester United players celebrate on the Anfield turf after a scarcely deserved smash and grab 1–0 victory against Liverpool, achieved thanks to a late goal from defender John O'Shea.*

LEFT BOTTOM: *Fulham defender Moritz Volz was the surprise scorer of goal number 15,000 in the Premier League when he found the net in a West London derby against Chelsea.*

OPPOSITE PAGE: *Wigan defender David Unsworth slams home a season saving penalty against relegation rivals Sheffield United under intense pressure. The barrel-chested defender knew a converted kick would keep the Latics in the Premiership and condemn his former club to the Championship.*

Despite dropping points at Newcastle and Arsenal, Manchester United remained six points clear of Chelsea at the end of January, as the Blues lost 2–0 at Liverpool. The Reds looked on course for a Champions League finish, largely thanks to the continued good form of Steve Gerrard. In a season filled with boardroom change, February saw American businessmen George Gillett and Tom Hicks complete their takeover of Liverpool.

Manchester United continued to show great consistency, thumping Spurs 4–0 and returning maximum points against Charlton and, in dramatic fashion, against Fulham when Cristiano Ronaldo scored a magnificent solo goal in the 88th minute to steal the points. Chelsea remained hot on their heels, also winning all three of their league fixtures.

## ⚽ INTERESTING INFO

In the Football League, Stockport County's 3–0 win over Swindon Town in March saw them set a record nine consecutive wins without conceding a goal.

March began with a huge clash between Manchester United and Liverpool at Anfield. The home side dominated possession without looking likely to score but with the match ticking into stoppage time, the unlikely hero was John O'Shea, who prodded home a last gasp winner in front of the Kop to send the United players and fans into delirium.

April began in nervous fashion for Manchester United who suffered a shock 2–1 defeat at Portsmouth when Rio Ferdinand's own goal proved decisive. Chelsea started the month well, recording victories over Tottenham and West Ham. United put the Portsmouth result behind them with a 2–0 home win over Sheffield United before dropping more points in a tense 1–1 draw with Middlesbrough. Their last fixture of the month saw them take a giant leap towards the title. Two goals behind to Everton with an hour played, United came back to win 4–2 thanks to goals from John O'Shea, Wayne Rooney, Chris Eagles and an own goal from Phil Neville.

Ady Boothroyd's Watford became the first side to drop out of the Premier League while lowly Fulham brought an end to Chris Coleman's managerial tenure, replacing him with Northern Ireland boss Lawrie Sanchez. Another managerial change was announced at the end of the month when Sam Allardyce resigned his role at Bolton after seven and a half years in charge. Sammy Lee was promoted from the coaching staff to take over as boss.

May featured a crucial Manchester derby that ended with Manchester United on the verge of being named champions. In a tight and often nasty affair, United ran out 1–0 winners thanks to a successfully converted penalty from Cristiano Ronaldo and Edwin van der Sar's save from Darius Vassell's spotkick. A day later, Chelsea failed to overcome Arsenal in a must-win encounter at the Emirates Stadium. The match ended 1–1 meaning that the Premier League title returned to Manchester for the first time since 2003.

## INTERESTING INFO

Manchester City set the record for lowest number of goals scored at home by a top-flight club when they found the net just 10 times on home soil during the 2006–07 season.

Charlton Athletic became the second team to suffer relegation following a 2–0 loss to Spurs at the Valley. A dramatic final day of the season saw the last two relegation places still up for grabs. West Ham ensured their safety after recording an unlikely 1–0 win against champions Manchester United at Old Trafford, thanks to the in-form Carlos Tevez. The other two clubs fighting for survival, Sheffield United and Wigan, met in a winner-take-all contest at Bramall Lane. Paul Jewell's Latics handled the pressure better with Paul Scharner and David Unsworth, who departed Sheffield United on a free transfer the previous January, scoring the goals in a 2–1 victory that sent the Blades back to the Championship.

Following Sheffield United's relegation, manager Neil Warnock resigned his post. Despite keeping the club in the top flight, Wigan boss Paul Jewell also walked away from his role as manager. He was replaced at the helm by assistant boss Chris Hutchings. Another end of season managerial change came at the City of Manchester Stadium where Stuart Pearce was sacked by Manchester City.

OPPOSITE PAGE: *The key man in West Ham's successful bid for Premiership survival, Carlos Tevez became a talismanic figure for team-mates and supporters and scored a host of match-winning goals in the final weeks of the season.*

BELOW: *Ryan Giggs and Gary Neville lift the Premiership trophy signalling an end to Manchester United's three-season title drought.*

# HONOURS LIST

## FA Barclays Premiership

**CHAMPIONS:** Manchester United
The Premier League trophy was returned to Manchester after a United team inspired by the attacking and big-match winning brilliance of Cristiano Ronaldo raised their game to overcome Chelsea.
**RUNNERS-UP:** Chelsea
**RELEGATED:** Sheffield United, Charlton Athletic, Watford
**TOP GOAL SCORER:** Didier Drogba (20 goals for Chelsea)

SHOOT MAGAZINE
2006–07

*Ahead of the new season, Shoot focused on some of the finest firepower available in the Premiership and interviewed the Tottenham pair of Dimitar Berbatov and Darren Bent, as well as Liverpool front man Peter Crouch. West Ham's Scott Parker also spoke about his England hopes and new Manchester United signing Michael Carrick was quizzed about reclaiming the Premiership title for the Red Devils.*

## 2006–07 SEASON TABLE

|    |                     | M  | W  | D  | L  | GF | GA | GD  | PTS |
|----|---------------------|----|----|----|----|----|----|-----|-----|
| 1  | Manchester United   | 38 | 28 | 5  | 5  | 83 | 27 | +56 | 89  |
| 2  | Chelsea             | 38 | 24 | 11 | 3  | 64 | 24 | +40 | 83  |
| 3  | Liverpool           | 38 | 20 | 8  | 10 | 57 | 27 | +30 | 68  |
| 4  | Arsenal             | 38 | 19 | 11 | 8  | 63 | 35 | +28 | 68  |
| 5  | Tottenham Hotspur   | 38 | 17 | 9  | 12 | 57 | 54 | +3  | 60  |
| 6  | Everton             | 38 | 15 | 13 | 10 | 52 | 36 | +16 | 58  |
| 7  | Bolton Wanderers    | 38 | 16 | 8  | 14 | 47 | 52 | -5  | 56  |
| 8  | Reading             | 38 | 16 | 7  | 15 | 52 | 47 | +5  | 55  |
| 9  | Portsmouth          | 38 | 14 | 12 | 12 | 45 | 42 | +3  | 54  |
| 10 | Blackburn Rovers    | 38 | 15 | 7  | 16 | 52 | 54 | -2  | 52  |
| 11 | Aston Villa         | 38 | 11 | 17 | 10 | 43 | 41 | +2  | 50  |
| 12 | Middlesbrough       | 38 | 12 | 10 | 16 | 44 | 49 | -5  | 46  |
| 13 | Newcastle United    | 38 | 11 | 10 | 17 | 38 | 47 | -9  | 43  |
| 14 | Manchester City     | 38 | 11 | 9  | 18 | 29 | 44 | -15 | 42  |
| 15 | West Ham United     | 38 | 12 | 5  | 21 | 35 | 59 | -24 | 41  |
| 16 | Fulham              | 38 | 8  | 15 | 15 | 38 | 60 | -22 | 39  |
| 17 | Wigan Athletic      | 38 | 10 | 8  | 20 | 37 | 59 | -22 | 38  |
| 18 | Sheffield United    | 38 | 10 | 8  | 20 | 32 | 55 | -23 | 38  |
| 19 | Charlton Athletic   | 38 | 8  | 10 | 20 | 34 | 60 | -26 | 34  |
| 20 | Watford             | 38 | 5  | 13 | 20 | 29 | 59 | -30 | 28  |

## PLAYERS OF THE SEASON

**PFA PLAYER OF THE YEAR:** Cristiano Ronaldo, Manchester United
**PFA YOUNG PLAYER OF THE YEAR:** Cristiano Ronaldo, Manchester United
**FOOTBALL WRITERS' PLAYER OF THE YEAR:** Cristiano Ronaldo, Manchester United

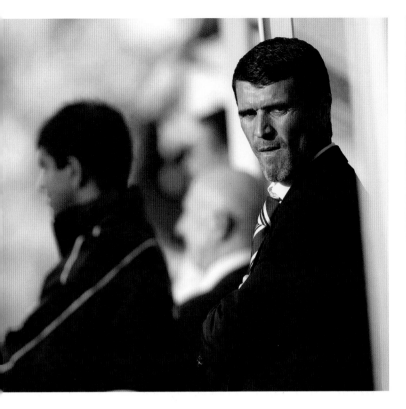

**FOOTBALL LEAGUE CHAMPIONSHIP CHAMPIONS:** Sunderland
**PROMOTED:** Birmingham City
**CHAMPIONSHIP PLAY-OFF WINNERS:** Derby County
**RELEGATED:** Southend United, Luton Town, Leeds United
**TOP GOAL SCORER:** Jamie Cureton (23 goals for Colchester United)

Sunderland enjoyed an amazing change in fortunes following Roy Keane's appointment as manager. After losing their first four matches and appearing primed for a relegation battle, the Black Cats showed a marked improvement under Keane's guidance. Backed by chairman Niall Quinn in the transfer market, Keane built an impressive team that lost just one of their final 20 fixtures to top the table with 88 points.

Steve Bruce's Birmingham City finished two points further back in second place, gaining automatic promotion after just a single season back in the second tier. The third promotion birth was occupied by Billy Davies' Derby County who defeated Tony Mowbray's West Brom 1–0 in the play-off final thanks to close-range winner from Stephen Pearson that was dubbed the '£60m goal' in reference to the estimated value of promotion to the Premier League.

**LEAGUE ONE CHAMPIONS:** Scunthorpe United
**PROMOTED:** Bristol City
**LEAGUE ONE PLAY-OFF WINNERS:** Blackpool
**RELEGATED:** Chesterfield, Bradford City, Rotherham United, Brentford
**TOP GOAL SCORER:** Billy Sharp (30 goals for Scunthorpe United)

Scunthorpe United, managed by former club physiotherapist Nigel Adkins, sealed the title to ensure progress out of the bottom two divisions for the first time since the 1960s. The goals of Billy Sharp proved crucial as the Iron won 26 of their 46 matches and clocked up 91 points. Gary Johnson's Bristol City claimed the second automatic promotion place to end an eight-year exile from the second tier while Blackpool, managed by Simon Grayson, defeated Yeovil Town 2–0 in the play-off final.

ABOVE TOP LEFT: *A picture of focus and intensity, Sunderland manager Roy Keane transformed the club's fortunes and guided the Black Cats to an unlikely title victory.*

ABOVE TOP RIGHT: *Scunthorpe United boss Nigel Adkins, the club's former physio, enjoys a cup of tea during the Iron's League One title winning campaign.*

**LEAGUE TWO CHAMPIONS:** Walsall
**PROMOTED:** Hartlepool United, Swindon Town
**LEAGUE TWO PLAY-OFF WINNERS:** Bristol Rovers
**RELEGATED:** Boston United, Torquay United
**TOP GOAL SCORER:** Izale McLeod (21 goals for MK Dons)

Three of the four teams relegated from League One at the end of the 2005–06 campaign completed an immediate return as Walsall, bossed by Richard Money, claimed the title by a single point from second-placed Hartlepool United, managed by Danny Wilson. Back in third place was Paul Sturrock's Swindon while Paul Trollope's Bristol Rovers ended six years in the fourth tier following a 3–1 play-off final victory over Shrewsbury Town.

Dropping out of the Football League were Torquay United and financially troubled Boston United who, as well as being docked 10 points for entering administration, were relegated two divisions for failing to pay creditors after previous financial irregularities that occurred during the 2001–02 campaign were taken into account by the authorities.

**FOOTBALL CONFERENCE CHAMPIONS:** Dagenham & Redbridge
**PROMOTED:** Morecambe

John Still's Dagenham & Redbridge stormed to the league title thanks to a return of 95 points to seal their first promotion to the Football League. Sammy McIlroy's Morecambe overcame Exeter City 2–1 in the play-offs.

# UP FOR THE CUP

**FA CUP WINNERS:** Chelsea

The first ever FA Cup final to be played at the new Wembley Stadium was won by Jose Mourinho's Chelsea who defeated Manchester United after Didier Drogba's well-taken extra-time goal proved decisive.

Chelsea reached the final following a 2–1 semi-final victory over Blackburn, which was achieved through Michael Ballack's extra-time winner while United overcame Watford 4–1 thanks to goals from Wayne Rooney, Cristiano Ronaldo and Kieran Richardson.

Shock results during the tournament included Plymouth Argyle overcoming Derby; Blackburn's victory over Arsenal; Birmingham knocking out Newcastle and non-league Basingstoke Town advancing past Chesterfield.

**LEAGUE (CARLING) CUP WINNERS:** Chelsea

Chelsea lifted the first major honour of the season following a bad tempered 2–1 victory over Arsenal. Both of Chelsea's goals were scored by their man for the big occasion, Didier Drogba, while Arsenal's reply came from Theo Walcott. The game was overshadowed by a mass brawl between both sets of players that led to Chelsea's John Obi Mikel and Emmanuel Adebyaor and Kolo Toure of Arsenal receiving red cards. Chelsea skipper John Terry also departed the action early in the game after an aerial collision with Abou Diaby left him unconscious and in need of hospital treatment.

ABOVE TOP RIGHT: *John Terry lifts another FA Cup for Chelsea after the Blues defeated Manchester United 1–0 thanks to a Didier Drogba goal in the first final played at the new Wembley stadium.*

OPPOSITE PAGE: *Didier Drogba converts another big game goal, this time against Arsenal in Chelsea's Carling Cup final victory.*

To reach the final, Chelsea completed a routine 5–1 aggregate victory over Wolves that featured braces from Andrei Shevchenko and Frank Lampard while Arsenal knocked out Tottenham 3–1 after extra time in the second leg thanks to a Jeremie Aliadiere strike and an own goal from Pascal Chimbonda.

Earlier in the competition, surprise results came in the form of Southend's 1–0 victory over a close to full-strength Manchester United at Roots Hall; Arsenal's 6–3 win at Liverpool, which featured four goals from Julio Baptista; Wycombe Wanderers' quarter-final win against Charlton and Chesterfield's win against West Ham.

**COMMUNITY SHIELD WINNERS:** Liverpool
Liverpool edged Chelsea 2–1 at the Millennium Stadium after goals from John Arne Riise and Peter Crouch. Chelsea's goal was scored by summer signing Andrei Shevchenko.

**THE FOOTBALL LEAGUE (JOHNSTONE'S PAINTS) TROPHY:** Doncaster Rovers
Sean O'Driscoll's Doncaster Rovers defeated Bristol Rovers 3–2 after extra time at the Millennium Stadium. The winning goal was scored by defender Graeme Lee.

# INTO EUROPE

### European Champions League

Liverpool were once again the Premier League's star performers as Rafa Benitez's team went on to reach the Champions League final for the second time in three seasons. The Reds comfortably topped a group that also featured PSV Eindhoven, Bordeaux and Galatasaray before enjoying a famous away goals victory over Barcelona in the knockout stages, which featured a 2–1 win over the Catalan giants at the Nou Camp, achieved through goals from Craig Bellamy and John Arne Riise.

Liverpool advanced past PSV 4–0 in the quarter-finals before beating Chelsea on penalties in the semi-final. The second time the two English clubs had met at that stage in the competition, the game was just as close with both home ties ending 1–0 to the hosts. The penalty shootout at Anfield ended in Liverpool's favour when Pepe Reina saved from Geremi and Dirk Kuyt drove home the winning kick.

Liverpool were again paired with AC Milan in the final, the side they had defeated in such dramatic fashion back in 2005. However, 2007 in Athens ended in disappointment when two goals from Filippo Inzaghi and a midfield masterclass from Kaka inspired the Italians to a 2–1 victory. Liverpool's late consolation goal came from Dirk Kuyt.

BELOW: *Led by penalty saving hero Pepe Reina, Liverpool celebrate their semi-final shootout victory over Chelsea at Anfield.*

Chelsea's progress to the latter stages of the competition saw them top a group featuring Barcelona and Werder Bremen, and knock out Porto and Valencia in the quarter and semi-finals.

Manchester United produced their best European showing for five years, reaching the quarter-final following a breathtaking 7–1 victory over Roma at Old Trafford. The Red Devils faced AC Milan in the semi-finals and recorded a 3–2 home victory inspired by the goals and work rate of Wayne Rooney before suffering a humiliating 3–0 loss in the San Siro which ended their progress in the tournament. Arsenal were the worst performing English team, crashing out to PSV Eindhoven 2–1 in the last 16 despite topping their group.

## UEFA Cup

The first English team to exit the competition were West Ham, who were soundly beaten 4–0 over two legs by Palermo, which meant they failed to progress to the group stages. Mark Hughes' Blackburn recorded victories over Wisla Krakov, Basle and Nancy to top their group but were knocked out by Bayer Leverkusen in the round of 32. Newcastle topped a group also containing Celta Vigo, Fenerbache, Palermo and Eintracht Frankfurt before defeating Belgium's Zulte Waregem in the knockout stages and losing to AZ Alkmaar in the round of 16. Tottenham went one step further, reaching the quarter-finals where they lost 4–3 on aggregate to cup holders and eventual winners Sevilla.

## THE INTERNATIONAL SCENE

Under new manager Steve McClaren, England began their qualifying campaign for Euro 2008 well, defeating both Andorra and Macedonia, before dropping points following a 0–0 home draw against the Macedonians. A 2–0 loss in Croatia and 0–0 draw with Israel, however, put England's hopes of qualification in jeopardy before a laboured 3–0 victory over Andorra saw the pressure build on McClaren.

*ABOVE: AC Milan striker Filippo Inzaghi scores a typical poacher's goal to help the Italian giants overcome Liverpool 2–1 in the Champions League final.*

# FERGUSON DOUBLES UP IN STYLE

The Premiership was rebranded as the Barclays Premier League to reflect a new sponsorship deal ahead of the new campaign. The money making machine that was the English top flight continued to churn as the so-called 'big four' clubs; Manchester United, Chelsea, Liverpool and Arsenal, buoyed by extensive revenue from their regular appearances in the latter stages of the Champions League, continued to monopolise the division's top four places.

In many ways, finances, multi-million pound takeovers and controversial transfer deals had taken over as the narrative of the English game. This was emphasised by the saga surrounding the Carlos Tevez and Javier Mascherano deals completed by West Ham United the previous summer.

After details of the signings were omitted from official records, a Premier League investigation found that West Ham had been guilty of breaching two rulings around transfers. The club was fined £5.5m but didn't receive a points deduction and Tevez was permitted to continue playing. This, and the perceived significant role played by Tevez in the club's successful avoidance of relegation the previous season, angered several clubs, particularly Sheffield United, one of those that did suffer relegation.

The Blades successfully appealed previous rulings that had been reached through the FA's arbitration procedure and sought £45m in compensation from West Ham for their loss of revenue from being relegated. The Hammers eventually went on to settle out of court, paying Sheffield United a fee in the region of £20m, but the whole affair left many in the English game with a bitter taste.

Champions Manchester United spent heavily in the summer and again looked the most likely to lift the Premier League trophy while their nearest neighbours Manchester City experienced a major change in identity following a multi-million pound takeover by Thai businessman Thaksin Shinawatra. City also hit the headlines with the appointment of former England manager Sven-Goran Eriksson.

OPPOSITE PAGE: *Wayne Rooney celebrates scoring for Manchester United against Manchester City during the Red Devils' title charge.*

BELOW: *Old blue eyes, Sven-Goran Eriksson, returned to English football as manager of Manchester City during pre-season.*

# TRANSFER TALES

After winning their first title in three seasons, Manchester United opted to add to their squad from a position of strength, bringing in England international midfielder Owen Hargreaves, as well as two promising talents from the Portuguese top flight in the form of skilful winger Luis Nani and Brazilian playmaker Anderson. After protracted negotiations with the Premier League and the third party owners of Carlos Tevez, MSI, United also completed the loan signing of the Argentine striker.

Other significant attacking additions were made by Liverpool who parted with £20m for Spanish striker Fernando Torres and £11.5m for Dutch youngster Ryan Babel. The Reds also brought in Ukrainian forward Andriy Voronin.

Tottenham paid relegated Charlton £16.5m for the sharp shooting Darren Bent and Everton broke their transfer record, spending £11.25m on Middlesbrough's Yakubu. The Toffees also moved for Sheffield United defender Phil Jagielka. Boro, meanwhile, splashed out £7m to end Jonathan Woodgate's spell with Real Madrid. Their local rivals Sunderland also made significant moves in the market, breaking the British record for a goalkeeper when they parted with £9m for Hearts' Craig Gordon and investing £5m in the striking talent of Michael Chopra.

Manchester City's new found riches saw them invest heavily in the likes of Italian striker Rolando Bianchi, Bulgarian winger Martin Petrov from Atletico Madrid and Brazilian schemer Elano from Shakhtar Donetsk. City also bolstered their ranks with the signings of Vedran Corluka, Valeri Bojinov and Javier Garrido.

Chelsea were relatively conservative spenders, bringing in Florent Malouda for £13.5m and acquiring Steve Sidwell, Tal Ben Haim and Claudio Pizarro on free transfers before adding Bolton striker Nicolas Anelka in January. Across London, Spurs invested £9m in Scottish right-back Alan Hutton and £5m in Southampton's promising youngster, Gareth Bale.

One of the Premier League's star turns left during the summer as Arsenal legend Thierry Henry departed for Barcelona. The Gunners swelled their ranks with the additions of Bacary Sagna, Lassana Diarra and Eduardo.

*Known as 'El Nino', which translates as 'the kid', Spanish striker Fernando Torres become a goal scoring sensation after joining Liverpool from Atletico Madrid during the summer.*

## BIGGEST TRANSFERS

**FERNANDO TORRES** – from Atletico Madrid to Liverpool – £20m

**OWEN HARGREAVES** – from Bayern Munich to Manchester United – £17m

**DARREN BENT** – from Charlton Athletic to Tottenham Hotspur – £16.5m

**ANDERSON** – from FC Porto to Manchester United – £16m

**NICOLAS ANELKA** – from Bolton Wanderers to Chelsea – £15m

**LUIS NANI** – from Sporting Lisbon to Manchester United – £14m

**FLORENT MALOUDA** – from Lyon to Chelsea – £13.5m

**RYAN BABEL** – from Ajax to Liverpool – £11.5m

**YAKUBU AIYEGBENI** – from Middlesbrough to Everton – £11.25m

**CRAIG GORDON** – from Hearts to Sunderland – £9m

**ALAN HUTTON** – from Rangers to Tottenham Hotspur – £9m

# TALES OF THE TURF

Chelsea began the season in good form, winning three of their first four games to top the table at the end of August. An injury-hit Manchester United endured a slow start, losing away to rivals Manchester City and dropping points against both Reading and Portsmouth. City, impressing under Sven-Goran Eriksson, Wigan and Liverpool made up the four.

September saw Chelsea lose to Aston Villa and stumble to consecutive home draws with Fulham in the league and Rosenborg in the Champions League, and the relationship between manager Jose Mourinho and owner Roman Abramovich became fractured to such a degree that the 'Special One' resigned from the club.

Chelsea appointed Israeli coach Avram Grant as their manager. His first game in charge ended in a 2–0 defeat to Manchester United, which featured goals from Carlos Tevez and Louis Saha. United's improved form saw them climb to second in the table, with Chelsea dropping off the pace and Arsenal storming to first place following a run of five successive victories. Manchester City's early season form continued as they occupied third place at the end of the month.

BELOW: *The goals of Cristiano Ronaldo were imperative to Manchester United as the Portuguese star began playing more centrally. Ronaldo was lethal from all distances and angles and, striking the ball in his own distinctive fashion, lit up the division with several breathtakingly brilliant free-kicks.*

In October Sammy Lee was sacked by Bolton and replaced by Gary Megson and Steve Bruce tendered his resignation at Birmingham. Tottenham sacked Martin Jol and brought in Juande Ramos who had previously managed Sevilla. Manchester United and Arsenal continued to impress with both clubs finishing the month level on points at the top of table. Chelsea found their feet under Avram Grant and joined Blackburn, Liverpool and Portsmouth in the chasing pack.

November saw the end of Chris Hutchings' tenure in charge of Wigan after less than six months. Steve Bruce was named as his successor. Time was also up for Billy Davies at Derby, after the Rams had won just one game in the opening three months of the season, the Scottish manager was sacked and replaced by former Wigan boss Paul Jewell. The Birmingham City managerial vacancy was filled by former Rangers boss Alex McLeish.

December brought another managerial casualty as Lawrie Sanchez was sacked by struggling Fulham. Vastly experienced former Blackburn boss, Roy Hodgson, was confirmed as his replacement.

With Cristiano Ronaldo in superb form, Manchester United won five of their six fixtures during December, with the Portuguese magician scoring seven goals. Arsenal dropped points at Portsmouth but still ended the year as the division's pace-setters, two points ahead of United. At the bottom of the table, the appointment of Paul Jewell failed to address Derby County's failings, as the Rams were marooned ten points from safety. The bottom three also contained Wigan and Fulham.

ABOVE: *Old Trafford pays tribute to those that lost their lives in the Munich air disaster. Half a century after the tragedy, which claimed the lives of eight Manchester United players, as well as staff members and journalists – including former Manchester City goalkeeper Frank Swift – both Manchester clubs met in this top-flight fixture.*

OPPOSITE PAGE:
*Chelsea midfielder Michael Ballack is congratulated by Ashley Cole after his goals inspired the Blues to a 2–1 home victory against title rivals Manchester United.*

It was a case of New Year, new manager for Newcastle who showed Sam Allardyce the exit door after just eight months in charge. The former Bolton boss paid the price for failing to get the fans onside with a brand of football they perceived as too defensive. The return of the man labelled 'the messiah' by Magpies fans – Kevin Keegan – was confirmed a couple of weeks later as the club's boss between 1992 and 1997 returned to St. James' Park for a second spell. Soon after Keegan's appointment, Newcastle owner Mike Ashley brought in Dennis Wise, who had been managing Leeds United, as the club's executive director.

Manchester United redressed the balance during January, picking up four successive victories, including a 6–0 thrashing of Newcastle that featured Cristiano Ronaldo's first hat-trick for the club. Dropped points against Birmingham, in a game that featured a sickening leg break for their striker Eduardo, saw Arsenal fall behind United on goal difference at the end of the month. A run of five consecutive victories enabled Chelsea to edge into title contention, as the Blues sat just four points off the summit.

*The ever-green Ryan Giggs celebrates scoring the goal that sealed the Premier League title for Manchester United on his record-equalling 758th appearance for the club.*

February was Arsenal's month as wins against Manchester City and Blackburn helped them regain a three point lead at the top. Manchester United lost ground following a 1–1 draw at Spurs and a 2–1 home defeat to Manchester City in a fixture that commemorated the 50th anniversary of the Munich air disaster. To mark the occasion both teams played in specially made retro style kits that featured the original 1–11 shirt numbers and both sets of supporters immaculately observed a minute's silence before the game began.

Manchester United found form in March, winning all six of their fixtures, including a 3–0 destruction of Liverpool at Old Trafford and a 4–0 thumping of Aston Villa, to open up a five-point advantage at the top of the table. The attacking trio of Ronaldo, Wayne Rooney and Carlos Tevez continued to terrorise defenders amidst comparisons with the club's holy trinity of the 1960s, which comprised the legendary Bobby Charlton, George Best and Denis Law.

Four consecutive draws and a 2–1 reversal to Chelsea saw Arsenal drop to third with the Blues replacing them as United's main challengers. Liverpool and Everton competed for fourth place,

with the red half of Merseyside looking most likely to succeed after Rafa Benitez's team opened up a five-point advantage over David Moyes' men.

Derby County's relegation was confirmed before the end of March, the earliest demotion in all 16 seasons of the Premier League. With just six games left to play, Fulham and Bolton appeared most likely to join them in the Championship.

A run of six wins from seven games saw Chelsea ratchet up the pressure on Manchester United in April. Draws with Middlesbrough and Blackburn, interspersed by a 2–1 win against Arsenal, knocked United slightly off-track. Chelsea defeated United 2–1 at Stamford Bridge thanks to two goals from Michael Ballack to put both teams level on 81 points with two games remaining.

The penultimate fixtures of the campaign saw United defeat West Ham 4–1 and Chelsea overcome Newcastle 2–0 to set up a dramatic final day decider. Manchester United's superior goal difference meant a win at Wigan would seal the title, while Chelsea needed to win their home clash with Bolton and hope that United faltered.

The Red Devils' nerves were settled after 33 minutes when Cristiano Ronaldo slammed home a penalty, his 31st goal of the season, to put United 1–0 ahead. Chelsea broke the deadlock in the second half through Andrei Shevchenko to set up a tense final 30 minutes of the season. Ryan Giggs, who joined the fray from the bench to equal Booby Charlton's record of 758 appearances for United, produced the deciding goal when he carefully guided home a left-footed drive into the net to double the Red Devils' advantage. The game finished 2–0, as United retained their title and lifted the Premier League trophy for the 10th time.

The final day also brought to a climax that season's relegation battle, with Bolton, Fulham, Birmingham and Reading all in contention for demotion. Roy Hodgson's Fulham completed their great escape by winning their last three fixtures, including a key 1–0 victory at Portsmouth achieved thanks to cool finish from Danny Murphy. Reading's 4–0 win against Derby proved too little too late as they dropped out of the division, alongside Birmingham's who also won 4–0 on the final day, against Blackburn. Bottom place Derby ended the season with a Premier League all-time low points tally of 11.

## ⚽ INTERESTING INFO

Manchester United winger Cristiano Ronaldo finished as the season's top scorer with 31 goals in 31 starts, equalling Alan Shearer's record for a 38-match season.

# HONOURS LIST

## Barclays Premier League
**CHAMPIONS:** Manchester United
Some breathtaking attacking football, combined
with typical end of season killer instinct, saw
Manchester United complete back-to-back titles
and firmly re-establish themselves as the Premier
League's dominant force.
**RUNNERS-UP:** Chelsea
**RELEGATED:** Reading, Birmingham City, Derby County
**TOP GOAL SCORER:** Cristiano Ronaldo (31 goals for
Manchester United)

SHOOT MAGAZINE
2007–08

*After the magazine
underwent a dramatic
re-brand and adopted a
more comic-like feel, more
players and a wider variety
of teams were featured on
the front cover. This edition
assessed the major transfer
business carried out by
Premier League clubs and
pictured the likes of Carlos
Tevez, Fernando Torres and
Craig Bellamy.*

## 2007–08 SEASON TABLE

| | | M | W | D | L | GF | GA | GD | PTS |
|---|---|---|---|---|---|---|---|---|---|
| 1 | Manchester United | 38 | 27 | 6 | 5 | 80 | 22 | +58 | 87 |
| 2 | Chelsea | 38 | 25 | 10 | 3 | 65 | 26 | +39 | 85 |
| 3 | Arsenal | 38 | 24 | 11 | 3 | 74 | 31 | +43 | 83 |
| 4 | Liverpool | 38 | 21 | 13 | 4 | 67 | 28 | +39 | 76 |
| 5 | Everton | 38 | 19 | 8 | 11 | 55 | 33 | +22 | 65 |
| 6 | Aston Villa | 38 | 16 | 12 | 10 | 71 | 51 | +20 | 60 |
| 7 | Blackburn Rovers | 38 | 15 | 13 | 10 | 50 | 48 | +2 | 58 |
| 8 | Portsmouth | 38 | 16 | 9 | 13 | 48 | 40 | +8 | 57 |
| 9 | Manchester City | 38 | 15 | 10 | 13 | 45 | 53 | -8 | 55 |
| 10 | West Ham United | 38 | 13 | 10 | 15 | 42 | 50 | -8 | 49 |
| 11 | Tottenham Hotspur | 38 | 11 | 13 | 14 | 66 | 61 | +5 | 46 |
| 12 | Newcastle United | 38 | 11 | 10 | 17 | 45 | 65 | -20 | 43 |
| 13 | Middlesbrough | 38 | 10 | 12 | 16 | 43 | 53 | -10 | 42 |
| 14 | Wigan Athletic | 38 | 10 | 10 | 18 | 34 | 51 | -17 | 40 |
| 15 | Sunderland | 38 | 11 | 6 | 21 | 36 | 59 | -23 | 39 |
| 16 | Bolton Wanderers | 38 | 9 | 10 | 19 | 36 | 54 | -18 | 37 |
| 17 | Fulham | 38 | 8 | 12 | 18 | 38 | 60 | -22 | 36 |
| 18 | Reading | 38 | 10 | 6 | 22 | 41 | 66 | -25 | 36 |
| 19 | Birmingham City | 38 | 8 | 11 | 19 | 46 | 62 | -16 | 35 |
| 20 | Derby County | 38 | 1 | 8 | 29 | 20 | 89 | -69 | 11 |

# PLAYERS OF THE SEASON

**PFA PLAYER OF THE YEAR:** Cristiano Ronaldo, Manchester United
**PFA YOUNG PLAYER OF THE YEAR:** Cesc Fabregas, Arsenal
**FOOTBALL WRITERS' PLAYER OF THE YEAR:** Cristiano Ronaldo, Manchester United

ABOVE LEFT: *Match-winner Dean Windass (left) and manager Phil Brown celebrate Hull City's Championship play-off final victory over Bristol City, which meant Premier League football for the first time in the Tigers' history.*

ABOVE RIGHT: *Powerful Swansea City striker Jason Scotland finished as League One's top goal scorer and inspired the Welsh club to the title.*

**FOOTBALL LEAGUE CHAMPIONSHIP CHAMPIONS:** West Bromwich Albion
**PROMOTED:** Stoke City
**CHAMPIONSHIP PLAY-OFF WINNERS:** Hull City
**RELEGATED:** Leicester City, Scunthorpe United, Colchester United
**TOP GOAL SCORER:** Sylvan Ebanks-Blake (23 goals for Wolverhampton Wanderers)

Tony Mowbray's West Brom registered 23 victories from 46 games and a total of 81 points to end a two-year exile from the top flight. Two points behind in second place were Stoke City, managed by Tony Pulis. The play-off final was won by Hull City who reached the top flight for the first time in their history following a 1–0 victory over Bristol City at Wembley. The winning goal was scored by 39-year-old hometown hero Dean Windass. The Tigers, managed by Phil Brown, completed their third promotion in just five seasons.

**LEAGUE ONE CHAMPIONS:** Swansea City
**PROMOTED:** Nottingham Forest
**LEAGUE ONE PLAY-OFF WINNERS:** Doncaster Rovers
**RELEGATED:** Bournemouth, Gillingham, Port Vale, Luton Town
**TOP GOAL SCORER:** Jason Scotland (24 goals for Swansea City)

Swansea City, guided by Roberto Martinez, stormed to the league title, amassing an impressive 92 points. Colin Calderwood's Nottingham Forest secured a return to the Championship, with a second place finish, while Doncaster Rovers, managed by Sean O'Driscoll, returned to the second tier for the first time in 50 years after defeating Leeds United 1-0 in the play-off final thanks to James Hayter's goal.

*In his second managerial role, former England midfielder Paul Ince guided MK Dons to League Two and Johnstone's Paints Trophy glory.*

**LEAGUE TWO CHAMPIONS:** MK Dons
**PROMOTED:** Peterborough United, Hereford United
**LEAGUE TWO PLAY-OFF WINNERS:** Stockport County
**RELEGATED:** Mansfield Town, Wrexham
**TOP GOAL SCORER:** Aaron McLean (29 goals for Peterborough United)

MK Dons, managed by Paul Ince, claimed the League Two title after amassing 97 points and losing just seven of their 46 games. Darren Ferguson, son of Sir Alex, guided Peterborough to automatic promotion at the end of his first season in charge. Third place was taken by Graham Turner's Hereford and Stockport County, managed by Jim Gannon, triumphed in the play-offs after defeating Rochdale 3–2 at Wembley. Dropping into the Conference, were Wrexham and Mansfield, who suffered relegation after 87 and 77 years in the Football League respectively.

**BLUE SQUARE PREMIER (FORMERLY FOOTBALL CONFERENCE) CHAMPIONS:** Aldershot Town
**PROMOTED:** Exeter City

Aldershot Town, the reincarnation of Aldershot FC, breached the barrier of a century of points to seal the Conference title under the guidance of Gary Waddock. Also returning to the Football League were Paul Tisdale's Exeter City who triumphed 1–0 over Oxford United in the play-offs.

# UP FOR THE CUP

**FA CUP WINNERS:** Portsmouth

Portsmouth's 58-year wait for a major trophy came to an end following 1–0 win over Cardiff at Wembley. The game's only goal was provided by veteran striker Nwankwo Kanu, who prodded home from close range in the first half.

Pompey reached the final following a 1–0 semi final victory over West Brom, when Kanu again scored the only goal, while Cardiff's progression was sealed by a 1–0 win over Barnsley, achieved through Joe Ledley's goal.

In a season filled with shock results, the quarter-finals brought two of the standout cup upsets, when Portsmouth knocked out Manchester United at Old Trafford following a 1–0 win and Barnsley, who had already triumphed over Liverpool at Anfield in the previous round, put paid to Chelsea's hopes following a 1–0 win at Oakwell. At the same stage, Cardiff ousted Middlesbrough from the competition. Surprise results earlier in the tournament included Bury's win over Norwich; Oldham's victory against Everton, Havant & Waterlooville advancing past Swansea and Bristol Rovers' defeat of Fulham.

*Portsmouth striker Nwankwo Kanu holds the FA Cup after his goal defeated Cardiff City 1–0 at Wembley.*

**LEAGUE (CARLING) CUP WINNERS:** Tottenham Hotspur

Tottenham ended their nine-year wait for a trophy by lifting the League Cup for the second time during the Premier League era. Spurs defeated Chelsea 2–1 at Wembley thanks to an extra-time winner from Jonathan Woodgate. Chelsea had taken a first-half lead through Didier Drogba before Dimitar Berbatov levelled matters for Spurs.

Tottenham's progress to the final saw them overcome local rivals Arsenal 6–2 on aggregate during the semi-finals, with Jermaine Jenas, Robbie Keane and Aaron Lennon amongst the scorers. Chelsea, meanwhile, defeated Everton 3–1 in a tie that featured goals from Shaun Wright-Phillips and Joe Cole.

The competition's standout results included Cardiff's defeat of West Brom, Luton's victories over Sunderland and Charlton and Coventry City's impressive 2–0 win against Manchester United.

**COMMUNITY SHIELD WINNERS:** Manchester United

Following a typically close affair between Manchester United and Chelsea, the scores were tied at 1–1 with Ryan Giggs and Florent Malouda scoring for their respective clubs. The hero during the penalty shootout was United goalkeeper Edwin van der Sar who saved spot kicks from Claudio Pizarro, Frank Lampard and Shaun Wright-Phillips.

**THE FOOTBALL LEAGUE (JOHNSTONE'S PAINTS) TROPHY:** MK Dons

MK Dons enjoyed Wembley glory after defeating Grimsby Town 2–0 thanks to goals from Keith Andrews and Sean O'Hanlon.

ABOVE: *Jonathan Woodgate celebrates with skipper Ledley King after his goal gave Tottenham an extra-time lead against Chelsea in the Carling Cup final.*

# INTO EUROPE

## European Champions League

Premier League clubs continued their dominance of the competition as both Manchester United and Chelsea reached the final to ensure the Champions League's first all-English showpiece.

Manchester United's passage to the final saw them dominate a group containing Roma, Sporting Lisbon and Dynamo Kiev before a routine 2–1 victory over Lyon in the last 16. The Red Devils then enjoyed a 3–0 quarter-final victory over Roma to set up a semi-final tie against a highly rated Barcelona side. After the first leg at the Nou Camp ended goalless, Paul Scholes settled the tie with a long-range half-volley that flew past Victor Valdes and into the roof of the Old Trafford net to seal a 1–0 aggregate win for the English club.

Chelsea's progress was equally impressive as the Blues topped a group that also contained Schalke, Rosenborg and Valencia, before overcoming Olympiakos and Fenerbahce to set up a third semi-final clash with Rafa Benitez's Liverpool. The Blues finally got the better of the Reds in the competition after two enthralling encounters ended 4–3 in their favour, with the second leg going to extra time and being settled by Didier Drogba's driven finish.

In the final, held in a rain saturated Moscow, Manchester United dominated the first half and took the lead following a typically powerful header from Cristiano Ronaldo. Chelsea reacted well after the interval and levelled the scores at 1-1 though Frank Lampard's deflected drive. The game went into extra time and saw Didier Drogba receive his marching orders following a petulant slap at Nemanja Vidic. United looked the more likely to score during the extended period but the contest went to penalties.

*BELOW: The net still bursting, Manchester United's midfield magician Paul Scholes heads for his team-mates after scoring the Champions League semi-final winning goal against Barcelona.*

The first man to miss from the spot was Ronaldo, who saw his hesitant strike well-saved by Petr Cech. Players from both sides continued to find the net, giving Chelsea captain John Terry the opportunity to win the competition with his penalty kick. United stopper Edwin van der Sar had gone the wrong way, but Terry, who slipped on the rain sodden surface when making contact with the ball, aimed his penalty onto the outside of the post and wide.

LEFT: *Chelsea captain John Terry loses his footing and misses the penalty that would've won the Champions League for the Blues.*

BELOW: *The contrast couldn't be more conspicuous as Manchester United goalkeeper Edwin van der Sar celebrates the crest-fallen John Terry's penalty miss.*

As the contest went into sudden death, Anderson, Salomon Kalou and Ryan Giggs, who set a new all-time appearance record for Manchester United, all converted their spot kicks before Nicolas Anelka had his shot saved by Van der Sar to ensure the third European Cup victory of United's history.

Liverpool had again impressed, finishing second to Porto in their group before disposing of Inter Milan and Arsenal to setup the semi-final clash with Chelsea. Arsenal also finished as group runners-up before knocking out AC Milan and succumbing to Liverpool in a memorable quarter-final encounter that ended 5–3.

## UEFA Cup

Of the four English teams participating, only Blackburn failed to qualify for the group stages after crashing out to Greek side Larissa 3–2 on aggregate. Bolton finished third in their group, picking up a credible 2–2 at Bayern Munich before beating Atletico Madrid in the first knockout stage and eventually losing 2–1 on aggregate to Sporting Lisbon. Tottenham, who finished second in their group, also crashed out during the last round of 16, suffering a penalty shootout defeat to PSV Eindhoven, while Everton reached the same stage before also losing out on penalties to Fiorentina.

ABOVE: *The Manchester United squad celebrate winning the third European Cup in the club's history.*

OPPOSITE PAGE TOP: *Bolton Wanderers striker Kevin Davies volleys home to secure a memorable 2–2 draw against Bayern Munich in the UEFA Cup.*

## THE INTERNATIONAL SCENE

England's dismal record under Steve McClaren continued, culminating in a 3–2 defeat against Croatia that ended the Three Lions' hopes of qualifying for the 2008 European Championships. McClaren was later sacked and replaced by Italian tactician Fabio Capello.

LEFT: *Holding an umbrella – a fashion decision that saw much ridicule from the tabloid press – Steve McClaren failed to weather the storm after England failed to qualify for Euro 2008 and was replaced by Fabio Capello.*

# ANOTHER TREBLE FOR THE RED DEVILS

**C**helsea began the new season with another new manager after Avram Grant was sacked despite taking the club to the Champions League final. Luiz Felipe Scolari was named as his successor. Sven Goran-Eriksson, who had lost out to Scolari at three major tournaments as England manager, was shown the door by Manchester City after just one season in charge. Blackburn Rovers boss Mark Hughes was appointed as his successor and coming in for Hughes at Ewood Park was his former Manchester United team mate, Paul Ince.

A change in the rules meant that English clubs could start naming seven substitutes on the bench instead of five, allowing the top-flight sides to keep more of the players from their ever-expanding squads happy and involved in first team affairs.

OPPOSITE PAGE: *The inspiration behind Manchester United's domestic dominance, Cristiano Ronaldo ended his last season in the red shirt with another Premier League winner's medal.*

LEFT: *Manchester United held off a late bid from Manchester City to secure the deadline day signing of elegant Bulgarian striker Dimitar Berbatov from Tottenham.*

# TRANSFER TALES

A multi-billion pound takeover of Manchester City by an Arabian consortium called the Abu Dhabi United Group, led by Sheikh Mansour bin Zayed Al Nahyan, whose family had made billions from the United Arab Emirates oil industry, meant that City boasted the richest owner in world football. Despite the takeover taking place at the beginning of September the club wasted little time investing funds in player acquisitions.

In fact, even before the takeover, City were spending heavily, bringing in the likes of Belgian defender Vincent Kompany for £6m from Hamburg, Argentine right-back Pablo Zabaleta from Espanyol and re-signing England winger Shaun Wright-Phillips from Chelsea in an £8.5m deal. Once the big money landed in the club's account, Mark Hughes was able to take this investment to another level, breaking the British transfer record to snare Brazilian forward Robinho from Real Madrid for £32.5m and also adding the likes of Joao Alves, Nigel de Jong, Wayne Bridge, Craig Bellamy and Shay Given.

Across Manchester, United broke their transfer record to sign languid Bulgarian striker Dimitar Berbatov from Spurs, holding off a late attempt to hijack the deal from City. As well as the departing Berbatov, Tottenham also lost his striker partner Robbie Keane to Liverpool for £20.3m but reinvested that money on Blackburn winger David Bentley, Croatian midfielder Luka Modric, Mexican youngster Giovani dos Santos, Wigan midfielder Wilson Palacios, Manchester City defender Vedran Corluka, Brazilian goalkeeper Heurelho Gomes and Russian striker Roman Pavlyuchenko.

Another Russian international arriving in the Premier League was diminutive playmaker Andrei Arshavin who joined Arsenal on deadline day of the August transfer window for £15m. The Gunners also brought in Mikael Silvestre from Manchester United and Cardiff City's promising midfielder Aaron Ramsey.

Chelsea's spending was relatively tame in comparison to the likes of Manchester City and Spurs, but they still added Portuguese pair Jose Boswinga and Deco. Liverpool's biggest signing was Robbie Keane from Spurs but the Reds also added Andrea Dossena and David N'Gog to their squad. Peter Crouch departed Anfield for Portsmouth, who also signed Younes Kaboul from Spurs.

Everton smashed their transfer record to sign Belgian midfielder Marouane Fellaini from Standard Liege for £15m. The Toffees also brought in Steven Pienaar from Borussia Dortmund and Louis Saha from Manchester United. Aston Villa completed the £12m addition of James Milner from Newcastle and signed Rangers defender Carols Cuellar, as well as Emile Heskey from Wigan and Chelsea's Steve Sidwell.

*Samba star Robinho became the first marquee signing of Manchester City's new regime as Mark Hughes attempted to build a team capable of challenging at the top of the Premier League.*

## BIGGEST TRANSFERS

**ROBINHO** – from Real Madrid to Manchester City – £32.5m

**DIMITAR BERBATOV** – from Tottenham Hotspur to Manchester United – £30.75m

**ROBBIE KEANE** – from Tottenham Hotspur to Liverpool – £20.3m

**JOAO ALVES** – from CSKA Moscow to Manchester City – £19m

**LUKA MODRIC** – from Dinamo Zagreb to Tottenham Hotspur – £16.5m

**JOSE BOSWINGA** – from FC Porto to Chelsea – £16.2m

**NIGEL DE JONG** – from SV Hamburg to Manchester City – £16m

**DAVID BENTLEY** – from Blackburn Rovers to Tottenham Hotspur – £15m

**ANDREI ARSHAVIN** – from Zenit St Petersburg to Arsenal – £15m

**JERMAIN DEFOE** – from Portsmouth to Tottenham Hotspur – £15m

**MAROUANE FELLAINI** – from Standard Liege to Everton – £15m

# TALES OF THE TURF

Chelsea started well under Luiz Felipe Scolari, winning two of their opening three games, including a 4–0 thumping of Portsmouth to top the table at the end of August. Champions Manchester United began with a home draw against Newcastle and a narrow victory over Portsmouth, before suffering a 2–1 defeat to Liverpool. United and Chelsea met at Stamford Bridge just a few weeks into the season in a game that ended in a 1–1 draw.

The season's first managerial change came in early September when West Ham boss Alan Curbishley resigned his post after 21 months in charge. His departure was soon followed by Kevin Keegan's exit at Newcastle as the former England coach resigned as Magpies manager for the second time. The man that replaced Keegan was former Wimbledon boss, Joe Kinnear, who took up the role on an interim basis. West Ham appointed former Chelsea forward, Gianfranco Zola, as their first ever non-British manager.

Newly promoted Hull City continued their impressive start to the season with a shock 2–1 victory over Arsenal at the Emirates Stadium, completing their first ever win against the Gunners thanks to goals from summer signings Geovanni and Daniel Cousin.

LEFT: *Brazilian midfielder Geovanni added South American flair to Phil Brown's hardworking Hull City and enjoyed impressive goal-scoring form at the beginning of the season.*

Chelsea and Liverpool were the early pacemakers and ended September tied on points at the top of the table. Blackburn and Hull continued to impress in the top ten while big-spending Tottenham surprisingly found themselves bottom of the table.

Spurs' bad form continued into October and signalled the end of Juande Ramos' spell in charge. The Spaniard was replaced by Portsmouth manager Harry Redknapp, who was succeeded at the south coast club by Tony Adams. Liverpool, inspired by the continued goal-scoring exploits of Fernando Torres, picked up three key victories on their travels during October, recording maximum points against Everton, Manchester City and Chelsea to end the month top of the table.

Liverpool and Chelsea continued to impress during November, but a defeat for Liverpool at Spurs and a loss to Arsenal for Chelsea allowed Manchester United to close the gap. Arsenal and Aston Villa completed the top four with Hull still punching above their weight in sixth.

Blackburn opted to make a managerial change before Christmas, giving Paul Ince his marching orders and replacing him with the more experienced Sam Allardyce. Roy Keane resigned his managerial role with Sunderland and was replaced by Ricky Sbragia. Liverpool drew three of their six fixtures in December but still finished the year at the top of the table. Chelsea were three points off the pace with Manchester United 10 points adrift.

United hit their straps in January, winning all five of their games, as Cristiano Ronaldo, Wayne Rooney and Dimitar Berbatov found their goal scoring form. Liverpool drew all three of their fixtures during the same period allowing their Manchester rivals to topple them from first place.

Portsmouth ended Tony Adams' 14-week reign in charge at the beginning of February, replacing him with Paul Hart. A day later, Chelsea parted company with Luiz Felipe Scolari who had been at the helm for just over half a season. The Brazilian was succeeded by experienced Dutchman Guus Hiddink on an interim basis.

Manchester United's good form continued to such an extent that they ended February seven points ahead of second place Chelsea. Liverpool dropped points to Manchester City and Middlesbrough. West Bromwich Albion, Blackburn Rovers and Stoke City remained in the relegation zone.

Rafa Benitez's Liverpool enjoyed a magnificent March, emphasised by a 4–1 thrashing of Manchester United at Old Trafford that shocked the United faithful. The Reds' goals were scored by Fernando Torres, who again terrorised the normally solid United defence, Steven Gerrard, Fabio Auerlio and Andrea Dossena. Home victories over Sunderland and Aston Villa ensure the Merseyside club closed the gap at the top to a single point after United suffered defeat at Fulham.

LEFT: *Steven Gerrard and Fabio Aurelio embrace after the Brazilian's free-kick extends Liverpool's lead during the Reds' 4–1 humiliation of Manchester United at Old Trafford.*

OPPOSITE PAGE TOP: *Teenage Italian striker Federico Macheda marked his Manchester United debut with a spectacular and crucial winning goal against Aston Villa during the title run-in.*

OPPOSITE PAGE BOTTOM: *Cristiano Ronaldo, who remained Manchester United's most dangerous attacking threat throughout the campaign, keeps his head to score against Tottenham at Old Trafford.*

*Russian playmaker Andrei Arshavin puts a major dent in Liverpool's title hopes after scoring all four of Arsenal's goals during a 4–4 draw with the Reds at Anfield.*

*A legend as a player, Alan Shearer failed to bring that match-winning magic into management, and Newcastle were relegated under the inexperienced caretaker boss.*

April saw a major turning point in the title race as Manchester United, who had been struggling for form, and found themselves trailing at home to Aston Villa for what would have been a third successive defeat, hit a late equaliser through Ronaldo and a stoppage time winner through 17-year-old debutant, Federico Macheda, who pirouetted on the edge of the box before guiding home a superb curling finish.

The Italian striker was also on target in United's next game against Sunderland which ended in a 2–1 victory before the Red Devils secured a 2–0 win over Portsmouth and a 5–2 victory over Spurs, in a match that saw them respond from being two goals down and fully demonstrated the match-winning brilliance of Cristiano Ronaldo.

Liverpool lost ground following a remarkable 4–4 draw with Arsenal at Anfield that featured a four-goal return from Gunners midfielder Andrei Arshavin. United ended the month three points clear and with a game in hand over Liverpool. Newcastle parted company with Joe Kinnear at the beginning of the month, replacing him with Alan Shearer for the remaining eight games of the season. However Newcastle, and their North East rivals, Middlesbrough, continued to struggle.

Liverpool recovered to record three successive victories over Hull, Newcastle and West Ham, but Manchester United also won their corresponding three games, against Middlesbrough, Manchester City and Wigan Athletic, meaning that a single point from their last two games would retain the Premier League title.

The Red Devils claimed the championship with a 0–0 draw against Arsenal at Old Trafford, meaning the title was won on the pitch at Old Trafford for just the second time since the Premier League started. A day later, West Brom became the first team to be relegated. Joining Newcastle and Middlesbrough in the battle to avoid the drop on the final day were Sunderland and Hull City. However, the bottom three remained unchanged after Newcastle suffered defeat at Aston Villa, ending their 16-year reign in the top flight, and Middlesbrough lost to West Ham.

The three remaining Champions League places were filled by Liverpool, Arsenal and Chelsea while Everton, Aston Villa and Fulham qualified for the UEFA Cup.

## INTERESTING INFO

Hull City endured an end of season collapse, winning just one of their final 22 league games. The Tigers eventually survived relegation by a single point.

# HONOURS LIST

## Barclays Premier League
CHAMPIONS: Manchester United
Manchester United's consistency and title winning experience proved decisive as they held off a late challenge from Liverpool.
RUNNERS-UP: Liverpool
RELEGATED: Newcastle United, Middlesbrough, West Bromwich Albion
TOP GOAL SCORER: Nicolas Anelka (19 goals for Chelsea)

SHOOT MAGAZINE 2008–09

With Shoot now reverting to its more traditional style, the front cover celebrated the longevity of Manchester United star Ryan Giggs and also featured an interview with Chelsea midfielder Joe Cole, who spoke about his return from injury. Arsenal's Brazilian midfielder Denilson disclosed his happiness at playing in England while Burnley defender Clark Carlisle assessed the newly-promoted Clarets' chances of Premier League survival.

## 2008–09 SEASON TABLE

|  |  | M | W | D | L | GF | GA | GD | PTS |
|---|---|---|---|---|---|---|---|---|---|
| 1 | Manchester United | 38 | 28 | 6 | 4 | 68 | 24 | +44 | 90 |
| 2 | Liverpool | 38 | 25 | 11 | 2 | 77 | 27 | +50 | 86 |
| 3 | Chelsea | 38 | 25 | 8 | 5 | 68 | 24 | +44 | 83 |
| 4 | Arsenal | 38 | 20 | 12 | 6 | 68 | 37 | +31 | 72 |
| 5 | Everton | 38 | 17 | 12 | 9 | 55 | 37 | +18 | 63 |
| 6 | Aston Villa | 38 | 17 | 11 | 10 | 54 | 48 | +6 | 62 |
| 7 | Fulham | 38 | 14 | 11 | 13 | 39 | 34 | +5 | 53 |
| 8 | Tottenham Hotspur | 38 | 14 | 9 | 15 | 45 | 45 | 0 | 51 |
| 9 | West Ham United | 38 | 14 | 9 | 15 | 42 | 45 | -3 | 51 |
| 10 | Manchester City | 38 | 15 | 5 | 18 | 58 | 50 | +8 | 50 |
| 11 | Wigan Athletic | 38 | 12 | 9 | 17 | 34 | 45 | -11 | 45 |
| 12 | Stoke City | 38 | 12 | 9 | 17 | 38 | 56 | -18 | 45 |
| 13 | Bolton Wanderers | 38 | 11 | 8 | 19 | 42 | 53 | -11 | 41 |
| 14 | Portsmouth | 38 | 10 | 11 | 17 | 38 | 57 | -19 | 41 |
| 15 | Blackburn Rovers | 38 | 10 | 11 | 17 | 40 | 60 | -20 | 41 |
| 16 | Sunderland | 38 | 9 | 9 | 20 | 34 | 54 | -20 | 36 |
| 17 | Hull City | 38 | 8 | 11 | 19 | 39 | 64 | -25 | 35 |
| 18 | Newcastle United | 38 | 7 | 13 | 18 | 40 | 59 | -19 | 34 |
| 19 | Middlesbrough | 38 | 7 | 11 | 20 | 28 | 57 | -29 | 32 |
| 20 | West Bromwich Albion | 38 | 8 | 8 | 22 | 36 | 67 | -31 | 32 |

# PLAYERS OF THE SEASON

PFA PLAYER OF THE YEAR: Ryan Giggs, Manchester United
PFA YOUNG PLAYER OF THE YEAR: Ashley Young, Aston Villa
FOOTBALL WRITERS' PLAYER OF THE YEAR: Steven Gerrard, Liverpool

**FOOTBALL LEAGUE CHAMPIONSHIP CHAMPIONS:**
Wolverhampton Wanderers
**PROMOTED:** Birmingham City
**CHAMPIONSHIP PLAY-OFF WINNERS:** Burnley
**RELEGATED:** Norwich City, Southampton, Charlton
Athletic
**TOP GOAL SCORER:** Sylvan Ebanks-Blake (25 goals
for Wolverhampton Wanderers)
Wolves, managed by Mick McCarthy, ended a five-year exile from the Premier League with a convincing league title win that saw them clock up 90 points and score 80 goals. Alex McCleish's Birmingham took second place to secure an immediate return to the highest level while Owen Coyle's Burnley defeated Sheffield United 1–0 in the play-off final, thanks to a spectacular strike from Wade Elliott. The win brought an end to the Clarets' 33-year top-flight absence.

**LEAGUE ONE CHAMPIONS:** Leicester City
**PROMOTED:** Peterborough United
**LEAGUE ONE PLAY-OFF WINNERS:** Scunthorpe United
**RELEGATED:** Northampton Town, Crewe Alexandra,
Cheltenham Town, Hereford United
**TOP GOAL SCORERS:** Simon Cox (Swindon Town) and
Rickie Lambert (Bristol Rovers) – both 29 goals
Nigel Pearson's Leicester stormed to the title, completing a 23-match unbeaten run and losing just four games all season. Peterborough, managed by Darren Ferguson, finished second to secure a second successive promotion while Nigel Adkins' Scunthorpe United overcame Millwall 3–2 in a thrilling play-off final that saw Martyn Woolford hit the winning strike.

**LEAGUE TWO CHAMPIONS:** Brentford
**PROMOTED:** Exeter City, Wycombe Wanderers
**LEAGUE TWO PLAY-OFF WINNERS:** Gillingham
**RELEGATED:** Chester City, Luton Town
**TOP GOAL SCORERS:** Simeon Jackson (Gillingham),
Grant Holt (Shrewsbury Town) and Jack Lester
(Chesterfield) – all 20 goals
With Andy Scott at the helm, Brentford returned to League One as champions, losing just seven of their 46 matches. Paul Tisdale's Exeter and Wycombe Wanderers, managed by Peter Taylor, advanced via automatic promotion. Mark Stimson's Gillingham defeated Shrewsbury 1–0 in the play-off final, with

Simeon Jackson scoring a last minute winner.

Luton, who were docked a massive 30 points, suffered a third successive demotion and were joined in the relegation standings by Chester City.

**BLUE SQUARE PREMIER CHAMPIONS:** Burton Albion
**PROMOTED:** Torquay United
Despite losing Nigel Clough to Derby Country during the season, Burton, under the experienced guidance of Roy McFarland, finally reached the Football League after finishing two points clear of second placed Cambridge United. The second promotion spot was taken by Torquay United who defeated Cambridge in the play-off final.

OPPOSITE PAGE TOP: *Chelsea striker Nicolas Anelka finished the season as the division's top scorer, netting 19 goals for the Blues.*

OPPOSITE PAGE BOTTOM: *Wolves striker Sylvan Ebanks-Blake wheels away to celebrate another goal during Wanderers successful promotion campaign.*

ABOVE: *Gillingham striker Simeon Jackson prepares to rejoice with Gills supporters after scoring a last-minute play-off winning goal.*

# UP FOR THE CUP

### FA CUP WINNERS: Chelsea

Temporary manager Guus Hiddink presided over another cup for success for Chelsea after they defeated Everton 2–1 at Wembley. The Toffees stormed into an early lead when Louis Saha found the net after just 25 seconds, setting a new record for the fastest goal ever scored in an FA Cup final. However, Chelsea responded through two of their men for the big occasion, Didier Drogba and Frank Lampard, who scored either side of half-time to complete a 2–1 victory for the London club.

The Blues reached the final following a 2–1 semi-final victory over Arsenal, achieved thanks to another winning goal from Drogba. Everton's progress was assured after a 4–2 penalty shootout win against Manchester United.

Shock results earlier in the competition included Nottingham Forest's 3–0 win at Manchester City, Coventry City defeating Blackburn, Burnley knocking out West Brom, Swansea ousting Portsmouth, non-league Blyth Spartans ending Bournemouth's run in the competition and Torquay United's defeat of Blackpool.

### LEAGUE (CARLING) CUP WINNERS: Manchester United

Manchester United lifted the League Cup for the third time in their history following a penalty shootout victory over Tottenham at Wembley. The Red Devils' crucial spot kick was scored by Anderson after goalkeeper Ben Foster impressed between the posts.

Eventual winners United progressed to the final thanks to a 4–3 aggregate victory over Championship side Derby, who had recorded a 1–0 first leg win at Pride Park, while Spurs overcame Burnley 5–4 after extra time thanks to goals from Roman Pavlyuchenko and Jermain Defoe.

Standout matches earlier in the tournament included victories for Burnley over Fulham in the third round, Chelsea in the fourth round and Arsenal in the quarter-finals, as well as Derby knocking out Stoke City; QPR seeing off Aston Villa and Northampton ending Bolton's interest in the competition.

### COMMUNITY SHIELD WINNERS: Manchester United

Following a drab 0–0 draw with Portsmouth, Manchester United won 3–1 on penalties to lift the Shield.

### THE FOOTBALL LEAGUE (JOHNSTONE'S PAINTS) TROPHY: Luton Town

Despite suffering relegation out of the Football League, Luton Town gave their supporters something to cheer for by defeating Scunthorpe United 3–2 after extra time to lift the Johnstone's Paints Trophy. The decisive goal was scored by Claude Gnakpa.

# INTO EUROPE

## European Champions League

Manchester United were again the Premier League's most impressive performers, reaching a second successive final. After topping a group that also featured Villarreal and Celtic, United defeated Jose Mourinho's Inter Milan and then FC Porto to set up an all-English semi-final clash with Arsenal.

The first leg ended 1–0 to United after a close range goal from John O'Shea but the second leg at the Emirates was a more one-sided affair. Sir Alex Ferguson's men took an early lead through a stunning Cristiano Ronaldo free-kick before exposing Arsenal on the counter attack in the second half with Ronaldo and Park Ji-Sung extending their advantage.

United were paired with Pep Guardiola's emerging Barcelona in the Rome final and despite bossing the early exchanges of the game, they were eventually given a lesson in possession by the Catalan club, who lifted the trophy thanks to a 2–0 victory that featured goals from Samuel Eto'o and Lionel Messi.

Barcelona had ended Chelsea's hopes in the semi-final, after a last minute away goal from Andres Iniesta sent them through at the expense of the Londoners to prevent a second successive all-English final. The Blues had previously beaten Liverpool in the quarter-finals, knocking the Reds out for the second season in a row. It proved another thrilling encounter as Chelsea won the first leg 3–1 at Anfield before Liverpool clawed

ABOVE: *With the pace and incisive passing of Wayne Rooney and Cristiano Ronaldo, Manchester United had developed into one of Europe's most devastating counter-attacking sides. Here, Park Ji-Sung is pictured scoring their third goal of a 3–1 away victory against Arsenal in the Champions League semi-final.*

ABOVE: *The incomparably gifted Lionel Messi demonstrates expert technique to score a rare headed goal and settle the Champions League final in Barcelona's favour.*

back the initiative at Stamford Bridge, hitting two unanswered goals before Chelsea steadied the ship to level the scores at 2–2. Neither side was finished there and four late goals shared between the rivals led to a final score of 4–4, which meant Chelsea advanced 7–5 on aggregate.

As well as competing in the Champions League, Manchester United's title as European champions saw them take part in the World Club World Cup in Japan. The Red Devils went on to lift the trophy, becoming the first English club to do so, following a 1–0 victory over Ecuadorian side Liga de Quito in the final, thanks to a precise and powerful strike from Wayne Rooney.

## UEFA Cup

England's best performing team were Manchester City who topped a group also containing Paris Saint-Germain and Twente before clocking up victories against three Danish sides, Aalborg BK, AaB Fodbold and Copenhagen, to reach the quarter-finals. However, Mark Hughes' men were unable to overcome Germany's SV Hamburg and went out 4–3 on aggregate. Aston Villa and Tottenham's hopes were ended in the round of 32 knockout stage, with Villa suffering defeat to CSKA Moscow and Spurs unable to progress past Shakhtar Donetsk. Portsmouth failed to progress through their group despite holding AC Milan to a famous 2–2 draw at Fratton Park.

## THE INTERNATIONAL SCENE

Fabio Capello's England completed a series of victories in their qualifying campaign for the 2010 World Cup. The Three Lions' most impressive display came against Croatia in Zagreb when a hat-trick from Theo Walcott inspired them to a 4–1 victory.

ABOVE TOP: *AC Milan superstar Kaka takes on Portsmouth's Nadir Belhadj during the south coast club's momentous 2–2 draw with the Italians in the UEFA Cup.*

ABOVE BOTTOM: *Arsenal's Theo Walcott grabs a clinical hat-trick in England's crucial 4–1 away victory against Croatia.*

# CARLO'S CHELSEA CRUISE TO THE TITLE

It was all change at Chelsea once again as temporary boss Guus Hiddink was succeeded by AC Milan's double Champions League winning boss Carlo Ancelotti. Steve Bruce resigned his role as Wigan manager during the summer to become Sunderland boss while Swansea City's Roberto Martinez succeeded Bruce at the JJB Stadium.

The biggest story of the summer was the loss of the Premier League's marquee talent, Cristiano Ronaldo, who left Manchester United for Real Madrid in a world-record £80m deal. Despite receiving such a substantial fee, United remained relatively frugal in the transfer market with many supporters and observers believing that the debt saddled on the club by the Glazer family was having a significant impact upon Sir Alex Ferguson's activity in the transfer market.

OPPOSITE PAGE: *The defensive abilities and leadership qualities of Chelsea captain John Terry were influential in the Blues reclaiming the Premier League title.*

BELOW: *Burnley's Robbie Blake celebrates his successfully converted penalty kick against Manchester United at Turf Moor.*

# TRANSFER TALES

As well as the departure of Cristiano Ronaldo, Manchester United also allowed Carlos Tevez to leave the club, a decision capitalised upon by their mega-rich local rivals Manchester City who bought the Argentine striker outright from his owners, Media Sports Investments. A notorious banner, emblazoned with Tevez's image was soon erected in the city with the wording 'Welcome to Manchester' causing a stir both locally and nationally as the blue half of the city looked to make an impression.

City breached the £100m transfer barrier, bringing in Arsenal striker Emmanuel Adebyor and his Gunners colleague Kolo Toure, Everton defender Joleon Lescott, Aston Villa's Gareth Barry and Roque Santa Cruz from Blackburn.

United's most significant addition was the £16m capture of pacey Wigan winger Antonio Valencia. The Red Devils also added former Liverpool and Newcastle striker Michael Owen on a free transfer and young French winger Gabriel Obertan.

Another significant talent departing England was classy Spanish midfielder Xabi Alonso, who joined Real Madrid from Liverpool for £30m. The Reds replaced him with Italian international Alberto Aquilani from AS Roma and also invested in Glen Johnson from Portsmouth and Greek defender Sotirios Kyrgiakos. Everton equalled their transfer record with the £15m signing of Russian midfielder Diniyar Bilyaletdinov and brought in Sylvain Distin and Johnny Heitinga.

Arsenal invested £10m in Belgian defender Thomas Vermaelen. The Gunners' local rivals, Spurs, brought in Portsmouth pair Peter Crouch and Niko Kranjcar, as well as Sheffield United youngsters, Kyle Walker and Kyle Naughton for a combined fee of £9m and Newcastle defender Sebastien Bassong for £8m.

It was another relatively quiet summer for Chelsea who added Russian utility player Yuri Zhirkov and young Manchester City striker Daniel Sturridge. Aston Villa again spent heavily, bringing in Stuart Downing from Middlesbrough for £12m, James Collins from West Ham, Manchester City's Richard Dunne, Stephen Warnock from Blackburn and Leeds youngster Fabian Delph.

Sunderland experienced a busy transfer window, spending £10m on Spurs striker Darren Bent, £6m on Wigan midfielder Lee Cattermole and £5m on Albanian international midfielder Lorik Cana.

Two former Manchester United fans' favourites, Manchester City manager Mark Hughes (left) unveils new signing Carlos Tevez. The deal caused controversy after the Blues erected a large banner featuring Tevez in Manchester city centre which was labelled 'Welcome to Manchester'.

## BIGGEST TRANSFERS

**EMMANUEL ADEBAYOR** – from Arsenal to Manchester City – £25m

**CARLOS TEVEZ** – from Media Sports Investments to Manchester City – £25m

**JOLEON LESCOTT** – from Everton to Manchester City – £22m

**GLEN JOHNSON** – from Portsmouth to Liverpool – £18m

**YURI ZHIRKOV** – from CSKA Moscow to Chelsea – £18m

**ROQUE SANTA CRUZ** – from Blackburn Rovers to Manchester City – £17.5m

**ALBERTO AQUILANI** – from AS Roma to Liverpool – £17m

**ANTONIO VALENCIA** – from Wigan Athletic to Manchester United – £16m

**DINIYAR BILYALETDINOV** – from Lokomotiv Moscow to Everton – £15m

**KOLO TOURE** – from Arsenal to Manchester City – £14m

# TALES OF THE TURF

Arsenal began the season in fine fettle, thumping Everton 6–1 at Goodison Park to record the biggest opening day top-flight victory for 15 years. Burnley started with a 2–0 loss to Stoke but enjoyed a famous victory in their first home fixture, beating champions Manchester United 1–0 thanks to a goal from Robbie Blake. The Clarets recorded a second victory in their next match against Everton, again by a 1–0 scoreline. Chelsea adjusted quickly to the methods of new manager Carlo Ancelotti, winning each of their opening four games. Manchester United won three of their first four, recording a 2–1 victory over Arsenal, but Chelsea ended August as league leaders.

September brought one of the most entertaining Manchester derbies in living memory when big spending Manchester City, referred to as 'noisy neighbours' by Sir Alex Ferguson, pushed United all the way at Old Trafford. In an end-to-end encounter littered with errors and great goals, United led 3–2 with the match ticking into stoppage time when a mistake from Rio Ferdinand was emphatically seized upon by Craig Bellamy who dribbled with pace past Edwin van der Sar before sliding the ball home from close range. With City poised to celebrate an unlikely point, United launched one final attack in the 96th minute when Ryan Giggs' incisive through ball found substitute Michael Owen, who instantly controlled the ball before prodding it past Shay Given to send the Stretford End into raptures.

The victory was key for United's title hopes but also illustrated that Manchester City were closing the gap in terms of quality. That momentous result helped United close the gap on Chelsea and both clubs ended the month level on 18 points.

Liverpool's indifferent start to the season took a comical turn in October as a beach ball thrown onto the pitch by one of their own supporters in a fixture against Sunderland was influential in deflecting a tame Darren Bent shot past Pepe Reina to gift the Black Cats one of the most extraordinary winning goals in Premier League history. The Reds then recorded a 2–0 victory over Manchester United at Anfield, giving Chelsea a two-point lead.

LEFT: *An incredulous looking Darren Bent celebrates with Sunderland team-mates after his shot deflected into the Liverpool goal off a rogue beach ball.*

The Blues maintained that advantage throughout November, picking up notable victories against Manchester United, when John Terry scored the only goal and away at Arsenal, when Didier Drogba scored twice in a 3–0 win. Portsmouth made another managerial change, replacing Paul Hart with former Chelsea boss Avram Grant.

Chelsea lost 2–1 to Manchester City at the beginning of December before drawing 3–3 with Everton, but Manchester United failed to fully capitalise and suffered a shock home defeat to Aston Villa. Despite an encouraging first half of the campaign and looking on course for their highest league finish for almost 20 years, Manchester City sacked Mark Hughes before Christmas, replacing him with Italian Roberto Mancini.

December brought another managerial change as struggling Bolton relieved Gary Megson of his duties. Chelsea ended the decade as league leaders, with a two-point advantage over Manchester United. Arsenal and Spurs completed the top four while Alex McCleish's Birmingham exceeded expectations and clocked up 32 points from their first 20 games. Portsmouth, Hull and Bolton completed the bottom three.

The New Year saw Owen Coyle leave Burnley to take over as manager of local rival Bolton. The Clarets moved for Brian Laws as his replacement. Three wins from four, including a dominant counter attacking inspired 3–1 victory against Arsenal at the Emirates Stadium, saw Manchester United cut Chelsea's lead to a single point.

In February, Portsmouth's financial struggles were matched by off field worries when they became the first Premier League club to go into administration. Pompey were deducted nine points, leaving them with a paltry total of seven that all but confirmed their relegation.

OPPOSITE PAGE: *Cutting an elegant figure on the touchline and showing he'd lost none of class associated with his playing career, Roberto Mancini was appointed Manchester City boss in December.*

BELOW: *Shielding the ball against Arsenal at the Emirates, Wayne Rooney scored a textbook counter-attacking goal against the Gunners to help Manchester United to victory.*

Manchester City recorded a memorable 4–2 victory over Chelsea at Stamford Bridge. As well as a superb performance form the visitors, which featured two goals from both Carlos Tevez and Craig Bellamy, the game was notable for two sendings off for Chelsea and Wayne Bridge snubbing John Terry's offer of a handshake before the game, following a highly publicised fallout between the ex-team-mates.

An upturn in form for Arsenal during March saw them enter the title picture alongside Chelsea and Manchester United as just three points separated all three clubs. Manchester United maintained their challenge winning all four of their March fixtures, including a 2–1 home triumph over Liverpool. Spurs and Manchester City were a further nine points off the pace in fourth and fifth respectively. Hull City, still struggling at the bottom of the division, opted to sack Phil Brown and name Iain Dowie as his successor.

Portsmouth's inevitable relegation was confirmed in early April as West Ham defeated Sunderland to mathematically rule out any slim hopes the south coast club had of avoiding the drop. Chelsea went from strength to strength in the closing weeks, thumping West Ham 4–1, Portsmouth 5–0 and Aston Villa 7–1 in the space of four games. The Blues also grabbed a crucial 2–1 victory over Manchester United thanks to Didier Drogba's winning goal before United suffered a disappointing 0–0 draw against Blackburn at Ewood Park. Those setbacks left the champions four points adrift after Chelsea beat Bolton 1–0.

United retained their slim title hopes with a dramatic last minute win against Manchester City when Paul Scholes headed home to seal the points. A 2–1 defeat for Chelsea against Tottenham gave United another boost, meaning a 3–1 victory over Spurs saw them reclaim top spot. Chelsea returned to form with a 7–0 drubbing of Stoke which left them a point clear of United and with a significantly better goal difference. Hull City edged closer to relegation following a 1–0 home loss to Sunderland while Burnley were demoted following a 4–0 defeat to Liverpool at Turf Moor.

May began with Spurs taking a big step towards securing fourth place after they recorded a 1–0 success against Bolton. The victory meant the Londoners required just a point from their crucial clash with Manchester City. In the penultimate round of fixtures, Chelsea recorded an impressive 2–0 win at Liverpool to put the title within touching distance and ended Liverpool's hopes of catching

Spurs in the process. Manchester United claimed a critical 1–0 win against Sunderland to ensure the title race went down to the final day.

Hull City's fate was confirmed before the final weekend when they were held to a 2–2 draw by Wigan, letting struggling West Ham, who later parted company with manager of Gianfranco Zola, off the hook. Tottenham recorded a key 1–0 victory at Manchester City thanks to a Peter Crouch goal and ensured their first top four finish for 20 years. It represented a debut qualification for the Champions League and the club's first European Cup campaign for 49 years.

Chelsea went into the final weekend knowing that victory against Wigan would secure them the title. Manchester United had to beat Stoke and hope for a favour from the Latics or a huge and unlikely swing in terms of goal difference. Chelsea took an early lead from the penalty spot as Wigan were reduced to 10 men. The home side eventually strolled to an 8–0 victory, rendering United's 4–0 win against Stoke irrelevant. The Blues lifted their third Premier League title to prevent United from claiming a record fourth successive championship. Arsenal finished third while Liverpool were seventh, their lowest league placing for 11 years.

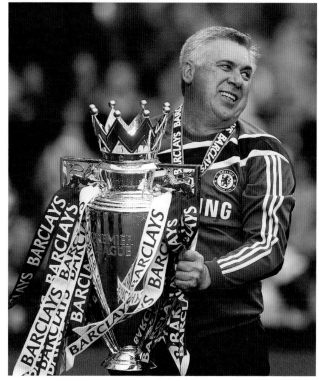

OPPOSITE PAGE TOP: *Craig Bellamy and Carlos Tevez inspired an ever-improving Manchester City to an impressive 4–2 win against Chelsea at Stamford Bridge.*

ABOVE TOP: *Still a potent threat in the Premier League, Chelsea powerhouse Didier Drogba was once again the division's most prolific scorer.*

ABOVE BOTTOM: *Chelsea manager Carlo Ancelotti lifts the Premier League title at the end of his first season in English football.*

# HONOURS LIST

## Barclays Premier League
**CHAMPIONS:** Chelsea
Chelsea showed devastating form in front of goal to score 103 times. They recorded 27 victories and 86 points to finish above Manchester United.
**RUNNERS-UP:** Manchester United
**RELEGATED:** Burnley, Hull City, Portsmouth
**TOP GOAL SCORER:** Didier Drogba (29 goals for Chelsea)

SHOOT MAGAZINE
2009–10

*During the season that saw Shoot cease as a printed publication, this new electronic version of the magazine was available for readers to access via the Shoot website or to download. The cover star was Aston Villa striker John Carew and other interview subjects included Patrice Evra and Florent Malouda. The magazine also focused on the highs and lows of David Beckham's momentous career after the former England captain had joined AC Milan on loan.*

## 2009–10 SEASON TABLE

|   |   | M | W | D | L | GF | GA | GD | PTS |
|---|---|---|---|---|---|---|---|---|---|
| 1 | Chelsea | 38 | 27 | 5 | 6 | 103 | 32 | +71 | 86 |
| 2 | Manchester United | 38 | 27 | 4 | 7 | 86 | 28 | +58 | 85 |
| 3 | Arsenal | 38 | 23 | 6 | 9 | 83 | 41 | +42 | 75 |
| 4 | Tottenham Hotspur | 38 | 21 | 7 | 10 | 67 | 41 | +26 | 70 |
| 5 | Manchester City | 38 | 18 | 13 | 7 | 73 | 45 | +28 | 67 |
| 6 | Aston Villa | 38 | 17 | 13 | 8 | 52 | 39 | +13 | 64 |
| 7 | Liverpool | 38 | 18 | 9 | 11 | 61 | 35 | +26 | 63 |
| 8 | Everton | 38 | 16 | 13 | 9 | 60 | 49 | +11 | 61 |
| 9 | Birmingham City | 38 | 13 | 11 | 14 | 38 | 47 | -9 | 50 |
| 10 | Blackburn Rovers | 38 | 13 | 11 | 14 | 41 | 55 | -14 | 50 |
| 11 | Stoke City | 38 | 11 | 14 | 13 | 34 | 48 | -14 | 47 |
| 12 | Fulham | 38 | 12 | 10 | 16 | 39 | 46 | -7 | 46 |
| 13 | Sunderland | 38 | 11 | 11 | 16 | 48 | 56 | -8 | 44 |
| 14 | Bolton Wanderers | 38 | 10 | 9 | 19 | 42 | 67 | -25 | 39 |
| 15 | Wolverhampton Wanderers | 38 | 9 | 11 | 18 | 32 | 56 | -24 | 38 |
| 16 | Wigan Athletic | 38 | 9 | 9 | 20 | 37 | 79 | -42 | 36 |
| 17 | West Ham United | 38 | 8 | 11 | 19 | 47 | 66 | -19 | 35 |
| 18 | Burnley | 38 | 8 | 6 | 24 | 42 | 82 | -40 | 30 |
| 19 | Hull City | 38 | 6 | 12 | 20 | 34 | 75 | -41 | 30 |
| 20 | Portsmouth | 38 | 7 | 7 | 24 | 34 | 66 | -32 | 19 |

## PLAYERS OF THE SEASON

**PFA PLAYER OF THE YEAR:** Wayne Rooney, Manchester United
**PFA YOUNG PLAYER OF THE YEAR:** James Milner, Aston Villa
**FOOTBALL WRITERS' PLAYER OF THE YEAR:** Wayne Rooney, Manchester United

**FOOTBALL LEAGUE CHAMPIONSHIP CHAMPIONS:**
Newcastle United
**PROMOTED:** West Bromwich Albion
**CHAMPIONSHIP PLAY-OFF WINNERS:** Blackpool
**RELEGATED:** Sheffield Wednesday, Plymouth Argyle, Peterborough United
**TOP GOAL SCORERS:** Nicky Maynard (Bristol City) and Peter Whittingham (Cardiff City) – both 20 goals.

Chris Hughton ensured that Newcastle's spell outside of the Premier League lasted just a single season by guiding the Magpies to a dominant Championship title. Inspired by the goal-scoring form of Andy Carroll and Kevin Nolan, Newcastle finished the campaign with 102 points, their highest ever return. Second place went to West Brom, managed by Roberto Di Matteo, who reached the Premier League for the fourth time in nine seasons.

Ian Holloway's Blackpool capped their end of season surge by defeating Cardiff City 3–2 in an end-to-end play-off final. Goals from Charlie Adam, Gary Taylor-Fletcher and Brett Ormerod helped the Tangerines end a 39-year top-flight exile.

**LEAGUE ONE CHAMPIONS:** Norwich City
**PROMOTED:** Leeds United
**LEAGUE ONE PLAY-OFF WINNERS:** Millwall
**RELEGATED:** Gillingham, Wycombe Wanderers, Southend United, Stockport County
**TOP GOAL SCORER:** Rickie Lambert (31 goals for Southampton)

Under manager Paul Lambert, who joined the club during the first week of the season, Norwich City topped the table with 95 points and scored 86 goals, 24 of which came from powerful striker Grant Holt. Simon Grayson's Leeds United, who led the table at Christmas, avoided an end of season collapse to take second while third place Millwall, bossed by Kenny Jackett, defeated Swindon 1–0 in the play-off final through Paul Robinson's goal.

ABOVE TOP LEFT: *Kevin Nolan (left) and Steven Taylor pose with the Championship trophy after Newcastle United finished top of the pile and confirmed an instant return to the Premier League.*

ABOVE TOP RIGHT: *Leeds United striker Jermaine Beckford celebrates another goal as the Yorkshire club gain promotion to the Championship.*

LEFT: *One of the youngest managers in the Football League, Eddie Howe erased memories of Bournemouth's financial struggles to guide the Cherries back into League One.*

**LEAGUE TWO CHAMPIONS:** Notts County
**PROMOTED:** Bournemouth, Rochdale
**LEAGUE TWO PLAY-OFF WINNERS:** Dagenham & Redbridge
**RELEGATED:** Grimsby Town, Darlington
**TOP GOAL SCORER:** Lee Hughes (30 goals for Notts County)

After six years in the fourth tier, Notts County achieved promotion in style under Steve Cotterill, accumulating 93 points and 96 goals. Eddie Howe completed a remarkable transformation at Bournemouth, having saved the Cherries from likely relegation during the previous campaign, the former club captain galvanised his troops to finish second in the table. Joining Bournemouth in the automatic promotion places were Rochdale, who, under Keith Hill, brought to an end their record 36-season spell in the basement division. John Still's Dagenham & Redbridge won the play-offs, defeating Rotherham United 3–2 thanks to Jon Nurse's crucial goal.

Dropping out of the Football League were financially stricken Darlington and Grimsby Town, the latter losing their league status for the first time in 99 years.

**BLUE SQUARE PREMIER CHAMPIONS:** Stevenage Borough
**PROMOTED:** Oxford United

Graham Westley's Stevenage Borough won 30 of their 44 games to seal the title and promotion to the Football League, 14 years after they were denied promotion due to the unsuitability of their stadium. Oxford United, managed by Chris Wilder, defeated York City 3–1 in the play-off final.

# UP FOR THE CUP

**FA CUP WINNERS:** Chelsea

In what was expected to be a largely one-sided encounter, already relegated Portsmouth gave a decent showing in their 1–0 loss to Chelsea. Blues striker Didier Drogba scored the only goal of the game with a measured free-kick. Pompey, who put in a spirited performance, even spurned the opportunity to take the lead when Kevin Prince-Boateng had his second half penalty saved by Petr Cech. Frank Lampard later missed a penalty for the Londoners, but Drogba's goal decided the contest and handed Chelsea their first league and FA Cup double.

The Blue's progress to the final was confirmed following a routine 3–0 victory over Aston Villa in the semi-final, achieved through goals from Drogba, Lampard and Malouda, while Portsmouth overcame Tottenham 2–0 after extra time, just hours after their Premier League relegation was confirmed, thanks to goals from Frederic Piquionne and Kevin Prince-Boateng.

The standout result in the early rounds of the competition came at Old Trafford where League One Leeds United recorded a shock 1–0 victory against Manchester United following Jermaine Beckford's smartly taken goal. Other impressive performers were Reading who defeated Liverpool 2–1 at Anfield, Stoke who overcame Manchester City and Arsenal and Notts County who ended Wigan's involvement in the tournament.

**LEAGUE (CARLING) CUP WINNERS:** Manchester United

Manchester United retained the Carling Cup with a 2–1 victory over Aston Villa at Wembley thanks to goals from Wayne Rooney and Michael Owen. Sir Alex Ferguson's men also owed a debt of gratitude to referee, Phil Dowd, after Nemanja Vidic miraculously avoided an early red card following a professional foul on Gabby Agbonlahor.

United reached the final following a titanic two-legged struggle against rivals Manchester City. After the first leg ended 2–1 to City, following two goals from Carlos Tevez against his former employers, the red half of Manchester responded in the second leg through Paul Scholes, Michael Carrick and a stoppage time goal from Wayne Rooney to win the tie 4–3. Villa also hit the goal trail to reach the final,

beating Blackburn 7–4 on aggregate, with the likes of James Milner, Emile Heskey and Ashley Young among the goals.

Shock results earlier in the tournament included Blackburn's quarter-final win over Chelsea, Blackpool's victory over Wigan and Barnsley's triumph over Burnley.

**COMMUNITY SHIELD WINNERS:** Manchester United
Chelsea gained revenge for defeat by United on penalties the previous summer, winning a shootout of their own to lift the shield. After an open game ended 2–2 after extra time, Ryan Giggs and Patrice Evra missed from the spot and Salomon Kalou scored the winner.

**THE FOOTBALL LEAGUE (JOHNSTONE'S PAINTS) TROPHY:**
Southampton
Alan Pardew's Southampton lifted the Football League Trophy following a 4–1 destruction of Carlisle United. The Saints goal scorers were Rickie Lambert, Adam Lallana, Papa Waigo and Michail Antonio.

### ⚽ INTERESTING INFO

Chelsea's 2010 FA Cup win was their third success in the tournament in four seasons.

ABOVE TOP: *Didier Drogba and Frank Lampard revel in Chelsea's League and FA Cup double success.*

ABOVE BOTTOM: *Manchester United captain, Nemanja Vidic, who was fortunate to avoid a red card earlier in the game, celebrates the Red Devils' Carling Cup final victory over Aston Villa.*

# INTO EUROPE

## European Champions League

The 2009–10 tournament was the first for six years that didn't feature an English team in the final, as the Premier League's leading lights struggled in the latter stages. 2006 finalists Arsenal were knocked out by reigning champions Barcelona in the quarter-finals, while 2008 winners Manchester United were outclassed by German champions Bayern Munich at the same stage. Both teams had topped their groups before Arsenal beat Porto 6–2 on aggregate and United comprehensively ousted AC Milan 7–2 in the last 32 knockout stage. Chelsea also finished on top of their group but bowed out in the first knockout stage to eventual winners Inter Milan, bossed by their former manager Jose Mourinho. Liverpool provided the biggest disappointment, crashing out at the group stage after registering just seven points.

## UEFA Europa League

Fulham were English football's standout performers in terms of European football for the 2009–10 campaign. The UEFA Cup had been rebranded as the UEFA Europa League and the Intertoto Cup was abolished. With the wily Roy Hodgson in the dugout, the London club progressed all the way to the UEFA Europa League final after a momentous, drama-filled campaign.

The Cotttagers' European adventure began as early as July in the competition's qualifying rounds. After successfully negotiating a two-legged tie with Lithuanian club FK Vetra, Fulham knocked out Russian side Amkar Perm to qualify for the group stage. They were then drawn alongside Roma, Basel and CSKA Sofia. Two wins over Basel and a draw with Roma helped Hodgson's men qualify as runners-up for the knockout fixtures. There, the west Londoners defeated Shakhtar Donetsk to set up a last 16 tie with Juventus. The Italian giants won the first leg in Turin 3–1 but Fulham put in a marvellous performance in the return match at Craven Cottage as goals from Bobby Zamora, Clint Demspey and a double from Zoltan Gera inspired them to a 4–1 win and a 5–4 aggregate victory.

ABOVE: *Simon Davies provides the equalising goal to give Fulham hope against Atletico Madrid in the Europa League final.*

Fulham faced German Bundesliga champions VfL Wolfsburg in the quarter finals and triumphed 3–1 on aggregate thanks to goals from Zamora and Damien Duff. The semi-finals pitted Fulham against another German club but the Londoners again ran out winners, as goals from Gera and Simon Davies sent them through to the final.

The English side faced an even tougher test in the final where they were paired with Spanish side Atletico Madrid. Atletico took a first-half lead through Diego Forlan but Fulham soon equalised through Simon Davies. The Cottagers took the game into extra time but their defences were eventually breached in the 116th minute by another deadly finish from Forlan, which settled the game.

Also reaching the latter stages were Liverpool, who progressed to the semi-finals where they were eliminated on away goals after extra time by Atletico. Of the other English clubs, Everton reached the last round of 32 where they succumbed to Sporting Lisbon and Aston Villa failed to qualify for the group stages.

BELOW: *Fulham midfielder Zoltan Gera celebrates scoring another crucial goal during the Cottagers' memorable UEFA Europa League run.*

# THE INTERNATIONAL SCENE

England maintained their unbeaten record to ensure qualification for the 2010 World Cup with an impressive 5–1 victor over Croatia at Wembley. At the tournament proper in South Africa, draws and largely drab displays against both the USA and Algeria put England's chances of advancing from the group in jeopardy but a crucial 1–0 win over Slovenia, marked by a goal from Jermain Defoe, sent Fabio Capello's men into the knockout stages. The Three Lions faced old foes Germany and were thoroughly outclassed following a disastrous defensive display that the Germans fully capitalised upon to win 4–1.

LEFT: *Gareth Barry and Matthew Upson of England get themselves into a muddle during the Three Lions' 4-1 World Cup drubbing by Germany, as the deadly Tomas Muller looks on.*

# UNITED BACK IN BUSINESS

Liverpool lost Rafa Benitez during the summer break after the Spaniard ended his six-season spell at Anfield. The Reds named Fulham boss Roy Hodgson as Benitez's successor. Fulham opted to bring in Mark Hughes, who had been out of work since departing Manchester City, as their new boss.

Another high-profile departure came on the eve of the season at Aston Villa, when Martin O'Neill decided he had taken the Midlands club as far as he could and tendered his resignation. The Villains promoted reserve team boss, Kevin McDonald, until a permanent successor could be found. West Ham filled their managerial vacancy with the appointment of former Chelsea and Portsmouth boss Avram Grant.

OPPOSITE PAGE: *Alongside Rio Ferdinand at the heart of Manchester United's defence, Serbian warrior Nemanja Vidic provided a solid and uncompromising foundation that allowed the Red Devils' attacking talents to flourish.*

BELOW: *Lively striker Javier Hernandez, also known as 'Chicharito', was one of Manchester United's shining lights during the season. The ultra-composed finisher is pictured during the Red Devils' home victory over Chelsea. The Mexican grabbed the game's opening goal with an unerring finish.*

# TRANSFER TALES

The season's biggest transfer stories took place during the January window when Chelsea's British record bid of £50m for Fernando Torres was accepted by Liverpool. The Reds immediately reinvested that money with the singings of Uruguayan forward Luis Suarez from Ajax for £23m and Newcastle striker Andy Carroll, who commanded a £35m fee.

Manchester City were once again the division's biggest overall spenders as Roberto Mancini strengthened his arm with the additions of Yaya Toure, Edin Dzeko, James Milner, David Silva, Aleksandar Kolarov and Jerome Boateng. In comparison, Manchester United's spending was relatively modest with Sir Alex Ferguson adding Mexican striker Javier Hernandez and young Fulham defender Chris Smalling.

As well as the addition of Fernando Torres, Chelsea looked to build on their League and Cup double success with the signings of Brazilian pair David Luiz and Ramires from Benfica and midfielder Yossi Benayoun from Liverpool.

Liverpool boss Roy Hodgson was extremely active in the market, adding Chelsea midfielder Joe Cole, Jonjo Shelvey from Charlton, Paul Konchesky from Fulham, Danish midfielder Christian Poulsen, Rangers defender Danny Wilson and Milan Jovanovic from Standard Liege.

Aston Villa invested £18m to acquire Darren Bent from Sunderland. The Black Cats strengthened significantly, adding Ghanaian World Cup star Asamoah Gyan for £13m, Wolves striker Steven Fletcher for £12m as well as Belgian goalkeeper Simon Mignolet and French winger Stephane Sessegnon.

Harry Redknapp continued to craft an exciting looking Tottenham squad with the signings of Dutch international Rafael van der Vaart from Real Madrid for £8m and former Chelsea and Arsenal defender William Gallas. Arsenal moved for French defenders Laurent Koscielny and Sebastien Squillaci, as well as Moroccan striker Marouane Chamakh.

Among the big names leaving the Premier League were Liverpool midfielder Javier Mascherano who joined Barcelona, Ricardo Carvalho who left Chelsea for Real Madrid and Manchester City flop Robinho who was loaned to AC Milan.

Manchester City showed they could compete with Europe's biggest clubs in the transfer market when they completed a move for Barcelona midfielder Yaya Toure. The Ivorian went on to become one of City's most talismanic talents.

## BIGGEST TRANSFERS

**FERNANDO TORRES** – from Liverpool to Chelsea – £50m

**ANDY CARROLL** – from Newcastle United to Liverpool – £35m

**JAMES MILNER** – from Aston Villa to Manchester City – £28.5m (including the exchange of Stephen Ireland)

**EDIN DZEKO** – from WfL Wolfsburg to Manchester City – £27m

**MARIO BALOTELLI** – from Inter Milan to Manchester City – £24m

**DAVID SILVA** – from Valencia to Manchester City – £24m

**YAYA TOURE** – from Barcelona to Manchester City – £24m

**LUIS SUAREZ** – from Ajax to Liverpool – £23m

**DAVID LUIZ** – from Benfica to Chelsea – £21.3m

**DARREN BENT** – from Sunderland to Aston Villa – £18m

OPPOSITE PAGE TOP: *In action for his new club Chelsea against his former employers Liverpool, Fernando Torres struggled to recapture the form he enjoyed at Anfield following a £50m move to Stamford Bridge.*

OPPOSITE PAGE BOTTOM: *A survivor of that dying breed of traditional English centre forwards, Andy Carroll joined Liverpool from Newcastle United in a £35m deal. The Reds were flush with cash after selling Fernando Torres to Chelsea and also swelled their ranks with the addition of Uruguayan forward Luis Suarez.*

# TALES OF THE TURF

Newly promoted Blackpool recorded the opening day's shock result, winning 4–0 at Wigan. Later in the month, the Tangerines came back to earth with bump when they were defeated 6–0 by Arsenal, in a game that featured Theo Walcott's first hat-trick for the Gunners. Reigning champions Chelsea ended August at the top of the table, winning all three of their fixtures and scoring 14 goals.

September saw Aston Villa appoint former Liverpool boss Gerard Houllier as manager. Chelsea lost their 100 per cent record after six games, when they went down 1–0 to Manchester City. Manchester United dropped points against Everton and Bolton but recorded an impressive 3–2 victory over Liverpool thanks to a classy hat-trick from Dimitar Berbatov. Chelsea remained the division's pacesetters at the end of the month, leading second placed United by three points.

At the beginning of October, the financial outlook at Liverpool looked bleak, when the club's directors came close to entering the Reds into administration in an attempt to oust the regime of Tom Hicks and George Gillett. That extreme measure didn't come to fruition but Liverpool were soon taken over by new US owners, New England Sports Ventures, who purchased the club for £300m. The off-field headlines continued when Sir Alex Ferguson announced Wayne Rooney's intention not to sign a new contract and leave Manchester United at the end of the season. However, after much media speculation, supporter outrage and extended talks with the club, the England striker made a shock u-turn and committed his future to the club.

Liverpool lost the Merseyside derby 2–0 to Everton and Newcastle hammered Sunderland 5–1 at St James' Park thanks to a Kevin Nolan hat-trick. Back-to-back draws with Sunderland and West Brom saw Manchester United fall further behind Chelsea, who defeated Arsenal, Blackburn and Wolves.

United began November brightly, defeating Wolves 2–1 the day before Chelsea were beaten, 2–0 by Liverpool. United capitalised thanks to a 7–1 thumping of Blackburn when the in-form Dimitar Berbatov scored five times. Chelsea suffered a shock 3–0 home loss to Sunderland and also lost 1–0 to Birmingham. The Blues dropped to second place, with Arsenal and Manchester City back in third and fourth respectively. The three W's of West Ham, Wolves and West Brom made up the bottom three.

BELOW: *Bulgarian striker Dimitar Berbatov looked right at home in a Manchester United shirt during the 2010–11 campaign. The languid forward hit a match-winning hat-trick against Liverpool and scored five goals during this win over Blackburn Rovers.*

*Liverpool legend Kenny Dalglish returned to manage the club for second spell after Roy Hodgson paid the price for a slow start to the season.*

*Liverpool forward Dirk Kuyt celebrates in front of the Kop after completing a hat-trick during the Reds' 3–1 victory over Manchester United at Anfield.*

Meanwhile, another Premier League takeover came to fruition at Ewood Park where the Rao family of India bought Blackburn Rovers for £43m. The new owners took the surprising decision to replace Sam Allardyce with Steve Kean as caretaker boss after Rovers were defeated 2–1 by the Allardyce's former club Bolton Wanderers.

December brought the shock sacking of Newcastle manager Chris Hughton, who had stabilised the Magpies in the top half of the table. His replacement was former Southampton boss Alan Pardew, who was appointed until the end of the season. Pardew's first game in charge ended in a 3–1 victory over Liverpool who continued to struggle for form.

Manchester City and Arsenal closed the gap on leaders Manchester United, but Chelsea fell further off the pace with three consecutive draws and a 3–1 defeat to improving Arsenal. United completed a narrow 1–0 win over the Gunners which helped them end the year in top spot.

A slow start to his tenure saw speculation about Gerard Houllier's position as Aston Villa manager. At the same time, his former club Liverpool parted company with boss Roy Hogdson after just six months. The Reds brought in former manager and club legend, Kenny Dalglish, who returned to the dugout after a 10-year absence. Manchester United won four of their five January fixtures to cement their standing at the top of the table.

February brought one of the more remarkable games of the season at St. James' Park when Arsenal surrendered a four-goal lead to Newcastle. The Gunners stormed 4–0 ahead after just 26 minutes before a spirited fight back from the hosts was completed by a vicious long-range volley by Cheick Tiote. It was the first time in Premier League history that a team with a four goal advantage had failed to win the game. On the same weekend, Everton defeated Blackpool 5–3 thanks to four Louis Saha goals and Carlos Tevez scored a hat-trick in Manchester City's 3–0 win over Wolves.

Manchester United experienced their first loss of the season, suffering a 2–1 defeat against Wolverhampton Wanderers at Molineux. Wolves' local rivals, West Brom, parted company with manager Roberto Di Matteo and replaced him with recently sacked Liverpool boss Roy Hodgson.

A crucial 2–1 win over Manchester City at Old Trafford, which featured a stunning overhead kick from Wayne Rooney, helped Manchester United retain their lead at the top of the table, while

### INTERESTING INFO

On Saturday 5th February 2011 a record 41 goals were scored in one day of Premier League action. The glut of goals came in just eight matches.

Wayne Rooney (centre) celebrates with Michael Carrick (left) and Rio Ferdinand after his penalty against Blackburn confirmed Manchester United's record 19th English top-flight title.

One of Blackpool's star performers in their refreshing approach to the Premier League, Gary Taylor-Fletcher celebrates a goal against Liverpool at Bloomfield Road.

Arsenal, who had recorded back to back home wins, became their nearest challengers.

Manchester United lost twice at the beginning of March when Chelsea beat them 2-1 at Stamford Bridge and Dirk Kuyt scored a hat-trick in Liverpool's 3–1 victory at Anfield. However, the Red Devils' lead at the top of table actually extended by the end of the month, as Arsenal drew against Sunderland and West Brom.

West Ham stormed into a two-goal lead against Manchester United in the opening weekend of April thanks to a pair of penalties from Mark Noble. However, United edged closer to the title with a second-half fight back that featured a Wayne Rooney hat-trick and saw them win 4–2. A week later, Andy Carroll finally bagged his first goals for Liverpool as Kenny Dalglish's men effectively ended Manchester City's faint title hopes with a 3–0 victory at Anfield.

Another expensive striker who ended his goal drought in April was Fernando Torres who scored his first in 13 appearances for Chelsea during a 3–0 win against West Ham. Further wins for Manchester United against Fulham and Everton left them on the verge of the title.

United made a further statement of intent in May when they defeated Chelsea 2–1 at Old Trafford thanks to goals from Javier Hernandez and Nemanja Vidic. It left the leaders needing just a single point from their final two fixtures to win the league. A 3–1

loss to Stoke ended Arsenal's slim hopes before United claimed a 1–1 draw at Blackburn thanks to Wayne Rooney's converted penalty. It meant that the Red Devils' could lift a record 19th league title.

The relegation picture remained unclear after Blackpool completed a dramatic 4-3 victory over Bolton in their penultimate game to maintain their hopes of survival. A win for Wolves against Sunderland boosted their chances but West Ham crashed to a 3-2 loss against Wigan, despite taking a two-goal lead, and became the first club to be relegated. Manager Avram Grant was sacked as a result.

The final day of the season brought relegation agony for both Blackpool and Birmingham. Ian Holloway's Tangerines, who had shown great spirit and attacking attitude during the season, suffered a 4–2 defeat to Manchester United, while a last minute goal from Tottenham condemned League Cup winners Birmingham to their fate. Joining United and Chelsea in the top four were Manchester City, who achieved their highest ever Premier League finish and Arsenal. Chelsea's failure to successfully defend their title saw Carlo Ancelotti sacked following the season's final fixture.

## INTERESTING INFO

A season filled with attack-minded teams the 2010–11 campaign saw a record 1,063 goals scored for a 38-fixture season.

# HONOURS LIST

## Barclays Premier League
**CHAMPIONS:** Manchester United
United claimed back the title and overtook Liverpool in terms of total championship victories thanks to the impressive goal-scoring form of Wayne Rooney, Dimitar Berbatov and Javier Hernandez.
**RUNNERS-UP:** Chelsea
**RELEGATED:** Birmingham City, Blackpool, West Ham United
**TOP GOAL SCORERS:** Dimitar Berbatov (Manchester United) and Carlos Tevez (Manchester City) – both 21 goals.

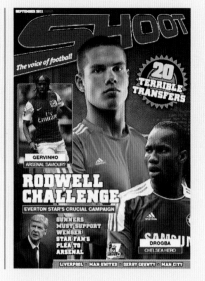

SHOOT MAGAZINE
2010–11

*Everton's highly-rated young midfielder Jack Rodwell gave an exclusive interview about his hopes for the future, while Ivorian stars, Didier Drogba of Chelsea and Gervinho of Arsenal were also featured, as was as a focus on 20 of the most 'terrible transfers' in Premier League history.*

## 2010–11 SEASON TABLE

| | | M | W | D | L | GF | GA | GD | PTS |
|---|---|---|---|---|---|---|---|---|---|
| 1 | Manchester United | 38 | 23 | 11 | 4 | 78 | 37 | +41 | 80 |
| 2 | Chelsea | 38 | 21 | 8 | 9 | 69 | 33 | +36 | 71 |
| 3 | Manchester City | 38 | 21 | 8 | 9 | 60 | 33 | +27 | 71 |
| 4 | Arsenal | 38 | 19 | 11 | 8 | 72 | 43 | +29 | 68 |
| 5 | Tottenham Hotspur | 38 | 16 | 14 | 8 | 55 | 46 | +9 | 62 |
| 6 | Liverpool | 38 | 17 | 7 | 14 | 59 | 44 | +15 | 58 |
| 7 | Everton | 38 | 13 | 15 | 10 | 51 | 45 | +6 | 54 |
| 8 | Fulham | 38 | 11 | 16 | 11 | 49 | 43 | +6 | 49 |
| 9 | Aston Villa | 38 | 12 | 12 | 14 | 48 | 59 | -11 | 48 |
| 10 | Sunderland | 38 | 12 | 11 | 15 | 45 | 56 | -11 | 47 |
| 11 | West Bromwich Albion | 38 | 12 | 11 | 15 | 56 | 71 | -15 | 47 |
| 12 | Newcastle United | 38 | 11 | 13 | 14 | 56 | 57 | -1 | 46 |
| 13 | Stoke City | 38 | 13 | 7 | 18 | 46 | 48 | -2 | 46 |
| 14 | Bolton Wanderers | 38 | 12 | 10 | 16 | 52 | 56 | -4 | 46 |
| 15 | Blackburn Rovers | 38 | 11 | 10 | 17 | 46 | 59 | -13 | 43 |
| 16 | Wigan Athletic | 38 | 9 | 15 | 14 | 40 | 61 | -21 | 42 |
| 17 | Wolverhampton Wanderers | 38 | 11 | 7 | 20 | 46 | 66 | -20 | 40 |
| 18 | Birmingham City | 38 | 8 | 15 | 15 | 37 | 58 | -21 | 39 |
| 19 | Blackpool | 38 | 10 | 9 | 19 | 55 | 78 | -23 | 39 |
| 20 | West Ham United | 38 | 7 | 12 | 19 | 43 | 70 | -27 | 33 |

## PLAYERS OF THE SEASON

**PFA PLAYER OF THE YEAR:** Gareth Bale, Tottenham Hotspur
**PFA YOUNG PLAYER OF THE YEAR:** Jack Wilshere, Arsenal
**FOOTBALL WRITERS' PLAYER OF THE YEAR:** Scott Parker, West Ham United

**FOOTBALL LEAGUE CHAMPIONSHIP CHAMPIONS:**
Queens Park Rangers
**PROMOTED:** Norwich City
**CHAMPIONSHIP PLAY-OFF WINNERS:** Swansea City
**RELEGATED:** Preston North End, Sheffield United,
Scunthorpe United
**TOP GOAL SCORER:** Danny Graham (24 goals for
Watford)

Queens Park Rangers, managed by Neil Warnock, ended a 15-year exile from the Premier League after claiming the Championship title. Warnock, who became the first Rangers boss in six years to complete a full season in charge, equalled the record for most promotions achieved by a single manager. Paul Lambert took Norwich to a second successive promotion, returning the Canaries to the Premier League for the first time since the 2004–05 campaign. Swansea City, managed by Brendan Rodgers, became the first Welsh club to earn promotion to the Premier League following a 4–2 victory over Reading in the play-off final.

**LEAGUE ONE CHAMPIONS:** Brighton & Hove Albion
**PROMOTED:** Southampton
**LEAGUE ONE PLAY-OFF WINNERS:** Peterborough United
**RELEGATED:** Dagenham & Redbridge, Bristol Rovers,
Plymouth Argyle, Swindon Town
**TOP GOAL SCORER:** Craig Mackail-Smith (27 goals for
Peterborough United)

Brighton, under the guidance of Gus Poyet, ended their final season at the Withdean Stadium with the League One title after accumulating 95 points. Southampton finished three points further back in second under new manager Nigel Adkins while Darren Ferguson's Peterborough ran out 3–0 winners against Huddersfield Town in the play-off final.

**LEAGUE TWO CHAMPIONS:** Chesterfield
**PROMOTED:** Bury, Wycombe Wanderers
**LEAGUE TWO PLAY-OFF WINNERS:** Stevenage
**RELEGATED:** Lincoln City, Stockport County
**TOP GOAL SCORER:** Clayton Donaldson (28 goals for
Crewe Alexandra)

John Sheridan's Chesterfield marked the first season at their new stadium with the League Two title after losing just eight of their 46 matches. Joining them in automatic promotion were Bury, under the recently appointed Richie Barker, and Gary Waddock's

ABOVE TOP: *A veteran of countless promotion bids, Neil Warnock celebrates guiding Queens Park Rangers back into the Premier League after a 15-year absence.*

ABOVE MIDDLE: *The distinctively chirpy expression of Gus Poyet was a familiar sight during the 2010–11 season as he guided Brighton back into the second tier as champions.*

ABOVE BOTTOM: *Crewe Alexandra striker Clayton Donaldson finished the season as League Two's most prolific scorer, having hit the target on 29 occasions.*

OPPOSITE PAGE: *Now established as one of the division's most dangerous attacking talents, Tottenham's Gareth Bale was recognised by his fellow professionals, who voted him their PFA Player of the Year.*

Wycombe Wanderers. The final promotion place was taken by Stevenage who defeated Torquay 1–0 in the play-off final thanks to John Mousinho's winning goal.

Dropping out of the Football League were Stockport County whose continued financial struggles led to a second successive relegation and Lincoln City who suffered demotion following a last day 3–0 loss to Aldershot.

**BLUE SQUARE PREMIER CHAMPIONS:** Crawley Town
**PROMOTED:** AFC Wimbledon

Experienced non-league boss Steve Evans guided Crawley into the Football League for the first time following an emphatic title victory that saw the West Sussex club garner 105 points and 85 goals, 37 of which were scored by striker Matt Tubbs. Another club gaining promotion to the Football League for the first time was AFC Wimbledon who, just nine years after their formation, defeated Luton Town 4–3 on penalties in the play-off final.

ABOVE: *Non-league goal poacher supreme, Matt Tubbs found the net 37 times to inspire Crawley Town to the Blue Square title.*

LEFT: *Obafemi Martins (centre) is pursued by Liam Ridgewell (left) and Barry Ferguson after scoring the goal that won the Carling Cup for Birmingham City.*

OVERLEAF: *Manchester City's Yaya Toure celebrates with Mario Balotelli after firing his side into the lead against Stoke in the FA Cup final.*

# UP FOR THE CUP

### FA CUP WINNERS: Manchester City

Manchester City lifted their first major honour for 35 years after Yaya Toure scored the only goal of their final clash with Stoke City. The trophy and a top four finish capped an extremely satisfying season for manager Roberto Mancini and confirmed City's place as the Premier League's emerging power.

Yaya Toure was also the hero in the semi-final as his goal settled matters against Manchester United at Wembley. Stoke, managed by Tony Pulis, reached their first ever FA Cup final following a 5–0 destruction of Bolton in their semi-final. The Potters' goals were supplied by Matthew Etherington, Robert Huth, Kenwyne Jones and Jonathan Walters.

The early rounds of the competition featured a number of cup upsets, including non-league Dover ousting Gillingham, Burton Albion knocking out Middlesbrough, Stevenage defeating Newcastle 3–1 and Sunderland crashing out to Notts County.

### LEAGUE (CARLING) CUP WINNERS: Birmingham City

Birmingham City won their first major trophy for 48 years after a shock 2–1 victory over much-fancied Arsenal in the final. Alex McLeish's Blues took an early lead through giant striker Nikola Zigic before Robin van Persie levelled for the Gunners.

The game was on the verge of entering extra time when substitute Obafemi Martins capitalised on a defensive error to guide the ball home and settle the contest.

Birmingham reached the final following a 4–3 extra-time aggregate victory over West Ham while the Gunners overcame Championship Ipswich at the same stage. Standout results earlier the competition included West Ham thumping Manchester United 4–0 in the fifth round, Ipswich knocking out West Brom and Northampton Town ending Liverpool's involvement, following a third round penalty shootout victory at Anfield.

### COMMUNITY SHIELD WINNERS: Manchester United

Manchester United outclassed Chelsea 3–1 at Wembley thanks to goals from Antonio Valencia, Javier Hernandez and Dimitar Berbatov.

### THE FOOTBALL LEAGUE (JOHNSTONE'S PAINTS) TROPHY: Carlisle United

Carlisle, bossed by Greg Abbott, claimed the trophy for the second time thanks to a 1–0 victory over Brentford. The only goal of the game was scored by defender Peter Murphy.

# INTO EUROPE

## European Champions League

Manchester United reached their third final in four seasons but again found Pep Guardiola's imperious Barcelona standing between them and glory. The Catalan giants came out on top following a 3–1 victory at Wembley. United went in level at half-time after Wayne Rooney equalised Pedro's opening goal but Barca showed their class in the second half as goals from David Villa and Lionel Messi settled the contest.

United reached Wembley after thumping German side Shalke 6–1 on aggregate in the semi-final, having overcome Chelsea 3–1 on aggregate in an all-English quarter-final. The Red Devils' goal scorers against the Blues were Wayne Rooney, Javier Hernandez and Park Ji Sung.

Of the other English sides, Arsenal were beaten in the quarter-finals by eventual winners Barcelona but Champions League debutants Tottenham enjoyed a superb tournament, reaching the quarter-finals where they were eventually knocked out by Real Madrid. Spurs, inspired by the pace and guile of Gareth Bale had recorded several impressive victories earlier in the competition, beating Inter Milan 3–1 at White Hart Lane and disposing of AC Milan 1–0 on aggregate in the last 16.

## UEFA Europa League

Following Fulham's exploits the previous season, English clubs failed to impress. The most notable performers were Liverpool and Manchester City who both progressed as far as the last 16. Liverpool, who had already beaten the likes of Napoli and Sparta Prague, were eventually eliminated by SC Braga of Portugal while City, who had topped a group including Juventus, succumbed to Dynamo Kiev. Aston Villa failed to even qualify for the group stages, crashing out to Rapid Vienna for the second successive season.

# THE INTERNATIONAL SCENE

Still smarting from another withering display at a major tournament, England began their qualifying campaign for Euro 2012 strongly with victories over Bulgaria and Switzerland. A 2–0 win over Wales in Cardiff lifted fans' spirits before manager Fabio Capello polarised opinion by reinstating John Terry as captain.

# CITY SEAL TITLE ON EPIC FINAL DAY

**B**efore the season began, Aston Villa boss Gerard Houllier left the club by mutual consent and was later controversially replaced by Birmingham City boss Alex McLeish. Mark Hughes opted to leave Fulham after less than a year in charge as the Cottagers moved for former Spurs boss Martin Jol.

Chelsea had yet another new manager as Andre Villas-Boas, a young Portuguese coach, seemingly in a similar mould to Jose Mourinho, who had also experienced success with FC Porto, was given the Stamford Bridge reins.

OPPOSITE PAGE: *Manchester City captain Vincent Kompany (left) and manager Roberto Mancini proudly display the Premier League trophy following City's dramatic title clinching victory against QPR.*

BELOW: *Arsenal's Robin van Persie, who ended the campaign as the Premier League's top scorer, skips around Chelsea's Petr Cech on his way to hitting a hat-trick against the Blues at Stamford Bridge.*

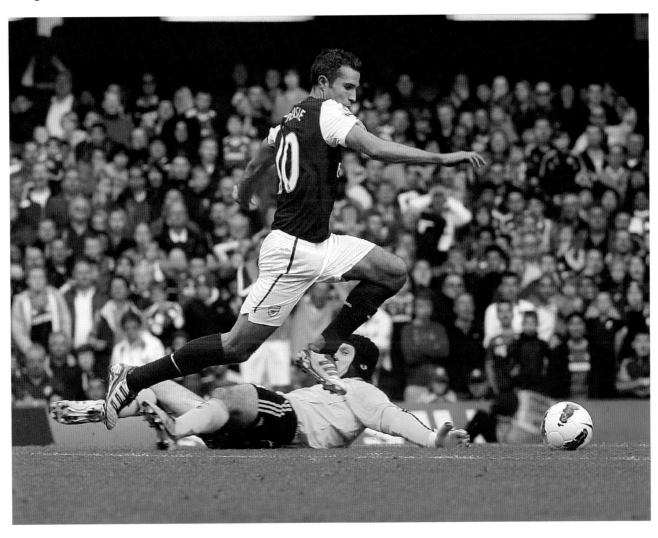

# TRANSFER TALES

Manchester City were again extremely active in the market, making Argentine striker Sergio Aguero their record signing for £38m and capturing two more Arsenal stars, in the form Samir Nasri and Gael Clichy. City also signed Stefan Savic from Partizan Belgrade, Romanian goalkeeper Costel Pantilimon and injury-plagued former Manchester United midfielder Owen Hargreaves.

Manchester United invested in two young English players, Blackburn defender Phil Jones and Aston Villa's Ashley Young, as well as bringing in teenage Spanish goalkeeper David de Gea as Edwin van der Sar's replacement between the posts.

Arsenal also invested in potential, acquiring teenage winger Alex Oxlade-Chamberlain from Southampton and added Ivory Coast forward Gervinho from Lille, Germany defender Per Mertesacker, Brazilian left-back Andre Santos and Everton's Mikel Arteta. Exiting the Emirates was club captain Cesc Fabregas, who returned to Barcelona in a £30m deal.

Chelsea strengthened in the form of Spanish midfielders Juan Mata and Oriol Romeu, Belgian striker Romelu Lukaku and Raul Meireles from Liverpool, while the Reds brought in Craig Bellamy, Charlie Adam and Jose Enrique, and also spent £20m on Middlesbrough's Stewart Downing and £16m on Sunderland's Jordan Henderson.

John O'Shea and Wes Brown both left Manchester United for Sunderland while David Vaughan, Ahmed Elmohamady, Connor Wickham, Sebastian Larsson and Craig Gardner also arrived at the Stadium of Light. Newcastle United brought in Yohan Cabaye from Lille, Sylvain Marveaux on a free transfer and Demba Ba joined from West Ham, with Kevin Nolan moving in the opposite direction.

Stoke signed Peter Crouch and Wilson Palacios from Spurs and brought in defenders Jonathan Woodgate and Matthew Upson. Tottenham added Manchester City striker Emmanuel Adebayor on loan and completed permanent deals for Brad Friedel, Louis Saha and Scott Parker.

Premier League newcomers Swansea brought in Michael Vorm, Danny Graham, Wayne Routledge and loaned Steven Caulker from Spurs. Newly-promoted QPR also swelled their numbers, adding Jay Bothroyd, Danny Gabbidon, Luke Young, Shaun Wright-Phillips, Anton Ferdinand, Armand Traore, Joey Barton and Kieron Dyer.

January saw an amazing u-turn from Manchester United legend Paul Scholes, who came out of retirement after hanging up his boots the previous summer. The winter window also saw a loan return to Arsenal for Thierry Henry, who arrived on a temporary deal from New York Red Bulls. Robbie Keane completed a similar deal, when he joined Aston Villa on loan from LA Galaxy.

## BIGGEST TRANSFERS

**SERGIO AGUERO** – from Atletico Madrid to Manchester City – £38m

**SAMIR NASRI** – from Arsenal to Manchester City – £25m

**JUAN MATA** – from Valencia to Chelsea – £23.5m

**STEWART DOWNING** – from Aston Villa to Liverpool – £20m

**DAVID DE GEA** – from Atletico Madrid to Manchester United – £18.9m

**PHIL JONES** – from Blackburn Rovers to Manchester United – £17m

**ASHLEY YOUNG** – from Aston Villa to Manchester United – £17m

**JORDAN HENDERSON** – from Sunderland to Liverpool – £16m

**ALEX OXLADE-CHAMBERLAIN** – from Southampton to Arsenal – £12m

**RAUL MEIRELES** – from Liverpool to Chelsea – £12m

# TALES OF THE TURF

Manchester City and Manchester United both began the season in emphatic goal-scoring form. City's new signings all adjusted well, as Sergio Aguero scored on his debut against Swansea and Edin Dzeko grabbed four in a 5–1 demolition of Tottenham. United, meanwhile, achieved one of the most notable results in Premier League history by embarrassing Arsenal, their closest rivals for many years, 8–2 at Old Trafford. The victory, which featured a hat-trick from Wayne Rooney, was United's highest scoring game since February 1999 and inflicted Arsenal's worst defeat in 116 years. United ended the month top of the table, only ahead of Manchester City on goal difference.

United maintained their impressive form in September, hammering Bolton 5–0 and beating Chelsea 3–1 at Old Trafford. City recorded home wins over Everton and West Brom to keep up the pace and both teams again ended the month level on points. Chelsea were third with Alan Pardew's Newcastle showing good form in fourth.

LEFT: *Tom Cleverley and Ashley Young celebrate with Wayne Rooney (centre) during Manchester United's 8–2 mauling of Arsenal at Old Trafford.*

A 1–1 draw between Liverpool and Manchester United at Anfield was overshadowed by alleged racist comments made by Reds striker Luis Suarez to United's Patrice Evra during the game. Following an FA investigation, Suarez was found guilty and subsequently banned for eight matches. In protest of Evra's allegations and the pending FA investigation, Liverpool caused a stir when the whole squad opted to wear t-shirts in support of Suarez during the warm-up of their next fixture against Wigan.

In their next fixture United faced another of their fierce rivals, Manchester City, and were on the wrong end of a humiliating scoreline at Old Trafford. Having gone down to ten men in the first half, the Red Devils were blown away 6–1 by Roberto Mancini's ruthless attacking force. The defeat was United's worst under Sir Alex Ferguson and their heaviest home loss since 1955. Chelsea lost ground following a 1–0 win at QPR in a game marred by an alleged racial slur made by Blues and England skipper John Terry to R's defender Anton Ferdinand.

Chelsea suffered a further loss in their following game, when Arsenal, inspired by a Robin van Persie hat-trick, completed a 5–3 victory at Stamford Bridge. October ended with Manchester City five points clear at the top of the table, with Manchester United second and Newcastle third.

In November, Steve Bruce was relieved of his duties by struggling Sunderland. A sequence of hard-fought 1–0 wins kept Manchester United in the title hunt, but the continued brilliance of Manchester City ensured they maintained a five-point lead. Tottenham rediscovered their form following a slow start and sat third, just two points behind United while Newcastle were fourth, with usual top four dwellers; Chelsea, Arsenal and Liverpool, all off the pace.

Manchester United enjoyed a positive December, winning five of their six fixtures, including back to back 5–0 home victories, as Manchester City suffered their first loss of the season against Chelsea before dropping points at West Brom. United ended the year on top of the table, but City had a game in hand. Spurs remained third with Arsenal fourth.

Manchester City started the New Year with a disappointing 1–0 loss at Sunderland, but four consecutive wins allowed them to top the table at the end of January. United suffered a 3–0 defeat at Newcastle but recovered to win their next three fixtures. QPR dispensed with Neil Warnock as manager and brought in Mark Hughes as his replacement.

ABOVE: *The rivalry between Liverpool's Luis Suarez and Manchester United's Patrice Evra intensified throughout the season.*

February saw John Terry stripped of the England captaincy in relation to his charge of racially abusing Anton Ferdinand in October. The outcome of the trial was still to be decided, leading to England boss Fabio Capello criticising the FA for the timing of their decision and tendering his immediate resignation.

*The subtle skills of Spanish international David Silva were key to Manchester City's domestic success during the season.*

*Concerned team-mates and opponents look on as Fabrice Muamba receives emergency treatment after collapsing on the pitch during an FA Cup tie between Tottenham and Bolton.*

West Brom deepened rivals Wolves' relegations concerns with a 5–1 victory against them at Molineux in the Black Country derby. The result led to the sacking of Wolves manager Mick McCarthy, who was replaced by assistant boss Terry Connor. Manchester City maintained their lead at the top of the table, winning each of their three fixtures, while Manchester United beat Liverpool 2–1 but dropped points in a 3–3 draw at Chelsea. The United Liverpool clash saw hostilities renewed between Luis Suarez and Patrice Evra, with the Uruguayan refusing to shake the Frenchman's hand before the game. A 5–2 loss to Arsenal left Spurs 10 points adrift in third.

March brought another managerial casualty as Chelsea showed Andre Villas-Boas the door following a 1–0 loss against West Brom. The Blues appointed former player Roberto Di Matteo, who had been acting as assistant manager, to the role until the end of the season. A 2–0 win for Manchester United over West Brom and a 1–0 loss for Manchester City at Swansea saw the Red Devils return to the top of the table for the first time since October. Wolves, who had registered just a single point since the sacking of Mick McCarthy, looked doomed to relegation as they stood six points adrift of safety with seven games to play.

The world of football held its breath in March after Bolton midfielder Fabrice Muamba collapsed on the pitch during an FA Cup tie between Tottenham and the Trotters at White Hart Lane. A severely ill Muamba had to be resuscitated several times and was taken to a nearby hospital where he lay in an induced coma before eventually recovering. Another Premier League footballer suffered a health scare when Aston Villa captain Stiliyan Petrov was diagnosed with acute leukaemia.

Wins against Blackburn and QPR at the beginning of April, combined with a 1–0 loss for Manchester City at Arsenal, left Manchester United eight points clear with six games to play. That gap closed to five points when United lost at struggling Wigan and City defeated West Brom 4–0. The next twist came when Manchester United were held to a 4–4 draw by an Everton buoyed by the impressive form of Marouane Fellaini, who terrorised the United defence at Old Trafford. Buoyed by that result, City defeated Wolves 2–0 to cut United's lead to three points in an outcome that also relegated Wolves. The month ended with a potential title decider between the two Manchester clubs. In a tight, tactical battle, City grabbed a 1–0 win thanks to a headed goal from skipper Vincent Kompany which left them top of the league with a goal difference of plus eight and two games left to play.

## INTERESTING INFO

In December the 20,000th Premier League goal was scored by Aston Villa midfielder Marc Albrighton against Arsenal.

May began with both City and United winning their penultimate games, with United defeating Swansea 2–0 and City winning by the same scoreline at Newcastle. Blackburn became the second team to be relegated when they lost 1–0 to Wigan, bringing an end to their 11-year stay in the top flight.

The final day saw Manchester City installed as odds on favourites to lift the title. With a hugely superior goal difference over Manchester United and facing relegation threatened QPR at home, the blue half of Manchester appeared to be the most likely to be celebrating at the final whistle. However, despite City taking the lead through Pablo Zabaleta, things didn't run that smoothly as QPR equalised through Djibril Cisse before taking an unlikely lead through Jamie Mackie. With United 1–0 up at Sunderland through Wayne Rooney, City needed two goals to maintain top spot.

A series of missed chances and a hugely tense atmosphere inside the Etihad stadium appeared to inhibit even the most talented players. But, after United's game ended 1–0, City scored a 92nd minute equaliser through Edin Dezko's header. They still needed another goal to lift the title and in their last attack of the game, that goal came when substitute Mario Balotelli fed Sergio Aguero inside the box. The speedy Argentine rode an apparent foul challenge before steadying himself and lashing the ball into the net to seal City's first Premier League title in the most dramatic fashion possible.

QPR's safety was assured despite the loss when Bolton only drew with Stoke and dropped out of the division. Elsewhere, Arsenal and Spurs joined City and United in the top four, with Newcastle fifth, Chelsea sixth, Everton seventh and Liverpool down in eighth.

## ⚽ INTERESTING INFO

Newcastle United manager Alan Pardew was named Premier League Manager of the Season, becoming the first Magpies boss and only the second Englishman, after Harry Redknapp, to receive the accolade.

ABOVE TOP: *Sergio Aguero celebrates one of the most memorable goals in Premier League history after keeping his composure to rifle the ball past QPR stopper Paddy Kenny to provide Manchester City with their first Premier League title in the most dramatic of circumstances.*

ABOVE BOTTOM: *Manchester City boss Roberto Mancini cuts a delirious figure as his club's Premier League title is confirmed.*

LEFT TOP: *The physical presence and goal-scoring ability of Everton's Marouane Fellaini put the title race cats firmly amongst the pigeons as the Toffees held Manchester United to a 4–4 draw at Old Trafford.*

LEFT BOTTOM: *Manchester City's Carlos Tevez attempts to break down the QPR defence as tension envelops the Eithad Stadium on the final day of the season.*

OVERLEAF TOP: *Manchester City's first team squad hold the club's first Premier League title aloft.*

OVERLEAF BOTTOM: *Newcastle enjoyed an impressive campaign under Premier League Manager of the Year Alan Pardew, narrowly missing out on a top four finish. Here, one of their most prolific performers, Papiss Cisse, scores one of the season's most spectacular goals against Chelsea at Stamford Bridge.*

# HONOURS LIST

## Barclays Premier League

**CHAMPIONS:** Manchester City
City claimed their first top-flight league title for 43 years and the third in their history following the most remarkable climax in Premier League history.
**RUNNERS-UP:** Manchester United
**RELEGATED:** Bolton Wanderers, Blackburn Rovers, Wolverhampton Wanderers
**TOP GOAL SCORER:** Robin van Persie (30 goals for Arsenal)

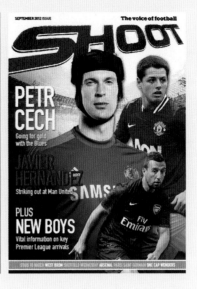

SHOOT MAGAZINE
2011–12

New Manchester United signing Javier Hernandez was joined on the front cover by Chelsea goalkeeper Petr Cech and Arsenal midfielder Santi Cazorla. The magazine assessed the summer's new arrivals and also ran features on England's 'one cap wonders' and the re-emergence of French club Paris Saint-Germain as a European force.

# 2011–12 SEASON TABLE

|   |   | M | W | D | L | GF | GA | GD | PTS |
|---|---|---|---|---|---|----|----|----|----|
| 1 | Manchester City | 38 | 28 | 5 | 5 | 93 | 29 | +64 | 89 |
| 2 | Manchester United | 38 | 28 | 5 | 5 | 89 | 33 | +56 | 89 |
| 3 | Arsenal | 38 | 21 | 7 | 10 | 74 | 49 | +25 | 70 |
| 4 | Tottenham Hotspur | 38 | 20 | 9 | 9 | 66 | 41 | +25 | 69 |
| 5 | Newcastle United | 38 | 19 | 8 | 11 | 56 | 51 | +5 | 65 |
| 6 | Chelsea | 38 | 18 | 10 | 10 | 65 | 46 | +19 | 64 |
| 7 | Everton | 38 | 15 | 11 | 12 | 50 | 40 | +10 | 56 |
| 8 | Liverpool | 38 | 14 | 10 | 14 | 47 | 40 | +7 | 52 |
| 9 | Fulham | 38 | 14 | 10 | 14 | 48 | 51 | -3 | 52 |
| 10 | West Bromwich Albion | 38 | 13 | 8 | 17 | 45 | 52 | -7 | 47 |
| 11 | Swansea City | 38 | 12 | 11 | 15 | 44 | 51 | -7 | 47 |
| 12 | Norwich City | 38 | 12 | 11 | 15 | 52 | 66 | -14 | 47 |
| 13 | Sunderland | 38 | 11 | 12 | 15 | 45 | 46 | -1 | 45 |
| 14 | Stoke City | 38 | 11 | 12 | 15 | 36 | 53 | -17 | 45 |
| 15 | Wigan Athletic | 38 | 11 | 10 | 17 | 42 | 62 | -20 | 43 |
| 16 | Aston Villa | 38 | 7 | 17 | 14 | 37 | 53 | -16 | 38 |
| 17 | Queens Park Rangers | 38 | 10 | 7 | 21 | 43 | 66 | -23 | 37 |
| 18 | Bolton Wanderers | 38 | 10 | 6 | 22 | 46 | 77 | -31 | 36 |
| 19 | Blackburn Rovers | 38 | 8 | 7 | 23 | 48 | 78 | -30 | 31 |
| 20 | Wolverhampton Wanderers | 38 | 5 | 10 | 23 | 40 | 82 | -42 | 25 |

# PLAYERS OF THE SEASON

**PFA PLAYER OF THE YEAR:** Robin van Persie, Arsenal
**PFA YOUNG PLAYER OF THE YEAR:** Kyle Walker, Tottenham Hotspur
**FOOTBALL WRITERS' PLAYER OF THE YEAR:** Robin van Persie, Arsenal

**FOOTBALL LEAGUE CHAMPIONSHIP CHAMPIONS:** Reading
**PROMOTED:** Southampton
**CHAMPIONSHIP PLAY-OFF WINNERS:** West Ham United
**RELEGATED:** Portsmouth, Coventry City, Doncaster Rovers
**TOP GOAL SCORER:** Rickie Lambert (27 goals for Southampton)

Champions Reading, managed by Brian McDermott, ended four years outside of the Premier League, after winning 27 of their 46 games. The Royals finished a point clear of Nigel Adkins' Southampton in second place. The Saints, inspired by the continued goal scoring form of Rickie Lambert, ended their seven-year exile from the top flight. Sam Allardyce and West Ham United took the third promotion place following a 2–1 play-off final victory over Blackpool, thanks to goals from Carlton Cole and Ricardo Vaz Te.

**LEAGUE ONE CHAMPIONS:** Charlton Athletic
**PROMOTED:** Sheffield Wednesday
**LEAGUE ONE PLAY-OFF WINNERS:** Huddersfield Town
**RELEGATED:** Wycombe Wanderers, Chesterfield, Exeter City, Rotherham United
**TOP GOAL SCORER:** Jordan Rhodes (36 goals for Huddersfield Town)

Managed by fans' favourite Chris Powell, Charlton Athletic accumulated 101 points to lift the League One title, losing just five games and finishing eight points clear of runners-up Sheffield Wednesday. The Owls, bossed by Dave Jones, gained automatic promotion ahead of neighbours Sheffield United following a final day victory over Wycombe Wanderers. The third promotion place was filled by Simon Grayson's Huddersfield Town who defeated Sheffield United 8–7 on penalties in the play-off final.

LEAGUE TWO CHAMPIONS: Swindon Town
PROMOTED: Shrewsbury Town, Crawley Town
LEAGUE TWO PLAY-OFF WINNERS: Crewe Alexandra
RELEGATED: Hereford United, Macclesfield Town
TOP GOAL SCORERS: Jack Midson (AFC Wimbledon), Izale McLeod (Barnet), Lewis Grabban (Rotherham United) and Adenayo Akinfenwa (Northampton Town) – all 18 goals.

Charismatic Italian Paolo Di Canio inspired Swindon to the title in his first season as manager, with the Robins clocking up 93 points and conceding just 32 goals. Second place was taken by Graham Turner's Shrewsbury Town, Crawley Town sealed back to promotions with a third place finish while Crewe defeated Cheltenham Town 2–0 in the play-off final through goals from Nick Powell and Byron Moore.

Macclesfield Town dropped back into the Conference after 15 years in the Football League and were joined by Hereford United.

BLUE SQUARE PREMIER CHAMPIONS: Fleetwood Town
PROMOTED: York City

Fleetwood Town stormed to the title to ensure league football for the first time in their history. Managed by Micky Mellon, the Cod Army accumulated 103 points and scored 102 goals. Joining them in the Football League were York City who overcame Luton Town 2–1 in the play-off final.

ABOVE TOP: *Showing every inch of the passion he exuded as a player, Paolo Di Canio salutes the Swindon Town fans after leading the Robins to the League Two title.*

ABOVE BOTTOM: *Club legend Chris Powell guided Charlton Athletic to the League One championship.*

# UP FOR THE CUP

### FA CUP WINNERS: Chelsea

Chelsea lifted their first trophy under interim manager Roberto Di Matteo after defeating Liverpool 2–1 in the final. The Blues took a first-half lead through Ramires before Didier Drogba doubled their advantage after 52 minutes. Andy Carroll reduced the arrears for Liverpool but the London club held on to lift the FA Cup for the seventh time.

Chelsea reached the final following a 5–1 mauling of Tottenham which featured goals from Drogba, Juan Mata, Ramires, Frank Lampard and Florent Malouda. Liverpool overcame Merseyside rivals Everton 2–1 at the same stage thanks to goals from Luis Suarez and Andy Carroll.

Earlier in the competition headlines were made by the likes of Crawley Town who advanced to the fifth round after defeating Hull City; Brighton, who knocked out Newcastle and Stevenage, who ended Reading's involvement in the competition.

### LEAGUE (CARLING) CUP WINNERS: Liverpool

Kenny Dalglish won the first trophy of his second spell as Liverpool manager after the Reds defeated Cardiff City 3–2 on penalties in the Carling Cup final. The game ended 1–1 after 90 minutes with Cardiff's opener coming from Joe Mason and Liverpool's late equaliser scored by Martin Skrtel. The teams shared another two goals in extra time after the Bluebirds' Ben Turner equalised Dirk Kuyt's effort. The drama from twelve yards was decided after Antony Gerrard, cousin of Liverpool captain Steven, had his penalty saved and Reds defender Glen Johnson made no mistake with his spot kick.

Liverpool progressed to the final thanks to a 3–2 aggregate semi-final victory over Manchester City while Cardiff ended Crystal Palace's hopes following a penalty shootout win. Standout results earlier in the competition included Palace's quarter-final victory against Manchester United at Old Trafford, Cardiff knocking out Blackburn and Rochdale ousting QPR.

ABOVE TOP LEFT: *Chelsea midfielder Ramires celebrates his FA Cup final goal against Liverpool.*

ABOVE TOP RIGHT:
*Liverpool players pose for photographs with the Carling Cup following their penalty shootout victory over Cardiff City.*

**COMMUNITY SHIELD WINNERS:** Manchester United

Manchester United won the Community Shield thanks to a 3–2 victor over Manchester City. The Red Devils had been two goals down, after City scored through Joleon Lescott and Edin Dzeko, but stormed back in the second half through goals from Chris Smalling and Nani, who bagged a brace.

**THE FOOTBALL LEAGUE (JOHNSTONE'S PAINTS) TROPHY:** Chesterfield

John Sheridan's Chesterfield defeated Swindon 2–0 at Wembley after an own goal from Oliver Risser and a late strike from Craig Westcarr.

# INTO EUROPE

## European Champions League

Against all odds Chelsea lifted the first European Cup of their history after a penalty shootout victory over Bayern Munich in the final. Bayern, playing at their Allianz Arena home stadium, bossed the game in terms of possession and attacking intent but it took the Germans until the 83rd minute to break the deadlock through Tomas Muller. Chelsea raised their game and with just two minutes left to play Didier Drogba rose at the near post to powerfully head home a Juan Mata corner.

BELOW: *Didier Drogba keeps his cool to side foot home the penalty that made Chelsea European Champions for the first time.*

*Chelsea players celebrate winning the Champions League for the first time in the club's history.*

Bayern were again the better side in extra time and had the opportunity to retake the lead when Drogba fouled Frank Ribery in the area and gave Arjen Robben a chance to score from the penalty spot. However, the former Chelsea winger fluffed his lines and saw his tame strike saved by Petr Cech. The game went into penalties, with Mata missing the Blues' first kick. However, Cech was again the hero as he saved penalties from both Ivica Olic and Bastian Schweinsteiger, giving Drogba the opportunity to win the contest for the Blues. The experienced Ivorian calmly stepped up, sent Manuel Neuer the wrong way and rolled the ball into the bottom left corner to realise Roman Abramovich's dream of winning Europe's premier competition.

The Blues' run to the final saw them top a group that also contained Bayer Leverkusen, Valencia and Genk. They then knocked out Napoli and Benfica over two legs to set up a semi-final tie against reigning champions Barcelona. Didier Drogba gave the Blues a narrow 1–0 lead following the first leg at Stamford Bridge before an incident filled second leg at the Nou Camp. Barca levelled the aggregate scores after 35 minutes through Sergio Busquets before John Terry saw red for an ill-judged kick on Barca's Alexis Sanchez that meant he would miss the final due to suspension.

Andres Iniesta gave Barca the lead before Ramires grabbed a crucial away goal on the stroke of half-time when he scooped a delicious chip over the advancing Victor Valdes. As the game ticked into stoppage time and with Barcelona seemingly running out of ideas, Chelsea launched a lightning quick counter-attack that freed Fernando Torres through on goal from just inside their opponent's half. The much maligned forward showed the speed and composure many thought he'd lost, rounding Valdes and stroking the ball home to send Chelsea into the final 3–2 on aggregate.

Of the other Premier League sides Arsenal again exited in the last round of 16, this time 4–3 on aggregate to AC Milan, while Manchester City and Manchester United both failed to qualify from their groups.

## UEFA Europa League

Fulham, Stoke, Birmingham City and Tottenham all progressed into the league stages of the tournament but only Stoke City managed to qualify for the knockout stages. Tony Pulis' side were knocked out 2–0 on aggregate in the last round of 32 by Valencia. Also joining the Potters at that stage of the tournament were Manchester City and Manchester United, following their elimination from the Champions League. City crashed out to Sporting Lisbon on away goals in the last 16 while United were defeated by Athletic Club.

## THE INTERNATIONAL SCENE

Wins against Bulgaria and Wales and a 2–2 draw with Montenegro saw England seal qualification for Euro 2012. Roy Hodgson, who had replaced Fabio Capello as manager in May just a few weeks before the European Champions, led the Three Lions to victories over Sweden and Ukraine and a draw with the France in the tournament proper. However, Hodgson's men failed to overcome Italy in the quarter-finals, crashing out on penalties following a 0–0 draw.

ABOVE LEFT: *Fernando Torres silenced many of his critics with a typically clinical counter-attacking goal against Barcelona at the Nou Camp, which confirmed Chelsea's passage to the Champions League final.*

LEFT: *England striker Danny Welbeck finds the net with an improvised back heeled finish during the Three Lions' topsy-turvy Euro 2012 group stage clash against Sweden.*

# VAN PERSIE PROVIDES 20/20 VISION

European champions Chelsea retained Roberto Di Matteo as manager going into the new season but Tottenham, who finished fourth but missed out on Champions League qualification due to Chelsea's success in the competition, took the surprising decision to sack manager Harry Redknapp, going on to replace him with former Blues boss Andre Villas-Boas.

Liverpool, who sacked Kenny Dalglish at the close of the previous campaign, named Swansea City manager Brendan Rodgers as his replacement. Succeeding Rodgers at Swansea was former Danish international forward Michael Laudrup. Another new boss for the new season was Steve Clarke, who was named as Roy Hodgson's replacement at West Brom. Aston Villa appointed Paul Lambert during the summer after parting company with Alex McLeish.

OPPOSITE PAGE: *Wearing number 20 on his back, Manchester United marksman Robin van Persie was the crucial attacking element in the Red Devils' securing their 20th English league title.*

LEFT: *After many of European football's biggest clubs attempted to add the spellbinding skill of young Belgian forward Eden Hazard to their ranks, Chelsea eventually won the race for his signature.*

# TRANSFER TALES

As well as the headline grabbing and much-protracted signing of Arsenal captain Robin van Persie for £24m, Manchester United also added Borussia Dortmund's Japanese playmaker Shinji Kagawa for £12m, Dutch left-back Alexander Buttner and young English midfielder Nick Powell from Crewe.

On the other side of Manchester, Roberto Mancini spent considerably less than usual, with the club conscious of UEFA's new financial fair play constraints and having to boost their English national contingent to meet other regulations. The Blues invested £12m in Everton's Jack Rodwell, as well signing Swansea forward Scott Sinclair, Brazilian right-back Maicon and Serbian defender Matija Nastasic.

Invigorated by their Champions League success, Chelsea again spent heavily, acquiring Belgian winger Eden Hazard for £34m, Brazilian midfielder Oscar for £19.35m, Cesar Azpilicueta from Marseille and Wigan forward Victor Moses for £9m, as well as adding Marko Marin and Demba Ba. The Blues lost Didier Drogba and sold Daniel Sturridge to Liverpool.

The Reds also moved for Roma striker Fabio Borini for £10.5m and loaned Nuri Sahin from Real Madrid but allowed Dirk Kuyt to depart for Fenerbahce, Andy Carroll to join West Ham on loan and Charlie Adam to sign for Stoke on a permanent deal. Stoke also brought in Blackburn midfielder Steven N'Zonzi and signed Michael Owen on a free transfer.

Arsenal's most expensive signing was French forward Olivier Giroud who joined for £12m from Montpellier. The Gunners also added German striker Lukas Podolski but lost midfielder Alex Song to Barcelona. North London rivals Spurs sold Luka Modric to Real Madrid but reinvested the money on the likes of French goalkeeper Hugo Lloris for £11.8m, Hoffenheim midfielder Gylfi Sigurdsson and Manchester City striker Emmanuel Adebayor.

Sunderland spent heavily, bringing in Steven Fletcher from Wolves for £12m and England winger Adam Johnson from Manchester City for £10m. Aston Villa made several significant additions, including Dutch defender Ron Vlaar and Belgian striker Christian Benteke. Everton strengthened with Kevin Mirallas, Steven Naismith and Bryan Ovideo joining the club, while Swansea signed Spanish striker Michu and his countrymen, Chico Flores and Pablo Hernandez.

QPR were one of the most active clubs in the market, adding Park Ji-Sung, Junior Hoilett, Julio Cesar, Rob Green, Jose Boswinga, Esteban Granero and Ryan Nelson. Elsewhere in London Mohamed Diame, Jussi Jaaskelainen, Matt Jarvis, Modibo Maiga and Alou Diarra signed for West Ham while Fulham brought in Dimitar Berbatov, Sascha Riether and Mladen Petric.

Highlights of the January transfer window included Mathieu Debuchy joining Newcastle and QPR spending £12.5m on former Blackburn defender Christopher Samba and £8m on French striker Loic Remy.

*Manchester United completed their determined pursuit of Arsenal captain Robin van Persie ahead of the campaign and the Dutchman soon justified Sir Alex Ferguson's great faith in his ability.*

## BIGGEST TRANSFERS

**EDEN HAZARD** – from Lille to Chelsea – £32m

**ROBIN VAN PERSIE** – from Arsenal to Manchester United – £24m

**OSCAR** – from Internacional to Chelsea – £19.35m

**MOUSA DEMBELE** – from Fulham to Tottenham Hotspur – £15m

**CHRISTOPHER SAMBA** – from Anzhi Makhachkala to Queens Park Rangers – £12.5m

**STEVEN FLETCHER** – from Wolverhampton Wanderers to Sunderland – £12m

**OLIVIER GIROUD** – from Montpellier to Arsenal – £12m

**SHINJI KAGAWA** – from Borussia Dortmund to Manchester United – £12m

**JACK RODWELL** – from Everton to Manchester City – £12m

**DANIEL STURRIDGE** – from Chelsea to Liverpool – £12m

# TALES OF THE TURF

Chelsea began the campaign strongly, achieving maximum points from their opening three games, which included 2–0 wins against Wigan and Newcastle. Everton and Swansea also started well, with Spanish striker Michu bagging an opening day brace in a 5–0 victory at QPR. Manchester United lost their opening fixture 1–0 to Everton but recovered with 3–2 victories against Fulham and Southampton, the latter featuring a hat-trick from summer signing Robin van Persie. Manchester City began with a 3–2 win over the Saints but dropped points against Liverpool.

September brought the first managerial departure of the season as under-fire Blackburn boss Steve Kean resigned. Chelsea maintained their impressive start, remaining unbeaten after six games and sat three points clear of second-place Everton. Manchester City drew with both Arsenal and Stoke while Manchester United grabbed a 2–1 win at Liverpool, but lost 3–2 to a Gareth Bale-inspired Spurs.

Manchester United enjoyed a comprehensive 3–0 win against Newcastle and defeated Stoke 4–2 before picking up a 3–2 win against leaders Chelsea to cut the Blues' advantage to a point. Manchester City went level on points with United after three successive wins. Spurs, who sat fourth, continued to impress under new boss Andre Villas-Boas.

November brought a significant dip in form for Chelsea as the European champions failed to win any of their five fixtures, drawing four and losing away to West Brom. Poor form in the Champions League, culminating in a 3–0 defeat to Juventus, led to Roberto Di Matteo being sacked by the club. His replacement, named on an interim basis, was former Liverpool boss Rafa Benitez. The appointment was far from popular with many Blues supporters who hadn't forgiven the Spaniard for derogatory comments he made about the club during his time at Anfield.

Manchester City remained the league's only unbeaten side during November as they recorded victories over Spurs and Villa, but Manchester United claimed top spot after registering four wins, including a 2–1 defeat of Arsenal that featured a goal against his former club from Robin van Persie. Four wins on the bounce saw West Brom move into fourth. QPR, who were eight points adrift at the bottom of the table, showed Mark Hughes the exit door, and replaced him with former Spurs boss Harry Redknapp.

The first Manchester derby of the season took place in December and saw United beat City 3–2 in a thrilling encounter. Wayne Rooney gave the Red Devils a two goal lead with a pair of smart finishes before City reduced the arrears through Yaya Toure and drew level thanks to Pablo Zabaleta. The game was won by the on-form Robin van Persie in the second minute of stoppage time after he guided home a curling free-kick. That result

TOP LEFT: *Spanish striker Michu proved to be one of the bargain buys of the season and marked his Swansea City debut with a brace of goals as the Swans defeated QPR 5–0 at Loftus Road on the opening day.*

TOP RIGHT: *Robin van Persie's wand of a left foot fires the ball past the Manchester City wall and into the net to give Manchester United a 3–2 victory over their local rivals at the Etihad Stadium.*

RIGHT TOP: *Pictured celebrating an important goal against Stoke City, Michael Carrick was the steadying influence of Manchester United's title challenging side.*

RIGHT BOTTOM: *Robin van Persie sealed Manchester United's 20th league title with one of the goals of the season after he met Wayne Rooney's long-range lofted pass with a sublimely timed and struck volley. The ball flew past Aston Villa goalkeeper Brad Guzan to give United a 2–0 lead at Old Trafford.*

OPPOSITE PAGE FAR RIGHT: *Arguably the greatest manager of all-time, Sir Alex Ferguson went out on a high after guiding Manchester United to a 20th top-flight title before retiring from football. Ferguson had been at United for over a quarter of a century and lifted 28 major honours as Red Devils boss.*

and wins against Sunderland, Newcastle and West Brom gave United a seven point gap over City at the end of the year. An improving Chelsea ended 2012 in third with Spurs in fourth.

The New Year signalled the end of Nigel Adkins' tenure in charge of Southampton, as the Englishman was replaced by Argentine coach Mauricio Pochettino. Manchester United maintained their title winning form during January, defeating Liverpool, Southampton and Wigan. City, still seven points adrift, enjoyed three wins of their own, which included a 2–0 triumph over Arsenal. However, the blue half of Manchester lost significant ground on the leaders the following month, drawing with both Liverpool and QPR and suffering a 3–1 loss at Southampton. Three wins from three for United enabled them to achieve a 15 point lead.

A March loss to Everton ensured Manchester City remained 15 points off United, having played their game in hand. A 13th Premier League title for the Red Devils looked inevitable as they won each of their three fixtures during the month; hammering Norwich 4–0 and recording 1–0 wins against Reading and Sunderland. The Royals lost patience with boss Brian McDermott, showing him the exit door and named Nigel Adkins, recently sacked by Southampton, as his replacement. Aston Villa, Wigan and Sunderland remained in trouble at the wrong end of the table. The Black Cats parted company with manager Martin O'Neill and replaced him with Paolo Di Canio.

Manchester City regained some pride in the second Manchester derby of the season, beating United 2–1 at Old Trafford at the beginning of April. However, United's inevitable record 20th title was confirmed a few weeks later following a 3–0 home win against Aston Villa that was lit up by a stunning volley from man of the moment, Robin van Persie, who met a lofted Wayne Rooney through ball with superb power and accuracy.

Liverpool striker Luis Suarez courted controversy again during April when he bit Chelsea defender Branislav Ivanovic on the shoulder during a league clash against Chelsea at Anfield. Taking his previous bad behaviour into account, the FA chose to ban the Uruguayan for 10 games. Before the month drew to a close, QPR and Reading became the first clubs to be relegated after they played out a draw. One of the month's standout results came at St. James' Park where Paolo Di Canio's Sunderland enjoyed a 3–0 victory over local rivals Newcastle.

With the title in the bag, Manchester United took their foot off the pedal in the remaining fixtures, unable to fulfil Sir Alex Ferguson's target of accumulating a tally of 100 points. The veteran manager shocked the world of football on May 8th when he announced his retirement from the game, after nearly 27 years in charge of United. The rumours immediately began about the likely identity of his successor.

Having experienced the joy of a shock FA Cup final victory over Manchester City days earlier, Wigan suffered the despair of relegation after a 4–1 loss to Arsenal on the final day of the season. Sir Alex Ferguson's final game as Manchester United manager ended in a 5–5 draw with West Brom. Manchester City finished second with Chelsea third and Arsenal fourth.

# HONOURS LIST

## Barclays Premier League

**CHAMPIONS:** Manchester United
United won an English record 20th top-flight title thanks to season characterised by the goal-scoring exploits of Robin van Persie. A 13th Premier League title provided the perfect swansong for the retiring Sir Alex Ferguson.
**RUNNERS-UP:** Manchester City
**RELEGATED:** Wigan Athletic, Reading, Queens Park Rangers
**TOP GOAL SCORER:** Robin van Persie (26 goals for Manchester United)

SHOOT MAGAZINE
2012–13

*Manchester United's title victory and Sir Alex Ferguson's retirement featured heavily on the cover of Shoot's season review of the 2012–13. Interviews with Everton defender Phil Jagielka, Arsenal midfielder Aaron Ramsey and Aston Villa's Christian Benteke are also showcased.*

# 2012–13 SEASON TABLE

|  |  | M | W | D | L | GF | GA | GD | PTS |
|---|---|---|---|---|---|---|---|---|---|
| 1 | Manchester United | 38 | 28 | 5 | 5 | 86 | 43 | +43 | 89 |
| 2 | Manchester City | 38 | 23 | 9 | 6 | 66 | 34 | +32 | 78 |
| 3 | Chelsea | 38 | 22 | 9 | 7 | 75 | 39 | +36 | 75 |
| 4 | Arsenal | 38 | 21 | 10 | 7 | 72 | 37 | +35 | 73 |
| 5 | Tottenham Hotspur | 38 | 21 | 9 | 8 | 66 | 46 | +20 | 72 |
| 6 | Everton | 38 | 16 | 15 | 7 | 55 | 40 | +15 | 63 |
| 7 | Liverpool | 38 | 16 | 13 | 9 | 71 | 43 | +28 | 61 |
| 8 | West Bromwich Albion | 38 | 14 | 7 | 17 | 53 | 57 | -4 | 49 |
| 9 | Swansea City | 38 | 11 | 13 | 14 | 47 | 51 | -4 | 46 |
| 10 | West Ham United | 38 | 12 | 10 | 16 | 45 | 53 | -8 | 46 |
| 11 | Norwich City | 38 | 10 | 14 | 14 | 41 | 58 | -17 | 44 |
| 12 | Fulham | 38 | 11 | 10 | 17 | 50 | 60 | -10 | 43 |
| 13 | Stoke City | 38 | 9 | 15 | 14 | 34 | 45 | -11 | 42 |
| 14 | Southampton | 38 | 9 | 14 | 15 | 49 | 60 | -11 | 41 |
| 15 | Aston Villa | 38 | 10 | 11 | 17 | 47 | 69 | -22 | 41 |
| 16 | Newcastle United | 38 | 11 | 8 | 19 | 45 | 68 | -23 | 41 |
| 17 | Sunderland | 38 | 9 | 12 | 17 | 41 | 54 | -13 | 39 |
| 18 | Wigan Athletic | 38 | 9 | 9 | 20 | 47 | 73 | -26 | 36 |
| 19 | Reading | 38 | 6 | 10 | 22 | 43 | 73 | -30 | 28 |
| 20 | Queens Park Rangers | 38 | 4 | 13 | 21 | 30 | 60 | -30 | 25 |

# PLAYERS OF THE SEASON

**PFA PLAYER OF THE YEAR:** Gareth Bale, Tottenham Hotspur
**PFA YOUNG PLAYER OF THE YEAR:** Gareth Bale, Tottenham Hotspur
**FOOTBALL WRITERS' PLAYER OF THE YEAR:** Gareth Bale, Tottenham Hotspur

**FOOTBALL LEAGUE CHAMPIONSHIP CHAMPIONS:** Cardiff City

**PROMOTED:** Hull City

**CHAMPIONSHIP PLAY-OFF WINNERS:** Crystal Palace

**RELEGATED:** Peterborough United, Wolverhampton Wanderers, Bristol City

**TOP GOAL SCORER:** Glenn Murray (30 goals for Crystal Palace)

Malky Mackay guided Cardiff City into the Premier League for the first time and back into the top flight after a 51-year absence. The Welsh club accumulated 87 points to finish eight clear of second place Hull City. The Tigers, managed by Steve Bruce, confirmed their Premier League return on the final day of the season. The last promotion place was taken by Ian Holloway's Crystal Palace who defeated Watford 1–0 after extra time in the play-off final, thanks to an ice cool penalty conversion from veteran striker Kevin Phillips.

## ⚽ INTERESTING INFO

In his final campaign, Manchester United manager Sir Alex Ferguson was named Premier League Manager of the Season. It represented the 11th occasion that Ferguson won the award during his career.

ABOVE TOP: *Exuding pace, skill and match-winning brilliance, Tottenham's Gareth Bale took his game to another level during the 2012–13 season and was named as the PFA and Football Writers' Player of the Year.*

ABOVE BOTTOM: *Veteran front man Kevin Phillips keeps his focus to successfully convert the penalty that sent Crystal Palace back into the Premier League.*

**LEAGUE ONE CHAMPIONS:** Doncaster Rovers
**PROMOTED:** Bournemouth
**LEAGUE ONE PLAY-OFF WINNERS:** Yeovil Town
**RELEGATED:** Scunthorpe United, Bury, Hartlepool United, Portsmouth
**TOP GOAL SCORER:** Paddy Madden (26 goals for Yeovil Town)

Doncaster, managed by Paul Dickov for the final few weeks of the season, following Dean Saunders' departure, confirmed the title on a dramatic final day thanks to a sensational 1–0 victory over Brentford, who were also in contention for first place. With the scores locked at 0–0 in stoppage time the Bees were awarded a penalty. On-loan Fulham striker Marcello Trotta took the kick but slammed the ball against the cross-bar. The power on the shot saw the ball rebound clear and set Doncaster on an unlikely counter attack. Brentford were unprepared and allowed Billy Paynter to surge forward and find James Coppinger in space, who steadied himself to score and seal Rovers' promotion and title victory in extraordinary fashion. Second placed Bournemouth, who would have claimed the title had Doncaster not scored, again owed their success to Eddie Howe, who had returned to the club following a brief spell at Burnley to once again galvanise a team struggling at the wrong end of the table. Brentford suffered further agony in the play-off final, where they were defeated 2–1 by Gary Johnson's Yeovil Town thanks to Dan Burn's winning goal.

**LEAGUE TWO CHAMPIONS:** Gillingham
**PROMOTED:** Rotherham United, Port Vale
**LEAGUE TWO PLAY-OFF WINNERS:** Bradford City
**RELEGATED:** Barnet, Aldershot Town
**TOP GOAL SCORER:** Tom Pope (31 goals for Port Vale)

Martin Allen's Gillingham lifted the title after winning 27 of their 46 league matches. Second place went to Steve Evans' Rotherham while Port Vale, bossed by Micky Adams, took third. The fourth promotion place was filled by Phil Parkinson's Bradford City who overcame Northampton Town 3–0 in the play-off final. Dropping out of the Football League were Barnet and Aldershot.

**BLUE SQUARE PREMIER CHAMPIONS:** Mansfield Town
**PROMOTED:** Newport County

Mansfield Town, managed by Paul Cox, ended their five-year exile from League Two by claiming the title while Newport County, bossed by former Spurs defender Justin Edinburgh, ended 25 years outside of the Football League after winning an all-Welsh play-off final against Wrexham 2–0.

TOP LEFT: *Doncaster Rovers celebrate their extraordinary last gasp League One title victory.*

TOP RIGHT: *Bradford City boss Phil Parkinson celebrates his team's second big day out at Wembley of the season after the Bantams overcame Northampton in the play-off final to seal promotion.*

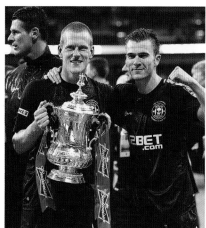

# UP FOR THE CUP

### FA CUP WINNERS: Wigan Athletic

Wigan Athletic completed the biggest FA Cup final shock since Wimbledon's victory over Liverpool in 1988 after defeating Manchester City 1–0 at Wembley. Roberto Martinez's side played with aggression and width, limiting City to precious few presentable chances and the favourites' hopes took a blow when defender Pablo Zabaleta was shown a second-half red card. After a goalless 90 minutes, with the contest on the verge of extra time, Shaun Maloney delivered an out-swinging corner that was met by a powerful near post header by Ben Watson. The ball flew into the net past Joe Hart, giving the Latics a famous victory.

Wigan reached the final after defeating Millwall 2–0 in the semi-final thanks to goals from Maloney and Calum McManaman. City progressed to the Wembley showpiece following a 2–1 victory over Chelsea, which featured goals from Samir Nasri and Sergio Aguero.

In a season filled with FA Cup upsets some of the most significant included non-league Luton beating Norwich in the fourth round, MK Dons knocking out QPR, Leeds seeing off Tottenham and Oldham disposing of Liverpool.

### LEAGUE (CAPITAL ONE) CUP WINNERS: Swansea City

Swansea claimed their first major English honour after a one-sided contest against League Two Bradford City at Wembley. The Swans ran out 5–0 winners thanks to doubles from Nathan Dyer and Jonathan De Guzman and a single strike from Michu.

The Welsh club reached their first major Wembley final following a two-legged semi-final win over Chelsea. The Swans settled the tie with a 2–0 win at Stamford Bridge in the first leg, achieved through goals from Michu and Danny Graham. Bradford became the first team from the fourth tier of the English game to reach a major final since Rochdale in 1962. The Bantams knocked out both Arsenal and Wigan before overcoming Aston Villa 4–3 on aggregate in the semi-final. The Yorkshire club's goal scorers included Nahki Wells and James Hanson.

Earlier in the tournament, one of the most memorable clashes saw Arsenal beat Reading 7–5 after extra time. The Gunners had trailed the Championship side 4–0 before a Theo Walcott hat-trick inspired them to complete an unlikely comeback. A number of lower league sides sprung shock results during the competition, including Leeds, who ousted Sunderland; Swindon, who knocked out Stoke and Sheffield Wednesday, who ended Fulham's interest in the tournament.

### COMMUNITY SHIELD WINNERS: Manchester City

Facing Chelsea at Villa Park, Manchester City showed their class with a 3–2 victory. The reigning champions' goals came from Yaya Toure, Carlos Tevez and Samir Nasri.

### THE FOOTBALL LEAGUE (JOHNSTONE'S PAINTS) TROPHY: Crewe Alexandra

Crewe Alexandra, managed by Steve Davis, defeated Southend United 2–0 in the final, scoring through Luke Murphy and Max Clayton.

# INTO EUROPE

### European Champions League

Premier League sides endured one of their most disappointing campaigns for years, demonstrated by Chelsea becoming the first reigning European champions to be eliminated in the group stages. Manchester City also crashed out at that stage after finishing bottom of a group that also contained Real Madrid, Borussia Dortmund and Ajax.

ABOVE: *Real Madrid's Cristiano Ronaldo forces the ball home to level the tie against his former club Manchester United. The Portuguese ace celebrated the goal in subdued and respectful fashion in front of the Old Trafford fans that used to worship him.*

Manchester United fared slightly better, topping their group before being paired with Real Madrid in the last 16. The clash brought a first return to Old Trafford for Cristiano Ronaldo following his 2009 move to the Spanish giants. United had taken the lead in the away tie through Danny Welbeck but Ronaldo later equalised for Real. In the return leg at Old Trafford, United again led following a Sergio Ramos own goal but a harsh red card for Nani transformed the balance of the tie and quick fire goals from Ronaldo and Luka Modric put Madrid through. Arsenal went out at the same stage after a second placed finish in their group set up a challenging tie against Bayern Munich. The German champions triumphed on away goals following a 3–3 aggregate scoreline.

*One of the best and most consistent defenders in European football, Branislav Ivanovic popped up with Chelsea's match-winning goal in the Europa League final.*

## UEFA Europa League

Dropping into the tournament following their Champions League exit, Rafa Benitez turned Chelsea's faltering European hopes around, overcoming Sparta Prague and Steaua Bucharest to set up a quarter-final tie with Russia's Ruban Kazan. The Blues went on to win 5–4 on aggregate with Fernando Torres scoring three goals. Paired with FC Basel in the semi-finals, the Blues won 5–2 with Torres again amongst the goals. The English club faced Benfica in the Amsterdam final and took the lead after an hour through Torres. Their Portuguese opponents soon levelled through Oscar Cardozo and the contest looked set for extra time until defender Branislav Ivanovic headed home a dramatic 93rd minute winner.

Of the other English sides, Liverpool were knocked out in the last 32 by Zenit Saint Petersburg while Tottenham and Newcastle both reached the quarter-finals. Spurs were beaten by Basel while Newcastle lost out to Benfica.

## INTERESTING INFO

In lifting the Europa League, Chelsea became the first English club to win all three of the major European club competitions.

## THE INTERNATIONAL SCENE

England made a positive if unspectacular start to their qualifying campaign for the 2014 World Cup, recording routine victories over San Marino and Moldova and completing hard fought 1–1 draws with Ukraine, Poland and Montenegro.

# CITY SUCCEED AS THE BIG LEAGUE OPENS UP

The build up to the 2013–14 campaign was dominated by the vastly changing managerial picture. It was the first ever Premier League season not to feature Sir Alex Ferguson as Manchester United manager, with the retired Scotsman replaced by his countryman David Moyes. The former Everton boss, who had developed an impressive CV during his Goodison Park tenure, was a surprise appointment for many, but he was Ferguson's hand-picked first choice and the United board awarded Moyes a six-year deal.

After Rafa Benitez's interim spell at Chelsea came to an end, Jose Mourinho completed a highly-anticipated return to the Premier League and to the Stamford Bridge dugout. It was also all-change at the Etihad stadium as the sacked Roberto Mancini was replaced by experienced Chilean coach Manuel Pellegrini. David Moyes' successor at Everton was Wigan's Roberto Martinez. With long-serving Stoke boss Tony Pulis stepping down during the summer, the Potters named Mark Hughes as his replacement.

left: An expression of familiar frustration, David Moyes' dream appointment as Manchester United manager turned into something of a nightmare as the season unfolded.

OPPOSITE PAGE: Sergio Aguero was again on target in the Manchester derby, this time helping City to a 4–1 victory over United as David Moyes' men started to struggle.

# TRANSFER TALES

Arsenal made significant moves in the market, smashing their transfer record to bring in German international midfielder Mesut Ozil from Real Madrid for £42.4m. After a summer filled with speculation, David Moyes waited until the last day of the transfer window to complete his first major addition for Manchester United, returning to Everton to sign Belgian midfielder Marouane Fellaini for £27.5m. Moyes again splashed the cash in January, persuading Chelsea to part with attacking midfielder Juan Mata in a £37.1m deal.

The Blues also spent heavily, adding Brazilian midfielder Willian for £30m, German forward Andrea Schurrle for £18m, Dutch youngster Marco van Ginkel and veteran Cameroon striker Samuel Eto'o. In January, Jose Mourinho also signed Nemanja Matic and Mohamed Salah.

The headline departure of the summer saw Tottenham sell Gareth Bale to Real Madrid in a world record £85.3m deal. Tottenham reinvested that money on the likes of Spanish striker Roberto Soldado, who cost £26m; Brazilian midfielder Paulinho, who cost £17m and Erik Lamela, who joined from Roma for £25.8m. Spurs also spent significantly on Nacer Chadli, Vlad Chiriches, Christian Eriksen and Etienne Capoue.

New Manchester City boss Manuel Pellegrini strengthened his squad with Brazilian midfielder Fernandinho for £30m, Fiorentina forward Stevan Jovetic for £22m, Spanish striker Alvaro Negredo for £20m, and also added Jesus Navas and Martin Demichelis.

Liverpool made several new signings, including French defender Mamadou Sakho and Sunderland goalkeeper Simon Mignolet. The Reds also completed loan and permanent deals for Iago Aspas, Tiago Ilori, Victor Moses and Kolo Toure.

Liverpool allowed both Andy Carroll and Stewart Downing to join West Ham, with Carroll moving for £15m. Everton, were also active in the market as new manager Roberto Martinez brought in James McCarthy, Arouna Kone and Antolin Alcaraz from his former club Wigan, as well as Spanish goalkeeper Joel Robles from Atletico Madrid. Martinez also completed season-long loan deals for talented Barcelona youngster Gerard Deulofeu, experienced Manchester City midfielder Gareth Barry and Chelsea powerhouse Romelu Lukaku.

*Arsenal demonstrated that they were once again able to compete at the top end of the transfer market with the club record £42.4m addition of German star Mesut Ozil from Real Madrid.*

## BIGGEST TRANSFERS

**MESUT OZIL** – from Real Madrid to Arsenal – £42.4m

**JUAN MATA** – from Chelsea to Manchester United – £37.1m

**FERNANDINHO** – from Shakhtar Donetsk to Manchester City – £30m

**WILLIAN** – from Anzhi Makhachkala to Chelsea – £30m

**MAROUANE FELLAINI** – from Everton to Manchester United – £27.5m

**ROBERTO SOLDADO** – from Valencia to Tottenham Hotspur – £26m

**ERIK LAMELA** – from AS Roma to Tottenham Hotspur – £25.8m

**STEVAN JOVETIC** – from Fiorentina to Manchester City – £22m

**NEMANJA MATIC** – from Benfica to Chelsea – £21m

**ALVARO NEGREDO** – from Sevilla to Manchester City – £20m

# TALES OF THE TURF

Liverpool grabbed an opening day victory over Stoke while Arsenal suffered a shock 3–1 home loss to Aston Villa. David Moyes' first game in charge of Manchester United brought a convincing 4–1 win at Swansea. Jose Mourinho's return to the Premier League was crowned with a 2–0 victory for Chelsea over Hull while Manuel Pellegrini began his Manchester City career strongly, masterminding a 4–0 home win over Newcastle. Chelsea led the table at the end of August after winning their second fixture against Aston Villa and drawing 0–0 at Manchester United.

Liverpool started September brightly, defeating Manchester United 1–0 at Anfield to top the table. Arsenal found their form as the month progressed, winning each of their four fixtures, including a 1–0 win against Tottenham. Manchester United struggled to adapt to the introduction of David Moyes as manager, suffering a 4–1 hammering against Manchester City and a surprise home loss to West Brom, which left them in 12th with just seven points from six games. It represented United's worst start to a season for 23 years. Another side struggling for form were Sunderland, who sat bottom of the table with just one point. Black Cats manager Paolo Di Canio paid the price, becoming the first Premier League manager to lose his job that season. The Italian was succeeded by Brighton boss Gus Poyet.

Arsenal enjoyed a productive October, defeating Norwich and Crystal Palace and topped the table at the end of the month. Chelsea, Liverpool and Spurs completed the top four. In the same month, Crystal Palace boss Ian Holloway tendered his resignation and the Eagles appointed former Stoke boss Tony Pulis as his successor.

ABOVE: *Liverpool striker Daniel Sturridge was in superb form throughout the season and formed a red hot partnership with Luis Suarez.*

ABOVE TOP: *Despite his advancing years Steven Gerrard remained one of Liverpool's most consistent performers. The club captain was on-hand to score a succession of crucial penalties, including this one against West Ham at Upton Park. Pictured either side of Gerrard are Raheem Sterling (left) and Jordan Henderson who both added energy and intensity to the Reds' pressing game.*

ABOVE BOTTOM: *The ubiquitous Uruguayan, Luis Suarez celebrates scoring against Cardiff during Liverpool's 6–3 destruction of the Bluebirds.*

Manchester City found their goal scoring form at the beginning of November, thumping Norwich 7–0 and hammering Tottenham 6–0. Chelsea dropped points against Newcastle and West Brom while Arsenal enjoyed a 2–0 home win over Liverpool and opened up a seven point lead at the top of the table.

Manchester City continued their impressive form during December, achieving notable home victories against title rivals Liverpool and Arsenal, the latter by virtue of a 6–3 scoreline at the Etihad. Everton ended the year in the top four, with Liverpool fifth. December brought a number of managerial changes as Martin Jol was sacked by Fulham and replaced by Rene Meulensteen, Steve Clarke was succeeded by Pepe Mel at West Brom, Andre Villas-Boas paid the price for Tottenham's poor form, with Tim Sherwood appointed as manager until the end of the season and Malky Mackay departed Cardiff City. Ole Gunnar Solskjaer was named as Bluebirds boss at the beginning of January.

Manchester City topped the table during January, winning all four of their games, which included a 5–1 victory against Spurs. Liverpool picked up a 5–3 win at Stoke and hammered Everton 4–0 in the Merseyside derby.

Three wins from four in February boosted Chelsea's title hopes and moved them to the summit of the Premier League. Jose Mourinho's men completed a tactical masterclass to defeat Manchester City 1–0 on their own ground and also defeated high-flying Everton by the same scoreline. Arsenal maintained their title challenge despite being hammered 5–1 at Anfield by Liverpool. It was an illustration of how the Reds had taken their pressing and attacking game to another level, as their lethal striker pairing of Luis Suarez and Daniel Sturridge caused defences nightmares. Swansea sacked Michael Laudrup and named Gary Monk as his successor while Fulham replaced Rene Meulensteen with Felix Magath.

March featured a 6–0 thrashing of Arsenal by Chelsea, marring the celebrations of Arsene Wenger's 1,000th game in charge of the Gunners. On-song Liverpool maintained their momentum, and recorded consecutive 3–0 victories against Southampton and Manchester United. A 6–3 win over Cardiff followed before a 4–0 trouncing of Spurs perfectly illustrated the Reds' swarming pressing game.

Everton continued to impress, playing a much more fluid, attacking style under Roberto Martinez than that associated with his predecessor, David Moyes. The Toffees recorded five successive victories during March. Chelsea added a 4–0 drubbing of Spurs to their 6–0 humiliation of Arsenal, but suffered a shock 1–0 loss at a much improved Crystal Palace. Manchester City retained their title interest with victories over Fulham, Hull and Manchester United.

Liverpool began April in positive mood, overcoming West Ham 2–1 at Upton Park thanks to a pair of penalties from Steven Gerrard. The victory boosted the Reds' morale further ahead of a crucial home clash with Manchester City the following week. Buoyed by vociferous home support, Liverpool again took an early lead through Raheem Sterling before Martin Skrtel added a second. City's passing game clicked into action in the second half and Manuel Pellegrino's men drew level after a goal from David Silva and an own goal from Glen Johnson. However, Liverpool had the last laugh when Brazilian playmaker Philippe Coutinho found the net with a classy finish to complete a 3–2 win for the leaders.

Everton continued to show their top four credentials with a 3–0 destruction of off-form Arsenal at Goodison Park, featuring yet another goal from the powerful Romelu Lukaku. The Belgian's parent club, Chelsea, got back on track with wins over Stoke and Swansea before suffering a surprise home loss to relegation threatened Sunderland. The Black Cats deservedly claimed a 2–1 win thanks to a late penalty from on-loan Liverpool forward Fabio Borini. Victory saw Gus Poyet's side pick up an unlikely four point haul in successive fixtures against title challenging sides, as the North East club had prepared for the Chelsea victory with a hard fought 2–2 draw at Manchester City.

BELOW: *Liverpool's Brazilian midfielder Philippe Coutinho volleys home the winning goal as the Reds defeat title challengers Manchester City 3–2 at Anfield.*

Sunderland's 2–1 victory over Chelsea was the first home loss that Jose Mourinho suffered as Blues manager.

Sunderland's positive results provided a real shot in the arm for league leaders Liverpool who defeated Norwich City 3–2 at Carrow Road. In-form Luis Suarez grabbed his 30th league goal of the season during the victory, becoming just the seventh player in the history over the Premier League player to have achieved that mi. The Reds were strong favourites to lift their first top-flight title since 1990.

The Easter weekend saw David Moyes former club Everton slam the final nail into the coffin of his Manchester United career following a 2–0 loss at Goodison Park. The result mathematically ended the reigning champions' chances of achieving Champions League qualification. Moyes was sacked two days later and replaced by Ryan Giggs until the end of the season. Another April managerial change came when Norwich replaced Chris Hughton with Neil Adams.

Sunderland picked up another key victory, winning 1–0 at Manchester United in Ryan Giggs' second game in charge. The result relegated both Fulham and Cardiff, who lost their respective fixtures to Stoke and Newcastle. United, who had begun Giggs' tenure with a 4–0 win against Norwich continued to show the inconsistent form that blighted them under Moyes, but went on to defeat Hull City 3–1 at Old Trafford in a game that featured two debut goals for teenage striker James Wilson and Ryan Giggs' last ever competitive appearance for the Red Devils.

April's biggest and potentially most decisive fixture came when title-chasing Liverpool met Chelsea at Anfield. Chelsea, with an upcoming Champions League semi-final against Atletico Madrid, made a number of changes to their line-up, including the introduction of Demba Ba in attack and a full debut

After a dream playing career for Manchester United, the legendary Ryan Giggs took over as the club's caretaker manager following David Moyes' dismissal. Here, Giggs is pictured in action during his last competitive appearance for United before retirement. The Red Devils' won the fixture against Hull City 3–1 at Old Trafford.

for young defender Tomas Kalas, who replaced the injured John Terry. Set up in an ultra-defensive formation by Jose Mourinho, Chelsea frustrated the hosts and the scoreline remained deadlocked until a rare error of judgement from Liverpool captain Steven Gerrard on the stroke of half-time. The experienced midfielder miss-controlled under pressure from Demba Ba on the halfway line and in his haste to recover he slipped, allowing Ba to prod the ball into space before bearing down on goalkeeper Simon Mignolet and guiding the ball into the net at the Kop End.

The second half brought plenty of Liverpool possession and multiple squandered long range strikes but no breakthrough before Chelsea countered in devastating fashion in the 93rd minute when former Red, Fernando Torres, ran clear on goal, committed Mignolet and squared to Willian who tapped into an empty net. Later that afternoon Manchester City defeated Crystal Palace 2–0 through goals from Edin Dzeko and Yaya Toure.

OPPOSITE TOP: *Belgian striker Romelu Lukaku enjoyed another productive campaign on loan from Chelsea. During the 2013–14 season, the powerful front man scored the goals that took Everton to a Europa League place.*

OPPOSITE BOTTOM: *Luis Suarez celebrates in distinctive fashion as Liverpool seized the title advantage with a key victory against relegation-threatened Norwich City at Carrow Road.*

OPPOSITE PAGE TOP LEFT: *Pictured seconds after his infamous slip, which handed Chelsea the lead in a crucial end of season clash at Anfield, Liverpool skipper Steven Gerrard struggles to accept what has happened.*

OPPOSITE PAGE TOP RIGHT: *A goal behind and with the clock ticking down, Liverpool's Steven Gerrard wrestles the ball from the king of gamesmanship, Chelsea manager Jose Mourinho.*

OPPOSITE PAGE BOTTOM: *Influential Ivorian Yaya Toure set Manchester City well on the way to the title with crucial goals against Crystal Palace and Aston Villa during the final week of the season.*

ABOVE LEFT: *Manchester City midfielder Samir Nasri strikes the opening goal as the Blues overcome West Ham on the final day to lift the Premier League title.*

ABOVE RIGHT TOP: *Second-half substitute Dwight Gayle popped up with two late goals to rescue a 3–3 draw with Liverpool for Crystal Palace, putting a serious dent in Liverpool's title challenge and handing the initiative back to Manchester City.*

ABOVE RIGHT BOTTOM: *Manchester City captain Vincent Kompany celebrates with manager Manuel Pellegrini after the club win their second Premier League title.*

## ⚽ INTERESTING INFO

After playing for Manchester United for almost 25 years, Ryan Giggs clocked up a club record 963 games and became the most decorated footballer in the history of the English game, lifting 22 major honours.

Liverpool's defeat handed the title initiative back to City who sat two points behind with a game in hand and a significantly superior goal difference.

The first weekend in May saw Manchester City take another step towards lifting their second Premier League title with a 3–2 victory over Everton at Goodison. City went level on points with Liverpool and topped the table on goal difference. The following night Liverpool faced a Crystal Palace side now free of any relegation concerns at Selhurst Park. The Reds gave a typically dynamic first-half display, taking a 1–0 goal lead through Joe Allen before storming forward in devastating style after the interval and extending their advantage through a Damien Delaney own goal and a Luis Suarez strike.

With Manchester City's significant goal difference advantage on their minds, the visitors continued to attack but Palace changed the momentum of the contest when Delaney scored at the right end before substitute striker Dwight Gayle added two goals in the last 10 minutes to register an unlikely 3–3 draw. Liverpool returned to the summit but City had an extra-game to play.

City won their game in hand in comfortable fashion, triumphing 4–0 over Aston Villa in a fixture that featured a barnstorming individual effort from Yaya Toure. Manuel Pellegrini's debut Premier League campaign ended in glory when City overcame West Ham 2–0 on the final day thanks to goals from Samir Nasri and Vincent Kompany. Liverpool also won their final fixture, beating Newcastle 2–1 and claimed second place.

Chelsea took third with Arsenal again finishing fourth, while Everton in fifth and Spurs in sixth took the two Europa League places. Seventh place represented Manchester United's worst ever Premier League showing and ensured the club's first season without European football during the Premier League era. At the wrong end of the table, the final relegation place was taken by Norwich after a 2–0 loss to Arsenal.

# HONOURS LIST

## Barclays Premier League
**CHAMPIONS:** Manchester City
A second Premier League title for the blue half of Manchester was delivered thanks to some superb attacking football, as the likes of David Silva, Yaya Toure and Sergio Aguero again showed their class.
**RUNNERS-UP:** Liverpool
**RELEGATED:** Norwich City, Fulham, Cardiff City
**TOP GOAL SCORER:** Luis Suarez (31 goals for Liverpool)

**SHOOT MAGAZINE 2013–14**

*During the summer between the 2013–14 season and the 2014–15 campaign, Shoot produced this special preview publication with the powerful headline of 'It's Back'. The cover star was newly-appointed Manchester United captain Wayne Rooney while each of the perceived title challengers; Chelsea, Arsenal, Manchester City and Liverpool, also graced the front page.*

## 2013–14 SEASON TABLE

|   |   | M | W | D | L | GF | GA | GD | PTS |
|---|---|---|---|---|---|----|----|----|-----|
| 1 | Manchester City | 38 | 27 | 5 | 6 | 102 | 37 | +65 | 86 |
| 2 | Liverpool | 38 | 26 | 6 | 6 | 101 | 50 | +51 | 84 |
| 3 | Chelsea | 38 | 25 | 7 | 6 | 71 | 27 | +44 | 82 |
| 4 | Arsenal | 38 | 24 | 7 | 7 | 68 | 41 | +27 | 79 |
| 5 | Everton | 38 | 21 | 9 | 8 | 61 | 39 | +22 | 72 |
| 6 | Tottenham Hotspur | 38 | 21 | 6 | 11 | 55 | 51 | +4 | 69 |
| 7 | Manchester United | 38 | 19 | 7 | 12 | 64 | 43 | +21 | 64 |
| 8 | Southampton | 38 | 15 | 11 | 12 | 54 | 46 | +8 | 56 |
| 9 | Stoke City | 38 | 13 | 11 | 14 | 45 | 52 | −7 | 50 |
| 10 | Newcastle United | 38 | 15 | 4 | 19 | 43 | 59 | −16 | 49 |
| 11 | Crystal Palace | 38 | 13 | 6 | 19 | 33 | 48 | −15 | 45 |
| 12 | Swansea City | 38 | 11 | 9 | 18 | 54 | 54 | 0 | 42 |
| 13 | West Ham United | 38 | 11 | 7 | 20 | 40 | 51 | −11 | 40 |
| 14 | Sunderland | 38 | 10 | 8 | 20 | 41 | 60 | −19 | 38 |
| 15 | Aston Villa | 38 | 10 | 8 | 20 | 39 | 61 | −22 | 38 |
| 16 | Hull City | 38 | 10 | 7 | 21 | 38 | 53 | −15 | 37 |
| 17 | West Bromwich Albion | 38 | 7 | 15 | 16 | 43 | 59 | −16 | 36 |
| 18 | Norwich City (R) | 38 | 8 | 9 | 21 | 28 | 62 | −34 | 33 |
| 19 | Fulham (R) | 38 | 9 | 5 | 24 | 40 | 85 | −45 | 32 |
| 20 | Cardiff City (R) | 38 | 7 | 9 | 22 | 32 | 74 | −42 | 30 |

## PLAYERS OF THE SEASON

**PFA PLAYER OF THE YEAR:** Luis Suarez, Liverpool
**PFA YOUNG PLAYER OF THE YEAR:** Eden Hazard, Chelsea
**FOOTBALL WRITER' PLAYER OF THE YEAR:** Luis Suarez, Liverpool

**FOOTBALL LEAGUE CHAMPIONSHIP CHAMPIONS:**
Leicester City
**PROMOTED:** Burnley
**CHAMPIONSHIP PLAY-OFF WINNERS:** Queens
Park Rangers
**RELEGATED:** Doncaster Rovers, Barnsley,
Yeovil Town
**TOP GOAL SCORER:** Ross McCormack (28 goals
for Leeds United)

Nigel Pearson's Leicester City stormed to the title and became the first team in the country to achieve promotion to ensure a Premier League return for the first time in a decade. The Foxes, who tallied 102 points, reached the division's summit on Boxing Day and remained there until the final week of the season. Joining them in the Premier League were Burnley who finished runners-up at the end of Sean Dyche's first season in charge. The third promotion spot was taken by Harry Redknapp's Queens Park Rangers who, despite being outplayed by Derby County in the play-off final, grabbed a last minute winner through Bobby Zamora to seal a 1–0 victory.

**LEAGUE ONE CHAMPIONS:** Wolverhampton
Wanderers
**PROMOTED:** Brentford
**LEAGUE ONE PLAY-OFF WINNERS:** Rotherham United
**RELEGATED:** Tranmere Rovers, Carlisle United,
Shrewsbury Town, Stevenage
**TOP GOAL SCORER:** Sam Baldock (24 goals for
Bristol City)

After two successive relegations, Wolverhampton Wanderers fared much better under the guidance of Kenny Jackett, storming to the League One title with a new record high of 103 points. Brentford, bossed by rookie manager Mark Warburton, took second place to reach the second tier for the first time in 21 years, while Steve Evans' Rotherham defeated Leyton Orient on penalties in the play-off final.

TOP: *Leicester City dominated the Championship to secure a long overdue return to the Premier League. Pictured celebrating another crucial goal are key performers Ritchie De Laet, Anthony Knockaert and David Nugent.*

RIGHT: *Dependable boss Kenny Jackett guided Wolverhampton Wanderers back into the second tier following an impressive first season in charge at Molineux.*

*Fleetwood Town manager Graham Alexander celebrates the club's play-off final victory against Burton Albion at Wembley.*

**LEAGUE TWO CHAMPIONS:** Chesterfield
**PROMOTED:** Scunthorpe United, Rochdale
**LEAGUE TWO PLAY-OFF WINNERS:** Fleetwood Town
**RELEGATED:** Bristol Rovers, Torquay United
**TOP GOAL SCORER:** Sam Winnall (23 goals for Scunthorpe United)

Chesterfield, managed by Paul Cook, achieved their second League Two title in three seasons, accumulating 84 points and losing just eight matches all season. Second place was occupied by Scunthorpe United whose form dramatically improved following the mid-season appointment of Russ Wilcox as manager. Keith Hill's Rochdale claimed third, completing the club's third ever promotion and the second under his stewardship. The play-off final was won by Fleetwood Town, led by Graham Alexander, who defeated Burton Albion 1–0 thanks to Antoni Sarcevic's goal.

Dropping out of the Football League were Torquay United and Bristol Rovers. It meant that the Pirates would face their first season outside of the top four divisions since 1920.

**FOOTBALL CONFERENCE CHAMPIONS:** Luton Town
**PROMOTED:** Cambridge United

Luton Town, managed by John Still, ended their five-year Football League exile, clocking up 101 points and losing just five of their 46 fixtures to top the division. Cambridge United defeated Gateshead 2–1 in the play-off final thanks to Ryan Donaldson's goal.

ABOVE TOP: *Arsenal midfielder Aaron Ramsey, who enjoyed a superb season in front of goal, celebrates hitting the strike that won the FA Cup for Arsenal.*

ABOVE BOTTOM: *Sunderland striker Fabio Borini, who scored a succession of crucial goals during the Black Cats' Premier League survival battle, gives his side a shock lead against Manchester City in the Capital One Cup final.*

## UP FOR THE CUP

**FA CUP WINNERS:** Arsenal

Arsenal and Arsene Wenger ended their nine-year wait for a major trophy following a dramatic 3–2 FA Cup final victory over Steve Bruce's Hull City. The Tigers stormed into a 2–0 first-half lead thanks to goals from James Chester and Curtis Davies before Santi Cazorla reduced the arrears with a stunning long-range free-kick. Laurent Koscielny levelled in the second half to force the contest into extra time. With Hull tiring, Arsenal took charge and grabbed the winner through Aaron Ramsey to lift the trophy for a record-equalling 11th time.

*Manchester City players celebrate with the League Cup after defeating Sunderland 3–1 at Wembley.*

The Gunners were pushed all the way to penalties by Wigan Athletic in the semi-final after a late Per Metesacker goal equalised a Jordi Gomez penalty to take the game into extra time. Arsenal triumphed after Gary Caldwell and Jack Collison missed for the Latics. Hull reached the FA Cup final for the first time in their history after defeating League One Sheffield United 5–3 thanks to goals from Yannick Sagbo, Matty Fryatt, Tom Huddlestone, Stephen Quinn and David Meyler.

Standout results earlier in the competition included Wigan ending Manchester City's hopes for the second season running, Sheffield United knocking out Aston Villa and Fulham, and Nottingham Forest thumping West Ham 5–0 at the City Ground.

### LEAGUE (CAPITAL ONE) CUP WINNERS: Manchester City

Manchester City claimed Manuel Pellegrini's first trophy in England following a 3–1 victory over Sunderland in the League Cup final. The Black Cats took an early lead through Fabio Borini but two goals in two second-half minutes turned the game for City as first Yaya Toure and then Samir Nasri found the net. The contest was settled in last minute when Jesus Navas clinically finished off a counter attack.

City enjoyed a comfortable route to the final, thrashing West Ham 9–0 over two legs. Sunderland experienced a tighter semi-final, eventually ousting Manchester United 2–1 on penalties following a 3–3 aggregate score.

Highlights earlier in the tournament included West Ham's 2–1 win at Tottenham in the quarter-final, Leicester knocking out Fulham, Birmingham defeating Swansea and Bristol City ousting Crystal Palace.

### COMMUNITY SHIELD WINNERS: Manchester United

Manchester United lifted their first silverware under David Moyes following a routine 2–0 victory over FA Cup winners Wigan, which featured a Robin van Persie brace.

### THE FOOTBALL LEAGUE (JOHNSTONE'S PAINTS) TROPHY: Peterborough United

Darren Ferguson's Peterborough defeated Chesterfield 3–1 thanks to goals from Josh McQuoid, Shaun Brisley and Britt Assombalonga.

# INTO EUROPE

## European Champions League

Chelsea were the Premier League's most impressive performers, advancing to the semi-finals where they were beaten 3–1 on aggregate by Atletico Madrid. Jose Mourinho's side had topped a group that featured Basel and Schalke before they advanced past Galatasaray and Paris Saint-Germain in the knockout stages. Manchester United also topped their group before knocking out Olympiakos but lost 4–2 on aggregate to Bayern Munich in the quarter-final. Manchester City qualified for the knock-out rounds for the first time, finishing second to Bayern Munich but lost 4–1 on aggregate to Barcelona in the last 16. Arsenal crashed out at the same stage, going down 3–1 to Bayern Munich.

## UEFA Europa League

Tottenham advanced to the last 16 where they lost to Benfica. Swansea gave a good account of themselves, finishing second to Valencia to advance through their group, recording a 3–0 away win against the Spaniards in the process, before losing 3–2 on aggregate to Rafa Benitez's Napoli in the last round of 32. Wigan, now playing in the Championship, finished bottom of their group.

# THE INTERNATIONAL SCENE

England wrapped up qualification for the World Cup and topped their group following a 4–1 victory over Montenegro and a 2–0 home win over Poland. However, the Three Lions once again failed to roar at the World Cup, losing two and drawing one of their three matches and being knocked out of a group that contained Italy, Uruguay and Costa Rica, after just two games.

OPPOSITE PAGE TOP: *A man never shy to show his emotions after a key Champions League goal, Jose Mourino sprints down the touchline to celebrate Demba Ba's quarter-final winner against Paris Saint-Germain at Stamford Bridge before giving an impromptu tactical team talk by the corner flag.*

OPPOSITE PAGE BOTTOM: *A rare high-point during David Moyes' Manchester United tenure, Patrice Evra celebrates scoring a spectacular volley against European Cup holders Bayern Munich in the Champions League quarter-final. The Red Devils ultimately lost the tie and, a few weeks later, Moyes lost his job.*

LEFT: *Wayne Rooney and his England team-mates celebrate his equalising goal against Uruguay during the group stages of the 2016 World Cup.*

# MORE GLORY FOR MOURINHO

The headline managerial appointment during the summer was that of Dutchman Louis van Gaal at Manchester United. The vastly experienced manager, who had previously led the likes of Ajax, Barcelona and Bayern Munich to domestic and European glory, seemed to be the ideal man to fill the vacancy left following the sacking of David Moyes. One of the game's more unique characters, Van Gaal started the United job fresh from a successful World Cup as head coach of Netherlands, having led his country to a third place finish.

OPPOSITE: *Arguably Chelsea's most potent attacking weapon, Belgian ace Eden Hazard scored a catalogue of crucial goals, including a sublime individual effort against Manchester United and a header against Crystal Palace that secured the title for the Blues.*

LEFT: *New Manchester United boss Louis van Gaal looks deep in thought alongside his assistant Ryan Giggs.*

# TRANSFER TALES

Huge increases in the level of global television revenue provided to Premier League clubs ensured that spending reached another level during the summer of 2014. Manchester United and Liverpool invested particularly heavily while usual big-spenders, Chelsea and Manchester City, had to be slightly more frugal to comply with the continuingly stringent Financial Fair Play regulations.

New Manchester United boss Louis van Gaal may have started his job late following the Netherlands' extended involvement in the World Cup, but he wasted no time sanctioning a couple of big-money deals that had already been lined up by the club. The Dutchman gave the green light for the additions of Southampton's teenage left-back Luke Shaw for £30m and Athletic Bilbao midfielder Ander Herrera for £29m.

Later on in the summer transfer window, Van Gaal identified his own targets and brought in one of the stars of his Dutch World Cup squad, Daley Blind, as well as another defender that impressed during the tournament, Argentine Marcos Rojo from Sporting Lisbon. Bigger deals followed for the Red Devils who smashed the British transfer record, splashing £59.7m on Real Madrid midfielder Angel Di Maria and completed the season-loan of Colombian striker Radamel Falcao for a significant salary investment. A number of players departed Old Trafford, including the experienced defensive trio of Rio Ferdinand, Nemanja Vidic and Patrice Evra, while youth product Danny Welbeck was surprisingly allowed to join Arsenal in a £16m deal.

Across Manchester, Manuel Pellegrini's Manchester City invested £32m on young French defender Eliaquim Mangala and £12m on his Porto team-mate, Fernando, and also brought in Bacary Sagna from Arsenal and experienced stopper Willy Caballero. Later on in the summer City also completed the unexpected loan signing of former Chelsea man Frank Lampard from their MLS franchise, New York City. The reigning champions were the division's biggest spenders during the January window when they spent £28m on powerful Swansea City striker Wilfried Bony.

Liverpool, City's main challengers during the previous season's title race, lost their most dangerous attacking threat after star forward Luis Suarez departed for Barcelona in a £75m deal. Brendan Rodgers was afforded the entire fee to reinvest in the team and the Northern Irishman wasn't shy in doing so. Close to £50m went to Southampton for the services of Croatian defender Dejan Lovren and England internationals Adam Lallana and Rickie Lambert, while a further £20m was spent on promising Benfica winger Lazar Markovic. The Reds also added German midfielder Emre Can for £10m, controversial Italian forward Mario Balotelli for £16m and Spanish left-back Alberto Moreno for £12m.

*Manchester United broke the British transfer record to sign Argentine winger Angel Di Maria from Real Madrid as the club tried to compensate for a below-par showing, both on and off the pitch, during the previous campaign.*

## BIGGEST TRANSFERS

**ANGEL DI MARIA** – from Real Madrid to Manchester United – £59.7m

**ALEXIS SANCHEZ** – from Barcelona to Arsenal – £35m

**DIEGO COSTA** – from Atletico Madrid to Chelsea – £32m

**ELIAQUIM MANGALA** – from FC Porto to Manchester City – £32m

**CESC FABREGAS** – from Barcelona to Chelsea – £30m

**ANDER HERRERA** – from Athletic Bilbao to Manchester United – £29m

**ROMELU LUKAKU** – from Chelsea to Everton – £28m

**WILFRIED BONY** – from Swansea City to Manchester City – £28m

**LUKE SHAW** – from Southampton to Manchester United – £27m

**ADAM LALLANA** – from Southampton to Liverpool – £25m

*Arsenal continued to spend big, adding Chilean World Cup star Alexis Sanchez for £35m.*

Chelsea brought in £50m from the sale of Brazilian defender David Luiz to Paris Saint-Germain and spent it extremely wisely. A shrewd operator in the transfer market, Jose Mourinho signed Spanish striker Diego Costa for £32m from Atletico Madrid and added his national colleague, former Arsenal midfielder Cesc Fabregas, for £30m from Barcelona. The Blues also brought in Brazilian left-back Filipe Luis from Atletico and French striker Loic Remy before signing Colombian winger Juan Cuadrado for £23.3m in January.

As well as the signing of Danny Welbeck from Manchester United, Arsenal made the marquee addition of Chile international forward Alexis Sanchez from Barcelona for £35m. The Gunners also moved for Mexican goalkeeper David Ospina, Newcastle right-back Mathieu Debuchy and young Southampton defender James Chambers.

Everton smashed their transfer record to sign Belgian striker Romelu Lukaku in a £28m permanent deal following his successful loan spell at Goodison Park. The Toffees also brought in Muhamed Besic and Samuel Eto'o. Newcastle were major movers again and signed the likes of Ayoze Perez, Jack Colback, Siem de Jong, Remy Cabella, Daryl Janmaat and Emmanuel Riviere. Their North East rivals, Sunderland, acquired West Brom's Billy Jones, Wigan's Jordi Gomez, and Jack Rodwell and Costel Pantilimon from Manchester City, before signing Jermain Defoe for £9m in January.

Southampton, who had lost so many players to other Premier League clubs, began filling the gaps in their squad once Ronald Koeman had his feet firmly under the St Mary's desk. The Saints' summer signings included Shane Long for £12m from Hull City, Serbian winger Dusan Tadic for £10.9m, lightning quick winger Sadio Mane for £10m and Italian striker Graziano Pelle for £8m. Koeman also worked the loan market well, bringing Ryan Bertrand from Chelsea and Toby Alderweireld.

Other headline signings included a real coup for Leicester City who added veteran Argentinean midfielder Esteban Cambiasso on a free transfer, West Ham's £12m addition of Ecuadorian World Cup star Enner Valencia, a return to Swansea City from Tottenham for Icelandic midfielder Gylfi Sigurdsson and Stoke City's move for former Barcelona starlet, Bojan.

Outside of the Premier League, recently relegated Fulham fully utilised the advantage of the 'parachute payments' they had received and generated shockwaves to the division above when they spent an incredible £11m on Leeds United striker Ross McCormack to smash the record fee ever spent by a Championship club. That single deal saw the value placed on almost every English-based player sky rocket.

## TALES OF THE TURF

Manchester United's new regime got off to a stuttering start after Louis van Gaal's first game at Old Trafford ended in a 2–1 opening day defeat to Swansea City. Arsenal began the season well, defeating Crystal Palace 2–1 while Chelsea overcame newly-promoted Burnley 3–1 at Turf Moor in a game that featured a debut goal for Diego Costa and an exquisite assist from Cesc Fabregas. The skilful Spaniard picked out Andrea Schurrle with a disguised pass that outfoxed the entire Burnley backline, allowing the German forward to do the rest with a drilled finish. Reigning champions Manchester City began with a 2–0 win at Newcastle while Liverpool triumphed 2–1 over Southampton at Anfield.

Appointed Manchester United captain by new manager Louis van Gaal, Wayne Rooney was also named skipper of the national team at the end of August after former captain Steven Gerrard announced his decision to retire from international football. Crystal Palace appointed Neil Warnock as Tony Pulis' successor which meant the veteran manager took charge of the Eagles for a second spell.

Chelsea led the way at the end of the opening month, after beating Leicester City 2–0 at home and having destroyed Everton 6–3 at Goodison Park. Added to the guile and imagination of attacking midfielders Cesc Fabregas and Eden Hazard, the ruthless finishing of Diego Costa saw the Blues play some of the most entertaining attacking football of all the teams previously managed by Jose Mourinho, including his title winning Chelsea sides of 2004–05 and 2005–06.

There was also a change in the dugout at White Hart Lane when Tottenham chose Southampton's Mauricio Pochettino as manager after caretaker boss Tim Sherwood failed to impress enough to be given the role on a full-time basis. Replacing Pochettino at Southampton was Dutchman Ronald Koeman, who immediately faced the impossible looking task of stabilising a club wounded by the exits of a cluster of key players.

On the eve of the new campaign, Crystal Palace were thrown into managerial turmoil when the previous season's Manager of the Year, Tony Pulis, resigned from his post, believing that the club's board hadn't supported him adequately in the transfer market. Long-serving coach Keith Millen was named caretaker boss.

### ⚽ INTERESTING INFO

The 2014–15 season saw Crystal Palace begin a second consecutive campaign in the Premier League for the first time.

LEFT TOP: *Chelsea striker Diego Costa adapted quickly to life in the Premier League and began the season in fine goal scoring form.*

LEFT BOTTOM: *Leicester City's waspish striker Jamie Vardy scores past Manchester United's David de Gea during the Foxes' famous 5–3 victory at the King Power Stadium.*

Swansea City and Aston Villa sat in second and third with Arsenal, Manchester City and Liverpool all in touching distance. Struggling to adapt to the coaching methods and the 3–5–2 formation implemented by Louis van Gaal, Manchester United remained winless at the end of the month after experiencing frustrating away draws with Sunderland and Burnley. The Clarets were rooted at the bottom of the table having registered just that single point against United.

Aston Villa recorded a shock 1–0 victory against Liverpool at the beginning of September and West Ham also took maximum points from the previous season's runners-up as the Merseyside club struggled in front of goal following the losses of Luis Suarez to Barcelona and Daniel Sturridge to injury. Arsenal found their form in September with a devastating attacking display against Aston Villa. The Gunners triumphed 3–0 at Villa Park in a game that featured Danny Welbeck's first goal for the club.

Manchester United got off the mark with a 4–0 home win over QPR that featured goals from summer signings Angel Di Maria and Ander Herrera. However, the following weekend, the Red Devils came back down to Earth with a bump after Leicester City put in one of the performances of the season to defeat United 5–3 at the King Power. Van Gaal's team had been in fine form in the first half, which featured a delicious chipped goal from Di Maria, and took a 3–1 lead in the second period. However, after a dubious penalty was awarded and converted, Leicester's worth ethic and tenacity, backed by vociferous support, saw them score a further three goals without reply to leave United and their new manager in a state of shock.

Under-fire Newcastle manager Alan Pardew saw his team rescue a 2–2 draw against Hull City after the Magpies had trailed the Tigers 2–0. Another manager in the firing line, West Brom's Alan Irvine, guided his team to a first victory of the season following a 1–0 win against Spurs at White Hart Lane while Crystal Palace defeated struggling Everton 3–2 at Goodison Park.

*ABOVE: Manchester City midfielder Frank Lampard embraces his former Chelsea team-mate Didier Drogba after scoring the goal that rescued a point for his current employers against his previous club.*

Towards the end of the month Chelsea and Manchester City met in a top of the table clash at the Etihad Stadium. Playing in a more typical pragmatic style, Chelsea took the lead with 20 minutes remaining through Andrea Schurrle before former Blues legend, Frank Lampard, came off the bench and scored a late equaliser against his old club to rescue a point for 10-man Manchester City. Chelsea remained top of the pile at the end of September, followed by Southampton who had gained many admirers under Ronald Koeman. The South Coast club were solid defensively and the attacking displays of summer signings Graziano Pelle and Dusin Tadic had inspired the Saints to notable victories against the likes of Swansea and Newcastle. The Magpies, yet to record a victory, sat second from bottom, only ahead of Burnley on goals scored.

Chelsea maintained their impressive form throughout October and recorded a 2–0 victory over Arsenal at Stamford Bridge, following goals from Diego Costa and Eden Hazard, as well as a 2–1 win at Crystal Palace. Manchester United overcame Everton 2–1 at Old Trafford thanks to Radamel Falcao's first goal for the club and a goalkeeping masterclass from young Spanish stopper David de Gea. It wasn't be the last time that De Gea's reflexes and gravity-defying shot-stopping were influential in a United victory during the campaign.

ABOVE: *Manchester United goalkeeper David de Gea produced a succession of match-saving displays that were influential in maintaining the Red Devils' top four challenge.*

Towards the end of the month United grabbed a late point against Chelsea at Old Trafford after Robin van Persie hit a stoppage time equaliser to cancel out Didier Drogba's opener for the Blues. Chelsea remained top at the end of October with Southampton, who recorded an 8–0 thumping over Sunderland during the month, still their nearest challengers in second. Manchester City were third, while Sam Allardyce's West Ham, who were playing some superb attacking football, sat fourth.

November saw Liverpool suffer three consecutive league defeats to Newcastle United, Chelsea and Crystal Palace as Brendan Rodgers' summer signings struggled to justify his faith in their ability. The Reds' great rivals, Manchester United, reached the top four for the first time after recovering from a 1–0 loss to Manchester City to defeat Crystal Palace, Hull City and Arsenal, the latter featuring a counter-attacking smash and grab victory at the Emirates thanks to a well-taken goal from Wayne Rooney. Chelsea remained on course for the title after opening up a six point lead from second place Manchester City.

Newcastle's form dramatically improved during November and December, as the Magpies recorded six successive victories in all competitions, which included a 2–1 win over league-leaders Chelsea. The previously under-fire Alan Pardew, who had been the subject of a vitriolic campaign for his sacking by Newcastle supporters, was named Premier League manager of the month as his team rocketed up the table and away from relegation concerns. However, Pardew remained on borrowed time and chose to depart the club during December to take the manager's job at his former side Crystal Palace, filling the vacancy left following the Eagles' sacking of Neil Warnock after less than four months in charge. Experienced coach John Carver was named as the Magpies' caretaker boss for the remainder of the season. December also brought an end to Alan Irvine's tenure as West Brom boss with the Baggies struggling in the bottom half of the table.

Manchester City enjoyed a productive December, recording impressive away wins at Southampton, West Brom and Sunderland, as well as home victories over the likes of Everton and Crystal Palace. Manuel Pellegrini's men closed the gap at the top to three points following Chelsea's defeat to Newcastle. Southampton suffered a loss of form which saw them drop down to fourth below Manchester United, who continued to struggle for consistency but maintained a decent points return. A high point for the Red Devils came when they defeated great rivals Liverpool 3–0 at Old Trafford thanks to goals from Wayne Rooney, Juan Mata and Robin van Persie. Despite the loss, Liverpool showed encouraging signs after Brendan Rodgers changed to a 3–5–2 line-up – a strategy that saw the Reds go on an improved run of results.

Arsenal, inspired by the attacking instincts of Alexis Sanchez, fared better as 2014 drew to a close and picked up a gutsy 2–1 win at West Ham which saw them leap-frog the Hammers into fifth place. The bottom three at end of the year comprised Crystal Palace, Leicester, who had gone into freefall following a promising start to the season, and Burnley.

January started with a new managerial appointment at West Brom after former Crystal Palace and Stoke boss, Tony Pulis, was named as Alan Irvine's successor. The form of Tottenham striker Harry Kane was one of the stories of the season. The young English striker, who had struggled to make an impact upon the Spurs first team for several years and following numerous loan spells at other clubs, was given an extended run in the side and grabbed it with both hands. His pace, power and growing influence was on show as Spurs were responsible for Chelsea's worst defeat of the season – 5–3 at White Hart Lane at the beginning of January. Chelsea's famously robust defence was taken apart by the speed and hunger of the Spurs' attack and Kane dominated the usually unflappable John Terry and Gary Cahill to score twice.

The Blues soon got back on track with a home victory over Newcastle and a stunning 5–0 win at Swansea City before a tense 1–1 draw with Manchester City at Stamford Bridge helped increase their advantage over the Manchester club to five points.

West Ham's early season form faded and they dropped out of the top seven to be replaced by an improving Liverpool. Southampton maintained their impressive performances and completed a shock 1–0 win over Manchester United at Old Trafford.

At the wrong end of the table, Leicester's rotten luck continued during February as they suffered losses to Crystal Palace and Arsenal. The Palace reversal featured a controversial coming together between Foxes boss Nigel Pearson, a man who faced the full glare of the media focus on several occasions during the season, and Eagles midfielder James McCathur. After McCarthur inadvertently upended Pearson on the touchline the City boss appeared to wrestle the opposing player whilst lying on the ground, a move that later saw him reprimanded by the FA.

Manchester United's midfield magician Juan Mata celebrates his second goal against Liverpool, a beautifully timed scissor kick, as the Red Devils overcame their great rivals 2–1 at Anfield.

Leicester City manager Nigel Pearson faced intense scrutiny from the media but maintained a steely focus on his team to keep the Foxes in the Premier League following arguably the greatest escape of all-time.

Speculation followed that Pearson was to be sacked by the club's owners but he was seemingly given a reprieve and retained his position despite his team's faltering form. One man to lose his job during February was Aston Villa manager Paul Lambert, who paid the price for overseeing another campaign that looked to be heading for a relegation battle. His successor was later named as former Spurs boss, Tim Sherwood.

Tottenham and Harry Kane continued to impress and grabbed a 2–1 win over Arsenal in the North London derby but were on the receiving end of a 3–2 to loss to Liverpool in what proved to be a rare high-point for Brendan Rodgers' team. Manchester City were held to a 1–1 home draw by Hull City but went on to record a 4–1 victory at Stoke and a 5–0 win at home to Newcastle. Manchester United suffered defeat to Swansea and drew 1–1 at West Ham but recorded victories over Burnley and Sunderland to remain in the top three at the end of the month. Chelsea maintained a five-point lead at the top of the table while Arsenal moved up to fifth.

March signalled the end of Gus Poyet's tenure as Sunderland manager as the Uruguayan paid the price for the Black Cats' poor performances. His replacement was later confirmed as veteran Dutch coach, Dick Advocaat. Liverpool began March with a 2–1 home victory over Manchester City that rekindled memories of the performances that characterised their title challenge the previous campaign. The Reds

then recorded back-to-back victories against Burnley and Swansea to set up a crucial looking contest against Manchester United at Anfield.

At Old Trafford there had been positive signs that Louis van Gaal's much-feted philosophy was beginning to bear fruit, as better defensive displays and dominant possession had been accompanied by goals and victories during a superb six-game spell during March and April.

United began their impressive run with a smash and grab 1–0 win against Newcastle at St James' Park, achieved thanks to a late goal from the markedly improved Ashley Young. A 3–0 home victory against Spurs followed, achieved thanks to goals from Juan Mata, Wayne Rooney and Marouane Fellaini. The physically imposing Belgian, like Ashley Young, was very much a figure of redemption during the campaign. Having been widely and harshly criticised by United supporters after struggling during the David Moyes' era, Fellaini became a crucial component of Louis van Gaal's revitalised team, offering height, strength and aerial prowess.

After defeating Spurs, United travelled to Anfield to face Liverpool, one of their rivals for a top four place; a battle that also featured Tottenham, Arsenal and Southampton and had been dubbed as a 'rat-race' by Louis van Gaal. Many pundits expected Liverpool to defeat United, but one of the Red Devils' most dominant and assured displays of the campaign followed. Juan Mata was the hero as he bagged a brace in a 2–1 win for United. The first goal was a smart finish following an incisive passing move and the second came in the form of a memorable scissor kick. The game also featured a bizarre red card for Liverpool captain Steven Gerrard. Having already announced he would depart the club at the end of the season, Gerrard ended his final clash against Manchester United in disappointing circumstances after being sent off just 45 seconds into his second-half substitute's appearance following a desperate lunge on Ander Herrera.

A 3–1 victory over Aston Villa followed before United impressed during a 4–2 win over title-challenging Manchester City at Old Trafford. Marouane Felliani was again in menacing mood and, alongside Ashley Young, Juan Mata and Chris Smalling, found the net to give United three crucial points.

While United made ground on Manchester City, Chelsea continued to impress at the top of the table, picking up key away victories against West Ham and Hull to finish March six points clear of City and with a game in hand. As well as the loss to Manchester United, City also suffered reversals to both Burnley, thanks to a classy finish from George Boyd, and away to a Crystal Palace side that had begun to impress under Alan Pardew. Arsenal closed the gap on City to a single point after a run of victories over the likes of Everton, QPR and Newcastle, achieved thanks to the in-form attacking duo of Olivier Giroud and Alexis Sanchez.

In April, Chelsea recorded a hard-fought 1–0 win against Manchester United at Stamford Bridge. The Red Devils dominated possession for large periods with the home side content to defend in numbers before the man that had made the difference on so many occasions throughout the season, Eden Hazard, produced a moment of magic to beat David de Gea and seal the three points. That victory helped the Blues end the month as huge favourites for the title, as they only needed a single victory from their final four fixtures.

Arsenal appeared the Blues' closest challengers but a 0–0 draw against Chelsea at the Emirates, in a display that again featured a dogged, defensive display from Jose Mourinho's men, effectively ended their slim hopes of causing an upset. One the same

The emerging and considerable talents of young Tottenham striker Harry Kane were showcased perfectly during Spurs' 5–3 victory over Chelsea at White Hart Lane.

afternoon, Manchester United were brushed aside 3–0 by Everton at Goodison Park, and the Red Devils' top four placing once again came into question.

At the foot of the table, Aston Villa, who had enjoyed an upturn in form following the appointment of Tim Sherwood, looked to be on a safer footing as the likes of Christian Benteke, Jack Grealish and Tom Cleverley began to find form. April brought one of the goals of the season when Stoke City's Charlie Adam scored from well inside his own half against Chelsea at Stamford Bridge.

*Stoke City's Charlie Adam is congratulated by his team-mates after scoring one of the goals of the season, from inside his own half, against Chelsea at Stamford Bridge.*

*One of the signings of the season, veteran Argentine midfielder Esteban Cambiasso was Leicester City's midfielder conductor during the Foxes fight for Premier League survival.*

Leicester City, who had appeared doomed since the turn of the year, recorded their first victory in nine league games following a 2–1 win over West Ham at the King Power Stadium. The game featured a classy goal from veteran midfielder Esteban Cambiasso who, alongside the hard working Jamie Vardy, was becoming crucial to any hopes the Foxes had of avoiding relegation.

The return to fitness of goalkeeper Kasper Schmeichel and the steadying influence of loan-signing Robert Huth as part of a three-man defence were also key elements to an amazing up-turn in form from the East Midlands club. Leicester went on to defeat West Brom 3–2 at the Hawthorns before overcoming Swansea 2–0 and Burnley 1–0 to move out of the bottom three for the first since November.

The Foxes went on to become one of the form teams in Europe, winning seven of their last nine games to complete one of the greatest escapes in Premier League history and avoid relegation with a game to spare. Aston Villa also secured their top-flight status in their penultimate league fixture, even though they were on the wrong end of a 6–1 scoreline against Southampton.

Manchester United continued to falter as much as they succeeded during the last month of the season, losing at home to West Brom before

recording a 2–1 win at Selhurst Park that almost secured a top-four finish. A draw for Liverpool at Chelsea the following day ensured United's return to a Champions League qualification spot, as the Reds, Spurs and Southampton ran out of steam.

Chelsea sealed the title with a 1–0 home win over Crystal Palace after Eden Hazard headed his rebounded, missed penalty into the net. It was the Blues' fourth championship in the Premier League era and their third under the guidance of Jose Mourinho. Manchester City went on to finish second, while Arsenal took third and Manchester United finished fourth. Tottenham ended fifth and qualified for the Europa League alongside sixth placed Liverpool and seventh placed Southampton.

Burnley became the first team to drop out of the division, despite a 1–0 win at Hull, while QPR followed them back into the Championship the next day after a crushing 6–0 loss to Manchester City. Defeat to Burnley left Hull perilously close to the drop while a run of eight straight defeats saw Newcastle firmly in the relegation picture.

A shirtless Jonas Gutierrez celebrates scoring the goal that preserved Newcastle United's Premier League status on the final day of the season.

An emotional Steven Gerrard salutes the Kop after his final appearance for Liverpool at Anfield.

## INTERESTING INFO

Frank Lampard is the highest goal scoring midfielder in the history of the Premier League. The former West Ham, Chelsea and Manchester City man scored a total of 177 goals in 609 games.

With a game in hand on their relegation rivals, Sunderland secured their top-flight survival following an edgy 0–0 draw against Arsenal at the Emirates. That left two teams, Newcastle and Hull City, fighting to avoid the final relegation place on the last day of the season. The Magpies knew a win over West Ham would ensure their safety while Hull had to beat Manchester United and hope that the Hammers could do them a favour at St James' Park. In the end, the highly-anticipated drama didn't unfold, as Newcastle won 2–0, with their second goal coming from Jonas Gutierrez, the Argentine midfielder who had returned to action earlier in the campaign after winning his battle with testicular cancer. Hull failed to break the deadlock in their game with Manchester United and ended up dropping out of the division with something of a whimper.

Anfield witnessed the end of an era in the penultimate weekend of the season as Steven Gerrard played his last game for Liverpool in front of the Kop. The occasion proved an anti-climax, however, as Crystal Palace played the role of party poopers to secure a 3–1 victory, achieved largely through the pace, trickery and attacking talents of entertaining wingers Yannick Bolaise and Wilfried Zaha. Gerrard received a wonderful reception from the Liverpool fans that was richly deserved, and gave an emotional farewell to the club he had served so well for 17 years.

Stoke City stunned Liverpool with a final day 6–1 drubbing at The Britannia Stadium. The only high point in an afternoon to forget for Reds fans was Steven Gerrard marking his last appearance for the club with a well-taken consolation goal. The result was far from a fitting send-off for the Reds' legendary captain and emphasised just how far the club had slumped following their title challenge the previous campaign. A true great of the Premier League era, Gerrard played a total of 503 games in the division, scoring 120 goals.

Another Premier League legend bowed out on the final day of the season, as Frank Lampard marked his final appearance for Manchester City with a goal in a 2–0 victory over Southampton. Like Gerrard, the former England man was set for a new career in the USA's MLS, after a glorious, trophy and goal-filled 20 years in English football.

# HONOURS LIST

## Barclays Premier League

**CHAMPIONS:** Chelsea

By the far the most dominant team in the division, Chelsea played with a more free-flowing style during the first half of the season before getting across the line in the final few months through a combination of rugged defending, tactical brilliance and ruthless finishing.

**RUNNERS-UP:** Manchester City

**RELEGATED:** Burnley, QPR, Hull City

**TOP GOAL SCORER:** Sergio Aguero (26 goals for Manchester City)

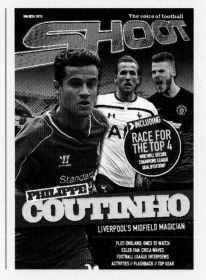

**SHOOT MAGAZINE 2014–15**

*Three of the stars of the 2014–15 season were afforded top billing as Shoot focused on the nip and tuck 'rat race' for the top four Premier League positions. Liverpool's Brazilian midfielder Philippe Coutinho was the most prominent player and was joined by on-form Spurs striker Harry Kane and Manchester United's ultra-consistent goalkeeper, David de Gea.*

## 2014–15 SEASON TABLE

| | | M | W | D | L | GF | GA | GD | PTS |
|---|---|---|---|---|---|---|---|---|---|
| 1 | Chelsea | 38 | 26 | 9 | 3 | 73 | 32 | +41 | 87 |
| 2 | Manchester City | 38 | 24 | 7 | 7 | 83 | 38 | +45 | 79 |
| 3 | Arsenal | 38 | 22 | 9 | 7 | 71 | 36 | +35 | 75 |
| 4 | Manchester United | 38 | 20 | 10 | 8 | 62 | 37 | +25 | 70 |
| 5 | Tottenham Hotspur | 38 | 19 | 7 | 12 | 58 | 53 | +5 | 64 |
| 6 | Liverpool | 38 | 18 | 8 | 12 | 52 | 48 | +4 | 62 |
| 7 | Southampton | 38 | 18 | 6 | 14 | 54 | 33 | +21 | 60 |
| 8 | Swansea City | 38 | 16 | 8 | 14 | 46 | 49 | −3 | 56 |
| 9 | Stoke City | 38 | 15 | 9 | 14 | 48 | 45 | +3 | 54 |
| 10 | Crystal Palace | 38 | 13 | 9 | 16 | 47 | 51 | −4 | 48 |
| 11 | Everton | 38 | 12 | 11 | 15 | 48 | 50 | −2 | 47 |
| 12 | West Ham United | 38 | 12 | 11 | 15 | 44 | 47 | −3 | 47 |
| 13 | West Bromwich Albion | 38 | 11 | 11 | 16 | 38 | 51 | −13 | 44 |
| 14 | Leicester City | 38 | 11 | 8 | 19 | 46 | 55 | −9 | 41 |
| 15 | Newcastle United | 38 | 10 | 9 | 19 | 40 | 63 | −23 | 39 |
| 16 | Sunderland | 38 | 7 | 17 | 14 | 31 | 53 | −22 | 38 |
| 17 | Aston Villa | 38 | 10 | 8 | 20 | 31 | 57 | −26 | 38 |
| 18 | Hull City | 38 | 8 | 11 | 19 | 33 | 51 | −18 | 35 |
| 19 | Burnley | 38 | 7 | 12 | 19 | 28 | 53 | −25 | 33 |
| 20 | Queens Park Rangers | 38 | 8 | 6 | 24 | 42 | 73 | −31 | 30 |

## PLAYERS OF THE SEASON

**PFA PLAYER OF THE YEAR:** Eden Hazard, Chelsea

**PFA YOUNG PLAYER OF THE YEAR:** Harry Kane, Tottenham Hotspur

**FOOTBALL WRITERS PLAYER OF THE YEAR:** Eden Hazard, Chelsea

*Bournemouth boss Eddie Howe worked miracles to deliver the Championship title and top-flight football for the first time in the club's history.*

*Bristol City boss Steve Cotterill returned the Robins to the second tier and also lifted the Johnstone's Paints Trophy.*

**FOOTBALL LEAGUE CHAMPIONSHIP CHAMPIONS:** Bournemouth
**PROMOTED:** Watford
**CHAMPIONSHIP PLAY-OFF WINNERS:** Norwich City
**RELEGATED:** Blackpool, Millwall, Wigan Athletic
**TOP GOAL SCORER:** Daryl Murphy (27 goals for Ipswich Town)

Bournemouth were the surprise Championship title winners after their free-flowing brand of attacking football saw them top the table on the final day of the season and reach English football's top flight for the first time in the club's history. Led by the highly-regarded Eddie Howe, who had worked miracles on a tight budget, the Cherries star performers included winger Scott Ritchie and strikers Callum Wilson and Yann Kermorgant. Second place went to Watford, who changed their manager four times in 35 days at the beginning of the season before settling on Slavisa Jokanovic, while Norwich City, who appointed Alex Neil as manager during the campaign, overcame Middlesbrough 2–0 in the play-off final thanks to goals from Cameron Jerome and Nathan Redmond.

**LEAGUE ONE CHAMPIONS:** Bristol City
**PROMOTED:** MK Dons
**LEAGUE ONE PLAY-OFF WINNERS:** Preston North End
**RELEGATED:** Notts County, Crawley Town, Leyton Orient, Yeovil Town
**TOP GOAL SCORER:** Joe Garner (25 goals for Preston North End)

Under the steady hand of Steve Cotterill, Bristol City stormed to the League One title to end their two-year exile from the Championship. The Robins topped the division for almost the entire season and became the first club in the country to achieve promotion. Second placed MK Dons, who finished as the top scoring side in any of the top four English leagues, took the second automatic promotion place, while Simon Grayson's Preston North End overcame Swindon Town 4–0 in the play-off final thanks to a hat-trick from Jermaine Beckford.

A mid-season replacement for the departing Gary Rowett, former Premier League star striker, Jimmy Floyd Hasselbaink, guided Burton Albion into League One for the first time.

**LEAGUE TWO CHAMPIONS:** Burton Albion
**PROMOTED:** Shrewsbury Town, Bury
**LEAGUE TWO PLAY-OFF WINNERS:** Southend United
**RELEGATED:** Cheltenham Town, Tranmere Rovers
**TOP GOAL SCORER:** Matt Tubbs (21 goals for AFC Wimbledon and Portsmouth)

Jimmy Floyd Hasselbaink, who succeeded Gary Rowett as manager during the season, guided Burton Albion to the title and into the third tier of English football for the first time in the club's history. The Brewers finished ahead of Micky Mellon's Shrewsbury Town and Bury, managed by Gary Flitcroft, who both secured automatic promotion. Phil Brown's Southend United overcame Wycombe Wanderers on penalties in the play-off final to take the fourth and final promotion place.

Dropping out of the Football League were Tranmere Rovers, who were relegated to the Conference for the first time in 94 years and Cheltenham Town, who returned to the non league scene after 16 uninterrupted years in the league.

**VANARAMA CONFERENCE CHAMPIONS:** Barnet
**PROMOTED:** Bristol Rovers

Martin Allen's Barnet secured the Conference title and became the first club to win promotion to the Football League on three separate occasions, following a dramatic 2–0 home victory against Gateshead on the final day of the season. Bristol Rovers, managed by Darrell Clarke, were narrowly pipped to the title but made amends in the play-off final, defeating Grimsby Town on penalties.

# UP FOR THE CUP

**FA CUP WINNERS:** Arsenal

In one of the most one-sided FA Cup finals in living memory, Arsenal tore into a below-par Aston Villa side from the kick-off. The Gunners took a first-half lead through a close-range Theo Walcott strike before Alexis Sanchez doubled their lead with a stunning second-half strike. Further goals from Per Metersacker and Olivier Giroud followed as the Gunners ran out 4–0 winners to lift the trophy for the second successive season and for a record 12th time.

Arsenal overcame plucky Championship side Reading in the semi-finals but were forced into extra time by Steve Clarke's team. The Gunners took a first-half lead through Alexis Sanchez before Garath McCleary shot home a shock equaliser. The Royals' goalkeeper Adam Federeci was in inspired form between the posts, miraculously preventing Arsenal's glut of attacking riches from finding the net. However, the Australian stopper went from hero to villain when he fumbled a tame Alexis Sanchez shot across his line to gift Arsenal a late extra-time victory.

Aston Villa secured their place in the final following an impressive display against Liverpool. Despite the Reds taking the lead through Philippe Coutinho, Villa fought back to win 2–1 thanks to goals from Christian Benteke and Fabian Delph.

Earlier in the competition, Manchester United negotiated several potential banana skins, overcoming League One Yeovil Town at Huish Park before being taken to a replay by League Two side Cambridge United, following a 0–0 draw at the Abbey Stadium. The Red Devils eventually progressed to the next round where they knocked out another League One side, Preston North End. While United remained in the competition, Premier League teams around them crashed out in a succession of shock results. Manchester City were beaten 2–0 at home by Championship side Middlesbrough, thanks to goals from Patrick Bamford and Kike, while two other second tier sides, Blackburn and Bolton, disposed of Swansea and Liverpool respectively.

However, the biggest giant slaying occurred at Stamford Bridge where League One Bradford City fought back from two goals behind to stun league-leaders Chelsea with a 4–2 victory. The Bantams' goals were scored by Jon Stead, Filipe Morais, Andy Halliday and Mark Yeates.

### LEAGUE (CAPITAL ONE) CUP WINNERS: Chelsea

Chelsea proved too strong for Tottenham and defeated their London rivals 2–0 to lift the first trophy of the season and the first silverware of Jose Mourinho's second spell at the club. The Blues claimed their fifth League Cup thanks to goals form John Terry and Diego Costa.

Chelsea reached the final following a 2–1 aggregate victory over Liverpool in the semi-final, when Branislav Ivanovic's extra-time goal proved crucial, while Tottenham overcame Sheffield United 3–2 across their two games, thanks to a late goal from Christian Eriksen.

The standout result in the competition took place in the second round when an under strength Manchester United team, which still featured numerous international players, was hammered 4–0 by League One side MK Dons. The Milton Keynes side played with power and determination and scored goals through a pair of braces from Will Grigg and Benik Afobe. Other shocks during the tournament included Sheffield Wednesday's victory over Burnley, Shrewsbury Town overcoming Leicester City and Sheffield United knocking out West Ham.

### COMMUNITY SHIELD WINNERS: Arsenal

FA Cup holders Arsenal lay down a marker for the new season with a comprehensive 3–0 victory over Manchester City at Wembley thanks to goals from Santi Cazorla, Aaron Ramsey and Olivier Giroud.

### THE FOOTBALL LEAGUE (JOHNSTONE'S PAINTS) TROPHY: Bristol City

Bristol City defeated Walsall 2–0 at Wembley Stadium to lift the Football League Trophy for a record third time. The Robins' goals were provided by Aden Flint and Mark Little.

RIGHT, FROM TOP TO BOTTOM: *Arsenal's Theo Walcott wheels away in delight after slamming home the opening goal of the 2015 FA Cup final; Bradford City players celebrate their remarkable FA Cup giant killing victory over Chelsea at Stamford Bridge; Chelsea skipper John Terry celebrates after scoring in the Capital One cup final against Tottenham; Benik Afobe slots another goal past a stunned David de Gea as Manchester United slump to an astounding 4–1 loss to MK Dons.*

# INTO EUROPE

## European Champions League

English teams endured another largely disappointing campaign in European football's premier competition, with only Chelsea emerging with any kind of credit. The Blues comfortably progressed through a group containing Schalke, Sporting Lisbon and Maribor but were given a tough draw in the last round of 16 where they met Paris Saint-Germain. The tie ended 3–3 on aggregate but Chelsea went out on away goals after former Blues defender, David Luiz, came back to haunt them with a late goal.

Manchester City qualified through the group stage of the competition but a runner's-up placing saw them paired with Barcelona in the last round of 16 tie. The Catalan club, boasting a trio of mesmerising attacking talent that comprised Lionel Messi, Luis Suarez and Neymar, were too strong for the English champions and ousted them 3–1 on aggregate.

Arsenal again disappointed in the knockout rounds of the competition, suffering a surprise 3–1 home loss to a Monaco side that featured former Tottenham and Manchester United striker Dimitar Berbatov, before ultimately crashing out on away goals following a 3–3 aggregate scoreline.

Participating in the competition for the first time since 2009, Liverpool endured a wretched campaign. The Reds were drawn against reigning European champions Real Madrid in the group stages, but were also paired with Swiss side FC Basle and European minnows, Ludogorets Razgrad. Brendan Rodgers' men went on to record just a single victory and suffered home defeat to Real Madrid and an away loss to Basle before being held at home by the Swiss side and dropping into the Europa League.

RIGHT: *Former Chelsea defender David Luiz is a picture of delight and intensity after scoring the goal that knocked the Blues out of Europe and sent Paris Saint-Germain into the quarter-final.*

## UEFA Europa League

Hull City, participating in the European competition for the first time in their history, failed to progress to the group stages following a play-off round exit at the hands of Belgian side Lokeren on away goals. Tottenham and Everton both took part in the group element of the competition. Spurs advanced to the last 32 where they were defeated 3–1 on aggregate by Fiorentina while the Toffees went one step further before being knocked out by Dynamo Kiev. Following their Champions League exit Liverpool were drawn against Besiktas in the knockout stages but went on to lose 5–4 on penalties to the Turkish side.

# THE INTERNATIONAL SCENE

England's European Championship qualifying campaign began well and included an impressive 2–0 away win over Switzerland that featured two decisive finishes from Arsenal striker Danny Welbeck. The Three Lions also enjoyed a 3–1 friendly victory over Scotland thanks to goals from Alex Oxlade Chamberlain and Wayne Rooney, who scored twice, and grabbed a 1–1 draw against Italy in Turin following a classy goal from Andros Townsend.

ABOVE: *Danny Welbeck, who signed for Arsenal during the summer, scores the first of a crucial brace for England against Switzerland.*

# THE SPENDING CONTINUES

The summer of 2015 saw the majority of Premier League teams once again tour the world to maximise commercial earnings and increase their appeal in Asia, the United States and Australia. Several clubs, including Manchester City and Tottenham Hotspur, began their globetrotting even earlier than usual, scheduling in post-season friendlies before the summer break to boost further enhance their bank balances.

Leicester City surprisingly parted company with Nigel Pearson during the closed season as the occasionally outspoken manager seemingly paid the price for a souring of his relationship with the club's Thai owners. This followed a controversial incident involving his son James during the Foxes end of season trip to Thailand that led to the younger Pearson having his playing contract cancelled. Leicester, who had completed one of the greatest ever Premier League survival bids at the end of the previous campaign, appointed former Chelsea boss Claudio Ranieri as Pearson's successor.

Following Sam Allardyce's end of season departure from West Ham, the Hammers moved for former Croatian international coach and one time central defender at the club, Slaven Bilic. Newcastle opted for another former international boss, Steve McClaren, who took up the reins at St James Park after John Carver returned to a backroom role. Newly promoted Watford appointed Spaniard Quique Flores as their boss after failing to agree a new deal with Slavisa Jokanovic, the man that had sealed second spot in the Championship.

OPPOSITE PAGE: *After a drawn out transfer saga that began during the 2014–15 campaign and dragged on throughout the summer, young England forward Raheem Sterling eventually signed on the dotted line at Manchester City after Liverpool agreed to sell him for £49m.*

LEFT: *A surprise appointment for many, veteran Italian coach Claudio Ranieri was named as Leicester City manager after the Foxes parted company with previous boss Nigel Pearson.*

# TRANSFER TALES

Of the promoted teams, Watford and Bournemouth – the latter preparing to play in the English top flight for the first time in their history – were widely tipped to struggle. Both clubs made significant additions with Bournemouth moving for the likes of veteran French defender Sylvain Distin, Norwegian winger Joshua King and Ipswich Town youngster Tyrone Mings, while Watford bolstered their ranks with several new signings, including Tottenham midfielder Etienne Capoue, Uruguayan defender Miguel Britos, Swiss utility man Valon Behrami and Spanish midfielder Jose Jurado. The third promoted club, Norwich City, took a more conservative approach to their transfer dealings but did add West Brom midfielder Youssouf Mulumbu on a free transfer.

Manchester United and Liverpool were again the most active clubs in the transfer market. United invested heavily to bolster their midfield with the signings of Germany's World Cup winning captain Bastian Schweinsteiger and the ever-improving Morgan Schneiderlin from Southampton. Further additions at Old Trafford included Dutch forward Memphis Depay and Italian full-back Matteo Darmian. United did allow a number of high profile players to depart, including striker Robin van Persie and winger Nani.

Liverpool offset the considerable losses of Steven Gerrard on a free transfer and the sale of Raheem Sterling to Manchester City with plenty of new additions. The Reds brought in experienced England international midfielder James Milner on a free transfer and also moved for young Burnley striker Danny Ings, promising Brazilian forward Roberto Firmino, Southampton's ultra-consistent right-back Nathaniel Clyne, Charlton youngster Joe Gomez, Bolton goalkeeper Adam Bogan and Aston Villa's powerful Belgian front man Christian Benteke for a staggering £32.5m.

As well as the protracted signing of Raheem Sterling, Manchester City added further young English talent in the shape of Fulham midfielder Patrick Roberts and Aston Villa captain, Fabian Delph, who went back on his decision of pledging allegiance to the Villains a few days before completing the move.

Arsenal pulled off one of the transfer coups of the summer, bringing in Chelsea's established stopper Petr Cech to fill their problem goalkeeping position. Chelsea signed Stoke City's Asmir Begovic as a replacement and also added Colombian striker Radamel Falcao – fresh from a disappointing season at Manchester United – on loan from AS Monaco.

Ronald Koeman's Southampton moved quickly in the market once again, signing Dutch midfielder Jordie Clasie from Feyenoord, Spanish striker Juanmi from Malaga, Portuguese defender Cedric Soares from Sporting Lisbon and experienced goalkeeper Maarten Stekelengburg on loan from Fulham.

# TOP TEN TRANSFERS

**RAHEEM STERLING** – From Liverpool to Manchester City – £49m

**CHRISTIAN BENTEKE** – From Aston Villa to Liverpool – £32.5m

**MEMPHIS DEPAY** – From PSV Eindhoven to Manchester United – £31m

**ROBERTO FIRMINO** – From Hoffenheim to Liverpool – £29m

**MORGAN SCHNEIDERLIN** – From Southampton to Manchester United – £25m

**MATTEO DARMIAN** – From Torino to Manchester United – £12.7m

**GREGORY WINALDUM** – From PSV Eindhoven to Newcastle United – £14.5m

**BASTIAN SCHWEINSTEIGER** – From Bayern Munich to Manchester United – £14.4m

**ALEKSANDAR MITROVIC** – From Anderlecht to Newcastle United – £13m

**TOBY ALDERWEIRELD** – From Atletico Madrid to Tottenham Hotspur – £11.5m

*Captain of the German national side and a Bayern Munich legend, Bastian Schweinsteiger joined Manchester United ahead of the new campaign as the Red Devils added depth and real quality to their midfield ranks.*

*Chelsea stalwart Petr Cech was snapped up by their London rivals Arsenal at the beginning of the summer. The giant Czech goalkeeper had been the Premier League's most consistent stopper for over a decade and looked set to add stability and assurance to a position that had caused the Gunners problems for several seasons.*

Everton signed Barcelona youngster Gerard Deulofeu for £4.3m after the Spaniard impressed during a loan spell at the club during the 2013-14 season and also added former Manchester United midfielder Tom Cleverley on a free transfer.

Tottenham snapped up promising right-back Kieran Trippier from relegated Burnley and moved for Belgian defender Toby Alderweireld after he impressed on loan at Southampton during the 2014-15 campaign.

West Ham brought in exciting French winger Dimitri Payet for £10.7m and Spanish midfielder Pedro Obiang from Sampdoria and agreed season-long loans with Arsenal's Carl Jenkinson and Argentine midfielder Manuel Lanzini.

Sunderland added to their defensive ranks in the shape of Younes Kaboul from Spurs and Sebastian Coates from Liverpool. The Black Cats also bought Dutch forward Jeremain Lens for £8m. Their great rivals Newcastle added a Dutchman of their own, bringing in £14.5m striker Gregory Winaldum. The Magpies further boosted their firepower with the £13m signing of Serbian front man Aleksandar Mitrovic.

Crystal Palace completed a real coup when they brought in France international midfielder Yohan Cabeye from Paris Saint-Germain for £10m. The Eagles also added Chelsea starlet Patrick Bamford on loan.

Leicester City finalised a permanent move for Stoke's Robert Huth and also added Austrian defender Christian Fuchs and Japanese striker Shinji Okazaki. Elsewhere Aston Villa brought in former Manchester City defender Micah Richards on a free transfer, Stoke swelled their ranks with the signings of former Liverpool full-back Glen Johnson and Spanish striker Joselu and Swansea moved for Portuguese striker Eder from Sporting Braga.

# STATISTICS

## Premier League Title Winners

1. Manchester United – 13
2. Chelsea – 4
3. Arsenal – 3
4. Manchester City – 2
5. Blackburn Rovers – 1

## All-time Premier League Goalscorers

1. Alan Shearer – 260 goals
2. Andy Cole – 187
3. Wayne Rooney – 185
4. Frank Lampard – 177
5. Thierry Henry – 175
6. Robbie Fowler – 162
7. Michael Owen – 150
8. Les Ferdinand – 149
9. Teddy Sheringham – 146
10. Robin van Persie – 144

## Premier League Appearance Records

**MOST PREMIER LEAGUE APPEARANCES:** 632, Ryan Giggs (Manchester United)

**OLDEST PLAYER:** John Burridge, 43 years and 162 days (Manchester City)

**YOUNGEST PLAYER:** Matthew Briggs, 16 years and 65 days (Fulham)

**MOST CONSECUTIVE PREMIER LEAGUE APPEARANCES:** 310, Brad Friedel (Blackburn Rovers)

**MOST SEASONS APPEARED IN:** 22, Ryan Giggs (Manchester United)

BELOW: *Michael Owen slots the ball past Shay Given and into the net to send the Stretford End into raptures and settle one of the most memorable Manchester derbies in the modern era in United's favour.*

# Professional Footballers' Association (PFA) Teams of the Season

## 1992–93

### PREMIER LEAGUE
1. Peter Schmeichel – Manchester United
2. David Bardsley – Queens Park Rangers
3. Tony Dorigo – Leeds United
4. Gary Pallister – Manchester United
5. Paul McGrath – Aston Villa
6. Roy Keane – Nottingham Forest
7. Gary Speed – Leeds United
8. Paul Ince – Manchester United
9. Alan Shearer – Blackburn Rovers
10. Ian Wright – Arsenal
11. Ryan Giggs – Manchester United

### DIVISION ONE
1. Ludek Miklosko – West Ham United
2. David Kerslake – Swindon Town
3. John Beresford – Portsmouth
4. Craig Short – Derby County
5. Colin Cooper – Millwall
6. Lee Clark – Newcastle United
7. Micky Hazard – Swindon Town
8. Martin Allen – West Ham United
9. John Aldridge – Tranmere Rovers
10. Guy Whittingham – Portsmouth
11. Gavin Peacock – Newcastle United

### DIVISION TWO
1. Marlon Beresford – Burnley
2. Scott Hiley – Exeter City
3. Vince Overson – Stoke City
4. Peter Swan – Port Vale
5. Simon Charlton – Huddersfield Town
6. Ray Walker – Port Vale
7. Ian Taylor – Port Vale
8. Darren Bradley – West Bromwich Albion
9. Mark Stein – Stoke City
10. Andy Walker – Bolton Wanderers
11. Bob Taylor – West Bromwich Albion

### DIVISION THREE
1. Mark Prudhoe – Darlington
2. Andy McMillan – York City
3. Paul Stancliffe – York City
4. Matt Elliott – Scunthorpe United
5. Damon Searle – Cardiff City
6. Kenny Lowe – Barnet
7. Derek Payne – Barnet
8. Gareth Owen – Wrexham
9. Gary Bull – Barnet
10. Darren Foreman – Scarborough
11. Carl Griffiths – Shrewsbury Town

## 1993–94

### PREMIER LEAGUE
1. Tim Flowers – Blackburn Rovers
2. Gary Kelly – Leeds United
3. Denis Irwin – Manchester United
4. Gary Pallister – Manchester United
5. Tony Adams – Arsenal
6. David Batty – Leeds United and Blackburn Rovers
7. Gary McAllister – Leeds United
8. Paul Ince – Manchester United
9. Alan Shearer – Blackburn Rovers
10. Peter Beardsley – Newcastle United
11. Eric Cantona – Manchester United

### DIVISION ONE
1. Nigel Martyn – Crystal Palace
2. Gary Charles – Derby County
3. Scott Minto – Charlton Athletic
4. Eric Young – Crystal Palace
5. Colin Cooper – Nottingham Forest
6. Mark Draper – Notts County
7. Scott Gemmill – Nottingham Forest
8. Jason McAteer – Bolton Wanderers
9. Stan Collymore – Nottingham Forest
10. Paul Walsh – Portsmouth
11. Chris Armstrong – Crystal Palace

### DIVISION TWO
1. Marlon Beresford – Burnley
2. Neil Aspin – Port Vale
3. Dylan Kerr – Reading
4. Adrian Williams – Reading
5. Dean Glover – Port Vale
6. Steve Castle – Plymouth Argyle
7. Ian Taylor – Port Vale
8. Ian Bogie – Port Vale
9. Jimmy Quinn – Reading
10. Andy Preece – Stockport County
11. Dean Windass – Hull City

### DIVISION THREE
1. Martin Hodge – Rochdale
2. Jason Cousins – Wycombe Wanderers
3. Terry Evans – Wycombe Wanderers
4. Alan Reeves – Rochdale
5. Roger Stanislaus – Bury
6. Steve Guppy – Wycombe Wanderers
7. Tony Rigby – Bury
8. Neil Lennon – Crewe Alexandra
9. Tony Ellis – Preston North End
10. Dean Spink – Shrewsbury Town
11. Dave Reeves – Carlisle United

## 1994–95

### PREMIER LEAGUE
1. Tim Flowers – Blackburn Rovers
2. Rob Jones – Liverpool
3. Graeme Le Saux – Blackburn Rovers
4. Gary Pallister – Manchester United
5. Colin Hendry – Blackburn Rovers
6. Tim Sherwood –Blackburn Rovers
7. Matt Le Tissier – Southampton
8. Paul Ince – Manchester United
9. Alan Shearer – Blackburn Rovers
10. Chris Sutton – Blackburn Rovers
11. Jurgen Klinsmann – Tottenham Hotspur

### DIVISION ONE
1. Shaka Hislop – Reading
2. Neil Cox – Middlesbrough
3. Ben Thatcher – Millwall
4. Alan Stubbs – Bolton Wanderers
5. Craig Short – Derby County
6. Alex Rae – Millwall
7. Jamie Pollock – Middlesbrough
8. Jason McAteer – Bolton Wanderers
9. Jan Age Fjortoft – Middlesbrough
10. John Hendrie – Middlsbrough
11. John Aldridge – Tranmere Rovers

### DIVISION TWO
1. Ian Bennett – Birmingham City
2. Gary Poole – Birmingham City
3. Tom Cowan – Huddersfield Town
4. Liam Daish – Birmingham City
5. Dean Richards – Bradford City
6. John Cornforth – Swansea City
7. Neil Lennon – Crewe Alexandra
8. Mark Ward – Birmingham City
9. Gary Bennett – Wrexham
10. Andy Booth – Huddersfield Town
11. Nicky Forster – Brentford

### DIVISION THREE
1. Gary Kelly – Bury
2. Duncan Jupp – Fulham
3. Tony Gallimore – Carlisle United
4. Dean Walling – Carlisle United
5. Russ Wilcox – Doncaster Rovers
6. Martin O'Connor – Walsall
7. Paul Holland – Mansfield Town
8. Wayne Bullimore – Scunthorpe United
9. Dougie Freedman – Barnet
10. Kyle Lightbourne – Walsall
11. Dave Reeves – Carlisle United

## 1995–96

### PREMIER LEAGUE
1. David James – Liverpool
2. Gary Neville – Manchester United
3. Alan Wright – Aston Villa
4. Tony Adams – Arsenal
5. Ugo Ehiogu – Aston Villa
6. Rob Lee – Newcastle United
7. Steve Stone – Nottingham Forest
8. David Ginola – Newcastle United
9. Ruud Gullit – Chelsea
10. Les Ferdinand – Newcastle United
11. Alan Shearer – Blackburn Rovers

### DIVISION ONE
1. Alan Kelly – Sheffield United
2. Dariusz Kubicki – Sunderland
3. Dean Gordon – Crystal Palace
4. Dean Richards – Wolverhampton Wanderers
5. Richard Rufus – Charlton Athletic
6. Alex Rae – Millwall
7. Lee Bowyer – Charlton Athletic
8. Garry Parker – Leicester City
9. Michael Gary – Sunderland
10. Dean Sturridge – Derby County
11. Steve Claridge – Leicester City

### DIVISION TWO
1. Darren Ward – Notts County
2. Chris Wilder – Rotherham United
3. Paul Bodin – Swindon Town
4. Shaun Taylor – Swindon Town
5. Ian Culverhouse – Swindon Town
6. Martin O'Connor – Walsall
7. Neil Lennon – Crewe Alexandra
8. Micky Mellon– Blackpool
9. Karl Connolly – Wrexham
10. Marcus Stewart – Bristol Rovers
11. Kurt Nogan – Burnley

### DIVISION THREE
1. Jim Stannard – Gillingham
2. Duncan Jupp – Fulham
3. Mike Heathcote – Plymouth Argyle
4. Paul Williams – Plymouth Argyle
5. Russ Wilcox – Preston North End
6. Simon Davey – Preston North End
7. Mark Kinsella – Colchester United
8. Roberto Martinez – Wigan Athletic
9. Ian Bryson – Preston North End
10. Andy Saville – Preston North End
11. Carl Dale – Cardiff City

## 1996–97

### PREMIER LEAGUE
1. David James – Liverpool
2. Gary Neville – Manchester United
3. Alan Wright – Aston Villa
4. Tony Adams – Arsenal
5. Ugo Ehiogu – Aston Villa
6. Rob Lee – Newcastle United
7. Steve Stone – Nottingham Forest
8. David Ginola – Newcastle United
9. Ruud Gullit – Chelsea
10. Les Ferdinand – Newcastle United
11. Alan Shearer – Blackburn Rovers

### DIVISION ONE
1. Alan Kelly – Sheffield United
2. Dariusz Kubicki – Sunderland
3. Dean Gordon – Crystal Palace
4. Dean Richards – Wolverhampton Wanderers
5. Richard Rufus – Charlton Athletic
6. Alex Rae – Millwall
7. Lee Bowyer – Charlton Athletic
8. Garry Parker – Leicester City
9. Michael Gary – Sunderland
10. Dean Sturridge – Derby County
11. Steve Claridge – Leicester City

### DIVISION TWO
1. Darren Ward – Notts County
2. Chris Wilder – Rotherham United
3. Paul Bodin – Swindon Town
4. Shaun Taylor – Swindon Town
5. Ian Culverhouse – Swindon Town
6. Martin O'Connor – Walsall
7. Neil Lennon – Crewe Alexandra
8. Micky Mellon – Blackpool
9. Karl Connolly – Wrexham
10. Marcus Stewart – Bristol Rovers
11. Kurt Nogan – Burnley

### DIVISION THREE
1. Jim Stannard – Gillingham
2. Duncan Jupp – Fulham
3. Mike Heathcote – Plymouth Argyle
4. Paul Williams – Plymouth Argyle
5. Russ Wilcox – Preston North End
6. Simon Davey – Preston North End
7. Mark Kinsella – Colchester United
8. Roberto Martinez – Wigan Athletic
9. Ian Bryson – Preston North End
10. Andy Saville – Preston North End
11. Carl Dale – Cardiff City

## 1997–98

### PREMIER LEAGUE
1. Nigel Martyn – Leeds United
2. Gary Neville – Manchester United
3. Graeme Le Saux – Chelsea
4. Gary Pallister – Manchester United
5. Colin Hendry – Blackburn Rovers
6. Nicky Butt – Manchester United
7. David Batty – Newcastle United
8. David Beckham – Manchester United
9. Michael Owen – Liverpool
10. Dennis Bergkamp – Arsenal
11. Ryan Giggs – Manchester United

### DIVISION ONE
1. Alan Miller – West Bromwich Albion
2. Kieron Dyer – Ipswich Town
3. Mauricio Taricco – Ipswich Town
4. Nigel Pearson – Middlesbrough
5. Colin Cooper – Nottingham Forest
6. Georgi Kinkladze – Manchester City
7. Lee Clark – Sunderland
8. John Robinson – Charlton Athletic
9. Paul Merson – Middlesbrough
10. Pierre van Hooijdonk – Nottingham Forest
11. Robbie Keane – Wolverhampton Wanderers

### DIVISION TWO
1. Alec Chamberlain – Watford
2. Gary Parkinson – Preston North End
3. Peter Kennedy – Watford
4. Shaun Taylor – Bristol City
5. Chris Coleman – Fulham
6. Kevin Donovan – Grimsby Town
7. Paul Bracewell – Fulham
8. Paul Groves – Grimsby Town
9. John Hodge – Walsall
10. Roger Boli – Walsall
11. Shaun Goater – Bristol City

### DIVISION THREE
1. Darren Ward – Notts County
2. Ian Hendon – Notts County
3. Dennis Pearce – Notts County
4. Gary Strodder – Notts County
5. Dean Walling – Lincoln City
6. David Farrell – Peterborough United
7. Jon Cullen – Hartlepool United
8. Martin Ling – Leyton Orient
9. Scott Houghton – Peterborough United
10. Jimmy Quinn – Peterborough United
11. Rodney Jack – Torquay United

# 1998–99

## PREMIER LEAGUE
1. Nigel Martyn – Leeds United
2. Gary Neville – Manchester United
3. Denis Irwin – Manchester United
4. Jaap Stam – Manchester United
5. Sol Campbell – Tottenham Hotspur
6. Patrick Vieira – Arsenal
7. Emmanuel Petit – Arsenal
8. David Beckham – Manchester United
9. Dwight Yorke – Manchester United
10. Nicolas Anelka – Arsenal
11. David Ginola – Tottenham Hotspur

## DIVISION ONE
1. Richard Wright – Ipswich Town
2. Gary Rowett – Birmingham City
3. Michael Gray – Sunderland
4. Darren Moore – Bradford City
5. Mark Venus – Ipswich Town and Paul
   Butler – Sunderland
6. Kieron Dyer – Ipswich Town
7. Lee Clark – Sunderland
8. Per Frandsen – Bolton Wanderers
9. Lee Hughes – West Bromwich Albion
10. Niall Quinn – Sunderland
11. Allan Johnston – Sunderland

## DIVISION TWO
1. Maik Taylor – Fulham
2. Steve Finnan – Fulham
3. Rufus Brevett – Fulham and Jamie
   Vincent – Bournemouth
4. Steve Davis – Burnley
5. Chris Coleman – Fulham
6. Darren Wrack – Walsall
7. Sean Gregan – Preston North End
8. Graham Kavanagh – Stoke City
9. Steve Robinson – Bournemouth
10. Mark Stein – Bournemouth
11. Geoff Horsfield – Fulham

## DIVISION THREE
1. Jon Hallworth – Cardiff City
2. Mark Delaney – Cardiff City
3. Paul Gibbs – Plymouth Argyle
4. Chris Hope – Scunthorpe United
5. Hermann Hreidarsson – Brentford
6. Jeff Minton – Brighton & Hove Albion
7. Jason Fowler – Cardiff City
8. Paul Evans – Brentford
9. Simon Davies and Matthew Etherington
   – both Peterborough United
10. Jamie Forrester – Bristol Rovers
11. Martin Butler – Cambridge United

# 1999–00

## PREMIER LEAGUE
1. Nigel Martyn – Leeds United
2. Gary Kelly – Leeds United
3. Ian Harte – Leeds United
4. Jaap Stam – Manchester United
5. Sammi Hyypia – Liverpool
6. Patrick Vieira – Arsenal
7. Roy Keane – Manchester United
8. David Beckham – Manchester United
9. Andy Cole – Manchester United
10. Kevin Phillips – Sunderland
11. Harry Kewell – Leeds United

## DIVISION ONE
1. Richard Wright – Ipswich Town
2. Gary Rowett – Birmingham City
3. Chris Powell – Charlton Athletic
4. Richard Rufus – Charlton Athletic
5. Chris Coleman – Fulham
6. Mark Kinsella – Charlton Athletic
7. Craig Hignett – Barnsley
8. John Robinson – Charlton Athletic
9. Andy Hunt – Charlton Athletic
10. Marcus Stewart – Huddersfield Town
11. Mark Kennedy – Manchester City

## DIVISION TWO
1. Roy Carroll – Wigan Athletic
2. Graham Alexander – Preston North End
3. Micky Bell – Bristol City
4. Steve Davis – Burnley
5. Michael Jackson – Preston North End
6. Darren Caskey – Reading
7. Sean Gregan – Preston North End
8. Graham Kavanagh – Stoke City
9. Jason Roberts – Bristol Rovers
10. Jon Macken – Preston North End
11. Glen Little – Burnley

## DIVISION THREE
1. Mike Pollitt – Rotherham United
2. Ian Hendon – Notts County
3. Matt Lockwood – Leyton Orient
4. Matthew Bound – Swansea City
5. Craig Liddle – Darlington
6. Tommy Miller – Hartlepool United
7. Nick Cusack – Swansea City
8. Darren Currie – Barnet
9. Marco Gabbiadini – Darlington
10. Richard Barker – Macclesfield Town
11. Neil Heaney – Darlington

# 2000–01

## PREMIER LEAGUE
1. Fabien Barthez – Manchester United
2. Stephan Carr – Tottenham Hotspur
3. Sylvinho – Arsenal
4. Jaap Stam – Manchester United
5. Wes Brown – Manchester United
6. Steven Gerrard – Liverpool
7. Roy Keane – Manchester United
8. Patrick Vieira – Arsenal
9. Teddy Sheringham – Manchester United
10. Thierry Henry – Arsenal
11. Ryan Giggs – Manchester United

## DIVISION ONE
1. Maik Taylor – Fulham
2. Steve Finnan – Fulham
3. Martin Grainger – Birmingham City
4. Henning Berg – Blackburn Rovers
5. Chris Coleman – Fulham
6. David Dunn – Blackburn Rovers
7. Lee Clark – Fulham
8. Sean Davis – Fulham
9. Matt Jansen – Blackburn Rovers
10. Louis Saha – Fulham
11. Damien Duff – Blackburn Rovers

## DIVISION TWO
1. Jimmy Walker – Walsall
2. Matt Lawrence – Millwall
3. Micky Bell – Bristol City
4. Arjan de Zeeuw – Wigan Athletic
5. Andy Tillson – Walsall
6. Scott Murray – Bristol City
7. Graham Kavanagh – Stoke City
8. Tim Cahill – Millwall
9. Neil Harris – Millwall
10. Martin Butler – Reading
11. Brian Tinnion – Bristol City

## DIVISION THREE
1. Mike Pollitt – Chesterfield
2. Josh Low – Cardiff City
3. Matt Lockwood – Leyton Orient
4. Danny Cullip – Brighton & Hove Albion
5. Steve Blatherwick – Chesterfield
6. Darren Currie – Barnet
7. Lee Hodges – Scunthorpe United
8. Tommy Miller – Hartlepool United
9. Paul Simpson – Blackpool
10. Bobby Zamora – Brighton & Hove
    Albion
11. Robert Earnshaw – Cardiff City

## 2001–02

### PREMIER LEAGUE
1. Shay Given – Newcastle United
2. Steve Finnan – Fulham
3. Wayne Bridge – Southampton
4. Rio Ferdinand – Leeds United
5. Sami Hyypia – Liverpool
6. Robert Pires – Arsenal
7. Roy Keane – Manchester United
8. Patrick Vieira – Arsenal
9. Ruud van Nistelrooy – Manchester United
10. Thierry Henry – Arsenal
11. Ryan Giggs – Manchester United

### DIVISION ONE
1. Russell Hoult – West Bromwich Albion
2. Graham Alexander – Preston North End
3. Neil Clement – West Bromwich Albion
4. Darren Moore – West Bromwich Albion
5. Joleon Lescott – Wolverhampton Wanderers
6. Eyal Berkovic – Manchester City
7. Ali Benarbia – Manchester City
8. Robert Prosinecki – Portsmouth
9. Shaun Goater – Manchester City
10. Dougie Freedman – Crystal Palace
11. Mark Kennedy – Wolverhampton Wanderers

### DIVISION TWO
1. Mark Tyler – Peterborough United
2. Graeme Murty – Reading
3. Micky Bell – Bristol City
4. Arjan de Zeeuw – Wigan Athletic
5. Danny Cullip – Brighton & Hove Albion
6. Scott Murray – Bristol City
7. Graham Kavanagh – Stoke City
8. Paul Evans – Brentford
9. Bobby Zamora – Brighton & Hove Albion
10. Nicky Forster – Reading
11. Jason Koumas – Tranmere Rovers

### DIVISION THREE
1. Romain Larrieu – Plymouth Argyle
2. Michael Duff – Cheltenham Town
3. Matthew Taylor – Luton Town
4. Paul Wotton – Plymouth Argyle
5. Graham Coughlan – Plymouth Argyle
6. Peter Beagrie – Scunthorpe United
7. Lee Hodges – Scunthorpe United
8. Lee Williamson – Mansfield Town
9. David Friio – Plymouth Argyle
10. Chris Greenacre – Mansfield Town
11. Nathan Ellington – Bristol Rovers

## 2002–03

### PREMIER LEAGUE
1. Brad Friedel – Blackburn Rovers
2. Stephen Carr – Tottenham Hotspur
3. Ashley Cole – Arsenal
4. Sol Campbell – Arsenal
5. William Gallas – Chelsea
6. Robert Pires – Arsenal
7. Paul Scholes – Manchester United
8. Patrick Vieira – Arsenal
9. Alan Shearer – Newcastle United
10. Thierry Henry – Arsenal
11. Keiron Dyer – Newcastle United

### DIVISION ONE
1. Shaka Hislop – Portsmouth
2. Denis Irwin – Wolverhampton Wanderers
3. Matthew Taylor – Portsmouth
4. Michael Dawson – Nottingham Forest
5. Joleon Lescott – Wolverhampton Wanderers
6. Muzzy Izzet – Leicester City
7. Michael Brown – Sheffield United
8. Michael Tonge – Sheffield United
9. Paul Merson – Portsmouth
10. Paul Dickov – Leicester City
11. David Johnson – Nottingham Forest

### DIVISION TWO
1. John Filan – Wigan Athletic
2. Nicky Eaden – Wigan Athletic
3. Micky Bell – Bristol City
4. Jason de Vos – Wigan Athletic
5. Fitz Hall – Oldham Athletic
6. Scott Murray – Bristol City
7. Jimmy Bullard – Wigan Athletic
8. Graham Kavanagh – Cardiff City
9. Robert Earnshaw – Cardiff City
10. Rob Hulse – Crewe Alexandra
11. Martin Bullock – Blackpool

### DIVISION THREE
1. Alan Fettis – York City
2. Carlos Edwards – Wrexham
3. Paul Underwood – Rushden & Diamonds
4. Graeme Lee – Hartlepool United
5. Chris Westwood – Hartlepool United
6. Paul Hall– Rushden & Diamonds
7. Mark Tinkler – Hartlepool United
8. Alex Russell– Torquay United
9. Ritchie Humphreys – Hartlepool United
10. Andy Morrell – Wrexham
11. Dave Kitson – Cambridge United

## 2003–04

### PREMIER LEAGUE
1. Tim Howard – Manchester United
2. Lauren – Arsenal
3. Ashley Cole – Arsenal
4. Sol Campbell – Arsenal
5. John Terry – Chelsea
6. Robert Pires – Arsenal
7. Steven Gerrard – Liverpool
8. Patrick Vieira – Arsenal
9. Frank Lampard – Chelsea
10. Thierry Henry – Arsenal
11. Ruud van Nistelrooy – Manchester United

### DIVISION ONE
1. Robert Green – Norwich City
2. Phil Jagielka – Sheffield United
3. Julia Arca – Sunderland
4. Danny Gabbidon – Cardiff City
5. Malky Mackay – Norwich City
6. Jason Koumas – West Bromwich Albion
7. Tim Cahill – Millwall
8. Michael Carrick – West Ham United
9. Andy Johnson – Crystal Palace
10. Robert Earnshaw – Cardiff City
11. Andy Reid – Nottingham Forest

### DIVISION TWO
1. Steve Phillips – Bristol City
2. Louis Carey – Bristol City
3. Gino Padula – Queens Park Rangers
4. Graham Coughlan – Plymouth Argyle
5. Dan Cullip – Brighton & Hove Albion
6. Carlos Edwards – Wrexham
7. David Friio – Plymough Argyle
8. Richie Wellens – Blackpool
9. Leon Knight – Brighton & Hove Albion
10. Scott Taylor – Blackpool
11. Brian Tinnion – Bristol City

### DIVISION THREE
1. Chris Weale– Yeovil Town
2. Nathan Stanton – Scunthorpe United
3. Andy Dawson – Hull City
4. Andy Crosby – Oxford United
5. Efe Sodje – Huddersfield Town
6. Liam Lawrence – Mansfield Town
7. Michael McIndoe – Doncaster Rovers
8. Alex Russell – Torquay United
9. David Graham – Torquay United
10. Lee Trundle – Swansea City
11. Peter Beagrie – Scunthorpe United

## 2004–05

### PREMIER LEAGUE
1. Petr Cech – Chelsea
2. Gary Neville – Manchester United
3. Ashley Cole – Arsenal
4. Rio Ferdinand – Manchester United
5. John Terry – Chelsea
6. Shaun Wright-Phillips – Manchester City
7. Steven Gerrard – Liverpool
8. Arjen Robben – Chelsea
9. Frank Lampard – Chelsea
10. Thierry Henry – Arsenal
11. Andy Johnson – Crystal Palace

### CHAMPIONSHIP
1. Kelvin Davis – Ipswich Town
2. Graham Alexander – Preston North End
3. George McCartney – Sunderland
4. Tom Huddlestone – Derby County
5. Gary Breen – Sunderland
6. Inigo Idiakez – Derby County
7. Jimmy Bullard – Wigan Athletic
8. Steve Sidwell – Reading
9. Julio Arca – Sunderland
10. Nathan Ellington – Wigan Athletic
11. Jason Roberts – Wigan Athletic

### LEAGUE ONE
1. Marlon Beresford – Luton Town
2. Ryan Taylor – Tranmere Rovers
3. Warren Cummings – Bournemouth
4. Curtis Davies – Luton Town
5. Chris Coyne – Luton Town
6. Ahmet Brkovic – Luton Town
7. Paul Merson – Walsall
8. Kevin Nicholls – Luton Town
9. Stuart Elliott – Hull City
10. Steve Howard – Luton Town
11. Leroy Lita – Bristol City

### LEAGUE TWO
1. Chris Weale – Yeovil Town
2. Sam Ricketts – Swansea City
3. Michael Rose – Yeovil Town
4. Adam Barrett – Southend United
5. Andy Crosby – Scunthorpe United
6. Lee Johnson – Yeovil Town
7. Darren Way – Yeovil Town
8. Kevin Maher– Southend United
9. Phil Jevons – Yeovil Town
10. Lee Trundle – Swansea City
11. Peter Beagrie – Scunthorpe United

## 2005–06

### PREMIER LEAGUE
1. Shay Given – Newcastle United
2. Pascal Chimbonda – Wigan Athletic
3. William Gallas – Chelsea
4. Jamie Carragher – Liverpool
5. John Terry – Chelsea
6. Cristiano Ronaldo – Manchester United
7. Steven Gerrard – Liverpool
8. Joe Cole – Chelsea
9. Frank Lampard – Chelsea
10. Thierry Henry – Arsenal
11. Wayne Rooney – Manchester United

### CHAMPIONSHIP
1. Marcus Hahnemann – Reading
2. Gary Kelly – Leeds United
3. Nicky Shorey – Reading
4. Ibrahima Sonko – Reading
5. Joleon Lescott – Wolverhampton Wanderers
6. Phil Jagielka – Sheffield United
7. Ashley Young – Watford
8. Steve Sidwell – Reading
9. Jason Koumas – Cardiff City (on loan from West Bromwich Albion)
10. Marlon King – Watford
11. Kevin Doyle – Reading

### LEAGUE ONE
1. Darryl Flahavan – Southend United
2. Greg Halford – Colchester United
3. Gareth Roberts – Tranmere Rovers
4. Sam Sodje – Brentford
5. Adam Barrett – Southend United
6. Andy Robinson – Swansea City
7. Neil Danns – Colchester United
8. Kevin Maher – Southend United
9. Lee Trundle – Swansea City
10. Billy Sharp – Scunthorpe United
11. Michael McIndoe – Doncaster Rovers

### LEAGUE TWO
1. Joe Hart – Shrewsbury Town
2. Danny Senda – Wycombe Wanderers
3. Matt Lockwood – Leyton Orient
4. Roger Johnson – Wycombe Wanderers
5. Gareth McAuley – Lincoln City
6. Josh Low – Northampton Town
7. Mark Jones – Wrexham
8. Ian Taylor – Northampton Town
9. Kevin Betsy – Wycombe Wanderers
10. Karl Hawley – Carlisle United
11. Michael Reddy – Grimsby Town

## 2006–07

### PREMIER LEAGUE
1. Edwin Van der Sar – Manchester United
2. Gary Neville – Manchester United
3. Patrice Evra – Manchester United
4. Rio Ferdinand – Manchester United
5. Nemanja Vidic – Manchester United
6. Paul Scholes – Manchester United
7. Steven Gerrard – Liverpool
8. Cristiano Ronaldo – Manchester United
9. Didier Drogba – Chelsea
10. Dimitar Berbatov – Tottenham Hotspur
11. Ryan Giggs – Manchester United

### CHAMPIONSHIP
1. Matt Murray – Wolverhampton Wanderers
2. Graham Alexander – Preston North End
3. Gareth Bale – Southampton
4. Darren Moore – Derby County
5. Curtis Davies – West Bromwich Albion
6. Dean Whitehead – Sunderland
7. Jason Koumas – Cardiff City (on loan from West Bromwich Albion)
8. Carlos Edwards – Sunderland
9. Gary McSheffrey – Birmingham Clty
10. Michael Chopra – Cardiff City
11. Diomansy Kamara – West Bromwich Albion

### LEAGUE ONE
1. Joe Murphy – Scunthorpe United
2. Jon Otsemobor – Crewe Alexandra
3. Matt Lockwood – Leyton Orient
4. Terry Skiverton – Yeovil Town
5. Ian Breckin – Nottingham Forest
6. Chris Shuker – Tranmere Rovers
7. Richie Wellens – Oldham Athletic
8. Wes Hoolahan – Blackpool
9. Luke Varney – Crewe Alexandra
10. Billy Sharp – Scunthorpe United
11. Matt Jarvis – Gillingham

### LEAGUE TWO
1. Clayton Ince – Walsall
2. Craig Pead – Walsall
3. Ritchie Humphreys – Hartlepool United
4. Michael Nelson – Hartlepool United
5. Chris Westwood – Walsall
6. Lee Frecklington – Lincoln City
7. Dean Keates – Walsall
8. Andy Monkhouse – Hartlepool United
9. Tommy Doherty – Wycombe Wanderers (on loan from Queens Park Rangers)
10. Izale McLeod – MK Dons
11. Jermaine Easter – Wycombe Wanderers

## 2007–08

### PREMIER LEAGUE
1. David James – Portsmouth
2. Bacary Sagna – Arsenal
3. Gael Clichy – Arsenal
4. Rio Ferdinand – Manchester United
5. Nemanja Vidic – Manchester United
6. Cesc Fabregas – Arsenal
7. Steven Gerrard – Liverpool
8. Cristiano Ronaldo – Manchester United
9. Emmanuel Adebayor – Arsenal
10. Fernando Torres – Liverpool
11. Ashley Young – Aston Villa

### CHAMPIONSHIP
1. Wayne Hennessey – Wolverhampton Wanderers
2. Bradley Orr – Bristol City
3. Paul Robinson – West Bromwich Albion
4. Ryan Shawcross – Stoke City (on loan from Manchester United)
5. Danny Shittu – Watford
6. Liam Lawrence – Stoke City
7. Brian Howard – Barnsley
8. Marvin Elliott – Bristol City
9. Jonathan Greening – West Bromwich Albion
10. Ricardo Fuller – Stoke City
11. Kevin Phillips – West Bromwich Albion

### LEAGUE ONE
1. Keiren Westwood – Carlisle United
2. Angel Rangel – Swansea City
3. Julian Bennett – Nottingham Forest
4. Gary Monk – Swansea City
5. Danny Livesey – Carlisle United
6. Andy Robinson – Swansea City
7. Ferrie Bodde – Swansea City
8. Richie Wellens – Doncaster Rovers
9. Kris Commons – Nottingham Forest
10. Jermaine Beckford – Leeds United
11. Jason Scotland – Swansea City

### LEAGUE TWO
1. Joe Lewis – Morecambe (on loan from Norwich City) and Peterborough United
2. Craig Pead – Brentford
3. Dean Lewington – MK Dons
4. Steve Foster – Darlington
5. Danny Swailes – MK Dons
6. Jason Puncheon – Barnet
7. Keith Andrews – MK Dons
8. Lloyd Dyer – MK Dons
9. George Boyd – Peterborough United
10. Jack Lester – Chesterfield
11. Aaron McLean – Peterborough United

## 2008–09

### PREMIER LEAGUE
1. Edwin van der Sar – Manchester United
2. Glen Johnson – Portsmouth
3. Patrice Evra – Manchester United
4. Rio Ferdinand – Manchester United
5. Nemanja Vidic – Manchester United
6. Ryan Giggs – Manchester United
7. Steven Gerrard – Liverpool
8. Cristiano Ronaldo – Manchester United
9. Nicolas Anelka – Chelsea
10. Fernando Torres – Liverpool
11. Ashley Young – Aston Villa

### CHAMPIONSHIP
1. Keiren Westwood – Coventry City
2. Kyle Naughton – Sheffield United
3. Danny Fox – Coventry City
4. Roger Johnson – Cardiff City
5. Richard Stearman – Wolverhampton Wanderers
6. Michael Kightly – Wolverhampton Wanderers
7. Joe Ledley – Cardiff City
8. Jordi Gomez – Swansea City (on loan from Espanyol)
9. Stephen Hunt – Reading
10. Sylvan Ebanks-Blake – Wolverhampton Wanderers
11. Jason Scotland – Swansea City

### LEAGUE ONE
1. Joe Murphy – Scunthorpe United
2. Neil Eardley – Oldham Athletic
3. Dean Lewington – MK Dons
4. Jack Hobbs – Leicester City (on loan from Liverpool)
5. Sean O'Hanlon – MK Dons
6. Fabian Delph – Leeds United
7. Matt Oakley – Leicester City
8. Chris Taylor – Oldham Athletic
9. George Boyd – Peterborough United
10. Rickie Lambert – Bristol Rovers
11. Matty Fryatt– Leicester City

### LEAGUE TWO
1. Scott Shearer – Wycombe Wanderers
2. Neil Austin – Darlington
3. Tom Kennedy – Rochdale
4. David McCracken – Wycombe Wanderers
5. Simon King – Gillingham
6. Omar Daley – Bradford City
7. Ben Davies – Shrewsbury Town
8. Dany N'Guessan – Lincoln City
9. Tommy Doherty – Wycombe Wanderers
10. Andy Bishop – Bury
11. Grant Holt – Shrewsbury Town

## 2009–10

### PREMIER LEAGUE
1. Joe Hart – Birmingham City (on loan from Manchester City)
2. Branislav Ivanovic – Chelsea
3. Patrice Evra – Manchester United
4. Thomas Vermaelen – Arsenal
5. Richard Dunne – Aston Villa
6. Darren Fletcher – Manchester United
7. Cesc Fabregas – Arsenal
8. Antonio Valencia – Manchester United
9. Didier Drogba – Chelsea
10. Wayne Rooney – Manchester United
11. James Milner – Aston Villa

### CHAMPIONSHIP
1. Lee Camp – Nottingham Forest
2. Chris Gunter – Nottingham Forest
3. Jose Enrique – Newcastle United
4. Fabricio Coloccini – Newcastle United
5. Ashley Williams – Swansea City
6. Graham Dorrans – West Bromwich Albion
7. Peter Whittingham – Cardiff City
8. Kevin Nolan – Newcastle United
9. Charlie Adam – Blackpool
10. Andy Carroll – Newcastle United
11. Michael Chopra – Cardiff City

### LEAGUE ONE
1. Kelvin Davis – Southampton
2. Frazer Richardson – Charlton Athletic
3. Ian Harte – Carlisle United
4. Patrick Kisnorbo – Leeds United
5. Gary Doherty – Norwich City
6. Wes Hoolahan – Norwich City
7. Jason Puncheon – MK Dons (on loan from Plymouth Argyle)
8. Robert Snodgrass – Leeds United
9. Nicky Bailey – Charlton Athletic
10. Rickie Lambert – Southampton
11. Grant Holt – Norwich City

### LEAGUE TWO
1. Kasper Schmeichel – Notts County
2. John Brayford – Crewe Alexandra
3. Tom Kennedy – Rochdale
4. Craig Dawson – Rochdale
5. Ian Sharps – Rotherham United
6. Ben Davies – Notts County
7. Stephen Dawson – Bury
8. Gary Jones – Rochdale
9. Nicky Law – Rotherham United
10. Lee Hughes – Notts County
11. Adam le Fondre – Rotherham United

# 2010–11

## PREMIER LEAGUE
1. Edwin van der Sar – Manchester United
2. Bacary Sagna – Arsenal
3. Ashley Cole – Chelsea
4. Vincent Kompany – Manchester City
5. Nemanja Vidic – Manchester United
6. Luis Nani – Manchester United
7. Samir Nasri – Arsenal
8. Jack Wilshere – Arsenal
9. Gareth Bale – Tottenham Hotpsur
10. Dimitar Berbatov – Manchester United
11. Carlos Tevez – Manchester City

## CHAMPIONSHIP
1. Paddy Kenny – Queens Park Rangers
2. Kyle Naughton – Leicester City (on loan from Tottenham Hotpsur)
3. Ian Harte – Reading
4. Ashley Williams – Swansea City
5. Wes Morgan – Nottingham Forest
6. Andy King – Leicester City
7. Adel Taarabt – Queens Park Rangers
8. Wes Hoolahan – Norwich City
9. Scott Sinclair – Swansea City
10. Grant Holt – Norwich City
11. Danny Graham – Swansea City

## LEAGUE ONE
1. Kelvin Davis – Southampton
2. Inigo Calderon – Brighton & Hove Albion
3. Dan Harding – Southampton
4. Gordon Greer – Brighton & Hove Albion
5. Jose Fonte – Southampton
6. Anthony Pilkington – Huddersfield Town
7. Adam Lallana – Southampton
8. Alex Oxlade-Chamberlain – Southampton
9. Elliott Bennett – Brighton & Hove Albion
10. Craig Mackail-Smith – Peterborough United
11. Bradley Wright-Phillips – Plymouth Argyle and Charlton Athletic

## LEAGUE TWO
1. Tommy Lee – Chesterfield
2. Damian Batt – Oxford United
3. Joe Skarz – Bury
4. Ian Sharps – Shrewsbury Town
5. Guy Branston – Torquay United
6. Danny Whitaker – Chesterfield
7. Jimmy Ryan – Accrington Stanley
8. Nicky Law – Rotherham United
9. Gareth Ainsworth – Wycombe Wanderers
10. Ryan Lowe – Bury
11. Craig Davies – Chesterfield

# 2011–12

## PREMIER LEAGUE
1. Joe Hart – Manchester City
2. Kyle Walker – Tottenham Hotspur
3. Leighton Baines – Everton
4. Vincent Kompany – Manchester City
5. Fabricio Coloccini – Newcastle United
6. Scott Parker – West Ham United
7. Yaya Toure – Manchester City
8. David Silva – Manchester City
9. Gareth Bale – Tottenham Hotspur
10. Wayne Rooney – Manchester United
11. Robin van Persie – Arsenal

## CHAMPIONSHIP
1. Kelvin Davis – Southampton
2. Nathaniel Clyne – Crystal Palace
3. Ian Harte – Reading
4. James Tomkins – West Ham United
5. Curtis Davies – Birmingham City
6. Adam Lallana – Southampton
7. Peter Whittingham – Cardiff City
8. Mark Noble – West Ham United
9. Matt Phillips – Blackpool
10. Rickie Lamber – Southampton
11. Jay Rodriguez – Burnley

## LEAGUE ONE
1. Ben Hamer – Charlton Athletic
2. Jack Hunt – Huddersfield Town
3. Rhoys Wiggins – Charlton Athletic
4. Michael Morrison – Charlton Athletic
5. Harry Maguire – Sheffield United
6. Johnnie Jackson – Charlton Athletic
7. Stephen Quinn – Sheffield United
8. Stephen Gleeson – MK Dons
9. Darren Potter – MK Dons
10. Jordan Rhodes – Huddersfield Town
11. Ched Evans – Sheffield United

## LEAGUE TWO
1. Bobby Olejnik – Torquay United
2. Paul Caddis – Swindon Town
3. Kevin Nicholson – Torquay United
4. Kyle McFadzean – Crawley Town
5. Ian Sharps – Shrewsbury Town
6. Matt Ritchie – Swindon Town
7. Marlon Pack – Cheltenham Town
8. Eunan O'Kane – Torquay United
9. Lee Mansell – Torquay United
10. Izale McLeod – Barnet
11. Tyrone Barnett – Crawley Town and on loan at Peterborough United

# 2012–13

## PREMIER LEAGUE
1. David de Gea – Manchester United
2. Pablo Zabaleta – Manchester City
3. Leighton Baines– Tottenham Hotspur
4. Rio Ferdinand – Manchester United
5. Jan Vertonghen – Tottenham Hotspur
6. Michael Carrick – Manchester United
7. Juan Mata – Chelsea
8. Eden Hazard – Chelsea
9. Gareth Bale – Tottenham Hotspur
10. Luiz Suarez – Liverpool
11. Robin van Persie – Arsenal

## CHAMPIONSHIP
1. Kasper Schmeichel – Leicester City
2. Kieran Trippier – Burnley
3. Wayne Bridge – Brighton & Hove Albion (on loan from Manchester City)
4. Wes Morgan – Leicester City
5. Mark Hudson – Cardiff City
6. Wilfried Zaha – Crystal Palace
7. Peter Whittingham – Cardiff City
8. Yannick Bolasie – Crystal Palace
9. Tom Ince – Blackpool
10. Glenn Murray – Crystal Palace
11. Matej Vydra – Watford

## LEAGUE ONE
1. Wes Foderingham – Swindon Town
2. Simon Francis – Bournemouth
3. Charlie Daniels – Bournemouth
4. Rob Jones – Doncaster Rovers
5. Harry Maguire – Sheffield United
6. Andy Ritchie – Swindon Town and Bournemouth
7. Luke Murphy – Crewe Alexandra
8. Alan Judge – Notts County
9. David Cotterill – Doncaster Rovers
10. Paddy Madden – Yeovil Town
11. Leon Clarke – Charlton Athletic, Scunthorpe United (on loan) and Coventry City

## LEAGUE TWO
1. Stuart Nelson – Gillingham
2. Sean Clohessy – Southend United
3. Joe Martin – Gillingham
4. Adam Barrett – Gillingham
5. Ryan Cresswell – Southend United
6. Jacques Maghoma – Burton Albion
7. Marlon Pack – Cheltenham Town
8. Gary Jones – Bradford City
9. Jennison Myrie-Williams – Port Vale
10. Tom Pope – Port Vale
11. Jamie Cureton – Exeter City

## 2013–14

**PREMIER LEAGUE**
1. Petr Cech – Chelsea
2. Seamus Coleman – Everton
3. Luke Shaw – Southampton
4. Gary Cahill – Chelsea
5. Vincent Kompany – Manchester City
6. Steven Gerrard – Liverpool
7. Adam Lallana – Southampton
8. Eden Hazard – Chelsea
9. Yaya Toure – Manchester City
10. Luiz Suarez – Liverpool
11. Daniel Sturridge – Liverpool

**CHAMPIONSHIP**
1. Kasper Schmeichel – Leicester City
2. Kieran Trippier – Burnley
3. Aaron Cresswell – Ipswich Town
4. Wes Morgan – Leicester City
5. Jason Shackell – Burnley
6. Will Hughes – Derby County
7. Danny Drinkwater – Leicester City
8. Craig Bryson – Derby County
9. Andy Reid – Nottingham Forest
10. Danny Ings – Burnley
11. Ross McCormack – Leeds United

**LEAGUE ONE**
1. Carl Ikeme – Wolverhampton Wanderers
2. Sam Ricketts – Wolverhampton Wanderers
3. Jake Bidwell – Brentford
4. Danny Batth – Wolverhampton Wanderers
5. Harry Maguire – Sheffield United
6. Bakary Sako – Wolverhampton Wanderers
7. Adam Forshaw – Brentford
8. Kevin McDonald – Wolverhampton Wanderers
9. Ben Pringle – Rotherham United
10. Britt Assombalonga – Peterborough United
11. Callum Wilson –Coventry City

**LEAGUE TWO**
1. Tommy Lee – Chesterfield
2. Michael Smith – Bristol Rovers
3. Michael Rose – Rochdale
4. Ian Evatt – Chesterfield
5. Liam Cooper – Chesterfield
6. Ian Henderson – Rochdale
7. John-Joe O'Toole – Bristol Rovers
8. Antoni Sarcevic – Fleetwood Town
9. Gary Roberts – Chesterfield
10. Sam Winnall – Scunthorpe United
11. Scott Hogan – Rochdale

## 2014–15

**PREMIER LEAGUE**
1. Petr Cech – Chelsea
2. Seamus Coleman – Everton
3. Luke Shaw – Southampton
4. Gary Cahill – Chelsea
5. Vincent Kompany – Manchester City
6. Steven Gerrard – Liverpool
7. Adam Lallana – Southampton
8. Eden Hazard – Chelsea
9. Yaya Toure – Manchester City
10. Luiz Suarez – Liverpool
11. Daniel Sturridge – Liverpool

**CHAMPIONSHIP**
1. Kasper Schmeichel – Leicester City
2. Kieran Trippier – Burnley
3. Aaron Cresswell – Ipswich Town
4. Wes Morgan – Leicester City
5. Jason Shackell – Burnley
6. Will Hughes – Derby County
7. Danny Drinkwater – Leicester City
8. Craig Bryson – Derby County
9. Andy Reid – Nottingham Forest
10. Danny Ings – Burnley
11. Ross McCormack – Leeds United

**LEAGUE ONE**
1. Carl Ikeme – Wolverhampton Wanderers
2. Sam Ricketts – Wolverhampton Wanderers
3. Jake Bidwell – Brentford
4. Danny Batth – Wolverhampton Wanderers
5. Harry Maguire – Sheffield United
6. Bakary Sako – Wolverhampton Wanderers
7. Adam Forshaw – Brentford
8. Kevin McDonald – Wolverhampton Wanderers
9. Ben Pringle – Rotherham United
10. Britt Assombalonga – Peterborough United
11. Callum Wilson –Coventry City

**LEAGUE TWO**
1. Tommy Lee – Chesterfield
2. Michael Smith – Bristol Rovers
3. Michael Rose – Rochdale
4. Ian Evatt – Chesterfield
5. Liam Cooper – Chesterfield
6. Ian Henderson – Rochdale
7. John-Joe O'Toole – Bristol Rovers
8. Antoni Sarcevic – Fleetwood Town
9. Gary Roberts – Chesterfield
10. Sam Winnall – Scunthorpe United
11. Scott Hogan – Rochdale